Fishguard & Rosslare Railways & Harbours Company

AN ILLUSTRATED HISTORY

ERNIE SHEPHERD

Dip. Loc. Hist. (NUI Maynooth)

COLOURPOINT

Published 2015 by Colourpoint Books
an imprint of Colourpoint Creative Ltd
Colourpoint House, Jubilee Business Park
21 Jubilee Road, Newtownards, BT23 4YH
Tel: 028 9182 6339
Fax: 028 9182 1900
E-mail: sales@colourpoint.co.uk
Web: www.colourpoint.co.uk

First Edition
First Impression

A catalogue record for this book is available from the British Library.

Designed by April Sky Design, Newtownards
Tel: 028 9182 7195
Web: www.aprilsky.co.uk

Printed by W&G Baird Ltd, Antrim

ISBN 978-1-78073-067-7

Front cover: GS&WR 4-4-0 No 309 at Waterford, about 1907, with the famous Cork–Rosslare boat express.
Painted by Jack Hill. *(Courtesy The Lord O'Neill)*

Rear cover: *Left:* Fishguard Harbour station in May 2011 with a two-piece Class 150 railcar set belonging to
Arriva Trains Wales preparing to depart for Cardiff on the 13:25 service following
the arrival of the *Stena Europe* from Rosslare. *(Ernie Shepherd)*
Right: 2700 Class Railcar leaving Campile for Rosslare Harbour. *(Ernie Shepherd)*

Contents

This book is dedicated to my wife Joy for her patience
and understanding for the long absences as research progressed.

Foreword

As I read the opening of Ernie Shepherd's history of the Fishguard & Rosslare Railways & Harbours Company I recalled my own surprise, upon taking up the position of General Manager Rosslare Europort in 2007, at being told that I would be appointed a director of a company listed on the London Stock Exchange. "What is it? What does it do?" I asked, but it took me a while to get my head around the idea of this company that holds assets and liabilities that are operated and managed by others.

In essence the F&RR&HCo is a late nineteenth century version of what corporate financiers would nowadays call a "special purpose vehicle" or SPV; a separate legal entity set up to hold and fund the specific assets of a joint venture between two separate and independent railway companies. There is a shareholders' agreement dated 27 May 1898 between the F&RR&HCo and its then shareholders, the GWR and the GSWR, amended by a supplementary agreement dated 14 February 1903 between the same parties, which provides *inter alia* that:

"… the [GSWR] shall work manage and maintain the portion of the [F&RR&HCo's] undertaking on the Irish side… and any loss incurred on the Irish side shall be made good and borne by the [GSWR]…

"… the [GSWR] shall subject to the payment of a due portion of the expenses of the administration of the [F&RR&HCo] be entitled to the receipts on the traffic on the portion of the… undertaking in Ireland and shall be responsible for… all working and other expenses incurred on that portion and shall indemnify and hold harmless the [GWR and the F&RR&HCo] and their respective undertakings from and against all actions, suits, claims and demands in respect of any liability whether in regard to capital or revenue for expenditure incurred on the Irish portion of the said undertaking.

"… the [GSWR] shall indemnify and hold harmless the [GWR and the F&RR&HCo] respectively against all losses, damages and expenses of every kind occasioned to them by reason of any act, default or omission of the [GSWR], their contractors, workmen or servants on the Irish side in the exercise of the powers of the [F&RR&HCo]"

As a result of these agreements, which were confirmed and made binding upon the parties by the F&RR&H Acts of 1899 and 1903, effective control and occupation of the railway and seaport on the Irish side was transferred from the F&RR&HCo to the GSWR. Of course the GSWR no longer exists, and Iarnród Éireann-Irish Rail as successor to that company is obliged to work, manage and maintain Rosslare Harbour and is entitled to all the Harbour's revenue and responsible for all of its expenses. IÉ is therefore the *de facto* port authority for Rosslare Harbour.

The use of the term "the Irish side" in the above extract is straightforward enough, but the agreements/legislation also refers to that part of the company's undertakings on the eastern side of the Irish Sea as "the English side", even though it is all in Wales! I recall a wry smile from a Welsh fellow-director when I referred to this at one of my early board meetings with the observation that the English always were a sensitive race! I was reminded of this incident in chapter one where Ernie presents a table of such "English" ports as Holyhead, Orme's Bay, Porth Dynllaen & Fishguard!

There were some fascinating insights into nineteenth century trade, for example the practice of sending goods from Cork to Wexford via Bristol (chapter 7); it reminds me of certain food and beverage products produced in County Wexford which in 2015 travel to the Continent via Dublin Port. *Plus ça change…*

In Chapter 22 Ernie describes the sinking of the *St Patrick* on 13 June 1941, *en route* from Rosslare to Fishguard. Ernie did not mention it because it occurred after he had completed his work, but on 13 June 2012 a plaque to commemorate the loss of the *St Patrick* was unveiled in the Rosslare Terminal Building by Ms Alice Hunt who lost her father and brother in the tragedy.

As someone now working in the ports and shipping industry, it is really interesting to note that in 1948 the gross tonnage of the ship on the Rosslare–Fishguard route was 3,500 tons; by way of comparison the ship on that route now has a GT of almost 25,000 tonnes, and the total gross tonnage of ships on regular service in and out of Rosslare in 2015 is almost 150,000 tonnes.

I am indebted to Ernie for knowledge of events in the decades immediately after World War II. I had no idea, for example, of the competitive threats to Rosslare from Waterford, but when you look at the relative traffic levels through the two ports today, it is clear that the right decisions were made back then. Other important innovations in those decades included the opening of the State's first RoRo ramp at Rosslare in 1965, the inauguration of the B&I line service between Rosslare & Swansea, the precursor to today's Irish Ferries service between Rosslare and Pembroke, and the Irish Continental Lines service to Le Havre in 1973, precursor to today's Irish Ferries service to Cherbourg/Roscoff.

As the General Manager of Rosslare Europort and a director of the F&RR&HCo I am immensely proud of the achievements of the Company and of CIÉ & Iarnród Éireann as the port authority at Rosslare Europort. Inevitably, a history book such as this must focus more on what happened 150 to 100 years ago rather than what happened in the last 50 years, although that is really rather impressive in my opinion. From the time when Rosslare had only one (Fishguard) service and Waterford Port was seeking to have that service transferred to Waterford, the Europort has grown to have five services to and from destinations as diverse as Fishguard & Pembroke in Wales, Cherbourg, Roscoff & St Nazaire in France and Gijon in Spain, it is the second largest passenger port in the State, the second biggest port in terms of ship movements, and the second biggest unitised freight port in the state, handling more unitised freight than the ports of Cork, Waterford and Shannon-Foynes put together. When Ernie's book is updated in 50 years time, there will be some story to tell!

I really enjoyed reading Ernie's history of this company. He has a nice style, easy to understand, and he has the gift of making a complex situation understandable. From time to time, when some technical issue to do with the port has come up, I have had occasion to refer to one or other of the F&RR&H Acts. It can sometimes be difficult to find the particular part you need in one of the acts, because so much of them relates to the financial affairs of various other predecessor railway companies which aren't relevant to the current port operation for which I am responsible. It is only when I read Ernie's history that I can begin to make head or tail of these various predecessor companies and the legacy they left the F&RR&HCo. It is an impressive feat of communication to turn such a spaghetti of railway aspirations, false starts, financial and other failures and achievements over about seventy years into an understandable narrative. Well done Ernie!

Finally, I would like to thank Ernie for undertaking this work, which I know is a labour of love. It is a fascinating insight into the history of this company of which I find myself a director. I must also thank Ernie for asking me to write this foreword. I am honoured to do so, and I hope that you, the reader, will get as much fascination and enjoyment from it as Ernie, I know, did in researching and writing it, and I did in reading the proof.

John P Lynch
General Manager Rosslare Europort
Director, Fishguard & Rosslare Railways &
Harbours Company

Introduction and Acknowledgements

Ask the average person in Ireland, or even the average railway enthusiast, how many companies own railways in the country and you will almost certainly be told that there are two, Iarnród Éireann (Irish Rail, generally shortened to IÉ [or IR in English]) and Translink, Northern Ireland Railways, with possibly Bord na Móna thrown in as an afterthought. It is almost certain that he or she will not make any mention of a Company which still technically owns the line from a point just south of Wexford Station to Rosslare Harbour a distance of some ten miles, and, although currently having no passenger service, the line between Rosslare Strand and Waterford; this is the Fishguard & Rosslare Railways & Harbours Company (F&RR&H). At the height of its existence, the Company owned a total of almost 104 miles of track in Ireland as well as just short of a mile of line at Fishguard Harbour. Although the Company is currently jointly owned by Irish Rail and Stena, board meetings are still held once a year and are attended by representatives of both of the owning companies.

When the author began his researches into the history of this Company, he was of the view that there would be little to record, bearing in mind the comparatively short mileage and the fact that the Company has only been in existence for a little over 100 years, but as time has gone by it has become patently obvious that the history of the F&RR&H is quite involved and full of interest and, at times, intrigue. To do full justice to the story, it has been found necessary to broaden the research beyond the actual Fishguard Company. For example, on the Irish side it has been necessary to begin the story with Brunel's original schemes for railways connecting Dublin with Waterford and the latter city with Cork. On the Welsh side, the original South Wales Railway played an important part in the story, as did the line from Clynderwen through the Preseli Mountains to Fishguard. Between those events of 160 years ago and the actual formation of the F&RR&H there were many schemes put forward, all of which deserve mention, albeit brief, for the part they have played in the unfolding drama. It is hoped that what is offered here does justice to gentlemen like Isambard Kingdom Brunel, Joseph Rowlands and James Cartland.

Although an important part of the Company's operations were, and are, based in Fishguard, this work is primarily intended as another in the series of Irish railway histories produced by the author during the past 20 years. To this end, the history of the various companies which predated the F&RR&H have been dealt with in some detail. It is to be regretted that no official records appear to have survived for the Cork & Youghal Railway, which was subsumed into the Great Southern & Western Railway (GS&WR) almost 150 years ago. Likewise, the Waterford & Wexford Railway (W&WR) became part of the old F&RR&H Syndicate in 1893/4 and it may be that the records were transferred to the Syndicate's offices in Birmingham and were destroyed when taken over by the new Fishguard Company in 1898. This view is strengthened by the fact that the Syndicate's own records prior to October 1898 are also no longer available. References in the following chapters to 'The Syndicate' allude to the Company formed by Rowlands and Cartland, which existed until its sale to Alexander Henderson was agreed in February 1898. It should at this juncture be pointed out that this history concentrates on the railway aspect of the Company's operations, although obviously some mention has to be made of the maritime side. This latter has, however, been dealt with in more detail by other authors and the reader is directed to the Bibliography for further information.

As is normal in such circumstances, the writing of this history would have been impossible without assistance from many sources. Córas Iompair Éireann (CIÉ) is the holding company for IÉ and has a statutory obligation to retain the records of the many Irish railway companies which eventually came together to form the Great Southern Railways in January 1925. In addition, as one of the Partners in the F&RR&H, they hold copies of the board minute books for that Company. These have been made freely available to the author. First and foremost must be mentioned Geraldine Finucane, the Secretary of CIÉ and her staff for allowing access to the board and traffic minute books of those of the constituent companies which have survived. Two Secretarial Services Managers, Frances Sugrue and the present incumbent Audrey Crowley must be mentioned specifically. The CIÉ Solicitor, Michael Carroll, now retired, went to a good deal of trouble turning out copies of various Acts of Parliament, while Vincent Brady in the Structural Design Office at Inchicore (also now retired) kindly produced drawings and photographs of bridges. John Lynch, the current General Manager, Rosslare, kindly photocopied copies of Acts of Parliament and other material which the author had not been able to otherwise obtain, and has also encouraged the author in his endeavours. Captain Aedan Jameson, the Harbour Master at Rosslare, kindly produced the aerial photograph of the port. Philip Quigley, the Operations Support Manager at Rosslare Harbour, has a fine collection of postcards of Rosslare and has kindly allowed the author to use scanned copies of these.

Having unsuccessfully attempted on a number of occasions to make contact with the F&RR&H Company, the author, almost in desperation, wrote to the (Pembrokeshire) *County Echo* enquiring whether there might be anybody in the Fishguard area who had any knowledge of the railway. The Editor kindly published my request and shortly afterwards I received an email from a gentleman who confirmed that he was the then Chairman of the Company. This was Gareth Williams, who confirmed the existence of material which might be of assistance in my researches. I eventually met up with Gareth at Fishguard in May 2008 and once again was given free access to the material available in Fishguard, some of which proved

extremely useful in the author's quest for detailed information. Gareth also took the trouble to take the author on a tour of the facilities at the port. During the course of that visit, the author also met up with local historian, Martin Lewis of Newport (Pembs.). I am extremely grateful to Martin for his kind hospitality and for showing me around the local facilities, including the Fishguard Bay Hotel, no longer of course in railway ownership. Martin also very kindly made available to me copies of old photographs in his collection; these were photocopied at short notice by Nigel Barrah in Fishguard and to him I am also grateful. Martin also kindly presented me with copies of his two books dealing with the history of Fishguard and district, referred to in the Bibliography.

Special mention must also be made of The National Archives at Kew, which as usual provided the author with access to not only the Board of Trade (BoT) papers relating to the various lines, but also GWR board minute books, maps etc. I would also like to thank the staff in the photocopying department for their assistance in scanning photographs and other material. Once again, the Irish Railway Record Society came to the author's assistance with the vast amount of material in their archival and library collections; I must here thank Brendan Pender and the Revd Dr Norman Gamble, past and present Archivists, and Timothy Moriarty, Librarian of that body. Individual members of the IRRS who assisted include Gerald Beesley, Barry Carse, Oliver Doyle, Seán Kennedy and Herbert Richards. Sincere thanks are due to the IRRS for allowing the author to use photographs from their extensive collection. Aside from providing the author with many biographical details of the various companies' engineers, Gerald encouraged me to continue my researches when, on occasions, there was a temptation to give it all up; he also very kindly, despite arduous work commitments, took a good deal of time to read through early drafts of the manuscripts and make constructive comments – we are, however, still not quite on the same wavelength as regards the use of the semicolon! Barry very kindly provided the author with photographs from his comprehensive collection along with permission to use them in this book.

Other individuals and bodies who have assisted in various ways include Birmingham City Archives; Brian and John Boyce of Rosslare; Richard Casserley; the Cropper family; Helen Roscoe of the Fishguard Library; Thomas Grennan of the Horeswood Historical Society; the GWR Society, in particular Graham Carpenter, John Lewis and Laurence Watson; House of Lords Record Office; Maria Kyte and Romina Germani of the Waterford & Suir Valley Railway; the National Library of Wales in Aberystwyth; Richard Parker; Nikki Bosworth of the Pembrokeshire Record Office in Haverfordwest; Kevin Robertson; University of Queensland; Waterford City Library; Waterford County Museum in Dungarvan; West Glamorgan Record Office; Wexford County Library. Websites from which useful material was gleaned include the British Newspaper Library, *The Irish Times*, *The London Gazette*, Dáil Éireann Debates, *Hansard*, Ancestry, *The Times of London*.

Finally, I would like to thank Colourpoint and in particular, Malcolm Johnston, the Commissioning Editor, for his faith in the project right from the beginning. Two other people at Colourpoint deserve mention, Rachel Irwin, my Editor, and Jacky Hawkes, who is responsible for the book's promotion and sales.

Any errors or omissions are the sole responsibility of the author; in the event that the assistance of any individual has not been noted, the author offers his sincere apologies. Errors or omissions or indeed any additional information or illustrations which might be included in a second edition should in the first instance be sent to the Publishers.

Ernie Shepherd

Maps of the Irish lines

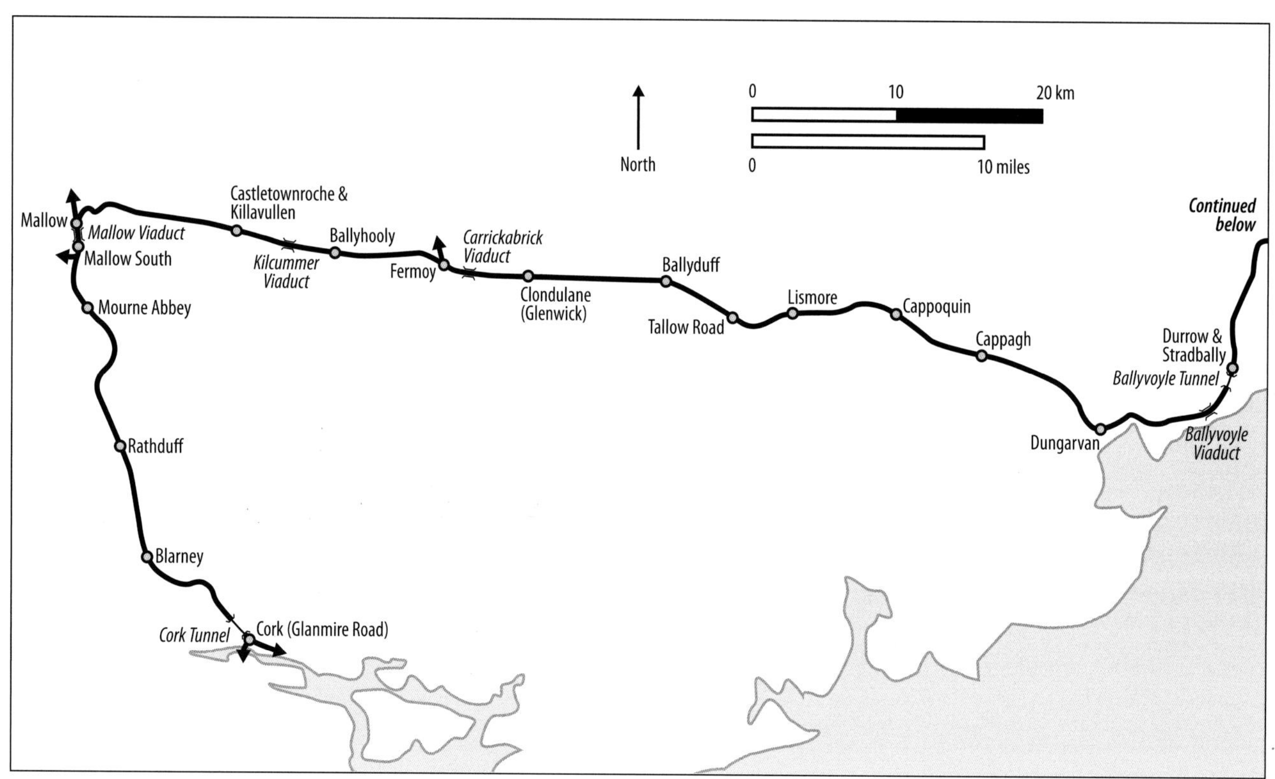

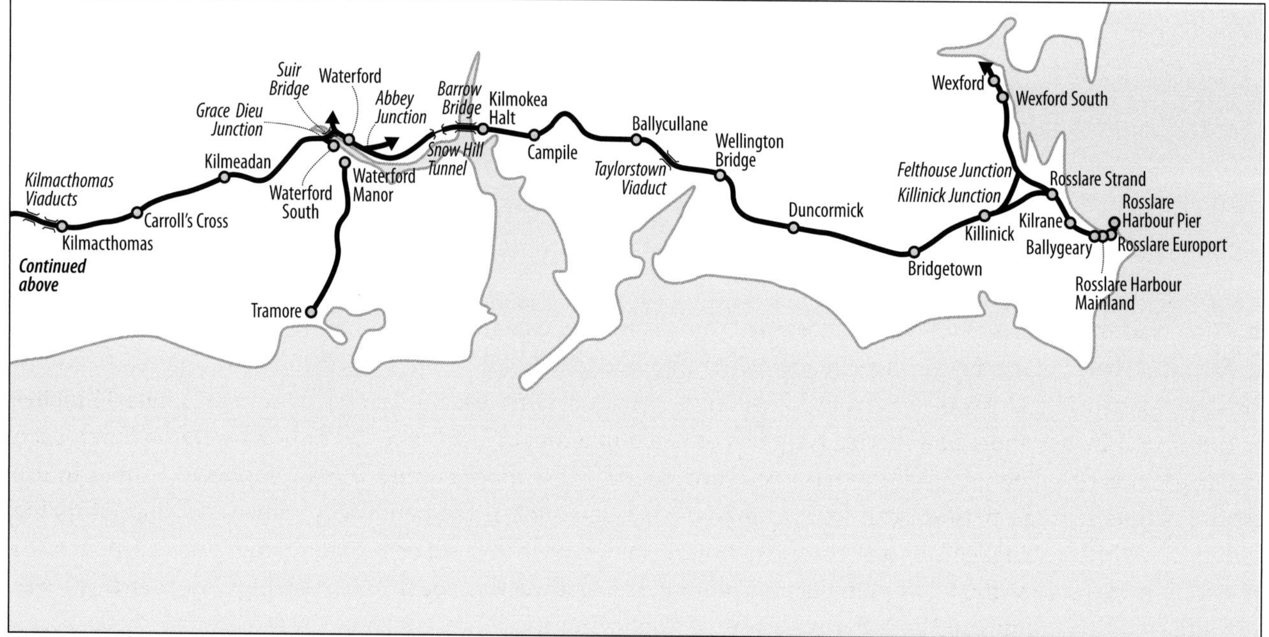

Map of the Welsh lines

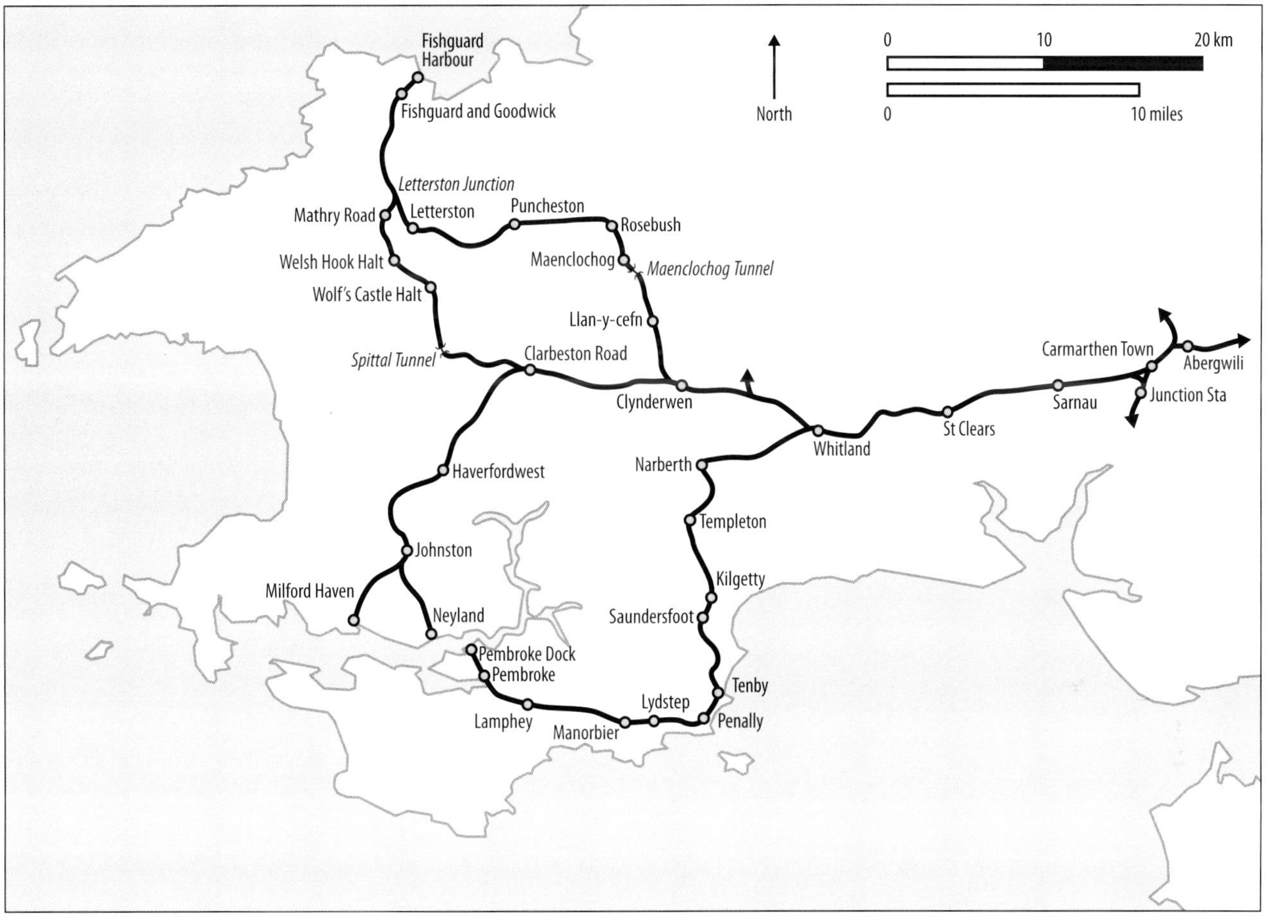

Note on Measurements

Now that Ireland has gone metric, it was felt that some brief explanation of imperial measurements might be useful, particularly for younger readers. The mile consisted of 8 furlongs, in turn consisting of 10 chains, the latter measuring 22 yards. A yard is divided into 3 feet, the latter each of 12 inches. A yard is thus 36 inches or just over 3 inches short of a metre. Weights consisted of a ton, comprised of 20 hundredweights (cwt), each of 112 pounds (lb). The imperial ton has been superseded by the metric tonne. Finally, monetary values in use for the majority of the period dealt with in this history consisted of the pound (£) (which for most of its life had parity with the English pound) comprised of 20 shillings (s), the latter in turn divided into 12 pence (d) or pennies; there were thus 240 pennies in a pound. The Guinea was equal to 21 shillings. The Euro (€) was introduced in Ireland in 2005 and floats against the Pound Sterling.

Abbreviations

ATW	Arriva Trains Wales
BoT	Board of Trade
BRB	British Railways Board
CB&PR	Cork, Blackrock & Passage Railway
CB&SCR	Cork Bandon & South Coast Railway
C&F&W&WR	Cork & Fermoy & Waterford & Wexford Railway (Act 1890)
CIÉ	Córas Iompair Éireann
CL&DR	Clonmel, Lismore & Dungarvan Railway
C&MDR	Cork & Macroom Direct Railway
CSÉ	Cómhlucht Siúicre Éireann Teoranta (The Irish Sugar Company)
C&WR	Cork & Waterford Railway
C&YR	Cork & Youghal Railway
D&SER	Dublin & South Eastern Railway
DW&WR	Dublin, Wicklow & Wexford Railway
EEC	European Economic Community
F&LR	Fermoy & Lismore Railway
F&RR&HC	Fishguard & Rosslare Railways & Harbours Company
GS&WR	Great Southern & Western Railway
GUV	General Utility Van
GW	First Great Western
GWR	Great Western Railway
HST	High Speed Train
IÉ	Iarnród Éireann (Irish Rail)
L&NWR	London & North Western Railway
MGWR	Midland Great Western Railway
NP&FR	North Pembrokeshire & Fishguard Railway
PWLC	Public Works Loan Commissioners
RHC	Royal Harbour Commissioners
RNAD	Royal Naval Armament Depot
W&CIR	Waterford & Central Ireland Railway
WD&LR	Waterford, Dungarvan & Lismore Railway
WHC	Wexford Harbour Commissioners
WL&FR	Waterford, Lismore & Fermoy Railway
WL&WR	Waterford, Limerick & Western Railway
W&WR	Waterford & Wexford Railway

CHAPTER ONE

In The Beginning

In the reign of Queen Elizabeth I, at a time when Irish affairs required regular communication between the Court and the Lord Lieutenant in Ireland, a postal service was established between Ireland and Britain. In October 1572 post stages were set up for a weekly mail service via Chester and the port of Liverpool to Howth, with a second route via Reading, Bristol and Swansea through Milford to Waterford. The northern route was redirected to the port of Holyhead in 1576, as this provided the shortest sea crossing. The General Letter Office, later to become the General Post Office (GPO) was officially established in England in 1660 by Charles II, but it was not until 1784 that a separate Irish Post Office was established with its own independent Post Master General of Ireland. The Act of Union in 1800 brought about a number of changes, the principal one as regards postal services being improvements in the road to Holyhead and the re-routing of coaches via Shrewsbury, so avoiding the North Wales coast road and the ferry crossing at Conway. It also resulted in the abolition of the office of Postmaster General of Ireland in 1831. An Act of 1810 authorised improvements in the harbours at Holyhead and at Howth. Steam ships began operating from Holyhead in 1819, the New Steam Packet Company offering to take the mails on its two paddle steamers, *Talbot* and *Ivanhoe*, but this was declined and the GPO introduced their own paddle steamers. In 1826 the GPO put on a steamer service from Liverpool to Kingstown via Holyhead, the Holyhead–Dublin steamers continuing, however, to use Howth until 22 January 1834 when Kingstown became the sole port.

At a meeting in Dublin on 9 August 1835, the Manager of the Ffestiniog Railway (FR), Dubliner, Henry Archer, proposed a rail and steamer link with London via Porth Dynllaen, about 20 miles southwest of Caernarvon, connecting en route with the FR at Porthmadog. Porth Dynllaen was regarded as a suitable location as it was capable of providing shelter from the prevailing southwest winds for the largest steam packets then in operation. The proposed rail connection to London was to be via Ludlow, Worcester, Stratford and Oxford, a distance of 220 miles. Two notable engineers, Charles Blacker Vignoles and John Urpeth Rastrick were requested to survey likely routes from Porth Dynllaen, these surveys being carried out in the first half of 1836. In all Vignoles considered four possible routes, his preferred option being 244 miles in length, and with very heavy gradients and a number of tunnels, including one of 2 miles in length.

In July 1836 Isambard Kingdom Brunel, the Engineer of the Great Western Railway (GWR), also surveyed a line from Gloucester to New Quay on Cardigan Bay; nothing further was heard of this scheme. Some nine years later the GWR Board were reported to be considering a broad-gauge line from Worcester to Porth Dynllaen. It is interesting that such a proposal was being put forward in 1845 as the South Wales Railway was very much alive by then.

The Irish Railway Commission was set up in December 1836 to consider and report on a general system of railways for Ireland, Vignoles being one of two engineers appointed to the Commission. As part of his brief he carried out additional surveys on the Welsh side; despite this he was still of opinion that his original survey of the Porth Dynllaen route was the most suitable. In all, six cross-channel routes were considered by the Commission as per the accompanying table overleaf.

As regards the use of Wicklow as a port, it would have required not only the construction of a new harbour but also a connecting railway line to the capital. As far as Fishguard was concerned, the possibility of a steamer service to Wexford was briefly considered but was dismissed as the port was not "adapted to the packet service", a remark which might

English Port	Distance from London in miles	Irish Port	Length of Voyage in miles	Total journey time
Holyhead	272	Kingstown	63	17h 53m
Liverpool	210	Kingstown	130	22h 17m
Orme's Bay	230	Kingstown	96	19h 37m
Porth Dynllaen	260	Kingstown	70	18h 8m
Porth Dynllaen	260	Wicklow	60	18h 1½m
Fishguard	260	Wicklow	79	19h 55½m

also have equally applied to Wicklow; it would require an even longer railway connection from Wexford to Dublin and was quickly ruled out. It is not clear from the report exactly where the service was to run from on the Welsh side, Goodwick or from the old harbour at Fishguard itself. However, as Holyhead was already the packet station for the mail steamers to and from Ireland, the argument came down to a choice between it and Orme's Bay, although Porth Dynllaen was to figure in future plans right up to the late 1880s. Captain (later Rear Admiral Sir) Francis Beaufort, RN, the inventor of the wind scale still in use today, came down strongly in favour of Holyhead. Lieutenant WL Sheringham of the Royal Navy reported in June 1838 in favour of Porth Dynllaen but it was Holyhead which eventually won out. The passing of the Chester & Crewe Railway Act in 1837 had really sealed the fate of the cross-channel service. With the opening of the Grand Junction Railway and the London & Birmingham Railway (L&BR) in July 1837, London was linked to Birmingham, Manchester and Liverpool by a mode of transport that was twice the speed of the road mail coaches. The GPO therefore decided to transfer the mails to rail transport, and with the opening of the Chester & Crewe Railway, the Dublin mails were carried by this route as from 6 April 1841.

A Select Committee of the House of Commons was set up in June of the following year to examine the question of postal communication with Ireland, Holyhead and Porth Dynllaen being again considered

on their respective merits. Holyhead was once more the preferred option despite the difficulties associated with the crossing of the Menai Straits en route from Chester. So it was that the Chester & Holyhead Railway Company (C&HR) lodged a Bill in Parliament in the spring of 1844, which received Royal Assent on 4 July of that year. Capital was set at £2.1 million, of which the L&BR was empowered to contribute £1 million. Included among the first Directors was Edward Cropper, a representative of the L&BR – a gentleman to whom we will return later in our narrative. The C&HR opened in stages between March 1848 and October 1850, with a 72-chain extension from Holyhead Station to the Admiralty Pier following on 20 May 1851. The detailed history of that particular company does not concern us further at this point and the reader is referred to the Bibliography for sources of further details.

Although the formation of the South Wales Railway (SWR) predates the Company that is the subject of this book by almost 60 years, it is important to relate the history of the SWR in some detail as it was the first serious attempt by GWR interests to establish a connection with the south of Ireland. Indeed, the early proposals for railway communication to and from the southeast of Ireland are an essential part of this history. Ireland's first railway, the Dublin & Kingstown (D&KR), was opened for traffic on 17 December 1834, connecting the city of Dublin with the harbour at Dunleary, a distance of a little under 6 miles. In May 1837 the line was extended the short distance to Kingstown to what is today the present station known as Dun Laoghaire.[1] Not content with terminating their line at Kingstown, the D&KR Directors set their sights on the township of Dalkey with its increasing population. There was already a double-track tramway in existence between Kingstown and the stone quarries at Dalkey, laid down in connection with the transport of stone for the construction of the harbour at Kingstown. That work was largely complete by the early 1840s and it was decided that one of the two tracks should be taken over and reconstructed for the

1 Dun Laoghaire as we know it today began its development with the construction of the new harbour. It was named Kingstown to celebrate the departure of King George IV through the port in 1821 and was renamed Dun Laoghaire (Laoghaire's Fort) in 1921.

use of the D&KR; to avoid having to go to Parliament for an Act, the existing route would be followed and horse power would be employed. This was to cause some difficulties due to the sharp curves and steep gradients of the tramway.

However, before any construction got under way the Directors and officers of the D&KR visited London to attend a demonstration of a new invention, which was to have far reaching consequences. This was the trial of a short Atmospheric railway at Wormwood Scrubs. Whilst the trials were apparently not an unqualified success, they appear to have had a great impact on the D&KR party. Where better to try out the new idea in ideal conditions but on the proposed line to Dalkey with its sharp curves and steep gradients? Construction proceeded apace and trials of the new system were carried out in the latter half of 1843 with the new line opening for public traffic on Friday 29 March 1844. Following the opening, the line was visited by many interested parties from Britain and further afield. One such was a group of GWR Directors and officers, including their Engineer, Isambard Kingdom Brunel, and Locomotive Superintendent, Daniel Gooch. Brunel was a man with an inventive mind, and was convinced of the merits of the Atmospheric system, although Gooch was reported to have had serious reservations. Despite these reservations, Brunel later persuaded his Directors to employ it on the South Devon Railway, although the outcome was never entirely satisfactory.

During the course of his visit to Dublin, Brunel took the opportunity to acquaint James Pim of the D&KR of the GWR Directors' desire to establish a new cross-channel shipping route to the southeast of Ireland. In connection with this venture they were anxious to see the establishment of a rail connection between Wexford or Waterford and Dublin and enquired whether the D&KR would be prepared to share in such a venture. In later chapters we will take a more detailed look into the affairs of what eventually became the Dublin & South Eastern Railway (D&SER) and another GWR-inspired scheme, the Cork & Waterford Railway which was intended to connect the two cities named in its title.

As early as October 1835, Brunel expounded his grand vision for the GWR by putting forward the idea of a steamship service from Bristol to New York, this leading to the setting up of the Great Western Steamship Company in 1836. The SS *Great Western* was launched on 19 July 1837 and departed on her first crossing to New York on 8 April of the following year.

Bristol was not, however, to be the end of Brunel's ambitions in regard to a transatlantic service, hence the plans for a line through South Wales and the construction of a new port at some suitable location. Brunel had carried out surveys in the summer of 1844 for the proposed line on the Welsh side, following which a prospectus was published in the name of the South Wales Railway for a line from Standish on the Cheltenham branch of the GWR, crossing the River Severn at Hock Cliff between Awre and Fretherne by means of a high bridge, and then following the coast to Newport. At the point of crossing the Severn the river was 1,100 yards wide. From Newport the line was to continue through Cardiff, Neath, Swansea and Carmarthen to Fishguard, where a new port would be established; a branch was also intended to run south from Eglwysfair Glan Taf to Pembroke, where the Admiralty had dockyard facilities. Much reference was made to communication with the south of Ireland, with the provision of a new port to the south of Wexford for cross-channel traffic. It is hardly surprising, therefore, that there were some Irish interests among the early promoters. It was clear that, whilst nominally independent, the SWR was, to all intents and purposes a subsidiary of the GWR; Brunel was appointed Engineer to the new company, which also shared a common Solicitor with the GWR, while its first Chairman was Charles Russell, Chairman of the GWR.

The course of the line west of Newport was generally approved of, but the inhabitants of Monmouthshire objected to the proposed line running along the coast where it would least serve their needs. It was suggested that it should run from Newport up the valley of the River Usk via Caerleon to Monmouth and thence to Gloucester, a line which would be 18 miles longer and with steeper gradients. The strongest opposition, however, was to the proposed crossing of the Severn,

Brunel suggesting, with the approval of the Severn Navigation Commissioners, a new navigable cut or ship canal across the Arlington promontory between Hock Cliff and Framilode Passage. Despite this the Admiralty were adamantly opposed to a bridge and this was to lead to a Bill being lodged for a line only as far as Chepstow.

The Act of Incorporation of the South Wales Railway Company received Royal Assent on 4 August 1845 with powers granted for a line from Fishguard to Chepstow with a branch from Newport to Monmouth; at the latter point the line was to connect with the Monmouth & Hereford Railway. Capital of the new company was to be £2.8 million, of which the GWR was to subscribe £600,000; this in due course proved to be a serious underestimation of the total cost of the line. No mention is made of the gauge for the new line, but it was clearly intended to be to the GWR broad-gauge of 7ft 0in from the outset. A further Bill was lodged in 1846 with alternative plans for the crossing of the Severn at the point originally proposed, one by a larger bridge, the second by a tunnel as recommended by James Walker on behalf of the Admiralty, but the Bill was rejected. Considering this a likely outcome, the SWR had already made provisional arrangements with the Gloucester & Dean Forest Railway to connect with the Monmouth & Hereford near Grange Court, about 8 miles from Gloucester, the necessary powers being obtained under another Act of 1846.

Some doubts appear to have existed from the outset regarding the suitability of Fishguard; although sheltered in part by high cliffs, there were no harbour facilities and it was exposed to certain wind directions. Milford Haven in the south of the county extolled the virtues of its safe anchorage for vessels. Another factor of concern to the inhabitants of Pembrokeshire was the fact that the proposed line was not intended to serve the county town of Haverfordwest, although this matter was resolved with the passing of the 1846 Act with powers granted for a branch from near Clarbeston Road to that town. The Act also allowed for two diversions, one between Carmarthen and Kidwelly to lessen earthworks and ease gradients; the second diversion was between Aberavon and Bridgend so as to avoid the coast with its shifting sands. Brunel

still appears to have had some reservations regarding the suitability of Fishguard as in November 1847 he advised the Directors that he had found another suitable location at Abermawr about 4 miles west of Fishguard, which would shorten the sea crossing by 5 miles. In fact, although powers were sought in the 1847 Session of Parliament, these were never actually granted for this diversion of the original line; nevertheless, some preliminary work was carried out and some of this can still be seen today beyond Welsh Hook and in the neighbourhood of Mathry Cross. The intention was to abandon some 6½ miles of the already authorised line.

Construction works began in the summer of 1846 and by August of the following year the entire line was under construction to within 7 miles of Fishguard. In the interim, an agreement had been concluded in December 1846 with the GWR for a perpetual lease of the SWR at a guaranteed rent of 5 per cent on a capital of £3 million in shares and £1 million in loans, together with half the surplus profits, the lease to come into effect with the completion of the entire line from Chepstow to Fishguard. However, events in Ireland were to have a considerable effect on the affairs of the SWR and we must briefly return across the Irish Sea to consider these in some detail.

It will be recalled that the GWR had sought to interest the D&KR Directors as Partners in a lengthy extension of their line southwards, it being announced in October 1844 that a deputation from the GWR was shortly expected. The D&KR Directors were a cautious group of Dublin businessmen, a number of them being of the Quaker tradition. Having given the matter due consideration, they decided that they would be stretching themselves too much by extending their 8 miles of line to one in excess of 100 miles. They therefore intimated that they were prepared to go as far as Wicklow, 30 miles south of the capital. The people at Paddington, probably correctly, took the view that having gone as far as Wicklow, the D&KR would not extend the line any further, and decided to go ahead without the D&KR. Early in November 1844 the *Wexford Independent* reported that maps and sections had been prepared by Brunel, for what became briefly known as the Wexford & Dublin Atmospheric

Railway. Rather than having a terminus in Wexford, the town was to be bypassed and Ballygeary selected as a packet station. The proposed line was to run to the east of the River Slaney, crossing to the west bank at Cullentra, a short distance from Ferrycarrig. By December the scheme had been revised to terminate in Wexford, near to the dockyard at the southern end of the quays. The plans to run down the east bank of the Slaney were effectively scuppered by the Admiralty, their Lordships insisting on the line crossing the river immediately below Enniscorthy by an opening bridge, this latter requirement later being rescinded.

An Act was obtained on 16 July 1846 incorporating the Waterford, Wexford, Wicklow & Dublin Railway (WWW&DR), generally referred to at the time as the 3Ws. Capital was set at £2 million with additional borrowing powers up to £666,000, subject to the usual provisos regarding borrowing. The 3Ws main line was to run from Dundrum, 3 miles from Dublin, to Grannagh, otherwise known as Granny Ferry, just outside the city of Waterford but actually situated in Co Kilkenny, where it was to connect with the proposed Waterford & Limerick Railway. At Dundrum the new line was to make an end-on junction with the Dublin, Dundrum & Rathfarnham Railway, the latter to run into Harcourt Road in the city of Dublin. The location for the city terminus was altered by an Act of 1847 to the west side of St Stephen's Green, although this was never actually built, but an extension to a new terminus situated in Harcourt Street was eventually completed in 1859. There were to be three branches, one to connect the D&KR line at Kingstown to the 3Ws at Bray, some 6 miles further south. A second line was to serve the town and port of Wicklow, while the third branch was to run to "a Pier in the Sea or on the Shore of Grenore (sic) Bay, near the Town and Port of Wexford." A further Act of 25 June 1847 made provision for a deviation of the line in Co Wicklow, one section stipulating that the pier at Grenore (sic) or South Bay was to be constructed of open piling.

Yet another Act of 30 June 1848 has some relevance to our narrative as it empowered the SWR to subscribe to the Irish undertaking and to appoint seven Directors to the 3Ws Board. As the number of Directors was in future to be limited to 12, it is clear that the SWR intended to have a controlling interest. More importantly, the Engineer was none other than IK Brunel. The ceremony of turning the first sod was carried out at Bray Head on 25 August 1848 by the 3Ws Chairman, the Earl of Courtown. Several contracts were entered into and work commenced at Bray Head and between Dalkey and Bray. Good progress was initially made but this was soon hampered by shortage of finance. Worse was to come. The potato crop had failed in Ireland in 1845, this being followed by a severe winter and then a complete crop failure in 1846. This had a devastating effect on the country's finances, while by 1851 the population had virtually halved. From that point onwards, emigration was to be a major part of Irish life. However, this crisis affected not only Ireland but it also had a deleterious effect in Britain.

Arising from the Great Famine the WWW&DR Directors took the decision to shorten their line to terminate at Wicklow. This was ironic, bearing in mind the GWR reservations on this very point only a few years previously in relation to the D&KR. In 1848 the SWR Directors also gave orders for a suspension of all work west of Swansea. As mentioned previously, the SWR were empowered under the 1848 Act to subscribe to the 3Ws. It had been the intention to subscribe a sum of £250,000 but, after only £33,000 had been advanced, the Welsh company had a change of heart. The SWR Directors wrote to the 3Ws in July 1850, strongly urging a suspension of all works in Ireland and a winding-up of the Company's affairs. They pointed out that they would strenuously oppose any Bill to terminate the line at Wicklow. Despite this warning, the 3Ws Board went ahead and successfully obtained an Act on 24 July 1851 for just such a move, the title of the Company being altered to the Dublin & Wicklow Railway. Later, the Company, re-titled in 1860 as the Dublin, Wicklow & Wexford Railway (DW&WR), extended its line in stages, eventually reaching Wexford in August 1872.

It will be recalled that the GWR lease of the SWR was only to come into effect on completion of the latter company's line to Fishguard, for which presumably Abermawr could have been substituted. However, when the decision was taken to restrict the works to Swansea the GWR quickly announced their unwillingness to complete the lease. Relations between the two companies soured, so much so that Charles Russell was replaced as Chairman of the SWR by Mr CRM Talbot of Margam Park, Lord Lieutenant of Glamorganshire. At the same time, it was reported that Mr Armstrong, the Company Secretary, had absconded with about £5,000 of the Company's money; he was replaced by Frederick George Saunders, Secretary of the Vale of Neath Railway and a nephew of Charles Saunders, the Secretary of the GWR.

The decision was now taken to resume the works west of Swansea, to which the line was opened in June 1850. Hardly had these works got under way when a fresh agreement was concluded with the GWR in March 1851 to lease the SWR for a period of 999 years. This lease was to come into operation with the completion of the line as far as Swansea, other sections being included as they opened for traffic. It was an unusual lease in that the line was to be worked by a joint committee of five Directors from each company; under its provisions the SWR was to receive two-thirds of the net profits after payment of working expenses and debenture interest. It was also decided that the line should now be built to Milford Haven rather than to Fishguard; as the section from Clarbeston Road as far as Haverfordwest had already been authorised in 1846, application was made to Parliament for construction of the remainder of the line, success being achieved in 1852. Under the same Act the 14 miles from Clarbeston Road to Fishguard were abandoned.

As regards the main line, the first section, from Chepstow to Swansea High Street, a distance of 75 miles, was opened on 18 June 1850, this section being double tracked with bridge rails. Locomotives and rolling stock were provided by the GWR along with the necessary staff, the remainder of the traffic staff being the responsibility of the SWR. The line was extended a further 30 miles to Carmarthen on 11 October 1852. Barlow rails were used in the construction of this section, laid direct on the ballast without any timber or other support; this led to problems later on. With the abandonment of the line to Fishguard, what had been a branch to Haverfordwest now became the main line, the 31 miles 14 chains

from Carmarthen to Haverfordwest being ready for a Board of Trade (BoT) inspection in December 1853. A ceremonial opening took place on 28 December, with scheduled services commencing on 2 January 1854; intermediate stations provided included Narberth Road and Clarbeston Road. Work then proceeded on the final extension to Milford Haven.

The location of the terminus was at Neyland, a single line being opened to this point on 15 April 1856. The port at Neyland was designed by Brunel and was more than adequate for the vessels of the period, with deep water available at all states of the tide. A twice weekly steamer service was quickly established between Neyland and Waterford, being operated by Messrs Ford & Jackson of London on behalf of the Company. The introduction of a second boat in May 1856 enabled a service to be provided on three days per week; in addition a service was also opened to Cork. Initially the port was called Milford Haven, being altered to Neyland in 1859. After a few months, however, the name was again changed and by December of that year it was known as New Milford, this name remaining in use until the facilities were transferred to Fishguard in 1906. The second line from Carmarthen to Milford Haven was completed on 1 July 1857, thus providing a double track all the way from Paddington.

A new agreement of 15 November 1861 provided for the GWR to take a lease of the South Wales Railway for six years from 1 January 1862 (or until an amalgamation between the GWR and West Midland Railway (WMR) had been sanctioned by Parliament), at a rent of £170,000 per annum and to work the line as part of their own system. A more formal agreement was drawn up in February 1862 and application was made to Parliament for its implementation; the subject of the GWR/WMR amalgamation was dealt with in a separate Bill. The Act received Royal Assent on 21 July 1863 and provided for the dissolution of the SWR as from 1 August of that year, thus ending the separate existence of the SWR.

To conclude this chapter, it is worth mentioning that the whole of the SWR section was converted from broad to standard (4ft 8½in) gauge during the month of May 1872. On the night of 30 April, the up line between New Milford and Grange Court was closed and handed over to the engineers, the down line being comprised of 14 sections, each in charge of a pilot engine and pilotman. At that point all broad-gauge rolling stock was worked out to Swindon, where extensive reception sidings had been installed. Large numbers of men were brought in and work commenced at daybreak on 1 May. Such was the pace of the work that the new up line was handed back for traffic on the night of Sunday 12 May. The down line was then converted, this in turn being completed by 22 May, double line working being reinstated by a special engine from New Milford that evening. The remainder of the line from Gloucester to Swindon was also converted to standard-gauge in May 1872.

Early Proposals for a Connection to Cork

The first reference to a railway involving Youghal, Co Cork, is to be found in the *Railway Times* for 10 March 1845 when details appeared of the prospectus for the Cork, Midleton & Youghal Railway Company. This was intended to connect the points named in its title, with branches to Cove (sic) and Fermoy. Total length was 50 miles; the proposed capital was to be £500,000 with Sir John Macneill acting as Consulting Engineer. The first section, the 12½ miles to Midleton, was to pass near to New Glanmire and Carrigtwohill; from Midleton, where the branch to Fermoy was to diverge, the line would continue via Castlemartyr and Killeagh to Youghal. Less than two weeks later, a more grandiose scheme under the title of the Cork & Waterford Railway (C&WR) was being put before the public. This line, which was intended to connect with the Waterford & Kilkenny Railway (W&KR), was to run from Cork to Waterford, with branches to Cove[1] and Fermoy, a total mileage of 100. Capital was to be £1 million in 40,000 shares. The offices were situated at 34 Broad Street Buildings in the City of London and, apart from a number of Directors of both the W&LR and W&KR companies, the provisional committee included Thomas Wyse, MP, as Chairman, the Earl of Desart, Viscount Duncannon and the mayors of Waterford and Kilkenny. Valentine Barry was appointed Provisional Secretary, and the Consulting Engineers were John Valentine and Denis Leahy.

The proposed line was to commence near Patrick's Bridge in Cork and, passing at the back of Glanmire, would run through Carrigtwohill, Midleton, Castlemartyr, Killeagh, Youghal, Tallow, Lismore, Cappoquin, Dungarvan, Stradbally, Bonmahon and Tramore. As we shall see, much of this proposed route was to be followed by the Waterford, Dungarvan &

Lismore Railway some 30 years later. It was reported in the *Railway Times* that the provisional committee had made contact with the Directors of the South Wales Railway with a view to forming a direct communication between the south of Ireland and England; the SWR agreed to subscribe a sum of £6,000 towards the new undertaking. The great intercourse of traffic between Cork and Cove was well known, while between Waterford and Tramore passenger traffic generating upwards of £7,000 existed during the summer months alone. There was a considerable source of revenue to be obtained if a westwards extension was also made. Apart from the tourist attraction of Killarney, there was the route to Valentia which could become a great high road of commerce between England and America. In addition to all of that, the mines at Bonmahon were believed by some to be a richer source of copper than any of the Cornish mines, a prophecy far removed from fact. All in all, prospects appeared to be most encouraging.

A special meeting of the C&WR shareholders was held early in February 1846 to consider and sanction an agreement with the Cork, Midleton & Youghal Railway (CM&YR) on terms which were considered to be equitable, viz holders of CM&YR scrip would, on payment of 5s be entitled to two C&WR scrip certificates for £25 shares with 30s paid on each. The capital of the two companies was to be consolidated with the new company to be known as the Cork & Waterford Railway, and IK Brunel had been retained as Consulting Engineer. It was reported that great co-operation was forthcoming from both the SWR and the GWR. By April, the C&WR Bill was under consideration in the House of Lords where it was being strenuously opposed by the newly formed Waterford & Tramore Railway (W&TR). That company's Engineer, Mr Townsend, believed that their line would be shorter and capable of being constructed

---

1 The original name of 'The Cove of Cork' was altered to Queenstown following the visit of Queen Victoria to Cork in August 1849. Following a resolution of the UDC in 1922, the Gaelicised version of Cobh was adopted.

more economically, in addition to which it would afford greater accommodation to the public. Apart altogether from the opposition in Parliament there was dissatisfaction amongst many of the shareholders who considered it expedient that all further progress be halted and the undertaking wound up.

The Cork & Waterford Railway Act received Royal Assent on 26 August 1846 for a mainline 78m 8c in length with branches to Fermoy and Tramore, representing a further 19m 16c. Barely a month later moves were once again being made to bring about the dissolution of the undertaking, a meeting to this effect being convened in Hitchcock's Hotel in Dublin; however, only a few shareholders turned up. The first ordinary proprietors' meeting was to have been held in London on 16 February 1847, having to be postponed to the following week due to a poor turnout. When the meeting did take place on 25 February, Thomas Wyse was elected Chairman of the Board. At the same meeting George Henry Layard was appointed Secretary at a salary of £600 per annum.

Addressing the meeting of 25 February, Wyse said there appeared to be two alternative courses of action open to the shareholders, one being to make a call of £1 per share, to be paid in 1848, and to proceed with construction of a small portion of the railway between Waterford and Tramore, thus ensuring a fair dividend which would enable commencement of the section from Cork to Midleton. The alternative was that everything should remain in abeyance until the next half-yearly meeting, a course recommended by the Directors, including those nominated by the GWR and SWR. Nothing was done, and when the proprietors next met in October 1847 they were informed that the Tramore line would cost about £95,000, viz £40,000 for earth works, £10,000 for land purchase and the balance for plant, rolling stock and stations. Whilst the line would initially be single, the earth works were to allow for doubling at some future date. The Directors then recommended proceeding with that section, no other portion of the line to be commenced until the propriety of proceeding be approved by the shareholders at a general meeting. One of the shareholders, a Mr Garrett, observed on the difficulties likely to be encountered in obtaining monies at that time, and suggested that the Directors refrain from making any calls on the shareholders until the end of March 1848 – a motion that was put to the meeting and passed.

By the time of the third shareholders' meeting in the following February, the Directors had found it necessary to apply to Parliament for an extension of time, but no works were proposed for at least 12 months, by which time it was hoped that the Company's financial position would be somewhat better. To show their good intention, the Directors decided to reduce the allowance to themselves by half; they did agree to maintain the Secretary's salary at £600, 12 months notice to be given of any proposed reduction. At the shareholders' meeting in March 1850, the Chairman in his report stated that there had been no significant changes in the Company's affairs in the interim. In response to a question from a shareholder, Wyse said the Directors would be glad for the passing of an Act giving them powers to wind up the Company's affairs.

Three months later, larger storm clouds loomed on the horizon when a prospectus was issued for the independent Waterford & Tramore Railway (W&TR) This was the section of the C&WR that had been regarded as the most lucrative and, although the half-yearly meeting scheduled for February 1851 once again failed to take place due to insufficient attendance, a special general meeting was held in the following month to consider the rival scheme. That resulted in a resolution empowering the Directors to seek a further Act to enable the C&WR to redefine its capital and, more importantly, to provide for the immediate completion of their line to Tramore. It was also resolved that, if deemed necessary, the W&TR Bill should be strenuously opposed, although it was felt that negotiations between the two parties might avoid a costly contest in Westminster.

The familiar pattern of having to postpone the half-yearly shareholders' meetings was repeated in September 1852. The *Railway Times*, commenting on the non-event, stated that whilst overtures had been made by respectable parties for the construction of the section of line as far as Youghal along with the Queenstown branch, no definite propositions were forthcoming as to the terms on which the line should be built. It also commented that no section of the Tramore line had been constructed, although it was confidently expected that work would commence in the following spring.

The people at the Waterford end decided to take the matter into their own hands and a provisional committee was formed in the spring of 1850 with William Peet as provisional Chairman of the W&TR. Offices were obtained free of charge at 55 The Quay in Waterford, a premises owned by Mr Harvey, the Provisional Secretary. The Provisional Committee included the Earl of Huntingdon, a local landowner. As mentioned earlier, a prospectus was issued in July 1850, showing a proposed capital of £90,000 for a line 7¼ miles in length. The Waterford & Tramore Railway Act received Royal Assent on 24 July 1851 with a capital of £48,000 in £10 shares, £10,000 Preference Shares and borrowing powers up to £19,350.

William Richard LeFanu was appointed Engineer-in-charge, and the contract for construction was awarded to William Dargan in an amount of £41,500. This latter figure was to include the purchase of land, responsibility for which was placed on Dargan. The first Chairman of the new company was Sir James Dombrain, who had for 20 years been Inspector General of the Coastguard Service. The first sod for the new railway was turned on 10 February 1853. Initially progress was slow due to adverse weather conditions, but the line was reported to be complete and ready for opening by the end of the following August. The line was duly inspected by Capt HW Tyler, who had been appointed Government Inspector of Railways at the BoT earlier in the year and he found it to be satisfactory. The first train left Waterford for Tramore at noon on 6 September 1853. The W&TR allocated 2,000 of their shares to the C&WR as part compensation for their use of the proposed route of the C&WR and also as a reward for not opposing the Tramore company's Bill in Parliament. Although the W&TR line always remained physically isolated from other Irish railways it subsequently became a constituent of the Great Southern Railways in 1925, later becoming part of the Córas Iompair Éireann (CIÉ) network in 1945, and continued in use until final closure on 31 December 1960.

Reverting to the affairs of the C&WR, compulsory powers for the acquisition of land had lapsed at the end of August 1853 and the time had then arrived when serious thought had to be given to whether work should proceed or the undertaking should be abandoned altogether as it had become clear that there was little or no prospect of a line being completed throughout from Cork to Waterford. The Directors decided that the line from Cork to Midleton as well as the branches to Fermoy and to Roche's Point in Queenstown should be constructed. Sir Charles Fox arrived in Cork early in October 1853 to make arrangements for going to Parliament for powers to construct the railway from Cork to Youghal with a branch to Queenstown and by that time the Company was being unofficially referred to as the Cork & Youghal Railway (C&YR). It was hoped to approach the baronies along the proposed line for guarantees, which, if forthcoming, would enable the contractors to enter on the works. All was not expected to be straightforward, as opposition was anticipated from the promoters of a line being sponsored by William Dargan, which was to run from Carrigaline to Queenstown and make a connection with the Cork, Blackrock & Passage Railway (CB&PR) by means of a 'steam bridge'. There were some who still firmly believed in a through railway from Cork to Waterford, a meeting held in Dungarvan towards the end of October 1853 passing a resolution drawing attention to the highly desirable nature of such a line.

By the following March it had definitely been decided to restrict the line to Youghal with a Queenstown branch and a Bill was promoted in Parliament to give effect to this. Although there was opposition from both the CB&PR and the GS&WR companies, the Bill proceeded through Parliament, the only major alteration being the dropping of the proposed Fermoy branch. The Cork & Youghal Railway Bill received Royal Assent on 31 July 1854; capital was reduced to £375,000 with borrowing powers not exceeding £125,000. It was agreed that two Directors from the SWR and one from the GWR should have places on the new company's board.

Meanwhile, IK Brunel arrived from England early in October 1854 to personally inspect the surveys which his staff had been conducting on the proposed Queenstown branch. Accompanied by Isaac Butt, MP, Chairman of the C&YR,[2] and the Resident Engineer, Osborne Cadwallader Edwards, he proceeded along the branch and, on his return to Cork, he carefully examined the approach of the line from Woodhill Terrace, later called Tivoli, the site of the terminus into King Street. On the next day, he proceeded to Youghal to inspect the line at the site marked out for the proposed terminus, then situated about 1½ miles from the town itself. These surveys were necessary as it was the intention to apply to Parliament for three extensions. Prior to Brunel's return to England, he was waited upon by Mr William Currey of Lismore Castle, agent for the Duke of Devonshire, in relation to the possibility of constructing a connecting line from Youghal to join the Waterford & Limerick Railway (W&LR) at or near Clonmel.

The contract for the construction of the C&YR line was initially let to Messrs Moore Brothers of Dublin on terms described as highly favourable to the Company, with an agreement that the portion between Dunkettle Bridge and Midleton should be opened for traffic by the end of 1855. The *Railway Times* noted that from the high character of the contractors, no doubt existed that they would execute the works in a most efficient and satisfactory manner, and it was confidently expected that work would commence within weeks, with all land expected to be in the contractor's hands by 1 March 1855 at the latest. There was a more confident mood at the half-yearly shareholders' meeting held in the King's Arms Tavern in London on 28 February 1855. Isaac Butt, in the chair, said that the contractors had agreed to accept a fair proportion of their payment in paid-up shares. Four miles of line were already in the contractor's possession and a Bill was before Parliament for the 5½ mile branch to Queenstown. Work in fact commenced on 26 March 1855 with 300 men reported to be employed at Dunkettle, some work also apparently being commenced at the Cork end of the line at New Glanmire. While this work was proceeding apace, the BoT was giving consideration to the company's Bill seeking the following extensions,

viz 73 chains to bring the line into the town of Youghal, and a branch 5 miles and 59 chains in length from Johnstown to Midleton Quay in Queenstown; in addition, a deviation of the authorised line between Clashduff and Burgess Lower was sought along with an increase in capital of £50,000. No problems were encountered in Parliament and Royal Assent was granted the following September.

The *Cork Reporter* announced in December that it was gratified to state that progress on the works was most satisfactory and there appeared to be no reason why the Dunkettle to Midleton section should not be opened for traffic in the summer of 1856, albeit somewhat later than originally envisaged. During harvest time, owing to the difficulty of procuring labour, except at exorbitant rates of pay, there had been a comparative lull in activity, but since the autumn, work had been vigorously resumed. The long embankment across the tidal water adjoining the village of Glountaine (today referred to as Glounthaune) had been completed, apart from a few yards at one point where a quantity of fill had been swallowed up by the slob. The portion of line from the point where it crossed the coach road at the east end of the embankment was almost equally advanced to within a very short distance of Midleton and the long clay cutting in the region of Carrigtwohill was ready for the laying of sleepers. The only rock cutting, at Water Rock, was in a similarly advanced state. Beyond Midleton, the greater portion of the line had been fenced while for over 2 miles at the city side of Glountaine much of the line was also fenced.

The half-yearly shareholders' meeting was held in Cork on 29 February 1856, the Chairman referring to the forward state of the works which would be completed for about £5,000 a mile and would yield an ample return as it would pass through a rich agricultural district and command the traffic between Queenstown and Cork. Under the existing circumstances, the Directors deemed it prudent to defer the construction of the Queenstown branch, instead devoting all their energies to the first portion of the main line to Midleton. Brunel's report for the meeting stated that of the 7½ miles upon which the contractor was at work, 5 miles were by then ready for

---

2 Isaac Butt was the first leader of the Irish Party in the British House of Commons.

ballasting. After some discussion as to the expediency of removing the Board from London to Cork, the report was adopted.

The company found itself in the Court of Common Pleas in June arising out of a dispute that had its origins in January 1846. As previously alluded to, two separate companies were registered in 1845, viz the C&WR and the CM&YR, both of which contemplated branches to Queenstown and Fermoy, the two undertakings having more or less similar proposed routes as far as Youghal. Following consultations between the two boards of Directors, an agreement had been reached on 23 January 1846 whereby the two companies and their subsidiaries were amalgamated under the title of the C&WR. The Waterford company's shares were valued at £25 with £1 10s 0d paid, while the Youghal shares were £50 with £2 15s 0d paid on each. The Directors arranged to convert each Youghal share into two C&WR shares, requesting a payment of 5s to equalise the deposits. The CM&YR shareholders felt that this was at variance with their subscription agreement which provided that no further calls should be made until the Act was obtained. The Court came out in favour of the Waterford company's view that an additional amount should in fact be paid.

June 1856 saw the C&YR receive Royal Assent for an Act which provided for a 1m 46c extension to St Patrick's Hill; this was the only Irish railway Act authorised in 1856. It had been unsuccessfully opposed by the GS&WR on the grounds that the extension was unnecessary and, more truthfully, it would interfere with their lines. Furthermore, they maintained that the estimates were too low and in any event the Youghal company had no funds. All perhaps to some extent true! Despite the success in Parliament, the Directors decided later in the year that, owing to the difficult state of the money markets, they would refrain from contracting any engagements or encouraging any unnecessary expenditure as a vigorous management might mean financial embarrassment and consequent permanent injury to the company. Towards the end of the year rumours were circulating of the possibility of the company falling into the hands of the GS&WR, a rumour strenuously denied by the Directors.

In December a large public meeting was held in Midleton to consider the propriety of consenting to a baronial guarantee in favour of the C&YR for 5% on the capital of £100,000 to enable the railway to be completed. In opening the proceedings Lord Fermoy stated that he would not attempt to influence the meeting one way or the other. Lord Shannon announced his opposition to a guarantee, while Mr Butt said that as public opinion was strongly divided on the issue, he had recommended to the Directors that they should not press for a guarantee. He did, however, point out that the ex-C&WR Directors had expended £60,000 with absolutely nothing to show for it, whereas the present company had only spent £40,000 and they had completed nearly 10 miles of railway.

The year 1857 saw the company's affairs in a state of disarray. At the half-yearly meeting in March, Butt announced that progress was steady but slow as the Directors felt it inexpedient to incur any larger expenditure to progress matters any faster. Further efforts were made during the year to remove the directorate from London to Cork, a move successfully opposed by the shareholders. The August half-yearly meeting was postponed due to insufficient numbers. The Chairman's report stated that resources were sufficient to enable the Directors to complete and open the first section from Midleton to Dunkettle. From the latter point to the city would be catered for by small steamers plying on the river. The next section to be completed would be that on to Killeagh, at which point there should be no difficulty in raising additional capital for the Queenstown branch. An event of August 1857, which was to be of considerable significance in later years, was the election of Sir Patrick Cusack Roney as a Director. Despite the apparent optimism of the report the company's financial affairs were far from healthy. In August, Thomas Brassey and his Partner, Mr Jackson, MP, arrived in Cork to consult with the Directors on the company's affairs and announced their interest in constructing the Queenstown branch due to their connections with the SWR. These discussions, and a meeting with the local gentry in November, led to an announcement to the effect that Messrs Brassey, Peto & Company had agreed to invest £120,000 in the company, subject to £80,000 being raised locally. The landed gentry appeared to look favourably on this idea and promises of assistance were made, some agreeing to accept shares in lieu of direct payment for land.

Work in fact ceased towards the end of 1857 due to shortage of finances, Messrs Moore Brothers relinquishing their contract as a result. By the time of the half-yearly meeting on 26 February 1858, Sir Cusack Roney was in the chair and he was able to report that an Act of Parliament had been obtained reducing the company's capital from £375,000 to £270,000 with powers to borrow correspondingly reduced to £90,000. The time limit for completion of the line was extended for a further two years. It was confirmed that the Directors had entered into an agreement to release Moore Brothers from their contract, by which time upwards of 9 miles of line was ready to receive permanent way. William Field & Co, (acting for Messrs Thomas Brassey & Co) agreed to complete the entire line from Cork to both Queenstown and Youghal, ready for public traffic, within two years, provided the company would re-issue shares to the extent of £70,000 and persuade land owners to take shares for their land to the extent of £25,000. In December, the *Cork Constitution* congratulated all concerned in the line and to all interested in the acceleration of communication between Cork and Youghal; the difficulties had been great but had been overcome.

By the following March prospects of opening the first section of line looked good, within six months between Dunkettle and Midleton, within twelve months between Midleton and Youghal, followed three months later by the entire line. The 1 June 1859 was a big day for the company when a fête on a grand scale was provided for the workmen engaged in the final stages of construction. The cost of the fête was borne by D Leopold Lewis of London, who had come to the aid of the financially embarrassed company and was to be closely associated with its affairs for some years to come. The *Illustrated London News* commented that the festivities were held on a piece of ground on the north side of the Glanworth Road, described as a kind of natural amphitheatre. Four large tables had been laid out to accommodate 800 people. At 4.00 pm the men marched to the tables preceded by a

German band and a banner consisting of long, curled, shavings floating from a pole and surmounted by a saw and hatchet. Rain delayed the commencement of the proceedings, dinner being followed by speeches and later still "fun and diversion". A large marquee had been erected and we are told that a liberal supply of cake and wine was provided for the ladies and gentlemen invited to witness the proceedings. The hungry navvies meanwhile had large quantities of beef, bacon, pork, potatoes and vegetables, liberally washed down with beer.

Some 1,200 men were employed on the works, and by August rails and fishplates were on hand, while three locomotives had been ordered from Messrs Neilson of Glasgow along with eight carriages from Ashbury & Co of Manchester. Wagons were later obtained from Long & Sons of Youghal. Mr D O'Sullivan, Station Master at the GS&WR terminus in Cork, was appointed to the position of Traffic Superintendent of the new line. Reporting in August on the state of affairs, Sir Cusack Roney stated that the first section would be ready for opening in the following month, but September came and went with further delays. He added that he expected a large local traffic on the line; the importance of the Queenstown branch could not be overstated; and further arrangements were in hand to raise capital so that the branch might be opened at the same time as the remainder of the main line.

The first items of rolling stock arrived from England in the closing days of September, in time to allow an opening to traffic on 10 November, following a BoT inspection and approval the previous week. The opening ceremony was performed by the Lord Lieutenant, the Earl of Carlisle, who was in Cork to lay the foundation stone for St Patrick's Bridge and also to confer a knighthood on John Arnott, the city's lord mayor (and a Director of the C&YR). The Earl travelled by road to Dunkettle, where he performed the ceremony, following which he and his party travelled by train to Johnstown where he turned the first sod of the Queenstown branch. Having completed the ceremonies, the party proceeded to Midleton where they retired to the engine house, which had been gaily decorated for luncheon for His Excellency and 200 guests. In his speech, the Earl said

Luncheon given to the Lord Lieutenant by the Directors of the Cork and Youghal Railway at the Midleton Station. *(Illustrated London News)*

that while 9 miles of line could not be considered as gigantic and "could be measured by a few puffs of the steam engine, it was nevertheless a promise of a more extended communication and had Europe behind it and America before it", a reference to the fact that the Queenstown branch would form part of the rail route from Dublin and was to be used for the mail traffic to and from America. His Excellency kindly gave permission for locomotive No 2 to be named *Carlisle*

after him, No 1 being named *Lewis* and No 3 *Roney*. The public opening took place two days later, on 12 November 1859. A service of four passenger trains each way daily with three on Sundays was provided, but there were no goods trains at first. A waiting room was provided at King Street with omnibuses running to Dunkettle in 40 minutes, and intermediate stations were provided at Island Bridge (later Little Island) and Carrigtwohill.

CHAPTER THREE

Waterford & Wexford Railway

It will be recalled from Chapter One that Messrs Ford & Jackson began operating a steamer service between New Milford and Waterford in August 1856 on behalf of the GWR and SWR with the SS *City of Paris*. The crossing, however, occupied 13 hours and an attempt was made to shorten this in 1861 with the introduction of proposals for the Waterford & Passage Railway (W&PR). This line, about 9 miles in length, was intended to diverge from the Waterford & Tramore Railway (W&TR) about ¾ mile south of its Waterford (Manor) Station and run eastwards through Woodstown and to terminate at Hackett's Quay in Passage East. There it was proposed to construct a jetty where, even at low water, there was a depth of 11 fathoms. It was estimated that this would reduce the journey time on the voyage from Waterford to New Milford by 1¼ hours. Powers were to be sought for the working of the new line by the W&TR and the doubling of the latter company's line as far as the point of junction. In the longer term, it was proposed to connect the W&TR line with the W&LR and W&KR systems on the north side of the River Suir.

The Act for the Waterford & Passage Railway received Royal Assent on 7 August 1862 with the Marquess of Waterford and Lord Templemore of Arthurstown being shown as patrons. Capital was fixed at £60,000 with additional borrowing powers up to one-third of that amount. The actual junction with the Waterford & Tramore Railway (W&TR) was to be located at a point 1,150 feet beyond the ½ milepost on the latter company's line. It was also proposed to introduce a steam ferry service across the estuary of the Suir from Passage East to Arthurstown in Co Wexford, thus reducing the travelling time by road between Waterford and Wexford by almost half.

Humphrey Williams Wood was appointed Secretary to the new company. Wood, who had connections with some English financiers, was also at the time Secretary to the Cork & Kinsale Junction and the Rathkeale & Newcastle Junction railways. Peter Roddy of Cork was appointed Engineer to the company. A contract for construction of the line was entered into with Messrs Wheatley Kirk & Company of Manchester; such was the nature of the works that it was confidently expected that the line would be completed within 12 months. It was reported that the first sod was turned near Waterford on 15 April 1863, although little or no construction appears to have been undertaken.

Nevertheless, ambitious extension plans were announced in 1863 and a fresh Bill was presented to Parliament. The proposed extensions included a connection with the W&LR at Newrath (Waterford). However, when the Act received Royal Assent on 28 July 1864, all that was sanctioned was a short extension at Passage East to a point on the southwestern shore of the estuary near the Tower (ruined) situated on the northeastern angle of the Quay adjoining a building known as 'the Garrison'. Powers were also granted to use and adapt for the conveyance of railway traffic, the Passage & Ballyhack Ferry, the latter Company to be vested in the W&PR. Notwithstanding the setback suffered in Parliament, yet another extension was announced, namely a railway from the Ballyhack ferry terminal on the Wexford side of the river through Duncormick to make a connection with the Wexford extension of the DW&WR, powers for which were also sought and obtained in the 1864 Session. It was also intended to construct a short branch to Ballygeary in Greenore (or South) Bay where a new harbour was to be constructed. These latter works, if sanctioned, were to be carried out by an independent company, the Waterford & Wexford Railway and Rosslare Harbour Company. There had even been talk in November 1863 of drawing up plans for a bridge across the River Suir in substitution for the Ballyhack ferry service.

The Waterford & Wexford Railway Company Act (W&WR) received Royal Assent on 25 July 1864. Section 17 of the Act authorised the making of two railways, viz one commencing on the tidal beach of the River Suir at Ballyhack and terminating at a point in the line of the proposed extension of the DW&WR in the parish of Carrick, just north of Wexford town; the second line was to be a branch to South or Greenore Bay. Powers were also granted for the construction of a pier or harbour at the latter point. Section 50 of the Act enabled the new company to enter into traffic arrangements with the DW&WR, while Section 55 granted running powers over all or any part of the latter undertaking. The DW&WR had received Royal Assent a month earlier, on 23 June, for the extension of their line from Enniscorthy to a terminus at or near the northwest side of Slaney Street in Wexford (roughly on the site today occupied by Dunne's Stores).

It is perhaps hardly surprising to record that two of the W&PR Directors acted in a similar capacity on the W&WR, namely Frederick William Sedgwick and Sir Cusack Patrick Roney, who was in fact the first Chairman of the W&WR. The two companies shared offices at 17 Gracechurch Street in the City of London. Apart from the foregoing individuals, a number of local gentry were also involved in the formation of the new company, including George Le Hunte of Artramont House near Castlebridge, Francis Augustine Leigh of Rosegarland near Wellington Bridge and John Thomas Rossborough Colclough (locally pronounced Coakley) of Tintern Abbey. Another ambitious scheme briefly surfaced in 1865, namely the Waterford & Wexford Junction Railway, to form a junction with the W&WR at Killesk to the east of Campile and terminate by a junction with the W&LR near its old terminus at Newrath; it failed, however, to materialise when the Bill was rejected on Standing Orders.

Little happened as regards either the W&PR or the W&WR during the ensuing five years, although both companies obtained Acts in 1867 granting extensions of time for construction. Roney died in 1868 and was replaced as Chairman of the W&WR by George Le Hunte, with Henry E Wynne of Wexford[1] becoming

Secretary. Despite obtaining their Act in 1867, the W&WR shareholders appeared to have little interest in the affairs of the company as it was reported that there was no attendance at either of the half-yearly meetings in that year. Some interest was shown in the following year when a meeting of supporters drew up a memorial for presentation to the Lord Lieutenant setting out the advantages of a harbour at Rosslare. This led to the appointment by the Public Works Loan Commissioners (PWLC) of an eminent engineer to inspect the area, this being carried out in August 1868. A further survey by the Admiralty Surveyor, Capt Edward K Calver, referred to the advantages of the site in terms of protection from prevailing winds. Resulting from these reports a Bill was prepared to set up a Harbour Authority to construct a curved pier 830 yards in length from the shore terminus of the authorised W&WR line. The Rosslare Harbour Commissioners (RHC) were established in 1869, taking over the railway company's powers in relation to the harbour. There were seven commissioners, viz the Mayor of Wexford, the MP for Wexford, a BoT appointee, a Wexford Harbour Commissioners (WHC) appointee and three representatives of the W&WR. The harbour works were estimated to cost £80,000 and a Government loan of £75,000 was sanctioned with the proviso that construction of the railway be carried out simultaneously with that of the pier.

Meanwhile, nothing at all had happened in relation to the W&PR and the decision was taken to abandon the undertaking. Sedgwick applied to the BoT in April 1869 for an abandonment warrant. Following an inspection of the company's books by Colonel Rich on 29 July 1869, the relevant warrant was granted on the following day. So came to an end the western portion of the proposed railway connection between Wexford and Waterford, and it was to be over 30 years before any further moves were made in that direction.

Hints of a change in the route of the proposed W&WR line surfaced early in 1869, about which time Martin John Farrell was appointed Resident Engineer.[2] The line as authorised was intended to run round the back of the town of Wexford, crossing over Grogan's

---

1 Henry Eckersall Wynne (1825–1895) was the son of the Revd Henry W Wynne, one-time Rector of the parish of Ardcolm, Co Wexford.

2 Martin John Farrell was the son of James Barry Farrell, County Surveyor for Wexford for upwards of 50 years.

Road and John Street. At a meeting of the WHC held in February it was reported that the W&WR wished the harbour commissioners to consider a proposal to run a tramway line "along the present Quay of Wexford." The tramway was intended to connect the W&WR and DW&WR companies' lines in Wexford and would afford facilities for shipping Ovoca ore[3] and pit props from Shillelagh, both in Co Wicklow. The tramway was intended to run from the DW&WR terminus at Slaney Street along the quays and across the Crescent, where there would be a 50ft wide swivel bridge with an opening in the centre to allow vessels into the Crescent. Finally, the tramway would run through the Liverpool Steam Packet yard and terminate at the end of the hill at William Street at the south end of the town; a contemporary newspaper report states that a line would be brought close to the water's edge at Fisher's Row, running along the bottom of Mr Stafford's place and into the Waterford line a little further on. Mr Le Hunte, on behalf of the W&WR, informed the WHC that horse traction would be employed on the tramway.

A lively discussion ensued with grave reservations being expressed regarding the crossing of the Crescent, which it was feared would severely impact on the shipping trade of the port. Mr Little, the WHC Solicitor, was of the view that whilst initially horses would be used, with any increase in railway traffic the company would seek to use locomotives. Despite these reservations the WHC agreed in principle with the tramway scheme, although it was not long before the two parties were embroiled in lengthy and at times acrimonious arguments over the quay line.

An inland route to Wexford

We must leave the Rosslare line again to take a brief look at another scheme for a railway to Wexford, as it was to have a bearing on the DW&WR's plans. The *Railway Times* of 4 January 1845 reported that Sir John Macneill had carried out a survey for a line to be known as the Wexford Carlow & Dublin Junction Railway (WC&DJR); at Carlow, it was to make connection with the GS&WR and thus provide access to Dublin. Passing through Ballon and Newtownbarry (now called Bunclody) the southern terminus was to be at Wexford. Following initial opposition to the scheme by the WWW&DR, an agreement was reached whereby the line would be restricted to run between Carlow and Enniscorthy. The Bill failed to get through Parliament in 1845 and was re-introduced in the 1846 session; the southern terminus was to be at Scarawalsh, some 3 miles north of Enniscorthy, at which point a connection would be made with the WWW&DR. Running powers were to be granted to the WC&DJR from Enniscorthy to Wexford, the 3Ws in turn receiving similar powers between Enniscorthy and Carlow. The scheme failed to proceed any further, but it was resurrected in 1854 as the Bagenalstown & Wexford Railway (B&WR) for a line from the former town via Goresbridge, Borris and Ballywilliam to Wexford.

The many difficulties which that company encountered are not relevant to the present history; suffice to say that the line was initially opened as far as Borris on 20 December 1858 and on to Ballywilliam on 17 March 1862, being worked by the GS&WR. Relations between the two companies were strained and the line closed on 1 January 1864. A disgruntled bondholder obtained a bankruptcy order in 1865 and the line was sold to an English barrister, Standish H Motte; by an Act of 1866 the company became the Waterford New Ross & Wexford Junction Railway (WNR&WJR), powers being granted to both the GS&WR and the DW&WR (as successor to the WWW&DR) to work it. The line was also to be extended to a point near the River Slaney known as Ballyhogue (Macmine). The line was opened in sections, viz to Borris on 5 September 1870, to Ballywilliam and Sparrowsland on 26 October 1870, and the final section, the 3½ miles from the latter point to the junction with the DW&WR at Macmine on 1 May 1873.

The line proved to be unremunerative to work, bearing the distinction of having the worst operating ratio of any Irish railway, at one point amounting to 204 per cent. Eventually, the PWLC announced their intention in May 1875 to auction the line. Both the GS&WR and the DW&WR inspected the line, the

---

3 The name Ovoca was used until 1912 when it was altered to the better known Avoca.

latter company, following consultations with the L&NWR, deciding against its purchase. However, following a meeting between the DW&WR and the GS&WR in October 1875, the latter company purchased the line, with the DW&WR having an option to purchase the section between Ballywilliam and Ballyhogue. The latter company agreed to work the line through to Bagenalstown, with the GS&WR paying a mileage rate.

The DW&WR then suggested the construction of a branch from Ballywilliam to New Ross, the GS&WR declining to become involved in such a venture. The DW&WR decided to go it alone and drew up plans for a New Ross extension, these being put to a meeting of the board in August 1876. The Act for this extension received Royal Assent on 6 August 1877, powers being granted for a line 7m 2f 27y long from a junction with the Ballywilliam to Macmine line at Palace East to the townland of Rosbercon in New Ross. The GS&WR took over the working of the Bagenalstown to Ballywilliam section in October 1884. Even before tenders were sought for the New Ross extension, the DW&WR board turned attention to a further extension of the line to Waterford, plans being submitted by the company's Engineer in September 1877. This line was to approach Waterford from the west side, with a bridge to be constructed across the River Suir to provide access to the Waterford, Dungarvan & Lismore Railway (WD&LR), which by that time was approaching completion. The Waterford Extension Act received Royal Assent on 22 July 1878, four lines being authorised. The principal one was to be 13m 7f 80y in length from the terminus of the authorised New Ross extension at Rosbercon and terminating a short distance to the north of Newrath House in Waterford. From there a branch was to cross the River Suir by means of an opening bridge and terminate by a junction with the WD&LR in the townland of Gibbet Hill, immediately to the west of the latter company's station. A connection was also to be made into the line of the Waterford & Central Ireland Railway (and presumably the W&LR, although not specifically mentioned) at Newrath.

The contract for the construction of the New Ross extension was awarded to Robert Worthington, the

line being opened on 19 September 1887. In the intervening 9 years the WD&LR had written on a number of occasions to the DW&WR enquiring when work was to commence on the latter's Waterford extension. Nothing was done to further the line, the powers eventually lapsing and it was not until April 1896 that Thomas Benjamin Grierson, the company's Engineer, produced fresh plans.

The Waterford & Wexford is completed

The various plans put forward for the line along the quay at Wexford included the provision of a solid quay wall, a new piled wharf 10ft wide, thus making provision for the loading and unloading of cargoes, the filling in of the Crescent, and the running of the railway around the inside of the Crescent on the public road. It was the piled wharf that was eventually chosen although this in turn involved many arguments as to the width to be allowed. The railway company proposed 10ft, the WHC insisted on 20ft and when the matter went to arbitration, 16ft was suggested as a compromise. The W&WR eventually won their argument in this regard and Wexford gained the famous 'wooden works', which were to be a feature of the town's quayside until comparatively recent times, giving it the air of a New England town.

At a meeting of the WHC in June 1871, consideration was given to the provision of a second line along the quays, to be used as a siding in connection with the loading and unloading of vessels alongside. The W&WR objected to this suggestion on the grounds of cost. They enquired about filling in the Crescent, this resulting in the Harbour Commissioners receiving a memorial in March 1873 from ship-owners and merchants strongly protesting against this idea. Even the Harbour Commissioners disagreed amongst themselves; Capt Fanning stated that half the vessels using the port tied up in the Crescent, Mr Allen said only about 10% used it, while Mr Armstrong was of opinion that it was used by nearly all the vessels.

Various plans for the transit of the quays were submitted to the Harbour Commissioners in September 1873, these being referred to Binden Blood Stoney, Engineer to the Dublin Port & Docks Board, for consideration and report. Reporting in November,

Wexford Quays with No 027 working a Waterford to Shelton Abbey empty train on 24 August 1980. This view shows the famous Wexford wooden works to good effect. These were later swept away when the town's main drainage system was renewed in the 1990s. *(Barry Carse)*

Stoney suggested filling in the Crescent and providing a wider and more substantial, concrete, quay; he also expressed himself in favour of two lines of rails along the quays.

While these matters were being considered, Messrs Barnett & Gale of London had been appointed in 1872 as contractors for the construction of a line "commencing by a junction with the works of the proposed Rosslare Harbour at a point in the cliff about 3½ chains north of the boundary line between the townlands of Bally Gillane Big and Bally Gillane Little in the parish of Kilraine (sic) and terminating at a point on the South Wall of the Packet Wharf in the parish of St Michael of Feagh" (Wexford). However, in March 1874 it was announced that the partnership had been dissolved, making it necessary to surrender the contract. By that time the earthworks on the section between the reclaimed lands and the terminus at Rosslare, a distance of 6½ miles, were well advanced and the bridges built, while 3 miles of fencing were also complete. Two months later, the DW&WR applied to

the WHC for permission to lay a temporary tramway from their goods depot along the quay to enable them to ship pit wood from Shillelagh and ores from Ovoca and to facilitate the loading and unloading of vessels. At a special meeting of the Harbour Commissioners it was agreed to grant the request, subject to the DW&WR agreeing to remove the tramway on 30 days notice and restoring the quay to its original state. The Town Commissioners also gave their blessing, asking that the tramway be brought down as far as the Crescent.

It was not until the end of December 1874 that a new contract was entered into for the completion of the line to Rosslare, this being awarded to Martin J Farrell, CE. Details were included of the stations at Ballygeary and Wexford. The former was to include a station house with one general waiting room (20ft × 12ft), one booking office (15ft × 10ft), one passenger platform 100ft in length, one goods platform 45ft long, two cattle pens, one watchman's and one porter's house, and a two-roomed house for the Station Master;

finally there were to be 220 lineal yards of sidings. The platform at Wexford was to be 150ft long; additionally there was to be an engine shed 100ft by 18ft (never built), a goods shed (25ft × 14ft) with a platform outside and quarter of a mile of sidings. The cost of Wexford Station was shown in the schedule of prices at £4,000 and that at Ballygeary at £1,500. It should here be mentioned that a separate station was not provided at Wexford until 1885. Permanent way was to consist of 69lb rail "to be of a character equal to those used upon the principal railways of England, with sleepers of Redwood Baltic timber from Memel, Stetton or Dantzic (sic), or approved native timber, 9ft long and not less than 9in wide". Coarse ballast of broken stone or coarse gravel, or any other hard coarse material not affected by wet such as cinders or slag, to a minimum depth of 15in was to be used. The contractor was obliged to afford facilities free of cost to the Rosslare Harbour Commissioners for the carriage of materials in connection with the harbour works.

An Act of 16 July 1874 granted a further extension of two years for completion of the works; the Act also gave powers for agreements to be made with the GWR, the RHC and the DW&WR. In the interim, the Company had applied to the PWLC for a loan of £26,700, this request being declined. At the half-yearly meeting in August the shareholders authorised the Directors to arrange construction of the main line to Ballyhack (on the Suir estuary), but in the following February the Directors decided against it on grounds of cost. About this time a further application was made to the PWLC; on this occasion, following assurances that the harbour works would be completed within a reasonable period of time and also confirmation that the GWR had agreed to allow generous rebates on through traffic, the PWLC recommended a loan. The Treasury, however, felt that the GWR offer was "too vague" and refused to accede to the loan, which was not finally granted until 1878.

Progress with construction of the W&WR was slow, the shareholders being informed at their meeting in February 1876 that 3 miles of line had been completed. MJ Farrell was also the contractor for Rosslare Harbour where a pier then extended 350 yards from an open viaduct 336 yards in length. It was confidently expected that both the railway and the

An early view of Rosslare Harbour. Whilst the signal cabin is in place on the pier, the lighthouse has not yet been completed. *(Philip Quigley Postcard Collection)*

harbour would be completed by the following autumn. The DW&WR agreed about this time to work the line when completed but refused to quote a rate until they had some idea of likely traffic returns.

Reference was made in August 1877 to a proposition from a Mr Sparks of London to finance the works. This offer fell through, but a year later another British firm, Messrs Watson, Smyth and Watson, made an offer to pay a sum of £27,000 in cash, being the Company's debts at that time, and to complete the railway. The firm was also to take over debenture capital as well as ordinary and preference shares, which would in effect have made them the owners of the W&WR, but once again, arrangements fell through. In January, the DW&WR finally made a firm offer for working the Rosslare line for a period of 14 years, subject to a minimum guaranteed payment of £4,000 per annum in return for providing a service of two mixed trains each way daily. All surplus receipts over £4,000 were to go to the W&WR until gross receipts exceeded £8,000 per annum, over which sum the DW&WR was to receive 50%. At the half-yearly shareholders' meeting at the end of February 1879, the Chairman referred to the fact that the agreement with the contractors had fallen through, a situation to be much regretted as by then the harbour works were progressing satisfactorily. There was no good news to report six months later for the works were still in abeyance; the only glimmer of light was that the Treasury, following an inspection by Robert Manning on behalf of the PWLC, had agreed to advance a loan of £53,000.

This lack of progress was most likely the reason for a poor attendance at the February 1880 meeting of shareholders. Finally, in April 1880 it was announced that a contract had been concluded with William Martin Murphy for the completion of the railway, agreement also finally having been reached with the WHC. The DW&WR were ordered in May 1880 to remove the temporary tramway, pursuant to the agreement dated 1 June 1874 with the WHC, so that Murphy could proceed with the laying down of permanent way on the quays at Wexford. In May 1880 the Company appointed WF Madden as Resident Engineer to superintend the construction of the line and of the pier at Rosslare in place of MJ Farrell;

Madden had just completed the Southern Railway line between Clonmel and Thurles. In July of the following year, the DW&WR agreed to loan a locomotive to Murphy in connection with the ballasting of the Rosslare line; three months later they also provided some wagons.

Further discussions with the DW&WR in February 1882 led to a revised offer to work the W&WR, based on a sum of £30 per week, terminable by either company on a month's notice; prior to commencement, the W&WR were to lodge a cheque for £120. By that time the Rosslare line was virtually complete and was first inspected in September 1881 by Maj Gen Hutchinson. He reported that it was 9m 41.4c in length, extending from an end-on junction with the DW&WR at Wexford, and terminating at the end of the pier at Rosslare Harbour. Sidings were provided at Wexford, Ballygeary Station, Ballygeary sidings and at Rosslare Pier, with stations at Rosslare, Ballygeary and Rosslare Pier. Permanent way consisted of flat bottomed wrought iron rails, fished at the joints, in lengths of 17ft and 23ft, weighing 65 and 69lb per yard. Sleepers were half round fir creosoted, 8ft in length with rails secured by a fang bolt and dog spike in each sleeper. Ballast consisted of broken stone, gravel and burnt clay, and was stated to have a depth of 12in below the under surface of the sleepers.

Bridges consisted of six overbridges, all of masonry and of 15ft span, nine underbridges, all with masonry or concrete abutments and timber beams. The most important were: one of nine spans (widest 42ft) "across a kind of timber pound at Wexford", with an opening span of about 40ft (the Crescent Bridge), the Coal Channel Viaduct, consisting of 22 spans of 19ft each, composed entirely of timber piles and timber top, and Rosslare Harbour pier, consisting of 13 spans of 35½ft, in which the piers were of concrete carrying wrought iron cross and main girders, and of 24 spans of 19ft, constructed entirely of timber. While the works generally appeared to have been substantially constructed and to be standing well, Hutchinson had no less than 11 requirements, most of which were expected to be completed within a few days. However, a parapet was called for on the pier at Rosslare due to its exposed location; this would take some time to provide, and in the interim Hutchinson felt that passenger services should only run as far as Ballygeary Pier siding.

A second inspection was carried out in March 1882, most of the previous requirements having been attended to satisfactorily. The only notable exception was that some of the occupation level crossing gates still opened inwards. As regards the parapet on Rosslare Pier, Hutchinson was still not happy with what had been provided as for a considerable part of its length it consisted of a row of girders placed on the tops of the girders carrying the line; these parapet girders had nothing but their own weight to prevent them from being blown over, and he felt it desirable that they should be clamped to the girders on which they rested. Nevertheless, BoT permission was given for the opening of the line for passenger traffic from Wexford right through to Rosslare Pier Head.

The line in fact opened for traffic on 19 June 1882, down trains departing Wexford (DW&WR) Station at 09.35 and 15.30 on weekdays and at 11.00 and 15.00 on Sundays. Return services departed Ballygeary at 10.30 and 16.30 on weekdays, and 14.00 and 18.00 on Sundays. Journey time was 40 minutes each way; all trains stopped at Rosslare, and provided first and third class accommodation only. On the opening day, a Saturday, the first train left Wexford at 10.30, those on board including Messrs Le Hunte and Wynne. The *Wexford Independent* reported that on the following day, over 700 people travelled, all being pleased with the trip. Within a week of the line opening, Wynne wrote to the DW&WR Secretary requesting the provision of a third train each way daily, this being provided at a rate of 18s per day. A revised timetable from 1 July shows departures from Wexford at 07.30, 13.30 and 18.20 and from Ballygeary at 09.00, 16.40 and 19.20. On Sundays, down trains left at 11.00 and 14.00, and up trains at 13.00 and 19.10. Sunday services proved very popular, with the DW&WR running seaside excursions from Gorey at substantially reduced fares; numbers travelling in early July quickly rose to in excess of 1,000, so much so that three trains were provided on Sundays by the end of that month. The weekday service was reduced to two trains each way for the winter months, this being the normal pattern for the future.

In August 1882 John Challoner Smith, the DW&WR Engineer, was authorised to lay in a siding at Rosslare, on condition that the W&WR deposited a sum equivalent to the estimated cost of labour and materials. The latter amounted to £150, which in fact exceeded the actual cost by £28 3s 8d, this latter figure being requested as a refund by the W&WR. It was also agreed to reduce the charge for supplying locomotive power for the winter months to 6d per mile.

Sunday services, which had been withdrawn for the winter months, were recommenced on 15 April 1883, connecting with the mid-day train from Gorey; it was announced in April that a well-appointed car would run between Ballygeary and Carne on Mondays, Wednesdays and Saturdays. Although traffic was healthy, the want of a refreshment room at Rosslare or Ballygeary, where ladies and children could be supplied with tea, coffee or milk, was much felt. A general meeting of shareholders of the W&WR was held early in June 1883 to consider what steps should be taken in support of an application for the necessary Government funds for the extension of the harbour at Rosslare. The PWLC had advanced £60,000, a sum totally inadequate for providing the necessary facilities, but had then stated that the harbour should be tried "in its present unfinished state and unsheltered condition to see what traffic (could) be found for it."

Traffic continued to grow and at the half-yearly meeting in August 1883 the Chairman confirmed that Messrs Cooper's cement and lime works at Drinagh, 3½ miles south of Wexford, was being connected with the railway. It was confirmed in March of the following year that the new siding had been connected, the railway company having reduced the rate for the carriage of lime to encourage the traffic. Maj Gen Hutchinson inspected the new facilities in January 1884, noting that the points connecting the siding to the main line were secured by Annets key attached to the train staff. The only criticism of the facilities was that the trap points were located too far from the main line and Hutchinson called for another set of trap points to be put in at the fouling point of the siding with the main line.

The *Wexford Independent* for 19 March 1884 referred to the Wexford & New Ross Tramway & Light

Railway Company, the northern terminus of which was to be located to the west of the main road leading to Drinagh, adjacent to the grounds of Rocklands Cottage; it was proposed to cross over the canal made for the convenience of Mr Cooper. Two further light railway schemes emerged in June, the South Wexford Light Railway and the Wexford & Duncannon Light Railway, both of which were intended to form junctions with the W&WR, the former 3¾ miles south of the W&WR's northern terminus, the latter at a point 150 yards from the level crossing leading from the grain warehouse at Felthouse. In the event, none of these schemes progressed any further.

Much of the March 1885 half-yearly meeting of shareholders was taken up with a discussion regarding the wreck of the steamer *Slaney*. This vessel had only been built several months previously for her owner, John Bacon of Liverpool, for the Liverpool–Wexford route. She ran aground on the night of 14 January 1885 while attempting to cross the bar of Wexford in an east-northeast gale with snow. Luckily, her 15 passengers and 18 crew were saved. Part of her 450 tons of general cargo, consisting of Indian corn and wheat, was auctioned at the end of March, while the 602 ton vessel herself was offered for sale by private treaty three months later. This and the subsequent wreck of the brigantine *Highland Mary* with a cargo of coal for Messrs Cooper once again brought home the urgent necessity of improving the port of Rosslare. The wreck of the *Slaney* led to a deputation of nearly 20 Irish MPs meeting the Treasury requesting a grant for the completion of the new port.

A new station was opened on 1 October 1885 at White Wall at the south end of Wexford, later to become known as South Wexford and later still Wexford South Station. From the same date the train service reverted to two trains each way daily, a pattern which was to follow in successive winters. Another improvement introduced with the summer timetable in May 1885 was the transfer of the southern terminus of the line from Ballygeary to Rosslare Harbour. By August 1886 it was reported that the pier extension at Rosslare was "going rapidly" with about 50 men permanently engaged making and placing in position large concrete blocks.

Henry Wynne wrote to the DW&WR early in February 1886 seeking to hire ballast wagons to enable the movement of stone to the Rosslare pier works; Wynne was informed that the DW&WR had no such wagons to spare. The half-yearly shareholders' meeting of the W&WR due to have been held on 6 August 1886 had to be postponed due to the non-attendance of sufficient people to form a quorum; this was to be the pattern for several subsequent meetings. The Chairman reported that while there had been a further increase in traffic, the annual earnings still fell below the level of working expenses. He also confirmed that cattle had been shipped through Rosslare on several occasions at the special request of traders. Work was proceeding on the pier extension with about 50 men permanently employed there making and placing in position large concrete blocks. The half-yearly report for the period ending 30 June 1888 made reference to the unseasonal weather, which had been unfavourable for tourists and

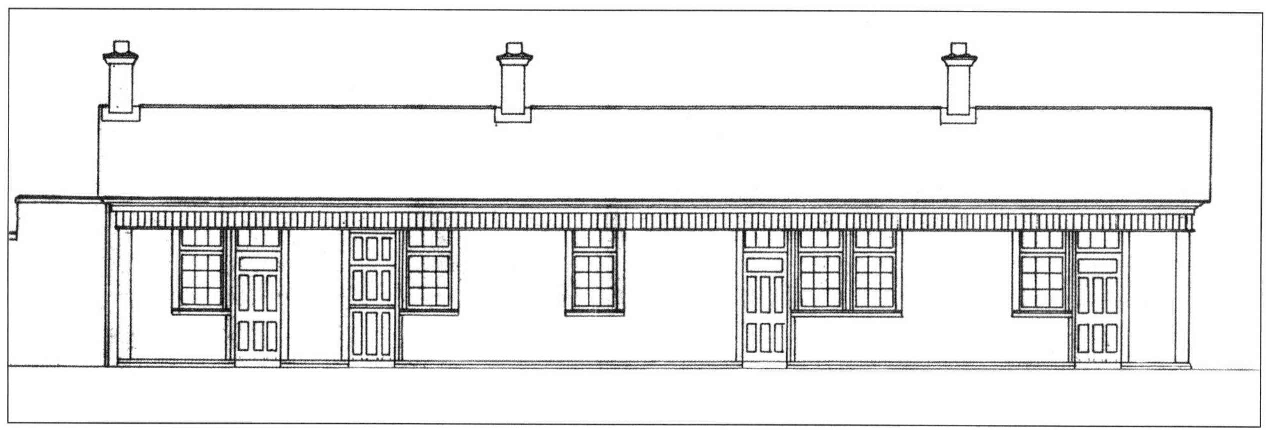

Wexford South station elevation, typical of many of the South Wexford line stations. *(Irish Rail)*

thus had affected receipts. The Chairman commented that the railway could not be kept open by the Directors at personal loss to themselves.

Little did the Chairman know at that point that the working of the line would come to an abrupt end less than 12 months later. It soon became clear that the Company had not been paying the DW&WR for working the line. The first hint of trouble came on 2 May 1889 when a deputation from the W&WR waited on the DW&WR Board urging that Company to continue to supply rolling stock. The latter Company declined to accede to the request unless satisfactory security was given for the payment of a large sum due in respect of past working. The deputation was told in no uncertain terms that the service would cease on Friday 17 May unless such a guarantee was given. A meeting was held in the Town Hall in Wexford, the result of which was a request that the line be kept open at least during the bathing season. One suggestion put forward at the meeting, but not followed up, was that the W&WR should issue debenture stock to enable them to purchase their own rolling stock. Henry Wynne wrote to the DW&WR on 16 May declining to give the necessary guarantee, possibly being of opinion that the working company was bluffing. The line duly closed on 17 May 1889, effectively remaining so for more than five years despite memorials presented at further public meetings in the ensuing days.

Even though the DW&WR had withdrawn their rolling stock from the W&WR line, they continued to bring their own wagons along the quays at Wexford, resulting some years later in an action being taken by the Wexford Harbour Commissioners before the Courts to restrain them. When the Bill for the Cork & Fermoy & Waterford & Wexford Railway (C&F&W&WR) was presented to Parliament in 1890, it brought some hope that the line might be re-opened as the promoters proposed to take running powers and make working agreements with both the W&WR and the DW&WR. Robert Worthington actually went as far as approaching the latter Company for the hire of rolling stock; this was approved, the charge to be not less than that previously made to the W&WR. By the time the C&F&W&WR Act received Royal Assent on 18 August 1890, reference to a working agreement with the DW&WR had been removed. At the half-yearly meeting held in August, Wexford Corporation urged the re-opening of the line, even if only on a temporary basis. Harry J Cooper, who operated the lime and cement works at Drinagh and which was connected to the W&WR line by means of a siding, reported on the great loss he was suffering by having to work his traffic with "an inferior class of engine". This latter appears to have been a four-wheeled machine, possibly designed by Cooper himself, and was used to haul wagons of cement from Drinagh to both Wexford and Rosslare, respectively to connect with the DW&WR and for export. It must have been relatively unusual for a private operator to use a commercial railway company's lines when the latter itself had no service operating.

A saturated boilered J15 0-6-0 works a mixed train northwards along Wexford Quays at an unknown date. *(J Macartney Robbins, courtesy IRRS)*

Some discussions took place at the beginning of 1891 which resulted in William L Payne, Traffic Manager of the DW&WR, being authorised to hire rolling stock to the W&WR, subject to the latter Company putting their line in order and to the accounts being settled weekly in future. Six months later the Wexford Harbour Commissioners raised concerns regarding the condition of the Quay line, some parts of which were considered to be dangerous; specific reference was made to the dilapidated state of the timbers on the Crescent Bridge, at least one beam of which was rotten. The Secretary of the WHC was ordered to request the railway company to execute the necessary remedial work.

In April 1892 the WHC requested the DW&WR to discontinue using the W&WR line along the Quays. At a subsequent meeting of the Harbour Commissioners in May, a memorial signed by a number of inhabitants of Wexford once again called on the Commissioners to do all in their power towards re-opening the Rosslare line. The WHC, however, considered the memorial should more correctly have been directed to the DW&WR as it was they "who are throwing obstacles in the way, as this Board from the beginning have done all they possibly could towards the re-opening of the line". It was a little unfair to entirely blame the DW&WR as the W&WR had precipitated the closure by not paying for the working of the line.

The WHC meeting of 28 June 1892 considered a letter from the Board of Works which expressed regret that the Commissioners had "on purely technical and unreasonable grounds determined to prevent the carrying out and completion of the working agreement for the W&WR now practically settled with the DW&WR, who have conceded all that fairly or reasonably might be expected of them". The letter went on to express the hope that better counsels would prevail and that the WHC would not persist in acting contrary to the views of the great majority of the people of Wexford. The WHC replied to the effect that they did not like the "objectionable tone" of the letter, which fell little short of accusing the Harbour Commissioners of being actuated by selfish if not dishonourable motives in dealing with the matter. The WHC were not prepared under any circumstances to

allow the DW&WR to levy rates on goods discharged or loaded at the legal quays to which goods landed at the railway jetties adjoining the DW&WR station were not subject – indeed the W&WR who had built the line derived no such rights under their Acts and had never attempted to make such charges. The WHC were now about to enforce notices resuming possession of the quay lines.

This threat was put into effect as the DW&WR Board, meeting on 3 November, ordered that notices be issued to the effect that as and from the following Monday they would discontinue sending wagons on to the Quay line. Despite this notification it would appear that the Company continued using the Quay lines as the *Wexford Independent* for 1 February 1893 referred to a case brought before the Vice-Chancellor's Court by the WHC seeking an injunction to restrain the DW&WR from exercising running powers over the Quay line and siding. Their argument was based on Section 8 of the W&WR Act of 1871 which provided that if, *inter alia*, the Company ceased or failed efficiently to work the lines of railway along the quay, the right of the Company to use them should cease and the Commissioners could resume possession. Not only had the W&WR failed to work the line, but they had also allowed it to fall into a state of disrepair. The Vice-Chancellor refused to hear the case without representatives of the W&WR being present and granted leave to add them as defendants to the action.

The DW&WR did finally desist from using the quay lines as witnessed by *The People* newspaper of 3 May which confirmed that they had refused to send their wagons down the quay pending a Court decision, despite a request from a prominent Wexford merchant. The only thing which kept the W&WR from falling into disrepair completely was the cement and coal traffic to and from Cooper's works at Drinagh.

The *Wexford Independent* for 24 June 1893 reported that a deputation from the Pembroke & Fishguard Railway Company (sic) had waited on the Board of the WHC seeking permission to use the Quay line in conjunction with the Rosslare Railway. The Commissioners decided to accede to the request, provided that the Company would not charge them anything for haulage. By that time it had become clear that the Rosslare line would soon be re-opened. Indeed, the *Wexford Independent* was able to report in its issue of 2 August that the negotiations between the Pembroke Railway Company (sic) and the W&WR "are finally closed" and that the former Company would shortly commence to put the line in thorough working order and would then place a line of steamers to run regularly between Fishguard and Wexford, presumably Rosslare.

The same newspaper reported in mid-November that the repair works were being pushed forward strenuously, and it was believed that the line would be open for traffic at the end of February 1894; this was to prove rather optimistic. There were about 40 men working daily under the supervision of Isaac J Mann, the W&WR Engineer. Although the line had lain virtually unused for more than four years, it was reported to be in fair condition, apart from the necessity to rebuild the Coal Channel bridge. Furthermore, apart from a few skilled hands, all the men belonged to Wexford, where labour was at that time scarce. The proposed February opening proved to be optimistic as it was announced in January that the repair works were proving to be more extensive than anticipated, the 1 April then being mentioned as an alternative. A closer examination of the Coal Channel bridge had led to a decision to completely renew it. Even if the line was not to be opened on 1 April, there was an anticipation that it would surely be ready by the summer for the inhabitants of Wexford "who appreciate a good bathe in the pure brine".

Despite the arrival on the scene of the Fishguard Bay Railway & Pier Company (FB&PR), the case against the DW&WR was pursued by the WHC. It was announced in April 1894 that the WHC were presenting a petition against the adoption of the Bill for the F&RR&H, unless the latter Company agreed to a clause in the Bill protecting the rights of the Commissioners in their action against the DW&WR and the W&WR. This was agreed to and was incorporated as Section 10 of the F&RR&H Act of 1894, thus enabling the petition to be withdrawn. The action against the DW&WR was heard in the Vice-Chancellor's Court in Dublin over three days in mid-April, judgment being given in favour of the defendants, and the action dismissed with costs.

The Commissioners rightly decided to discontinue any further action.

The *Wexford Independent* reported on 16 June that a locomotive had arrived in Wexford from Leeds for the new owners of the Rosslare line[4] on the previous Wednesday. On the following morning it was sent down to Ballygeary to assist in the construction of the new 'elbow' being added to the extremity of the pier; it was also to be used as a general shunting engine on the line. This was *Erin*, which was in due course to work the opening train. IJ Mann wrote to the BoT on 25 June requesting an inspection of the line "which has not been worked for passenger traffic since 1889".

Hutchinson came to Wexford in July and once again inspected the line. He confirmed that the line had now passed into other hands, who were to provide new rolling stock of their own. Hutchinson was not enamoured with *Erin*, declaring it unsuitable for passenger traffic. The second locomotive, as yet undelivered, was a six-wheeled tank and would suffice in the short term, although another locomotive would be required to adequately work the traffic. Otherwise, in the event of a breakdown, the service would have to be suspended. At one point the Company endeavoured to evade the requirement to provide vacuum brakes on the rolling stock in view of the short length of line involved, this being given little sympathetic consideration by the BoT. Hutchinson confirmed that the Coal Channel viaduct had been thoroughly overhauled, with new timbers supplied where necessary. He went on to say that works were still ongoing to adapt the pier for the reception of passenger and other traffic, although the Company wished only to work traffic as far as Ballygeary (known as Harbour) Station. In the circumstances, permission was given for opening to that point, subject to certain requirements being completed.

Maj Marindin made the next inspection on behalf of the BoT when he visited in June 1895 to inspect the works at Rosslare Harbour. The only work of importance on the section of line between Rosslare Harbour Station and Rosslare Pier was the pier itself,

---

4 The W&WR was generally referred to locally as the Rosslare Railway. An early photograph of Rosslare harbour shows one of the locomotives bearing the letters R&WR on its buffer beam. As far as is known they never carried the initials of the F&RR&H Company.

Left: The only known photograph of a passenger train on the W&WR section during the period between 1882 and 1889 when that line was worked by the DW&WR. The date is believed to be 1886 and the location is Ballygeary. The locomotive is most likely DW&WR No 1, which is known to have worked on the line. The carriage appears to be a four-compartment six-wheeler built by Ashbury of Manchester. *(Courtesy Hotel Rosslare)*

Right: This photograph of Rosslare pier is only one of two known to show one of the F&RR&H's two locomotives, in this case *Erin*. Later allocated the number 300 by the GS&WR, the number was never actually carried. Of note are the initials R&WR on the buffer beam, applied for accounting purposes. The second known copy of an F&RR&H locomotive appears opposite page 53 of HC Casserley's *Outline of Irish Railway History*. (Oliver Doyle Collection)

which was confirmed to be in good order. There was a platform at the landing stage and a ticket platform at the shore end of the pier. All points were locked by the train staff, Marindin requesting an undertaking extending the staff working over the new section of line.

During the course of the visit, Marindin made reference to some rails between the station and the signal cabin at Wexford over which Rosslare trains had to travel, and which were deemed to be in an unsafe condition. Moreover, the working in the signal cabin was also unsatisfactory as it appeared that the levers were worked by two different men, one on behalf of the DW&WR and one on behalf of the F&RR&H; in fact it transpired that the signals for the latter Company's trains were often not worked at all. The DW&WR responded to the comments by pointing out that the rails in question had been quite adequate for goods traffic, although they conceded that they were inadequate for passenger trains. However, as the passenger trains in question were the responsibility of the Fishguard Company, they felt that that Company should pay for any work required; likewise, that Company should also pay for putting the signals and the cabin in proper working order.

CHAPTER FOUR

The Fermoy & Lismore Railway

As already mentioned in the Introduction, any information that we have to hand on the history of the Fermoy & Lismore Railway (F&LR) is very sparse, no board minutes having apparently survived. What follows has been put together from newspaper abstracts and the Board and Traffic Committee minutes of the GS&WR and the WD&LR companies. A preliminary scheme for connecting Mallow with the garrison town of Fermoy had been promoted in 1846, but it was the Mallow & Fermoy Railway which was granted the necessary powers in 1854. Those powers were eventually taken over by the GS&WR in 1857 and they constructed the 17-mile branch, which opened on 17 May 1860.

Several schemes for railways to the east of Fermoy predated the F&LR proper, the first of which was the Brunel inspired C&WR of 1845. The GS&WR board minutes refer to a letter received from Lord Lismore on 22 November 1861 in which he enquired whether the Company would do anything to promote a railway from Fermoy to join up with the W&LR between Cahir and Clonmel; the GS&WR declined to become involved. Three years later, Messrs Barrington & Jeffers, the GS&WR Solicitors, advised the Company that they were about to apply to Parliament on behalf of an independent company for the construction of a line of railway from Fermoy to Lismore. They required to know if the GS&WR would be prepared to offer a working agreement similar to that which they had recently entered into with the Cork & Limerick Direct Railway. On this occasion the GS&WR confirmed that they would be prepared to offer a five-year working agreement when the line was made.

In point of fact, three schemes inspired by the prospect of a new steamer service between Milford and Rosslare were proposed for the 1865 Session of Parliament. Two companies, the Waterford, Lismore & Fermoy Railway (WL&FR) and the Clonmel, Lismore & Dungarvan Railway (CL&DR), had the enthusiastic backing of the Duke of Devonshire who had his Irish seat at Lismore Castle. The Engineers for both of these schemes were Wellington Arthur Purdon and William Bourne Lewis, and Edmond Power of Clonmel was to act as Solicitor. The former scheme proposed a line of railway from Bilberry Rock in Waterford to Dungarvan, in addition to a line from Lismore to a junction with the GS&WR at Fermoy. Working and traffic arrangements were proposed with both the W&LR and the GS&WR. The Act received Royal Assent on 5 July 1865 with the Earl of Huntingdon, Sir Richard Musgrave, Deputy Lieutenant for Co Waterford[1], John Esmonde, John Bagwell and James Galwey being shown as the first Directors. The WL&FR held the necessary statutory meetings in London, many of which were reported to have been poorly attended. No contract for construction was ever awarded and in 1868 the Company sought permission to abandon its powers, this finally being granted in December 1869 following a report from Colonel FS Rich of the BoT to the effect that no capital had actually been subscribed.

The CL&DR was intended to bridge the gap between the two portions of the WL&FR scheme. It envisaged a line from Clonmel southwards to Whitechurch; at the latter point two lines would diverge, westwards to Cappoquin and Lismore, and eastwards to Dungarvan. The total length of the line was to be 37¾ miles, including the 8-mile branch to Dungarvan, and the total estimated cost was £257,144. Apart from the Duke of Devonshire, who initially subscribed £35,000 towards the scheme, later increased to a shareholding of £60,000 and a loan for a similar amount, it was reported that both lines had the support of the W&LR and the GWR. In particular, the W&LR Board announced that they were willing to

---

1 Sir Richard Musgrave was the 4th Baronet of Tourin in Co Waterford (1820–74).

aid the CL&DR project with a working agreement on the usual mileage basis for 20 years, although when a further sum of £4,000 was requested from them they stated that they would rather not subscribe beyond the plant outlay for working the line. The provisional committee included the Chairman and Deputy Chairman of the W&LR, and Sir Richard Musgrave.

At the same time, a rival scheme to the CL&DR had been submitted to Parliament under the grandiosely titled Southern Railway Company of Ireland (SR). This company proposed a railway from Thurles on the GS&WR Dublin–Cork main line to Clonmel, and from the latter town via Whitechurch to Youghal. To enable faster running over easier gradients the line was intended to take a different route to that of the CL&DR between Clonmel and Whitechurch. The junction between the two companies' lines would have formed a cross, centred on the town of Cappoquin, and the SR planned to construct tramways at various locations. It was envisaged that the SR would be worked either by the GS&WR or the W&LR.

When the two schemes were being debated in Parliament it quickly became clear that heavy cuttings and an extensive viaduct on the SR scheme would increase the cost over its rival by £94,000. Apart from this, several prominent witnesses questioned the necessity for a line between Cappoquin and Youghal, which was already adequately served by a steamer service on the River Blackwater. Waterford was the natural port for the district and a connection to a second port, at Cork, was not considered necessary. Towards the close of the debate on the CL&DR, Counsel for the SR offered to confine their line to the section between Clonmel and Thurles, but with mutual running powers. This offer was turned down by the CL&DR, but was subsequently accepted when the SR agreed to drop the running powers clause. The subsequent history of the SR is described in the author's history of the Waterford, Limerick & Western Railway (WL&WR) (see Bibliography). Whilst Purdon & Lewis had prepared detailed plans, and the line had been marked out by the end of 1865, no contract was ever awarded for construction of the CL&DR.

The collapse of these schemes came as a disappointment to the residents of Dungarvan, the result of which was the formation of the Waterford & Lismore Road Steamer Company Limited to run road-trains in the area. They ordered a 12hp steam road locomotive from RW Thompson of Edinburgh, which was manufactured by Robey & Company of Lincoln and named *Shamrock*. In addition, four wagons were obtained from the South of Ireland Wagon & Wheel Company of Cappoquin. The locomotive arrived in Waterford on 23 March 1871, shortly afterwards commencing a service between Waterford and Dungarvan. However, it turned out to be a failure due to being under-powered and, after suffering a number of breakdowns, the service was discontinued. It was reportedly out of use by May of that year, but we do not know when exactly the company went out of business.

By 1868 it was clear that the Duke of Devonshire had turned his attention to connecting Lismore with the GS&WR at Fermoy. It has been said that what was to become known as 'The Duke's Railway' was inspired by his desire to improve the lot of the tenants on his vast estate around Lismore. On 29 July 1868, Francis E Currey, the Duke's Agent at Lismore, wrote to Messrs Barrington & Jeffers stating His Grace's views as to raising capital for the proposed line. In response to this, the GS&WR, whilst fully appreciating the liberal support that the Duke of Devonshire was prepared to give to the new undertaking, said the state of their Company's finances was such that they could not assist financially. They were, however, prepared to work the line for ten years from its being opened for traffic at 40 per cent of gross receipts, or, if preferred, by providing a service of three trains each way daily at a rate of 1s 6d per train mile.

Success was achieved on 24 July 1869 with the passing of an Act incorporating the Fermoy & Lismore Railway Company and authorising a railway 15m 2f 4c in length between the two places named in its title. Capital was to be £100,000 with borrowing powers up to one-third of that figure. The first Directors were shown as the Duke of Devonshire, Lord Frederick Cavendish[2], Francis E Currey, James (later Sir James)

---

2 Frederick Charles Cavendish was the second son of William Cavendish, 7th Duke of Devonshire. He was appointed Chief Secretary for Ireland in May 1882 but was assassinated along with his Permanent Under Secretary on Saturday 6 May 1882 by a group calling itself the Irish National Invincibles while walking close to his residence in the Phoenix Park, Dublin.

Fermoy station looking towards Waterford and showing overall roof, photographed in 1963. Just visible in the bay platform beside the signal cabin is ex GS&WR 0-6-0T No 90. The central signal cabin was erected in 1921, replacing two earlier cabins, one at the west end controlling the Mitchelstown branch, the other out beyond the goods store (left of overall roof). *(T Cott, IRRS Collection)*

Ramsden and Francis J Howard. Sir James Ramsden, whom we shall meet again in connection with the WD&LR, was closely involved with the history of the Furness Railway, holding the positions of Locomotive Engineer and Chairman of that concern; he was also responsible for the development of the town of Barrow-in-Furness. He would also have known the Currey family and the Duke of Devonshire; the Duke had large estates in the area and was also closely involved with the Furness Railway. A Mr George Noble was appointed Secretary to the new Company and the Engineers were our old friends WA Purdon & WB Lewis.

In Vol 10 of the *Journal of the Irish Railway Record Society* George Mahon states that the contract for construction of the line was awarded to Thomas Brassey in 1869, and this may well have been the case. He was one of the greatest railway builders and was the contractor for the Furness Railway, so it may have been at Ramsden's suggestion that it was proposed that his firm should carry out the construction work. However, Brassey was diagnosed with cancer in early 1870 and was to die in December that year, and this probably explains how John J Bagnell came to take up the contract. Bagnell commenced work in the latter half of 1870, the GS&WR agreeing to provide him with an open fortnightly account during the time he was constructing the F&LR. Tracings of the new line, showing gradients and curves as prepared by the engineers, were submitted to the GS&WR in January 1871, these being passed to Charles G Napier, that Company's Divisional Engineer in Cork, for his approval. Following receipt of these drawings, authority was given to Bagnell to proceed with the connecting works at Fermoy Station.

During 1871 a contract was signed with the firm of McKenzie, Clunes & Holland (later to become simply McKenzie & Holland) of Worcester for the provision of interlocking and signals for the new line. Reporting in May 1871, the Duke of Devonshire, who had been elected Chairman, said that the works were progressing rapidly, with all the bridges and fencing completed, while rails and sleepers were on the ground ready for laying. The *Waterford News* was able to report that the heaviest work on the line was a large iron viaduct some 100ft above the ground over the River Blackwater at Carrick-a-bric Castle (also spelt Carrickabrick), just outside Fermoy. By then it was confidently expected that the line would be completed by the following spring.

A formal working agreement was signed between the GS&WR and the F&LR on 12 August 1871, valid for ten years from the date of opening. The GS&WR agreed to provide not less than three trains each way on weekdays and one each way on Sundays. They were to have the power to determine the hours of starting

Ballyduff station looking towards Waterford. The building on the left hand side is the goods store. Just beyond the signal cabin and out of view around the curve the line crossed over the Ballyduff to Tallow road. The six-lever signal cabin was at the Mallow end of the up platform. *(T Cott, Courtesy Irish Railway Record Society)*

and arrival of each train. They were also to provide additional facilities at their Fermoy Station, the F&LR agreeing to construct the line into, and the junction at, Fermoy in a permanent and substantial manner. Stations were only to be opened at Clondulane, Ballyduff Bridge, Glencairn (Tallow Road) and Lismore, any others to be with the prior consent of the GS&WR. That at Clondulane was only to be a flag station for passenger traffic, with a siding for goods traffic from Clondulane Mill, if agreed; a more complete station was to be provided if mutually agreed between the two companies. The GS&WR were to provide all necessary locomotives, rolling stock and locomotive crews, while the F&LR were to provide sufficient station facilities at Lismore, including engine shed, carriage shed, goods shed, cattle pens, turntable and water tanks. This agreement was subsequently renewed on 17 February 1883.

It was reported in February 1872 that the GS&WR had made overtures to the F&LR in regard to purchasing the new line, although this progressed no further. Following an inspection of the line by the GS&WR Directors and officers on the morning of 30 July 1872, the Duke of Devonshire laid on a sumptuous déjeuner at Lismore Castle. In his speech to the assembled guests, the Duke praised the GS&WR Directors for agreeing to work the line at cost. He went on to comment that it was "impossible for him

to describe the (GS&WR) Board as a body for which everyone had a good word", a phrase which caused some mirth among his listeners. William Haughton, the GS&WR Chairman, responded by saying that his Company always acted for the benefit of both the shareholders and the public, despite having to contend with many difficulties. There were many people who would have agreed wholeheartedly with the first part of this statement, but who would have found it difficult to accept that the Company really had the public's interest in mind.

The first of two BoT inspections was carried out on 24 August by Lieutenant Colonel CS Hutchinson.[3] In his report, Hutchinson stated that the permanent way consisted of 69lb flat-bottomed rail in 17ft, 20ft and 23ft lengths, fish-plated on (mostly Baltic) creosoted cross-sleepers, set 3ft apart except at rail joints. Ballast consisted of broken stone 15in deep below the sleepers. The ruling gradient was 1 in 81½ and the sharpest curve was of 23 chains. Stations were provided at Clondulane, Ballyduff, Tallow Road and Lismore, and there was one level crossing. There were 11 over and 17 under bridges. The viaduct over the River Blackwater was of 7 spans, 1 of 156ft, 1 of 31ft and 5 of 45ft. While the works were substantially constructed they were "generally very incomplete."

---

3 The titles of BoT inspecting officers are shown as they were at the times of inspection.

Hutchinson called for a second platform at Fermoy, with loop points interlocked with the distant signal. At the other end of the line he required an unnecessary crossover road at Lismore to be removed and trains worked in and out on the same line, so as to avoid a set of facing points. Lismore Station was described as a beautiful structure of brown sandstone quarried locally, with walls and pillars artificially finished and carved; these pillars were adorned with the Duke of Devonshire's family crest, while the engine shed was said to have the appearance of a small church.

The GS&WR wrote to the BoT on 20 September confirming that they had agreed to work the new line when it had been completed to the satisfaction of their officers, undertaking to work it on the train staff system. Four days later Hutchinson returned for his second, and final, inspection of the line, and it was reported that he had six locomotives placed on the Blackwater Bridge to test its strength. Despite one or two minor matters, including a deficiency of ballast in a number of places, and the necessity for clocks at stations, the line was pronounced in order for opening. Traffic commenced on 27 September 1872 with a service of three trains each way daily.

Only three months after the opening of the line it was reported on 4 December that a cutting and two embankments had failed, the GS&WR Board asking their Engineer to report on whether or not the line was dangerous for the public; pending receipt of this report, they informed Mr Currey that they might have to suspend the working of the line until repairs were carried out. There was also an on-going problem with ballast, the F&LR offering to pay £2,000 to the GS&WR to complete proper ballasting, this offer being rejected. (Another serious slip occurred in a bank at an unspecified location towards the end of January 1877, the matter being referred to the F&LR for their urgent attention.)

The question of providing additional accommodation for locomotives at Lismore was raised with the F&LR in February 1873. Not having had a reply to their letter, Alexander McDonnell, the GS&WR Locomotive Engineer, raised the matter again early in May, pointing out the great inconvenience and loss to the Company. The Secretary was directed to write

to Mr Currey "insisting that suitable accommodation be at once provided for two more locomotives." This was absolutely essential and failure to provide it would leave the GS&WR no option but to reconsider the working agreement.

With the working agreement nearing the end of its term, a deputation from the WD&LR, consisting of three Directors, Messrs Currey, Ramsden and Goff, accompanied by Messrs O'Malley (Secretary), Otway (Engineer) and Power (Solicitor) met with the GS&WR Board on 10 March 1882 to discuss proposals for the working of both the F&LR and the WD&LR. The GS&WR offered to work the two lines for 65 per cent of gross traffic receipts, the two companies supplying permanent way materials. The service was to consist of three trains each way on weekdays and one or two on Sundays as deemed necessary, 5 per cent additional to be allowed for specials. Rates and taxes were to be the responsibility of the two companies. The deputation was informed that if both companies were worked by the GS&WR, every fair advantage would be offered to the port of Waterford. Any agreement was to run for ten years, the GS&WR offering to take over such of the WD&LR rolling stock, at a valuation, as might be approved by their Locomotive Engineer.

Nothing further was done as regards the working of the WD&LR, so the GS&WR wrote to Currey on 19 May drawing his attention to the fact that the working agreement with the F&LR was due to terminate on 1 October 1882. Currey responded in June to the effect that the working arrangements were considered to be "very unfair, if not prohibitive", and suggesting a rate of 50 per cent of gross receipts for a period of three or five years. The GS&WR responded in October offering 65 per cent for five years to 60 per cent for a ten-year agreement, the former being reluctantly accepted and incorporated in a new agreement dated 17 February 1883.

Some other minor events might be mentioned at this juncture. Currey approached the GS&WR in August 1876 seeking the free carriage of a quantity of materials and workmen engaged in providing a water supply at Clondulane Station, this being sanctioned by the Board. Clondulane Station was in the news again

Lismore station with its ornate station building on the right and goods store on the left. This view is looking towards Tallow Road. Beyond the platform on the right were a single road locomotive shed and turntable. There was also a carriage dock. *(T Cott, IRRS Collection)*

at the beginning of June 1878 when it was broken into; Currey was duly informed of the unprotected state of the station. Lismore Station was the scene of another attempted robbery on the night of 22 February 1882, Currey being requested to have bars or shutters placed on the windows of the goods store. Six years later, on 3 February 1888, it was the turn of Fermoy Station when a sum of £22 4s 6d in cheques, notes and coin was stolen from the safe. On that occasion the Station Master, Mr Duggan, was asked to explain why he had given up the key of the safe when it was his duty to retain it in his own custody.

Currey wrote again to the GS&WR in November 1879 suggesting that a refreshment stall should be opened at Lismore Station. The idea was approved of in principle, but the Directors refused to allow the Station Master to take charge of it. It was reported on 10 December 1879 that the locomotive of the 17:00 Lismore to Cork train had run off the turntable and into a field at Lismore, injuring the driver, who was considered to be at fault. As this was the second derailment involving the Lismore turntable, it was considered unsafe and the matter was duly referred to Mr Currey for attention.

The remaining items all involve the station at Fermoy. Additional signalling was provided there in March 1881 at a cost of £65. In July of the following year the GS&WR Engineer, Kennett Bayley, submitted a plan and estimate for a coal store at Fermoy, this work being approved at a total cost of £606. The store was reported to be ready for use in July 1882, being let to a Mr Daniel O'Keeffe in the following October at a rent of £30 per annum for ten years. O'Keeffe objected to the terms of the lease, the Company refusing to alter the terms of the agreement.

In connection with the visit of the Prince and Princess of Wales in May 1886 the GS&WR were asked to contribute towards the expense of decorating the station at Fermoy; the Station Master was requested to report on the matter. It would appear that the station at Fermoy did not have a water supply, water for the use of the locomotive department being supplied by means of a travelling tank. It was suggested in May 1883 that the locomotive department be requested to leave any surplus water in the station, an old tank being provided for this purpose. The Station Master reported in July 1884 that work on the town supply was nearing completion and recommended that the station be connected up. However, following a report from Messrs Aspinall and Ilberry that their particular departments might require 10,000 and 200 gallons per day respectively, there proved to be some difficulty in finalising an agreement with the Fermoy Water Company. Finally, in April 1886 an agreement similar to that arranged with the authorities in Tralee was completed.

The five-year working agreement fell due for renewal on 1 October 1887. In this context, Kennett Bayley reported that if the F&LR line was relaid at the rate of one mile per year for the following thirteen years, the annual cost of maintenance would work out at £2,250; after that period the annual charge should not exceed £1,200. The agreement was duly renewed for a further five years. The GS&WR advised in August 1891 that following the termination of the agreement on 30 June 1892 they would require a rent of £500 per annum for a minimum period of ten years. This figure included a sum of £300 a year to cover alterations necessary at Fermoy Station, but excluded telegraph services and block working. The upshot of this demand was that the F&LR gave formal notice on 30 December 1891 of their intention to terminate the agreement as from 30 June 1892. Dissatisfied with the GS&WR's attitude to working their line, an agreement was concluded with the WD&LR whereby the latter Company took over the working.

It is clear that the idea of the F&LR being worked by the WD&LR was being seriously considered prior to December 1891 as Otway, the WD&LR Engineer, had requested, and been granted, permission from the GS&WR on 7 December 1888 to inspect the F&LR line. Possibly following this inspection he submitted plans on 11 December 1890 to the WD&LR Board of a proposed new station at Fermoy and of the existing passenger accommodation at the GS&WR station; this was followed up a month later with plans for proposed new buildings and sidings for the goods and cattle station. It is, therefore, hardly surprising to find the WD&LR Board discussing the question of a working agreement with the F&LR at a joint meeting of Directors on 19 February 1891. Their Secretary was instructed to prepare a statement embodying the framework of a working agreement and then to discuss the matter with the Board of Works.

There are few references to the F&LR in the WD&LR minute books from which we can assume that the working was carried out in a satisfactory manner. While the Dungarvan Company's own line was being relaid with steel rails, the F&LR line was not overlooked; Otway reported in November 1894 that he had relaid ½ mile of the latter Company's line during the previous half-year.

CHAPTER FIVE

Early Schemes for Dungarvan

A number of early schemes were proposed to connect towns like Dungarvan and Lismore with Waterford and Cork, or to provide alternative access to Dublin, some of them by circuitous routes. One of the earliest schemes brought forward was in 1861, for a tramway to connect Dungarvan with the River Blackwater at Villierstown Quay, about 5 miles to the south of Cappoquin. It was intended to bring the town of Dungarvan into connection with Cork by means of the steamer service plying between Villierstown and Youghal, and from the latter over the C&YR to the city of Cork. The steamer service had first been introduced in 1843 and operated for several years, being resurrected in the early 1860s when the C&YR advertised a service with the tug *Daisy*, replaced a few years later by the *Fairy*. A Bill appeared in the 1862 Session for the Fermoy, Lismore & Dungarvan Railway, which hoped to obtain baronial guarantees. It failed to progress any further, the withdrawal of the Bill prompting the *Railway Times* to comment that; "the countenance of established interest has not shone upon the project with warmth sufficient to bring it into life"! A more ambitious scheme, which had the support of the Waterford Grand Jury, was intended to connect Fermoy with both Cork and Waterford, with a connection to the steamer service to Milford.

In Chapter Four we have already noted proposals for the WL&FR and CL&DR aimed at connecting Waterford with Cork that had failed to get off the ground, In any event, by the early 1870s steps were being taken for the formation of a railway company to provide the necessary connections, which was to be called the Waterford, Dungarvan & Lismore Railway (WD&LR). As originally envisaged, it was intended to link the towns named in its title, with a branch across the River Suir at Waterford to provide a connection with the Waterford & Limerick and Waterford & Kilkenny lines. Although slightly out of context chronologically,

mention should here be made of a proposal put forward at the end of 1872 for the Waterford, Wexford & Rosslare Junction Railway for the construction of a connecting railway from the proposed W&WR line near Campile to the W&LR near Waterford, in effect a resurrection of the W&WJR mentioned previously, but promoted by the W&WR. The construction of this line and the completion of the W&WR to Ballyhack would have provided continuous rail communication between Rosslare and Mallow, and thus with Cork, Tralee and Killarney, as well as an alternative route, albeit roundabout, from Cork to Dublin.

A meeting was held in the County Courthouse in Waterford on Saturday 2 March 1872 to consider the provisions of the WD&LR Bill in Parliament. The local press reported a large attendance at the meeting, including the Marquess of Waterford, the Earl of Huntingdon, Lord Hastings, Sir John Keane, Sir Nugent Humble, James Delahunty, MP for Waterford, Abraham Denny, Frederick and William Malcomson, Ambrose Congreve, Revd John Medlycott and James Strangman, all either important landowners or merchants associated with the county and city of Waterford. The High Sheriff of the county, Percy Smith, took the chair. A resolution was passed pledging the ratepayers of the county to guarantee a dividend of 5 per cent on the proposed capital of £280,000, until such time as the traffic should pay a dividend. Mr Delahunty expressed his conviction that the traffic would be so great that, instead of the guarantee ever being demanded, the shareholders would find it a very profitable investment. Sadly, as we shall shortly discover, the reality was to be very different.

The Act of Incorporation for the WD&LR received Royal Assent on 18 July 1872, capital being set at £280,000 in £10 shares, with additional borrowing powers up to £93,300. It was stipulated that the baronies of Middle Third, Decies Without, Decies

Within, Drum, Coshmore and Coshbridge in the county of Waterford should contribute to provide a dividend equal to 5 per cent; the guarantee was to apply for 22 years from the date of opening of the line. The first meeting of Directors following the passing of the Act was held on 16 September 1872 with the Marquess of Waterford in the chair. The attendance included Sir John Keane, James Galwey, Francis E Currey, Henry White and Edmond Power, the latter gentleman in the combined roles of Solicitor and acting Secretary to the new Company. Also in attendance were the Engineers, Wellington Purdon and Charles Tarrant, and RM Muggeridge, the Parliamentary Agent. Richard Muggeridge had previously been Secretary to the Waterford, Wexford, Wicklow & Dublin (later Dublin & Wicklow) Railway from 1849 to 1856.

One of the items discussed was the raising of funds so that construction could be commenced at the earliest opportunity; additionally, some thought was given to whether a suitable contractor could be found and on what terms. The remainder of the meeting was taken up with a discussion regarding two proposed deviations in the authorised line through the estates of Sir Nugent Humble and Ambrose Congreve immediately to the west of Waterford. In the latter instance, Congreve had been offered a sum of £10,000 compensation, much of the deviation being planned alongside the River Suir. In all, three deviations were sought when notice for a Bill was published in November 1872. In total, a length of some 36 miles was involved, the longest being that from the townland of Killoteran about 4 miles from the terminus at Waterford to a point west of Dungarvan, near to the site of the later Ballymacmague level crossings. These deviations and the payment to Congreve were given effect to by a further Act of 7 July 1873, which also extended the baronial guarantee to nine baronies and the city of Waterford and the period of the guarantee from 22 to 35 years.

Early in November an agreement was reached with a Mr French for the lease of a property in Cathedral Square in Waterford to be used as the Company's offices; the agreement was for a term of 35 years from 1 November 1872 subject to an annual rent of £42. French had some reservations about the house being used as offices on the grounds that the colour of the paintwork and the possibility of office papers being stuck on the walls would militate against it being used as a dwelling-house at the expiration of the lease! The Directors agreed that the only structural alteration required was the removal of a partition separating the back bedroom from the dining room attached to it; in addition a new water closet was required. In August of the following year a Mr Michael Hourigan was appointed caretaker of the offices at a wage of £1 13s 4d per month, plus coal and candles, he being required to reside in the house. James Scott was paid an amount of £173 3s 6d in March 1874 in respect of board room and office furniture, while Messrs J & E Maher received £5 in respect of hearth rugs. Hourigan's stay was relatively short as in April 1875 James Daly was appointed housekeeper and office messenger at 10s per week, payable monthly; he was ordered to keep the premises clean and in order.

At about the same time as Hourigan was appointed, advertisements were placed in the local press for the position of Secretary. In all, 45 applications were opened at the board meeting on 3 September 1873, these being quickly whittled down to four, viz Messrs Naan, Jacob, Madden and Dobbs; of these the first two had connections with the W&LR. However, when the matter was considered again a fortnight later, a fifth name had been added to the shortlist, namely George Willis. Willis, who was described as being very experienced and had previously been with the GWR and the DW&WR, was duly appointed to the post, his duties to commence on 10 November 1873. He was granted a salary of £400 per annum, and was instructed to reside permanently in or near Waterford and to confine himself exclusively to the duties of his office.

Meanwhile, Messrs Purdon and Tarrant, the Engineers, had reported to the Board on 12 August 1873 with proposals for finding a suitable contractor. It was decided to contact Messrs Harrison and Ogilvie, both trusted Partners of the late Thomas Brassey.[1] They also suggested that the construction works be divided into three divisions; if that course was adopted, then the tenders should be confined to works only, the

---

1 Henry Harrison was in fact Brassey's brother-in-law.

Company itself supplying the permanent way. It was to be 16 March 1874 before it was announced that the negotiations with Messrs Harrison and Ogilvie had been concluded, they having been unsuccessful in persuading their friends to subscribe to the capital of the Company. It was then decided to approach Joseph Philip Ronayne; Ronayne, however, declined to submit a tender, again for financial reasons, and it was, therefore, decided to re-advertise; with tenders to be submitted to the Secretary by Wednesday 13 May.

The year 1874 saw two tramway schemes proposed for the city of Waterford, notices for which were published in the previous December. The Waterford Railways Junction Railway & Tramway Bill planned a main line of tramway commencing by a junction with the W&LR about 7 furlongs west of that Company's terminus, crossing the River Suir on a new bridge and connecting with the authorised line of the WD&LR. From the latter Company's terminus, a further tramway, approximately a mile in length, was to run along the South Quays to the GWR yard at Adelphi Wharf. The Engineers for this scheme were our good friends, Messrs Purdon and Tarrant. The second scheme, under the title of the Waterford Free Bridge Railways Bridge and Tramways, with Sir Charles Fox as Engineer, envisaged no less than nine tramways, the principal one running from the W&LR Company's Kilkenny Goods Yard gate, crossing the River Suir on a new toll-free combined road and rail bridge, and along the South Quays to Adelphi Wharf. One of the branch tramways was to terminate at Bilberry Road adjoining the WD&LR terminus, while another was to go as far as the W&TR terminus in Manor Street. On the north side of the river, tramway No 8 was to run along the Dockyard and Sion Row to a terminus at the Ferry Slip near Abbey Road. This latter line was therefore to follow closely the course of the joint DW&WR/F&RR&H line that was constructed some 30 years later.

Despite the fact that both schemes passed Standing Orders in March 1874, they caused much controversy in both railway and public circles in Waterford. The Secretary of the WD&LR reported to the Board meeting on 4 April that a clause had been introduced into the 'Waterford Tramways Bill, known as Scheme No 2' (the Free Bridge scheme), conferring working powers on the WD&LR. It was decided that it would be necessary to convene a Wharncliffe[2] meeting for the purpose of considering it. However, there is no further mention of the matter, either in the Board minutes or in the General Meetings book, so we do not know the outcome of these deliberations. What we do know is that neither tramway scheme ever progressed any further.

Five tenders for construction of the line were opened and considered at the Board meeting on 13 May 1874. The Engineers and Solicitor were instructed to communicate with two of the contractors to ascertain if they were prepared to modify their tenders. Messrs Smith, Finlayson & Company agreed to reduce their tender for the first division (Waterford to Kilmacthomas, a distance of 14 miles 67 chains) from £71,700 to £69,698 and on the second division (Kilmacthomas to Dungarvan, 13 miles 49 chains) from £105,100 to £97,400. It was decided to award these contracts at the amended figures. The third division (Dungarvan to Lismore, 14 miles 35 chains) was awarded to JW Stanford[3] of Dublin for £49,149 6s 10d (unaltered).

Towards the end of May, the Marquess of Waterford announced his intention to resign as Chairman of the Board. The Directors endeavoured to persuade the Duke of Devonshire to accept the vacant position, but he expressed himself unhappy with the wording of the prospectus regarding the provision of capital for rolling stock. He was, however, unwilling to allow the line to be abandoned on those grounds. If parties could be found to co-operate with him, the Duke would himself provide £20,000 towards the amount that would be required in excess of the £280,000, either for the construction of the line or for the provision of rolling stock; furthermore, as regards the £20,000, he would be willing to forego interest thereon. Abraham Denny was elected Chairman of the Board at a meeting

---

2 A Wharncliffe meeting was a meeting of shareholders of a railway company, called for the purpose of obtaining their assent to a Bill in Parliament bearing on that company's railway. So called after Lord Wharncliffe, its originator.

3 John Woodward Stanford was actually a Partner with Travers Hartley Falkiner and although the tender was submitted under his name it was Stanford and Falkiner who carried out the works. The contractor's Resident Engineer on the third division was Samuel Gordon Fraser.

held on 14 July, a position which he was to hold until 1891. At the same meeting, Sir James Ramsden of Barrow-in-Furness and Abraham Stephens of Duncannon, were appointed as Directors. Abraham Stephens was at that time a Director and Chairman of the W&LR. He was not, however, destined to remain long as a WD&LR Director, as in January 1875 he announced that family arrangements had prevented him paying the £1,000 required of him towards the share capital, and he, therefore, reluctantly tendered his resignation.

A conference was held on 13 June 1874 at New Milford between representatives of the WD&LR and the GWR, which resulted in the latter company agreeing to provide an annual rebate of £1,000 for 21 years on through traffic between the two systems. As a result, the GWR became entitled to nominate a Director to the WD&LR board, this position in due course being filled by Sir Charles Alexander Wood, Deputy Chairman of the GWR from 1865 until his death in April 1889. At the Board meeting on 16 June a memorandum from Sir James Ramsden was read explaining that if satisfactory arrangements were made for the working of the line, the Duke of Devonshire would be prepared to increase his subscription towards the capital of the line from £5,000 to £20,000, in addition to which he would provide a further sum of £20,000 towards the cost of rolling stock. This led to a discussion as to whether the line should be worked by the WD&LR itself, by another railway company, or by a contractor. As regards the latter, this was a method of working favoured in the 1850s, but since that time its popularity had waned.

In July 1874 Purdon was ordered to communicate with South Wales iron-makers for the supply of about 5,000 tons of rails. However, arising from a fall in the price of iron, delays in the contract works meant that the Company saved quite an amount when these were finally ordered from Messrs Guest & Company in December for delivery over a two-year period commencing on 1 May 1875. The actual order placed was for 5,200 tons of flat-bottomed rails weighing 70lb per yard at a cost of £8 7s 6d per ton, along with 225 tons of fishplates, 354 tons of fastenings and 49 tons of spikes. At the Board meeting on 21 July a letter was read from Sir John Coode regarding his proposed visit to Waterford for the purpose of advising on some general scheme for providing railway accommodation for the city. In his letter he requested the various railway companies and the Waterford Harbour Board to furnish him with detailed statements embodying any points considered relevant to his inquiries. Later, the WD&LR was requested to pay a proportion of Sir John's fees for production of the report, a request to which they strenuously objected on the grounds that they had not authorised his visit, nor indeed had they ever been consulted about it in advance. The Board minutes remain silent on whether or not they ever did contribute.

By the time the order was placed for permanent way materials, plans had been prepared and submitted for both intermediate and terminal stations, these plans being "generally approved." Correspondence from the Guardians of Kilmacthomas Union was considered in February 1875 in relation to land being compulsorily taken for construction of the railway. It was suggested that the Company should close the existing burial ground and enclose another plot of land in substitution at their own expense. It was also suggested that the Company should provide a level crossing and pay the Guardians a sum of £50 in compensation for the inconvenience caused. Another land dispute at Kilmacthomas ended up in the legal system. In the case of Ardagh v WD&LR, the plaintiff, a County Magistrate, sought an injunction restraining the Company from holding on to certain lands compulsorily taken. The judge agreed with the plaintiff, commenting that it was "amazing such a thing could go on in this country as the taking of property with a strong hand. Such conduct could not be tolerated." The judge went on to say that he thought the Company's offer was "absurd and illusory."

At the sixth half-yearly meeting of shareholders held in March 1875 at the Company's offices in Cathedral Square, Alderman Denny congratulated the large attendance of shareholders on the very satisfactory progress of the works. Works had been started at Ballyvoyle on 4 December and at Kilmacthomas a week later. John Blake, a major shareholder, expressed regret that the people of the city and county were not

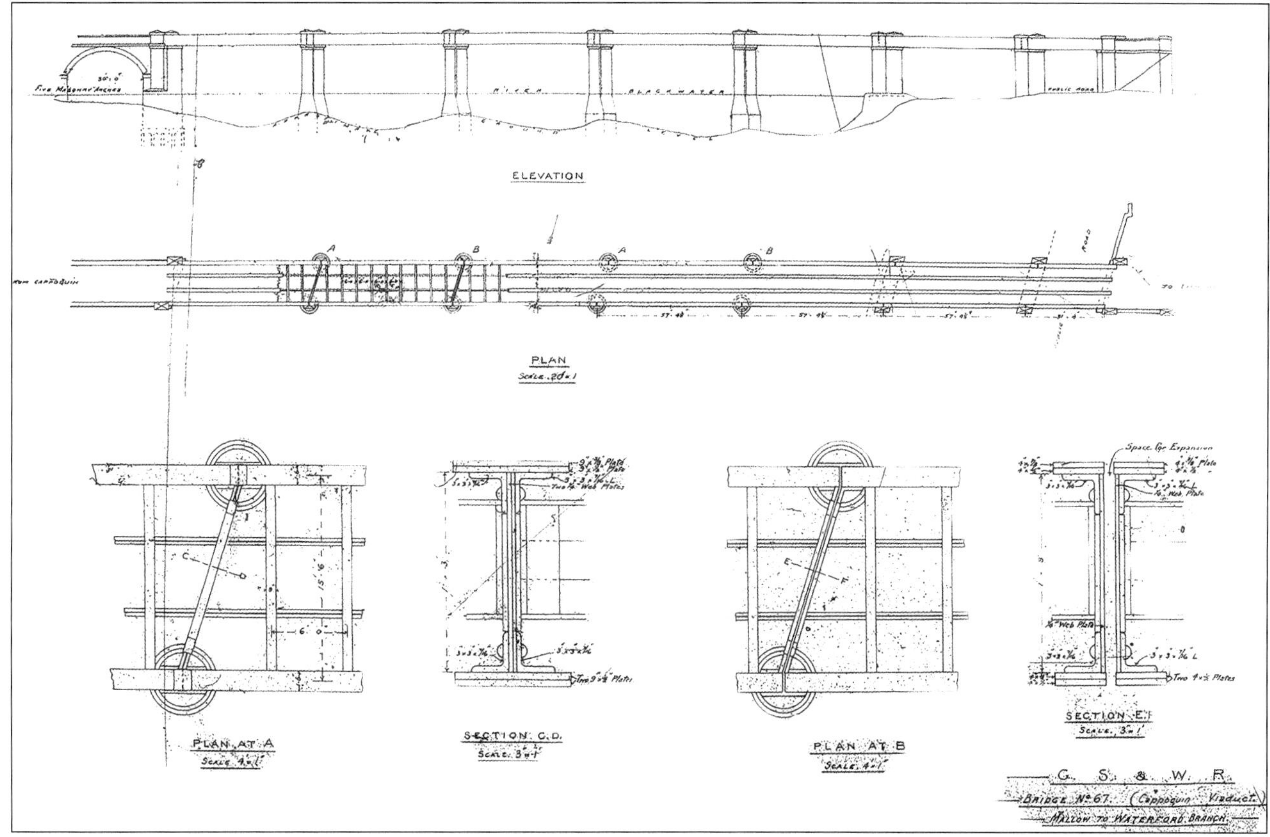

Plan drawing of Cappoquin Viaduct. (*Author's Collection*)

coming forward more numerously to support the undertaking.

Shortly after that meeting, disaster struck when the Blackwater Bridge at Cappoquin, only just completed, was severely damaged by floodwaters on 27 September 1875, some discussion taking place in October regarding its reinstatement. Mr Stanley, Secretary of the South of Ireland Wagon and Wheel Company, wrote to the Board in March of the following year enquiring as to "certain (unspecified) arrangements" in connection with the reconstruction of the bridge, he being informed that no decision had yet been taken. A committee was appointed in April 1876 with power to decide the question of any extra works required. The committee reported to the Board on 11 May and it was decided to substitute iron cylinders filled with concrete in lieu of the piers in the old structure; it was also agreed that an extension of 150ft be provided by means of five continuous masonry arches of 30ft span. Messrs Purdon and Tarrant were ordered to prepare detailed plans and estimates based on these proposals.

Meanwhile, the matter of lining Ballyvoyle tunnel was considered at a Board meeting on 13 July, it being agreed that it be lined with brick of the same quality as Youghal bricks shown to the Directors by Mr Ashwell, representative of Smith, Finlayson & Co.

The question of making provision for rolling stock was brought before the Board in November and December 1876, these deliberations resulting in the Chairman and FE Currey being requested to communicate with Mr Ilberry of the GS&WR to ascertain upon what terms that Company might be disposed to work the line, a proposition that was declined. Approaches were also made to the GWR in January 1877 enquiring if they would either work the line or make some provision for rolling stock. The GWR replied in March stating that they had some redundant broad-gauge stock which could be converted for use on the WD&LR. We shall return to the whole question of rolling stock in Chapter 19.

At the Board meeting on 8 June 1876, the engineer submitted plans for first and second class stations along with a tender from David Moran of Waterford as follows:

First class station at Cappoquin £500
Second class station at Cappagh £400

Moran's tender was accepted, but in March 1877 we find the Engineer's attention being called to the matter of stations with a view to having them ready for the opening of the line. Reporting back to the Board on 12 April, Purdon confirmed that he had ordered foundations to be laid for stations at Durrow & Stradbally, Kilmacthomas, Kill & Bonmahon, Kilmeaden and Dungarvan. Plans for a goods shed at the latter station at an estimated cost of £679 9s 8d were approved in July. However, in October 1877 it was reported that Mr John Sheehan, the contractor for the stations at Stradbally, Durrow and Kilmacthomas, had yet to commence work. Whilst on the subject of stations, reference should be made to a request first made in May 1875 by Mr Power O'Shee of Gardenmorris for a flag station at Kill, situated about 12 miles west of Waterford. Whilst the Board confirmed their willingness to provide such a station, which they considered to be both convenient and advantageous for the district, they were not prepared to guarantee its permanent continuance as requested by O'Shee. Following a number of such requests, the station was provided at Carroll's Cross, being opened in 1882.

It was reported in April 1877 that the Duke of Devonshire, in company with the Directors, had inspected the works between Lismore and Dungarvan, during the course of which he had walked into Ballyvoyle tunnel. Only a month later, an embankment collapsed about half a mile west of Dungarvan, burying three workmen in the debris. Luckily, on being extricated, it was found that their injuries were not life threatening. Signals and other fixed plant were ordered from the Ashbury Railway Carriage & Iron Company Ltd. Later, however, it appears that the Company had a change of heart and approached Messrs McKenzie & Holland, who declined to entertain a system of deferred payments for signalling. So in March 1878 the tender of the

Gloucester Wagon Company[4] at £3,732 was approved for the supply of interlocking equipment, erection of signals and signal cabins. Later still this Company tendered successfully for the erection of the station at Waterford at £1,500 as well as three of the smaller stations at Kilmacthomas, Durrow and Kilmeaden at £230 each, and an engine shed at Lismore for £430.

Also in May William Forsyth, Chief Engineer of the Board of Works, was appointed to inspect the line in relation to the Company's application for a Treasury loan. Having inspected the entire line, Forsyth expressed himself favourably impressed with the progress and stability of the works. Pending receipt of this loan, the Duke of Devonshire advanced a further sum of £10,000 to keep the works in progress. The Directors expressed some dissatisfaction with Ashwell's progress in August and threatened to take the contract from him. Purdon, however, expressed every confidence in his ability to complete the two divisions under his control by 1 April 1878 and it was agreed to leave matters stand *pro tem*.

In August 1877 tenders were received for the supply of four locomotives, details of these being further dealt with in Chapter 19. With the approaching completion of the works, it was decided in December to advertise for the services of a competent engineer to take charge of the Locomotive, Carriage & Wagon Department, applications to be in the hands of the Secretary by 31 December. Upwards of 50 applications were received and it was decided to seek the advice of Henry Waugh, Locomotive Superintendent of the Waterford & Tramore Railway since 1860. In due course the names of William Wakefield, foreman in charge of the DW&WR works at Grand Canal Street in Dublin, and Edward Graves, foreman in charge of the C&YR workshops at Midleton, were short-listed for interview. William Wakefield was duly appointed Locomotive Superintendent of the WD&LR on 4 March 1878 at a salary of £300, being informed that his services might be required "at an early period". He had commenced his career at the Inchicore Works of

---

4 The Gloucester Wagon Company had been founded in 1860, diversifying into signalling in 1876, when George Edwards, Signal Superintendent of the L&NWR, was persuaded to join them. He patented a new signal interlocking frame in March 1877. They later expanded the business to include the provision of station buildings etc.

the GS&WR under his father, John Wakefield, and later became Locomotive Draughtsman with the Midland Great Western Railway at Broadstone. After spending a period running a foundry he joined his father on the DW&WR in 1871. Reverting to August 1877, the DW&WR obtained an Act for an extension of their line to the townland of Rosbercon on the Waterford side of the River Barrow at New Ross. The decision to locate their terminus at that point was clearly made with the future prospect of extending further to Waterford itself; the DW&WR decided to go back to Parliament in the 1878 Session seeking such powers. When the matter was first raised in October 1877 it was considered by the WD&LR Board, who were of opinion that it would be of mutual interest and they agreed to provide half of the necessary capital for the erection of the bridge to connect with the proposed extension of the DW&WR and also to pay half of the maintenance costs, in return for which the Company would take half of the tolls for 'foreign companies' using the bridge.

The WD&LR proposed that station accommodation should be provided on the south side of the river, either by a station to be erected at the joint expense of the two companies or by the DW&WR paying rent for the use of a station entirely provided by the WD&LR. It was suggested that permissive powers be taken in the Bill for the DW&WR to work the WD&LR. Writing to the DW&WR in November, the WD&LR sought that company's co-operation in extending their line into the city and also the making of an extension from Fermoy to Cork. When the Act was finally obtained on 22 July 1878, running powers over the Dungarvan line were authorised in Section 38, while Section 41 empowered the DW&WR to contribute any sum not exceeding half of the cost of construction of the junction line and the terminal station at Waterford, as well as to any extension of the WD&LR into the city which might be authorised in that Company's 1878 Act. In turn, the WD&LR were required to contribute half of the cost of two of the DW&WR's four authorised lines.

Railway No 2 is of particular relevance to our story. It was to be 5 furlongs, 4 chains and 7 yards in length from the terminus of Railway No 1 (the main line from New Ross) near Newrath House, crossing the River Suir by means of an opening bridge, and terminating by a junction with the WD&LR close to its terminus at Bilberry. However, the DW&WR suffered from the same basic problem as the WD&LR, namely a shortage of funds and, as a result of this, no work was done on the Waterford extension. Jumping ahead chronologically, correspondence passed between the two companies during 1880 and 1881, the upshot of which was that the Dungarvan Company stated that the maximum amount to which they were prepared to contribute half was £40,000. By that time it had been agreed that a joint station would be provided on the site of the WD&LR terminus at the expense of both companies. The powers for the Waterford extension eventually lapsed and the DW&WR had to go back to Parliament in 1897 to revive them; indeed the New Ross extension was not opened until September 1887. In the interim, in February 1882 they had offered to work both the WD&LR and the F&LR, but that matter was also shelved.

Mention has been made previously to the proposed extension of the WD&LR from its terminus at Bilberry into the city. Notice of a Bill to effect this was published towards the end of 1877. Leaving the existing terminus, the line was to fall on a gradient of 1 in 800 for about a furlong, then horizontal to the mouth of a 90-yard long tunnel through portion of Gibbet Hill, from which point it would be on a falling gradient of 1 in 200, roughly to the 3 furlong mark, the last portion being level. The line was to terminate in Bridge Street, approximately half way between Mary Street and Dyehouse Lane, a good portion of which was to be closed. It was also intended to divert a portion of Bilberry Road.

In addition to the extension, the Waterford City Tramway was to form a junction with the extension to the west of Gibbet Hill, initially running on the north side of Bilberry Road. It was then to take to the centre of the road as far as the Bridge, run along Merchants' Quay, past the Clock Tower, along Coal Quay, Custom House Quay, Parade Quay and Adelphi Quay, and terminate at the end wall of the GWR Steam Packet Office. The total length of the proposed tramway was to have been 1 mile 2 furlong & 2½ chains, and was to have been double-track throughout; it was apparently intended for goods traffic, providing a connection with the GWR steamers. At a meeting of Waterford Corporation held on 8 January to urge the adoption of the Bill, James Delahunty, MP, took the opportunity to state that the city was being deprived of its right to appoint Directors to the WD&LR by the County Grand Jury, "to enable Englishmen to step in and take £14,000 per annum out of their county railway."

When the Bill for the WD&LR extension came to be debated by the House of Commons Select Committee, petitions against it had been lodged by the Corporation of Waterford and Messrs Davis, Strangman & Company, who operated a brewing business at Bilberry close to the course of the proposed extension. It was confirmed that the promoters had agreed to keep the costs of the extension separate from those of the rest of the Company's capital. Despite this there were calls for the line not to be authorised as ratepayers were reported to be "almost maddened at the prospect of the proposed imposition on them," and it was also strongly felt that the ratepayers should be represented on the board. It was also confirmed that the extension did not actually interfere with the brewery premises.

With the WD&LR line nearing completion, the Duke of Devonshire signified his desire to inspect the works over the entire line on Monday 24 April. Orders were therefore given for the necessary arrangements to be made. A saloon carriage was placed at the Company's disposal by the GS&WR, which was attached to Mr Stanford's engine[5] for the journey. The train departed Lismore at 10 o'clock and proceeded to Dungarvan, picking up Sir John Keane at Cappoquin along with Edmond Power, the Company's Solicitor. At the Tay viaduct, to which they had been compelled to travel from Dungarvan by road in consequence of a short break in the permanent way, they were met by Abraham Denny, George Willis and Thomas O'Malley. From here the journey proceeded with Mr Ashwell's engine and several ballast wagons with a wagonette and seats for the occasion. A heavy downpour of rain prevented a close inspection of portion of the works but the party reached the Company's offices at 14.30, where luncheon was provided by the Directors. His

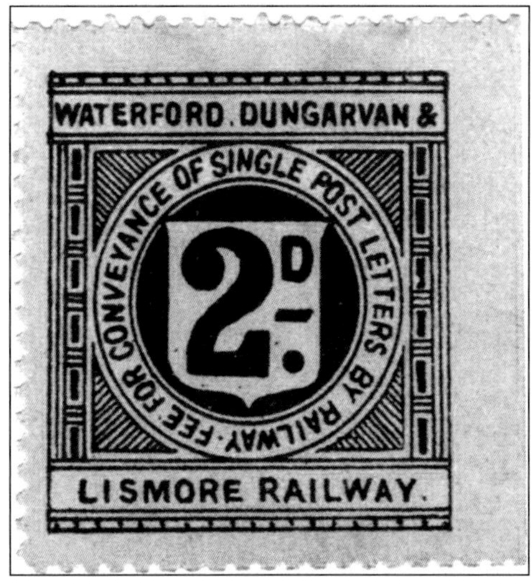

WD&LR Letter Stamp. *(Author's Collection)*

Grace expressed himself quite satisfied with the state of the works.

The question of appointing a Traffic Manager was discussed at the Board meeting on 4 March 1878, the name of Thomas O'Malley, formerly of the Limerick & Ennis Railway, being considered. Ten days later O'Malley was appointed to the position at a salary commencing at £200 per annum plus travelling expenses, he to take up his position on Monday 18 March. It was decided in April to set up a Traffic Committee to arrange matters regarding services, fares and the like. It was agreed that the Committee should consist of the Chairman along with Messrs Goff, Power and White. The matter of passenger fares was in fact brought up on 22 June, the following rates being agreed:

First Class   2d per mile with an addition of 10%
Second Class 1½d per mile with an addition of 10%
Third Class   1d per mile

It was agreed that the train service would consist of two trains each way, from Waterford at 10:10 and 14:50, from Lismore at 07:20 and 15:20.

At the half-yearly shareholders' meeting in June 1878, Denny stated that the greater part of the loan from the Board of Public Works had been received, with the balance of about £10,000 expected in the

---

5 Ex-GS&WR 2-2-2 No 13 – see Chapter 19 for further details.

course of the following month. He confirmed that the Bill for the extension to Bridge Street was then at its second reading in the House of Commons and was expected to become law very shortly. It was also confirmed that the majority of the rolling stock had arrived, but due to a strike in the iron trade in England their locomotives had been delayed. In this context it was arranged that the DW&WR would provide the Company with the loan of two locomotives, pending receipt of their own; likewise, the GS&WR offered the loan of one locomotive.

An inspection was carried out on 12 June by Colonel FH Rich on behalf of the Board of Trade, but a few matters required attention, and permission to open the line was refused. Colonel Rich arrived back in Waterford on the Milford ferry on the morning of 8 August to carry out a more detailed inspection of the line over a period of two days. On the first day he went as far as Durrow, from whence he returned to Waterford. On the second day he re-inspected the works beside the river at Mount Congreve, and then proceeded to Lismore, completing his inspection at about 18.00. On this occasion he found the arrangements more or less complete and satisfactory. The report confirmed the length of the new line at 42 miles 30 chains, single throughout, but with passing loops at Kilmacthomas and Dungarvan. Permanent way consisted of Vignoles rail weighing 70lb per yard, fished and fixed with spikes and fang bolts to sleepers laid at an average of 3ft apart; the latter being 9ft × 10in × 5in. Colonel Rich confirmed that the line was generally well ballasted and fenced. The ruling gradient was 1 in 66 and the sharpest curve of 18 chains radius.

There were 13 under and 8 over bridges, all but one constructed of stone, the exception being of wrought-iron girders. In all there were 18 viaducts and one tunnel 418 yards in length, lined throughout with stone. There were 27 authorised level crossings and one which was not authorised, the latter at 35m 40c. He confirmed that clocks were required at stations, to be either put up outside or arranged inside the windows so that they might be seen from the trains; in addition some ballasting was required. Colonel Rich also requested that Lismore Station should be worked entirely by the GS&WR. Permission was given for the opening of the line to traffic, this taking place on Monday 12 August. In the interim, Mr Currey had been in consultation with the GS&WR regarding the Company's use of the latter's station at Lismore. Arrangements regarding its use were incorporated in an agreement dated 31 October 1878.

The *Waterford News* of 16 August reported on the opening of the line, the first train, well-filled and with the locomotive decorated with flags, departed at 10:30. The rolling stock, especially the second-class, drew favourable comment, as did the stations. The temporary terminus was admired for its convenience and neatness, Kilmeaden was much neater and better fitted up than expected, while Durrow was regarded as being the best-finished on the line. The correspondent commented that the line would take time to develop traffic. However, within a year, the WD&LR was reporting the third worst working ratio in Ireland, 98 per cent, but we shall continue the saga of the Dungarvan company following its opening in the next chapter.

CHAPTER SIX

Opening and Sale

Within days of the line opening for traffic a Mr Williams of Shandon approached the Board on 3 September 1878 offering to manage a refreshment room at Dungarvan Station, presumably intended to be in premises provided by the Company. The Board, however, failed to see the necessity for such an establishment and declined the request. John Fitzpatrick of Dungarvan sought permission in May 1880 to open a similar establishment there, the Board again deciding that it was both unnecessary and undesirable; they did, however, suggest that a refreshment room might be considered at Lismore, as it would be "an accommodation to passengers". None was ever provided at either location. Also in September 1878 a Mr JW Cooper offered a sum of £40 per annum for the privilege of selling books and providing advertising at stations. This offer was accepted, provided Cooper located bookstalls at Waterford, Dungarvan and Cappoquin; he was also required to sell newspapers. Cooper gave notice on 15 June 1882 of his intention to terminate the contract, the Secretary being ordered to communicate with Messrs WH Smith & Son[1] to see if they would be interested in continuing the bookstalls as from 1 June 1883. There is no further mention of the matter in the board minutes, so it seems likely that nothing further transpired in this regard; in any event it can hardly have been particularly remunerative.

A more pressing matter occupied the Directors' attention at their meeting on 10 October 1878, namely the consideration of tenders for the erection of locomotive workshops and related offices at Waterford. Three tenders had been submitted, viz from Matthew Hunt at £840, John Ashwell (the contractor who had worked on the first and second divisions)[2] at £1,071

and Messrs Ryan & Son at £1,052. Before coming to a decision, the Board considered how they could effect a saving by adopting a cheaper mode of roofing, the matter being referred to the Engineer, James Otway, for a report. Otway reverted to the Board a fortnight later when it was agreed that a patent covering known as 'Malcomson's Roof' be adopted. Early in November it was decided to postpone the erection of the locomotive workshops and carriage shed until the line was formally taken over from the contractors. In any event it was reported in December that an amended plan for a fitting shed and office had been submitted, the contract for the work being awarded to a local builder, John Hearne, in an amount of £660 18s 0d.

A number of other building matters occupied the Board's attention about that time. In December Otway was instructed to inspect a hut at Kilmeaden offered for sale by John Ashwell. If deemed suitable, and if it could be obtained at a fair price, it was to be used as a temporary abode for the Station Master, James Connington. It would appear as if the 'temporary abode' became somewhat more permanent as Connington wrote to the Board in April 1889 offering to erect, at his own expense, a dwelling house at the station on the understanding that he be repaid the cost and interest by annual payments, when he would become owner of the property. Surprisingly, this was agreed to, Otway being instructed to choose a suitable site. The Board agreed to guarantee a yearly payment of £16 for 12 years, on the understanding that the house did not cost more than £150. In the event, John Hearne successfully tendered at £217, the Directors agreeing to pay Connington £20 per annum for 15 years.

The signal cabin at Durrow was burned down on 26 December 1878, and Otway was requested

---

1 Charles Eason was the Manager for the WH Smith business in Ireland, which in 1886 was transferred to Eason & Son.
2 John Ashwell had been the contractor on the spectacular Ribblehead viaduct and Dent Head viaduct for the Settle & Carlisle section of the Midland Railway in England, but his financial difficulties led to the MR taking over the works in 1871.

A very old view of staff at Dungarvan station on an unknown date. *(Waterford County Museum)*

to submit a design for a structure of a "more solid permanent nature." Approval was given for this on 17 January 1879 at an estimated cost of £95, this work also going to John Hearne, and he submitted his account for £98 5s 8d in the following May. This explains why the signal cabin at Durrow differed in appearance from others on the line, which were supplied by the Gloucester Wagon Company. Finally, following correspondence with Alfred Currey of the F&LR, it was agreed that a reasonable rent for the use of Lismore Station would be £250 per annum.

A deputation from Youghal Harbour Commissioners waited on the Board on 13 February 1879 regarding the proposed introduction of a daily steamer service on the River Blackwater between that town and Cappoquin. The deputation enquired whether the Company would be disposed to contribute towards the dredging of the river, the Commissioners expressing their willingness to bear "a very liberal proportion of the expense." The Board agreed to a survey being made of the river bed so as to ascertain an approximate estimate of the expense involved. It would appear that the survey was not carried out as the matter was raised again in the following June, when Otway was requested to report on the likely

cost of such a survey. There the matter rested until May 1887 when the Deputy Chairman was requested to meet with a party from the Blackwater Navigation Company regarding the taking of a piece of land below the railway bridge at Cappoquin for use as a general wharf and landing place. A formal agreement was signed on 1 July of that year for the use by the Blackwater Navigation Company of a piece of ground on the west side of the river adjoining the railway bridge, the annual rent to be 5s, payable annually on 1 July. There is reference to the use by the Navigation Company of the steamer *Avonmore*.

Francis Keane wrote to the Board in January 1890 regarding the improving of the landing place for the river steamer, the Company declining to incur any outlay, but agreeing instead to grant the use of the landing place on the same conditions as to the former company. McNeill (see Bibliography) states that a service first began operating between Youghal and Cappoquin in 1843, a service which lasted for only a few years, being revived again in the early 1860s by the C&YR. That service in turn lapsed after about ten years, being once again revived in 1893. Following a further break, the Youghal & Blackwater Tourist Steamer Company began a summer-only service in

1907 using the paddle-steamer *Dartmouth Castle*. Railway records would appear to suggest, however, that there may have been some activity on the river in the late 1880s as witness the reference to the *Avonmore* in 1887.

Otway reported to the Board in March 1879 on the condition of certain of the bridges on the line. This report was most likely prompted by his letter to the Board two months earlier on the Mahon Viaduct and one of the arches in the Dalligan Viaduct. Regarding the former, Otway had reported that the work which had given way there had been "judiciously dealt with and the road rendered perfectly safe." At Kilmacthomas there had been some settlement of the embankment between the station and the river viaduct and he recommended that longitudinal timbers be placed under the sleepers. With reference to Ballyvoyle tunnel, Otway reported that it was very wet and that lime had washed from the mortar. At Dungarvan the east abutment of the bridge had settled unequally, producing an ugly crack in the small arch.

Turning finally to the Dalligan Viaduct, the largest such on the line, Otway advised that it was causing him the most anxiety. The mortar used in its construction was made of local white lime and sea sand, and had shown a reluctance to set. This had led to the opening up of the east and west wings which had required shoring up, some of the spandrils having bulged. He recommended that without delay the east wings and all the spandrils be tied together and the arches protected from the action of water by a layer of puddle[3], where it could be employed, and of pitch and tar or asphalt where there was insufficient room for the puddle. The engineer reported further in May 1880 that the small arch at the Waterford side of the Colligan Viaduct was showing increasing signs of failure. He was instructed to watch the structure closely and, if deemed necessary, to put in rolled iron beams to carry the rails over the arches. All of these bridge defects coming to light within nine months of the opening of the line clearly were worrying developments and pointed to poor workmanship or materials in the

original construction of the line, reinforcing the view expressed by some that insufficient capital was raised in the first instance, and we shall now consider this latter point in a little more detail.

The Secretary informed the Board on 13 February 1879 that a sum of £6,800 had been received from the Board of Works, representing the third instalment of the Treasury loan of £93,000. Despite this the Company's financial position was in a poor state, so much so that it was announced in July that Messrs Craig Gardner, Public Accountants of Dublin, had been called in to investigate the Company's accounts and report to the Board as soon as possible. This request coincided with a letter from the Gloucester Wagon Company regarding the Company's dishonoured acceptances due on 4 July for £4,850 8s 7d, representing the Wagon Company's account, with interest, for station buildings. The Secretary was instructed to seek renewal for three months, by which time it was confidently expected that the Company's financial arrangements would have been sorted out. There was also an account owing to Messrs Sharp Stewart in an amount of £8,832 14s 8d for four locomotives. So bad were matters that some consideration was given to a temporary suspension of the working of the line, but it is difficult to see what advantage would have been gained from such action. Pending receipt of Craig Gardner's report, the question of a reduction in the working expenses was considered; the Directors made a token gesture by agreeing not to take any fees "till further notice." Mr Shanks of Craig Gardner attended the board meeting on 5 August and produced a financial statement of the Company's position. Having fully considered this report it was arranged that the accountants send a brief statement to shareholders outlining the position and urging them to attend a meeting in the Imperial Hotel in Dublin on 27 August.

There was a crowded attendance at the Dublin meeting. The letter to shareholders had outlined how the Directors had ineffectually endeavoured to grapple with the Company's financial difficulties, which largely resulted from the unforeseen costs of the line. These included the reconstruction, at a cost of £13,699, of the bridge over the River Blackwater at Cappoquin following its virtual destruction by

---

3 Puddle was clay with sand or gravel with water added and thoroughly mixed so that it became watertight. Generally used in the construction of canals, the term was first used in 1762 by the canal builder, James Brindley, although its use goes back to Roman times.

flood on 27 September 1875 when it had just been completed, the necessity of lining Ballyvoyle tunnel in brick at a cost of £7,200, the extension of Whelan's Pill Viaduct at £5,000 and additional earthworks at £27,603. The accounts exhibited a deficit of £124,932. It was agreed that insufficient capital had initially been provided, the works having been more costly than anticipated, and subsequently receipts had failed to live up to expectations. However, the Directors expressed confidence for the future; the DW&WR had obtained powers in 1878 for a Waterford extension, powers which enabled them to cross the River Suir and join up with the Company's line at Waterford. At the western end, a continuation of the line from Fermoy to Cork would also help to boost receipts.

One of the shareholders present at the meeting, a Dr Reynett, enquired if the sum of £125,000 now proposed to be raised would be sufficient to pay off all of the Company's debts. A Major Borrowes asked about passenger traffic, the Traffic Manager reporting that the summer average was about 1,400 per week, with between 600 and 800 in winter. The Company's Solicitor, Edmond Power, commented that the line was largely a tourist line, hence the difference in summer and winter figures; livestock also tended to be more numerous in summer. The Directors were accused of not supplying traffic returns to the newspapers as other companies did, and it came as a big surprise to many shareholders that the Company was in such a difficult financial situation. Another shareholder, William Findlater, suggested the setting up of a committee of independent shareholders to confer with the Directors and consider the best course to be pursued for the future. Another suggestion was that the line should be worked by the GS&WR; this matter was raised once more towards the end of 1880, going as far as having heads of an agreement drawn up. Legal opinion was taken regarding the suggested closure of the line, this opinion being to the effect that the baronies could not be compelled to pay dividends if the line was closed. It went on to state that the sums payable under the guarantee had to be paid in the manner laid down in the 1873 Act and could not be accessed by any of the Company's creditors.

At a further meeting between the Directors and shareholders early in December, the Solicitor put forward proposals worked out by the Directors. These involved the preference shareholders abating their dividends from 5 per cent to 4 per cent per annum and the deferred shareholders from 5 per cent to 3½ per cent. The contribution from the baronies should be reduced from £14,000 to £10,800 per annum, while additional preference capital to the extent of £135,000 at 4 per cent should be issued to rank next after the debenture stock; finally, the liability of the baronies should be extended to 40 years from 7 August 1882. Counter proposals were put forward but no consensus could be achieved. The Solicitor also advised the meeting that Ashwell had presented a petition for a receiver over tolls and profits and the baronial guarantees, the latter being successfully opposed, although not before it had been brought before the Courts.

Reverting to August 1879, it was decided to reduce the head-office staff by combining some posts and doing away with others. The positions of Traffic Manager and Secretary were combined at a salary of £250 per annum, likewise those of Accountant and Cashier. It was also decided that the locomotive and permanent way departments should be placed under the control of one officer, who was also to take charge of the stores department. Arising from this decision, William Wakefield was informed on 18 September 1879 that, owing to the financial difficulties and the necessity for the strictest economy in working expenses, it had been decided that the Board had very reluctantly been obliged to dispense with "his valuable services" as from 31 December; likewise Mr Mills, the cashier, was given similar notice.

There is little doubt that the Company's financial position was parlous as witnessed by a board minute of 30 September referring to the Sheriff's possession at Waterford Station at the suit of a Mr Morris of Kilkenny. The Sheriff apparently withdrew his Bail from "the coal and other property seized" in October, although we have no further details. At the same meeting the Secretary was instructed to seek renewals of various Bills. Even Messrs Craig Gardner had to wait for payment of their account for £95 12s 9d until "the Traffic Committee are able to find funds for its liquidation." Possibly arising from the notification of his impending

A Dungarvan to Waterford goods train crossing over the Shandon Bridge shortly after leaving Dungarvan. *(Waterford County Museum)*

dismissal, Wakefield lodged a claim for £13 19s 8d, representing his expenses for travelling to Manchester to inspect the locomotives under construction, and a further claim for £11 15s 0d for replacing drawing instruments lost in a fire at the Company's offices. It was agreed to pay the former amount but as regards the instruments he was informed that the Company had no funds available. Both Wakefield and Mills unsuccessfully sought substantial compensation for their dismissal. Wakefield returned to work under his father on the DW&WR at Grand Canal Street, eventually taking charge there, while Mills moved to a post on the Waterford & Limerick Railway. Thomas O'Malley was duly appointed Manager and Secretary on 22 December 1879 at a salary of £250 per annum, and James Otway as Engineer and Locomotive Superintendent at the same salary.

A settlement was finally made with the Gloucester Wagon Company following a judgment in July 1880 for £6,206 6s 5d, this figure including £852 in respect of signals. The first of a number of communications from the Board of Trade urging the application of continuous brakes was received in July, the Secretary being ordered to communicate with other companies; the Engineer was also requested to report on the likely cost of carrying this into effect.

Nearly two years after the embarrassment of having to bring in outside auditors the Company's financial position was still cause for concern. The Solicitor, Edmond Power, met with the Secretary on 7 April 1881 to consider the "financial embarrassment of the Company." Later that day Power attended a Board meeting and informed the Directors that a sum of £40,000 would be required to arrange all the liabilities of the Company. Arising out of this, Denis Crofton, Chairman of the Preference Shareholders' Defence Committee, handed in a resolution at the next Board meeting on 12 May requesting that the Board should notify both the GWR and the GS&WR that they were prepared to enter into negotiations with either company with a view to a sale of the line. However, as the Company Chairman was away in America, a decision was deferred awaiting his return.

At a further meeting held a week later, it was suggested that if the Duke of Devonshire would advance a sum of £42,000 or thereabouts to discharge the liabilities of the Company, exclusive of his own claim, and accept as security an assignment of the debts to be so discharged, the appointment of a Receiver and Manager as ordered by the Vice-Chancellor would be obviated. In the absence of a response, the Chairman and Secretary were respectively appointed as Receiver and Manager of the line on 12 July; this news led to a further resolution from Crofton for negotiations to be opened with the GWR and the GS&WR, a suggestion that was declined by the Board. Following a meeting between representatives from the three boards, the GS&WR offered in March 1882 to work the F&LR and the WD&LR for a period of ten years. Specifically in relation to the WD&LR, the GS&WR agreed to take over such portion of that Company's rolling stock as might be approved by the GS&WR Locomotive Engineer at an agreed valuation.

Despite, or perhaps because of, the difficulties in which the Company found itself, the Directors considered approaching the F&LR with a view to working that line. However, in November the matter was again raised and it was decided that in view of the financial difficulties facing the WD&LR the time was not right for such a move. Should the DW&WR proceed with their extension line, then the situation might have improved, but in the interim thoughts once again turned to a possible working of both the WD&LR and the F&LR by the GS&WR, the Solicitor being instructed to seek a temporary working agreement. In due course representatives of the two companies met and an offer was made by the GS&WR, an offer which drew strenuous opposition from the Grand Jury of Waterford and other parties. These negotiations finally came to an end in May 1882, following the intervention of the Duke of Devonshire. The DW&WR meanwhile now sought a guarantee that the WD&LR would pay half the cost of two of the lines authorised in their Act of 1878, a guarantee they refused to consider unless the total cost of the two lines in question was limited to £40,000.

Leaving aside for the moment the Company's financial woes, we must record some other happenings. Sanction was given by the BoT in January 1881 for the use of a new loop and platform at Durrow Station pending a re-inspection by Colonel Rich. The re-inspection was carried out at the beginning of March when Colonel Rich found everything in order. As far back as May 1875 a Mr Power O'Shee had requested an open or flag station at Kill to the west of the site of Kilmeaden Station. This request was initially declined although an agreement was eventually

signed in July 1876. A year later the ratepayers of the district requested a station at Carroll's Cross instead of at Kill, O'Shee seeking to hold the Company to their agreement. In the following October a further deputation attended the Board and presented another memorial urging the necessity of a flag station at Carroll's Cross. Otway reported that the adverse gradients at that location made it difficult to accede to the request and as an alternative a flag station was suggested at a point 8¾ miles from Waterford. The Company offered in June 1878 to provide O'Shee with passes for life for himself and his wife over the entire line, along with free passes once a week on relevant market days between Kilmacthomas and Waterford for four of his tenants. Eventually, in April 1886, he accepted payment of a sum of £100 in full settlement.

Finally in February 1882 the Board approved the construction of a station at Carroll's Cross at a cost of £270, although instructions were given not to commence work "till further orders." Instructions to proceed with the work were eventually given three months later, and on 20 April. Maj Gen Hutchinson inspected the new station on behalf of the BoT at the end of October 1882, quoting its location as being at a point 11m 43c from Waterford. He confirmed that arrangements at the new station were sufficient and he recommended that the BoT sanction its opening.

The first of a number of approaches regarding the construction of a tramway to connect the station at Dungarvan with the quay there was made to the Board in August 1882, the Directors expressing themselves in favour of such a scheme. As a result, Otway was instructed to prepare a survey for a tramway, to be worked by horse power. Nothing further transpired at that time and the matter was again raised in August 1885; on that occasion the Company stated that they had no powers to give any financial assistance. Notice of an application for the construction of a tramway under the Tramways (Ireland) Acts was published in November 1885, the promoters being shown as Abraham Denny, Francis E Currey, Sir Richard F Keane, Henry White and William Goff Davis Goff, all Directors of the WD&LR. The proposed tramway was to be 2f 65y in length, commencing by a junction with a siding of the WD&LR close to Shandon Road and terminating on the Quay about 190ft southeast of the northeast corner of the Fish Market abutting on the quay. The tramway was never constructed, although further approaches were made in the mid-1890s and to the GS&WR as late as February 1902.

The Secretary informed the Board in May 1884 that the powers taken in the Company's Act of 1882 (extending the time for construction under the 1878 Act) for an extension of the line from the terminus at Gibbet Hill into the city, and the authorised extension of the DW&WR to Waterford, were both due to expire in 1885. O'Malley was duly instructed to enquire whether the DW&WR intended to keep their parliamentary powers alive. In June the latter company confirmed that their New Ross extension was by then under construction, although destined not to open for another three years, and that the Waterford extension was still under consideration. However, in the following November the DW&WR advised that the extension had been "indefinitely postponed." The result of this was that the Dungarvan Company decided not to proceed with their own extension into the city of Waterford.

The possibility of the GS&WR working the line was revisited again towards the end of 1887, the Board of Works making enquiries in this regard early in October. As the GWR agreement of January 1874 was likely to impact on any decision, the matter was discussed with Sir James Ramsden. He in turn made contact with James Grierson, the General Manager of the GWR. Regrettably, Grierson passed away on 7 October, only three days short of his sixtieth birthday, after a long and distinguished career with the GWR. This delayed a response from the Paddington authorities, but when it did come it was to the effect that the GWR were not prepared to consider any modifications to the 1874 agreement; one can understand their concerns as they undoubtedly anticipated the loss of traffic from the WD&LR passing through the port of Waterford to New Milford. Despite this setback, an approach was made to the GS&WR in November. They confirmed they were prepared to consider working the WD&LR subject to the provisions of the GWR agreement. They did, however, suggest that the Dungarvan Company might consider whether it would be to their advantage

to forego the annual subsidy of £1,000, assuming the GWR would agree to cancel it.

The GS&WR Engineer, Kennett Bayley, was instructed at the end of November to carry out a full inspection of the WD&LR, his report being submitted to the GS&WR Board at their meeting of 30 December. A copy of that report, which outlined what would be required in the way of future maintenance, was sent to the WD&LR suggesting that Abraham Denny should attend a board meeting at Kingsbridge to discuss the matter further. It is clear from a further letter sent to Denny at the end of January 1888 that considerable maintenance would be required over the ensuing ten years or so, particularly in respect of 1888 and 1889, with outlay amounting respectively to 103.22 and 103.50 per cent of gross receipts being quoted. The result of this was that the GS&WR stated that they were prepared to work the line in perpetuity at a rate of 79.50 per cent. Whilst the GS&WR were prepared to take over the WD&LR rolling stock at an agreed valuation, they were not keen on inheriting the associated leasing arrangement. There matters rested until Otway requested permission in December 1888 to inspect the F&LR line, this being granted; it is clear that the WD&LR had decided not to avail of the GS&WR offer and were apparently giving serious consideration to working the Lismore Company's line. What is not clear is whether any approaches had been made at that time from the latter Company or if it was a predatory move on the part of the Dungarvan Company.

A different scenario presented itself in November 1888, when a shareholder, Richard Ussher of Cappagh House and soon to become a Director, wrote enquiring as to the position if the Board of Works forced a sale or lease of the railway to the GS&WR, as foreshadowed in correspondence dated 28 September between the Treasury and the Duke of Devonshire. A partial solution was to bring about the strictest economy in working expenses and outlay on repairs and renewals, so as to keep these items within the revenue, and, hopefully, forestall any action from the Treasury. However, having closely examined their departments, both O'Malley and Otway confirmed that they could make no meaningful reductions. Instead, it was decided to communicate to the Board of Works how injurious it would be, not only to the future interests of the Company, but also to the commercial welfare of the district, if a sale or lease was forced on the Company. This letter was followed up on 27 November by a face-to-face meeting with the Board of Works. The WD&LR deputation left Dublin with the feeling that they had put their arguments forcefully enough, and that they had secured the immediate future of the Company.

However, in December the Board of Works complained of the high working expenses as compared with the Sligo Leitrim & Northern Counties Railway (SL&NCR), a line of similar length and also in receipt of a Treasury loan. In 1886, the last year for which final figures were available, working expenses on the SL&NCR were £10,502 as against £15,052 on the WD&LR, respectively £244 and £354 per mile. There was no denying the figures and the Directors decided to bring in a railway expert to undertake a detailed examination, the Board of Works agreeing to this and proposing that it be carried out by either EJ Cotton or JE Ward, respectively Managers of the Belfast & Northern Counties and the Midland Great Western Railways. The inspection of the line was carried out in March 1890 by Cotton, a copy of his report being passed to the Secretary and Engineer early in April.

In view of the possibility of working the F&LR, Otway submitted plans and estimates for works considered necessary at Fermoy, including a separate passenger platform, goods and coal stores, cattle pens and an engine shed, along with additional siding accommodation, all estimated to cost £3,500. As there were no intermediate crossing places on the Lismore line, a second platform and loop were recommended at Ballyduff Station at a cost of £600. The Board of the WD&LR agreed that if they were to work the F&LR, it should be done based on actual outlay. An inspection of the F&LR was carried out by the Directors in March 1889, Otway pointing out the facilities for providing a goods station at Fermoy independent of the existing GS&WR facilities. The Secretary was instructed to ascertain terms on which a site, then in the occupation of a Mr Newstead, could be obtained. Newstead offered to sell the land with a house for a sum of £1,000, reserving portion of the land so he could build a new residence for himself. This offer was

recommended to the Duke of Devonshire, and was approved by him. Detailed plans of the proposed new facilities at Fermoy were approved by the Board on 11 December 1890, Otway being instructed to obtain tenders for goods and coal stores, engine shed and turntable. However, in the interim the plans had been submitted to Alfred Currey on behalf of the F&LR; having consulted with Sir James Ramsden, the latter gentleman suggested some modifications, which were to be referred to the Marquis of Hartington, the Duke of Devonshire's eldest son, who was shortly to become the eighth Duke of Devonshire.

Negotiations between the two companies reached a successful conclusion and a ten-year working agreement was signed on 22 March 1892, to come into effect on the termination of the existing agreement with the GS&WR, and the WD&LR began working the F&LR as from 1 March 1893. There was a proviso in the agreement that if any new line of railway be constructed between Cork and Fermoy, then it would be lawful for either party to determine the agreement on one month's notice. A service of three trains each way daily was to be provided on weekdays with at least one passenger train on Sundays, to be run at mutually agreeable times. As envisaged, the WD&LR had no desire to make any profit in working the 'Duke's Railway' and so the line was to be worked at cost. In order to provide adequate passenger facilities at Fermoy, the GS&WR proposed erecting the necessary facilities at a cost of £1,887, charging a rent of £200 plus a further £300 per annum for station services. The latter was considered to be excessive by the F&LR.

Dr Currey, the Company's Medical Officer, wrote to the Board in November 1882 complaining of the condition of the station house at Cappoquin, which he described as unhealthy to reside in. Otway was instructed to report as to the measures deemed necessary to render it fit for occupation; meanwhile, perhaps as a sweetener, the Station Master's salary was increased to £70 per annum, apparently having been reduced from the figure of £80 originally approved in June 1878 when a Mr J Thompson was appointed to the post. It was not until 7 November 1883 that Otway was able to confirm that repairs had been completed and the house ready for occupation. Two stations came up for mention in October 1883. Consideration was given to the provision of a second platform at Kilmeaden to allow trains to cross there; the Board authorised expenditure of £200 in this regard. Carroll's Cross Station had been opened the previous year for passenger traffic, but the local farmers now sought the provision of a siding, the Board seeing no reason to provide the facility. Otway in due course prepared a plan and estimate, the latter in an amount of £200. However, the Board decided in July 1884 that further consideration be postponed as works of "a more pressing character claim attention." A carriage shed was also proposed for Lismore Station in July 1884 but this was never provided. Instead, the WD&LR decided to request the GS&WR to have their locomotive shunt the Dungarvan Company's carriages under the existing (train) shed, "which would afford partial shelter whilst they are standing at the station"; we do not know what the GS&WR's reaction was to this request, but it can hardly have been very favourable.

Waterford Station was in the news on several occasions, the first in January 1887 when Otway submitted plans for the erection of 14 workmen's houses, along with gate keepers' houses at five level crossings, at a total cost of £2,720. The Secretary was directed to communicate with the Board of Works as to whether they would be prepared to advance a loan to the Company for this outlay. The Board of Works offered to provide half of the cost but enquired how the Company intended to procure the other moiety; this appears to have put an end to the matter. In July 1890 the Engineer reported the necessity for a new shed at Waterford so as to carry out wagon repairs, which were on the increase as stock aged; the Board authorised expenditure of £70. This was presumably the small wagon shop just beyond the turntable at the eastern end of the station. The station at Waterford at that time suffered from the inconvenience of having only one platform for passenger traffic, it being suggested in March 1891 that a second one be provided. A short bay platform for departing trains was brought into use later in the year. Cappoquin Station also acquired a second platform, expenditure of £360 in this regard being approved by the Board on 18 December 1891.

Whelan's Pill viaduct, near milepost 69½, had been the subject of a report presented to the Board on 12 March 1885 as it was causing some concern as to its safety; Otway was instructed to proceed at once with the necessary repairs. Reporting again in October, Otway referred to the difficulties involved in repair work due to subsidence and the subsequent twisting of part of the structure. A more detailed report was submitted to the Directors in October 1886, with some subsidence still reportedly taking place, although this was expected to abate in the coming months. While the bridge had been repaired as ordered by the Board, Otway drew attention to the necessity for the viaduct's complete renewal within two or three years, the likely expense of an iron bridge being about £1,200 plus £500 or £600 for erecting it. When Otway reported once again in January 1889, he quoted a figure of £3,000 for an iron bridge, half that amount if it was constructed of timber. The replacement rested on whether the Board of Works would provide assistance.

Tenders were submitted to the Board which met on 26 April 1889 as undernoted:

Company	Location	Erection work	Iron work only
John Cunningham	Dublin	£3,584 0s 0d	–
Alfred Thorne	London	£3,734 0s 0d	£1,250 0s 0d
John Lysaght Ltd	London	£4,016 10s 0d	£1,000 0s 0d
A Handyside & Co	Derby	£4,050 0s 0d	–
EC & J Neary	Birmingham	£4,277 0s 0d	£1,300 0s 0d
J Goodman & Co	Motherwell	–	£1,315 0s 0d

The tender of Messrs Lysaght Ltd for ironwork only was accepted, the remaining work to be carried out by Mr Otway under the superintendence of Montague Mandeville at a rate of £4 4s 0d per week during its execution. The new viaduct was in place by November 1890, the Board commenting that Mr Otway was entitled to much credit for having brought the work to such a satisfactory conclusion, both financially and structurally, ably assisted by Mr Mandeville.[4]

---

4 Montague Mandeville subsequently joined the staff of the GS&WR as Assistant District Engineer at Cork, and was appointed District Engineer in Dublin in 1901, transferring to a similar position at Cork in 1904.

A Mr David Kiersey applied to the Board in October 1889 for a site on waste ground belonging to the Company at Kilmacthomas on which to construct a butter factory. Following an inspection of the proposed site by Otway it was agreed to lease the ground at an annual rent of 5s; Kiersey had to agree to the buildings being solely used as a butter factory, and he was not permitted to erect any further buildings without prior written permission. He did apply again in November 1890 for permission to erect a shed, this also being granted. Likewise he was authorised to add a grinding mill in April of the following year, the annual rent for which was set at £5. However, when Kiersey sought authority in November 1893 to make further additions, including the erection of a manure factory, the latter was turned down; indeed it is not clear how this type of activity would have fitted in with a creamery.

The question of providing a turntable and weighing machine at Cappoquin was referred to the Engineer in January 1895 for a report. Following confirmation from the BoT in March that the Company could substitute the electric train staff for the ordinary train staff and ticket system then in use between Waterford and Lismore, both matters were referred to the Board of Works seeking their approval for the necessary expenditure. The latter body replied in June to the effect that the Treasury had declined to sanction the application of the net revenue for this purpose. The Board of Works were unimpressed by pleadings from the Company, the Directors going as far as suggesting in July 1896 that they would themselves provide half of the cost of the two items if the Treasury would allow the balance to be charged as working expenses. A turntable was eventually installed at Dungarvan by the GS&WR in 1908.

Messrs George Keogh & Sons, Solicitors for the DW&WR, wrote to the WD&LR in December 1894 regarding the proposed extension of their line from New Ross to Waterford, seeking approval of certain clauses in that Company's proposed Bill, which would allow the WD&LR to subscribe capital and allow working arrangements. While the Board had no objections to a working agreement being entered into, they were not prepared to agree to the clauses in relation to subscribing capital or guaranteeing dividends. Further correspondence in 1895 urged the Board to secure financial support from the Duke of Devonshire for the New Ross & Waterford Extension Railway; Messrs Keogh were politely informed that the Duke's advisors – Sir James Ramsden in effect – were not prepared to recommend that the Duke should subscribe to the undertaking. A further, more personal attempt was made in May 1896, when Colonel Tighe, Chairman of the DW&WR, wrote directly to Sir James Ramsden, but yet again the Company declined to assist financially. In December 1896 the Board responded to further correspondence from the DW&WR, in which they notified the WD&LR that they were about to seek compulsory running powers over both the WD&LR and the F&LR, both companies absolutely declining to assent to this.

Francis Currey, the Chairman of the Board since 1891, but also connected with the Company from its earliest days, wrote to his colleagues on 17 August 1895 stating that on health grounds, and on the advice of his medical adviser, he felt it necessary to tender his resignation. The Directors persuaded Currey to remain on the basis that the work of the Board was of a more routine nature than in previous years and did not demand the Chairman's personal attendance at all meetings. However, Currey passed away on 6 June 1896 at the age of 82 at Lismore, mention being made of his long and arduous service to the Company. Another similar loss occurred with the death on 19 October 1896 of Sir James Ramsden, a man who had also given a great deal of his time to the undertaking. The Company had on 21 December 1891 lost another person of considerable standing in the form of the seventh Duke of Devonshire. Currey was replaced as Chairman by William Goff Davis Goff, who was to remain in that position until the demise of the Company itself in 1898.

The Chairman in his statement to shareholders at their half-yearly meeting on 29 May 1897, referred to the falling off in livestock receipts, mainly due to the unsettled condition of the bacon trade in Waterford, livestock numbers carried being down from 27,031 to 23,833, a reduction of 3,198 over the corresponding period in 1895. Further mention was made of this in the following December with carryings down more than 1,500. A dispute had arisen from the fact that the large pig merchants in Waterford decided at the beginning of the year to purchase pigs direct from farmers rather than through the pig buyers.[5] Considerable ill-feeling followed, resulting in some of the firms' principals being assaulted, and in at least one instance an Assistant Manager at Messrs Matterson was stabbed to death. Resulting from the dismissal of one of the pig butchers, the employees at Messrs Denny went on strike, while the pig buyers in all three bacon curing factories also ceased work. The upshot of this was the practical extinction of pig fairs along the line and the consequent non-attendance of buyers had a detrimental effect. The dispute was finally settled at the end of June 1897 and Goff expressed a hope that a recovery would soon follow. Military traffic was also down, the result of which was a reduction in passenger receipts under all headings. However, by that time the end of the WD&LR as an independent company was also very much on the cards and we must therefore follow subsequent events in that regard.

Shock news for the Company came on 16 September 1896 when the Board of Works informed the Directors that, acting on instructions from the Treasury, they intended to at once advertise the line for sale in order to realise the mortgage loan with overdue interest. This was all the more surprising since, only a year previously, the Treasury had agreed to the net earnings being used for the complete relaying of the line over a period of nine years. Following protests from the Directors and the raising of the matter in Parliament, the sale was postponed to allow the Treasury more time to come up with an alternative plan. The GS&WR Board Minutes for 25 November 1896 include an interesting entry. Mr Colhoun, the GS&WR General Manager, drew his Board's attention to the proposed DW&WR Bill to extend their line from New Ross to Waterford, a scheme which envisaged a bridge across the River Suir at Waterford and a connection with the WD&LR, and he suggested that the time had then come for the GS&WR to "endeavour to get possession

of the WD&LR unless they decide to take over the line to New Ross." In the absence of the Chairman, consideration of the matter was postponed for further discussion. It is not clear exactly at what point negotiations were opened with the GWR regarding a possible joint purchase of the WD&LR but this had become a reality only eight months later.

Details were published in the press on 23 July 1897 outlining two competing tenders for the purchase from the Government of the mortgaged WD&LR, one a joint offer from the GWR and GS&WR, the other from the F&RR&H. The GWR alliance agreed to pay the Treasury a sum of £75,000 in addition to a figure of £7 12s 6d per £10 share. The Treasury was to collect from the baronies and pay to the two companies, half-yearly, the annual sum of £8,400 in discharge of the existing liability of the baronies to pay £14,000. The two companies were obliged to provide a direct and efficient service of trains between Cork and Waterford via Mallow, at rates and fares based on the lower mileage as if the direct Fermoy to Cork line were constructed. However, if, in the opinion of an arbitrator appointed by the BoT at the insistence of the baronies affected, a direct line was considered desirable, then the companies would construct and work such a line, provided a 2 per cent perpetual guarantee was forthcoming from the baronies. The GWR undertook, upon completion of their new South Wales direct line, then under construction, to improve and expedite both their train and steamer services; in the case of the latter the Company would introduce new and improved steamers. The entire offer was conditional on a satisfactory arrangement being made with the Duke of Devonshire for the acquisition of the F&LR.

The Fishguard Company's offer involved the purchase of the Government mortgage of £93,000, all arrears of interest being cancelled. Pending the completion by the F&RR&H of their proposed lines from Rosslare to Waterford, including the bridge across the River Suir, and the line from Fermoy to Cork, the earnings of the WD&LR were to continue to be paid to the Treasury. Assuming these lines were completed and opened for public traffic by 1 August 1903, a payment equivalent to 2 per cent on the Dungarvan

---

5 This dispute had in fact been simmering since February 1890 when quay porters at Waterford refused to handle a cargo of bacon en route from Limerick to London.

capital of £280,000 would be paid, increasing to 2½ per cent per annum after the guarantee from the baronies expired in August 1913.

The details of the two offers left the WD&LR Chairman, William Goff Davis Goff, in no doubt that the ratepayers of the county and city of Waterford would be better off accepting the GWR offer. Not only was it financially advantageous, but the Fishguard offer was dependent on a large amount of capital being raised to finance the new lines. It was quite possible at the end of the day that the F&RR&H might fail to raise this capital, or might in a few years decide not to proceed with construction of the lines. The assets of the F&RR&H consisted of a breakwater and a few miles of railway in Co Wexford. Goff did, however, concede that the F&RR&H had one major advantage, namely the proposed short sea crossing. There were many who loathed the idea of spending upwards of eight hours on the crossing from Milford to Waterford, particularly in the GWR steamers of the period. Robert Ussher, one of Goff's fellow Directors held an opposing view, being strongly in favour of a Fishguard takeover. He was not alone in this, as public bodies from Youghal and Queenstown to Wexford were of like mind. Typical of comments made were those of the Youghal Board of Guardians, who were of opinion that the interests of the GS&WR were "wholly opposed to such railway extension and competition."

Within days of the publication of these offers, Robert Hanbury, Secretary to the Treasury,[6] met two influential deputations in London. The first included Sir Richard Musgrave, a large landowner in the Dungarvan and Lismore Unions, CW Humble, another landowner, Frederick Keane of the Cappoquin Foundry, Robert Ussher, Patrick Meade, Mayor of Cork and Thomas Healy, MP for Wexford.

The deputation was introduced by Mr Power, MP, who apologised for the absence of Mr Shee due to his steamer being seven hours late, a point not lost by the members of the deputation in putting across their arguments. Ussher informed Mr Hanbury that whilst the deputation were fully desirous that the Treasury should approve of the scheme which would be of greatest service to the country, they passionately believed this would be best secured by the acceptance of the F&RR&H offer. They wished to be relieved from the monopoly of the GS&WR and the new Company would provide welcome competition. Hanbury informed the deputation that he was due to receive a second deputation from the city of Waterford and he had no doubt their views would be opposed to those now put forward. He was sure, therefore, that the deputation would be patient until he had considered both points of view.

John Redmond, MP for Waterford, introduced the second deputation, which included representatives of Waterford Corporation, Waterford Chamber of Commerce, Waterford Board of Guardians and the Waterford Harbour Board. Their views were, as anticipated, totally opposite to those of the earlier deputation, considering a takeover of the 'County Railway' by the F&RR&H would be disastrous for the interests of Waterford. Also in attendance, to protect the interests of the GWR, was Joseph Wilkinson, that Company's General Manager. On being questioned by Mr Hanbury, Wilkinson confirmed that his Company had reconsidered their earlier offer and were now prepared to increase their contribution from 2 to 2½ per cent, thus increasing their annual contribution from £5,600 to £7,000, further reducing the liability of the ratepayers. Wilkinson confirmed the Company's current interest in the WD&LR; apart from an annual subsidy on traffic receipts worth £1,000 a year under the agreement of January 1874, they also held £5,500 worth of shares.

---

6 Robert William Hanbury (1845–1903) was elected to the House of Commons in 1872 as Member for Tamworth. Under the Conservative Government elected in 1895, he was appointed Financial Secretary to the Treasury and President of the Board of Agriculture in 1900.

CHAPTER SEVEN

Cork to Waterford & Wexford

As early as 1864 the Aberystwyth & Welsh Coast Railway (A&WCR) submitted a Bill to Parliament seeking powers to operate a cross-channel service from Porth Dinlleyn and the setting up of a terminal at Aberdovey. There was strong opposition from established shipping interests and the Bill was withdrawn before it even reached the Committee stage. In the next year the Bill was reintroduced with plans for a service from Aberystwyth and Aberdovey to Waterford and Wexford; the Waterford & Kilkenny Railway were keen to see this service established as rival lines were diverting traffic via the L&NWR through Kingstown and Holyhead. This time the Bill got through the Committee stage in the House of Commons but was thrown out by the Lords in June 1865. Briefly in 1880 some discussions took place between the A&WCR and the Manchester & Milford Railway for a transatlantic service from Aberdovey, nothing further being heard of this ambitious scheme.

Under an Act of 29 June 1883 the Cambrian Railways, as successors to the A&WCR, got powers to improve the harbour at Aberdovey, improvement works being carried out in 1885/6. Messrs Conacher and Owen, respectively Secretary & General Manager and Engineer of the Cambrian Railways (CR), held talks with the Waterford & Limerick Railway (W&LR) Board in August 1886 regarding the prospects of a proposed morning steamer service between Aberdovey and Waterford in competition with the GWR service, further negotiations taking place in the following December. An independent company, the Aberdovey & Waterford Steam Ship Company (A&WSS), but sponsored by the CR, was formed to commence a service between the two ports. The first crossing from Aberdovey was made on 19 April 1887, operated by the paddle steamer *Liverpool*. Nine sailings a month were operated and after a period the *Liverpool* was replaced by the former Belfast Steamship Company's

Magnetic.[1] The GWR raised objections to the new service on several occasions, claiming that through booking arrangements were contrary to the terms of the 1872 agreement between that company and the W&LR. Despite this the service, intended mainly for cattle, lasted until 'temporarily' withdrawn as from 1 December 1888.

Not content with the revenue it was receiving from the A&WSS Company, the CR promoted a Bill in the 1889 Session to run its own cross-channel service from Aberdovey. Despite strenuous opposition in Parliament, the Cambrian Railways (Steamboats) Act received Royal Assent on 9 July 1889. Powers were granted to allow the company "to provide or build, work, let and use steamers" between any of four Welsh ports, including Aberdovey, and Wicklow, Arklow, Wexford and Rosslare. The ports of Waterford and Cork were excluded since they were already used by established operators. It was intended initially to purchase one paddle steamer of about 800 tons, but this was left in abeyance.

At this point in our narrative, the reader is most likely wondering why we have gone off on an apparent tangent to look at the Cambrian Railways and their steamer interests. It is clear, however, that the Cambrian Railways were behind a scheme which was brought before Parliament in 1890, a scheme which was very similar to that put forward by the F&RR&H Company eight years later. It is time, therefore, to take a look at this scheme.

It should here be pointed out that the Government of the day had set up a Royal Commission on Irish Public Works on 16 October 1886 under the chairmanship of Sir John Allport, General Manager of the Midland Railway (of England), to inquire into

---

1 Although not a sister ship to the F&RR&H steamer *Voltaic*, both were owned by the Belfast Steamship Co and had almost identical dimensions. The two ships came from different builders.

the fisheries, harbours, canals, arterial drainage and railways of Ireland. With regard to the railways, the Commissioners were instructed to inquire "whether increased facilities could be afforded to trade or commerce by any changes, legislative or otherwise, in the organisation or management of the Irish railway system." The Commissioners issued their second report in January 1888 in which they recommended, *inter alia*, the connection of Wexford and Rosslare with the whole of the southwest of Ireland, albeit by means of an extension of the DW&WR company's New Ross branch to Waterford. It also suggested a connection between the lines of the CB&SCR and the GS&WR in Cork so as to promote the interests of the fisheries. Here was the impetus for the scheme being put forward.

Notice was published in November 1889 of intention to seek a Bill for the construction of a railway to connect all the lines having termini in Cork with the exception of the Cork & Muskerry Light Railway. By an extension of this circular route, a line was to run to a junction with the F&LR. Making a connection with the WD&LR in Waterford, another line was to cross the River Suir, make a connection with the W&LR and then proceed to two separate connections with the W&WR; branches to Ramsgrange and Kilmore Quay were also envisaged. We shall look at these proposals of the Cork & Fermoy and Waterford & Wexford Railway (C&F&W&WR) in somewhat more detail a little later in our narrative.

The W&LR received a letter early in February 1890 from the Secretary of Waterford Corporation inviting a representative of the Board to attend a meeting in opposition to the new scheme; this invitation was declined as was a request in March for information in respect of their traffic, presumably through the port of Waterford. In April, the W&LR Board considered holding a Wharncliffe meeting to approve the C&F&W&WR Bill, subject to the prior approval of the GWR. The latter company confirmed in May that they had no objection to the W&LR taking whatever steps were considered desirable in their own interests (and by inference those of the GWR); however, the Directors decided against putting the matter before the shareholders at that time as they were otherwise engaged in other more pressing parliamentary business of their own.

In evidence before the Select Committee of the House of Commons in May 1890, John Conacher, the Secretary and General Manager of the CR, confirmed that the scheme first came to his attention through William Bailey-Hawkins, a CR Director. Bailey-Hawkins was one of the promoters named in the Cork & Fermoy & Waterford & Wexford Railway Bill, and was later to become Chairman of the CR from 1905 to 1909. The other promoters were our old friend, Sir James Ramsden, and John Barry, the MP for South Wexford between 1880 and 1893. Also closely involved at the early stage was the Irish railway contractor, Robert Worthington, who appears to have been involved in some of the early negotiations.

The Select Committee was chaired by Mr Arthur Brend Winterbotham, the MP for Cirencester, and when the C&F&W&WR Bill came before the Select Committee in May 1890, the opening speech, on behalf of the promoters, was made by Mr Littler, QC. He pointed out that the scheme was essentially brought forward for the development of Irish industries and fisheries in West Cork. By 1890 there were five separate railways having termini in the city, none of which were at that time connected. They were the GS&WR, Cork Blackrock & Passage Railway (CB&PR), Cork Bandon & South Coast Railway (CB&SCR), Cork & Macroom Direct Railway (C&MDR) and the Cork & Muskerry Light Railway (C&MLR). Of these, the CB&SCR (Cork & Bandon Railway prior to 1888) and the C&MDR had had a physical connection at Ballyphehane Junction between 1866 and 1879, but in the latter year, following ever increasingly acrimonious disputes, the C&MDR had removed the connection and extended their line to a new terminus at Capwell.

The proposed new line would enable fish to be brought from the West Cork ports to Waterford and Rosslare, saving cartage across the city of Cork. Apart altogether from the cost of cartage, physical damage was caused to the fish, particularly mackerel, due to the jolting of the carts; in addition, connections were sometimes missed and ice melted, meaning that fish was not as fresh as it might have been when it reached Birmingham or London. It was intended that traffic for the English Midlands would be shipped via Aberdovey and the CR, while south of England traffic would go via Milford or even a new port at Fishguard.

Another important aspect of the proposed new line was that it would considerably shorten the journey time between Cork and Wexford. At that time, someone wishing to send a ton of goods between the two places sent it from Cork to Bristol by steamer and it was then brought back on a second steamer to Wexford. Railway passengers for Wexford had to endure a journey of 11¾ hours via Dublin, whereas the new route would reduce this to about 5 hours. Littler made reference to the powers already obtained by the CR to operate steamers to Rosslare; the only reasons they had not yet built steamers were the inordinate and unexpected price rises and the fullness of all the shipbuilding yards with orders.

Littler then moved on to briefly list the petitions that had been lodged against the Bill. To enable us to better understand the relevance of some of these, we must take a slightly more detailed look at the proposed scheme. The Bill for the C&F&W&WR, as originally put forward, included no less than 13 separate railways in the Cork and Fermoy section and 7 in the Waterford and Wexford section.

Railway No 1 was to commence at a point in the City Park, where there was to be a station, and was to terminate close to the old CB&PR terminus beside Victoria Road. The main line (Railways 2, 4, 10 & 11) then ran round in a kind of horseshoe past the gas works, the Fever Hospital on the Douglas Road, passed over Evergreen Road, then turned north over the Bandon Road. It then crossed over the South and North channels of the River Lee at high level respectively adjoining Erinville House and the Mardyke, where there was to be a second station. Finally, it turned northeast, tunnelling through Sundayswell Hill, before finally heading more or less east for Fermoy, where it was to terminate at a point 373 yards east of the bridge carrying that railway over the mail coach road from Fermoy to Clonmel and Mitchelstown. En route around the city it was to make connections with the CB&PR (Railway No 3), CB&SCR and C&MDR (Railways 5, 6, 7, 8 & 9) and finally the GS&WR (Railway No 13). Railway No 13 was to diverge at Farrancleary Cottage, turn north and terminate by a junction with the up line of the

GS&WR about ¼ mile north of that company's tunnel. This proposed junction with the GS&WR was to be the cause of some dispute as we shall shortly see.

In regard to the W&WR section, the line was to commence by a junction with the WD&LR in the townland of Gibbethill at a point in its main line opposite the northeast corner of that company's engine shed at Waterford, then cross the River Suir by an opening bridge, cross over the W&LR line, through a short tunnel and then connect with the W&LR company's goods extension line some 312 yards east of the toll house at the north end of the wooden road bridge over the Suir, affectionately known to residents of Waterford as 'Old Timbertoes'. The line was then to closely follow the north bank of the river as far as Snow Hill, through which it would tunnel. Emerging from the tunnel, it would cross the River Barrow by another opening bridge to pass into County Wexford. Passing close to Dunbrody Abbey, the line was to run to the townland of Orristown in the parish of Kilmacree. There, the line was to divide in two, the northern arm running roughly northeast for a distance of 2m 1f 3c to a junction with the W&WR, 150 yards southeast of an occupation level crossing leading from warehouses at Felthouse on the Wexford Harbour South Reclamation (2m 0f 2c from Rosslare Station – now Rosslare Strand). The southern portion was to continue east for 3m 3.6c to join up with the W&WR at Rosslare (now Rosslare Strand) Station. Branches were to run from near Dunbrody via Arthurstown to Ramsgrange and Kilmore Quay, the latter line finishing up on the quay some 45ft from its outer end.

The GS&WR objected to the proposed line on several grounds. In the first instance, the new line would be a direct competing route between Cork and Fermoy, being some 14 miles shorter than the GS&WR route via Mallow. They also argued that the new line would form part of a competing route between Cork and Dublin, something that the residents of Cork would have been quite happy to see. Later, in evidence to the Committee, Alexander McCarthy, the Town Clerk of Cork, would testify that the GS&WR did not appear to favour any extension of the trade of Cork and were regarded with "very great dissatisfaction." The GS&WR also complained of the proposed point

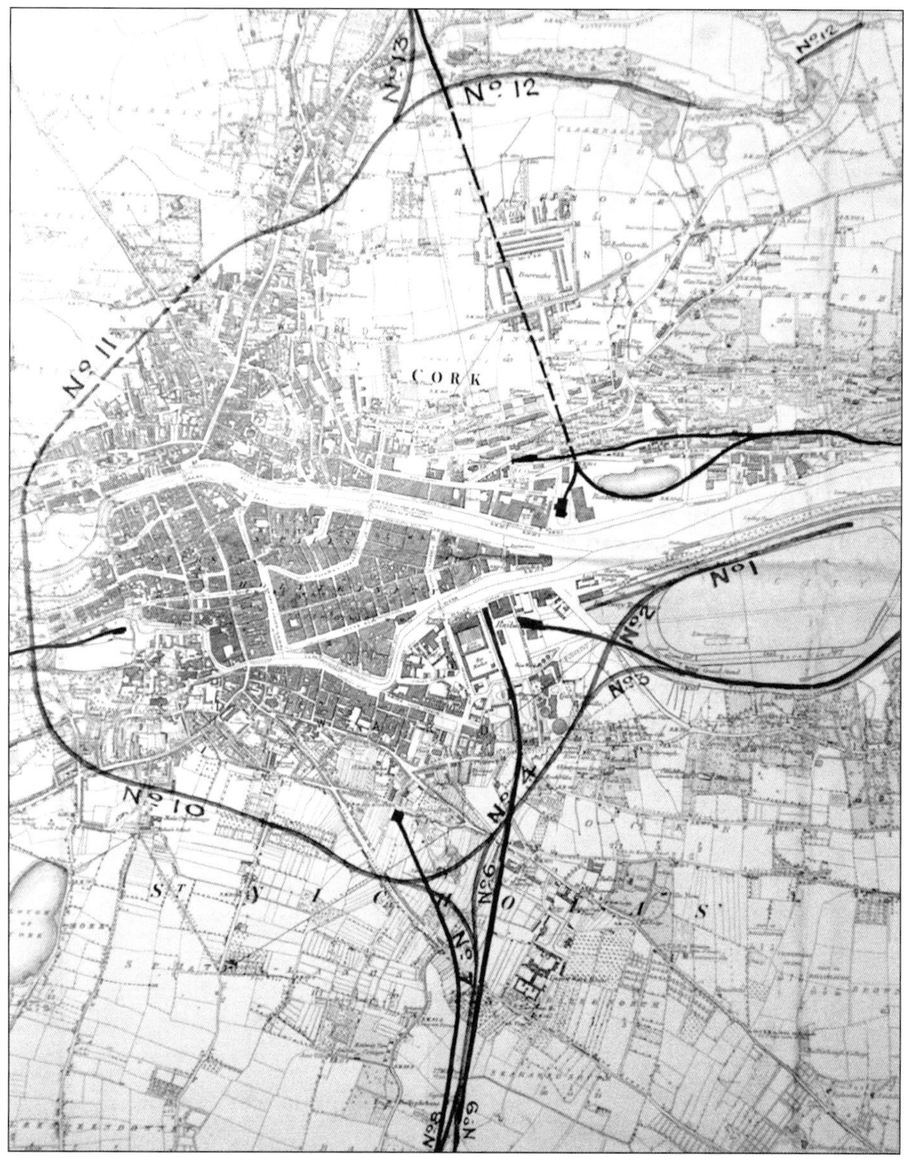

Map of (part of) Cork city showing the proposed connections of the railways envisaged by the Cork & Waterford and Waterford & Wexford Railway scheme of 1891. Railway No 12 was to form a connection with the WD&LR. This scheme was in effect the forerunner of the later F&RR&H scheme of 1898. *(Courtesy IRRS Archives)*

of junction between the two lines about ¼ mile north of the tunnel; Counsel pointed out that the GS&WR had themselves had a temporary terminus near there for some years prior to the completion of the tunnel. Both Robert Colhoun and Kennett Bayley, respectively General Manager and Engineer of that company, were called to give evidence against the junction which was to be on a gradient of 1 in 65, considerably steeper than that which the BoT would approve for a station site. Bayley also cast some doubts on the estimates for land and property to be acquired in Cork. Not only did he consider that the estimates were out by more than £30,000, but in addition there was a shortfall in the amount of land which he estimated would be required.

Finally, Colhoun tried to counter criticisms of the manner in which the company worked the F&LR; complaints had been made in the rate for working the line, which Colhoun put down to the necessity for relaying. He confirmed in addition that improvements had been made at Mallow Station to enable Fermoy line trains to run through without changing locomotives, although this method of working was on hold pending the outcome of the C&F&W&WR Bill. He confirmed that the service between Cork and Fermoy consisted of four passenger trains each way daily, with three on the Duke's line from Fermoy to Lismore. However, it was to be regretted that the WD&LR only saw fit to provide two trains each way between Lismore and Waterford, which did not make connections with the GS&WR service, being instead worked in connection with the GWR shipping route from Waterford.

Father Charles Davis, parish priest of Baltimore in West Cork, was called to give evidence regarding fish traffic and confirmed that he was the Founder and Manager of the Baltimore Industrial Fishing School, to which Baroness Burdett-Coutts had generously advanced something like £10,000.[2] Father Davis confirmed that a great deal of the fish landed at Baltimore was exported to England but, when questioned further, he had to concede that much of it was sent out of west Cork ports by steamer to Milford, while some went by rail from Cork to Dublin for export via Holyhead. About 500 tons had gone by this route in 1889.

The Marquess of Hartington, MP, soon to become the 8th Duke of Devonshire, confirmed that his father, the 7th Duke, had constructed the F&LR virtually at his own expense, outlay having been of the order of £130,000. He had done this to develop his estate and for the benefit of his tenants; he had also contributed largely to the construction and equipping with rolling stock of the WD&LR, a figure of £190,000 being quoted. The Marquess was somewhat disparaging of the facilities provided by the GS&WR; whether or not this was part of a strategy that led to an agreement in March 1891 whereby the WD&LR took over the working of the F&LR as from 1 March 1893 is not known. However, he was of the view that the proposed Cork and Fermoy direct line would be a decided advantage, and by bringing additional traffic to the Dungarvan line would thereby increase receipts and relieve to some extent the county guarantee.

John Barry, MP for South Wexford, stated that railway communication in the county was bad. He had approached the Treasury on several occasions seeking

assistance to complete the harbour at Rosslare. He referred to the plans of the Cambrian Railways to operate a steamer service, this having influenced his decision to become involved in the railway project. He was convinced that if a steamer service was inaugurated between Rosslare and Fishguard, then there was little doubt but that the GWR would complete the railway to the latter point. Barry referred to a recent trip he had made from Wexford to Waterford, which clearly showed the difficulties involved; he had travelled via Ballywilliam to New Ross, stayed there overnight and then continued to Waterford by steamer, a total journey time of 21 hours. He maintained that the feeling in New Ross was generally in favour of the new line, apart from some objections regarding the location and height of the proposed bridge over the Barrow. As we shall shortly see the objections expressed by the New Ross traders and merchants were rather more vociferous and widespread than suggested by Barry.

Michael Whelan, Manager of Messrs Philip Pierce & Company of the Mill Road Iron Works in Wexford, confirmed that much of their agricultural machinery for Wales was brought to New Ross and Waterford for shipment to Milford Haven, a most circuitous and very expensive route. Some items went from Wexford by steamer to Bristol, but that steamer only operated from Wexford on Mondays and was frequently unable to accommodate their business. Mr Thompson of Thompson Brothers, who experienced similar difficulties, backed him up in his evidence.

Samuel Gordon Fraser, the Engineer for the proposed line, was next called to give evidence. He confirmed that some consideration had been given to making connection with the 3-ft gauge C&MLR, possibly laying down a third rail, but the difference in elevation between the two lines would have made it difficult. Asked about a possible central station in Cork, Fraser confirmed that it had been considered, but the cost of acquiring property was prohibitive compared with the circular route. He also confirmed that the Cork to Fermoy section would pass through the villages of Rathcormac and Castle Lyons. Regarding the bridge over the River Barrow, he stated that the original scheme put forward by the DW&WR in 1878 had proposed a bridge rather higher up the

---

2 Angela Georgina Burdett-Coutts, 1st Baroness, was born on 24 April 1814, daughter of Sir Francis Burdett, MP, and Sophia Coutts, who was the daughter of Thomas Coutts, Founder of Coutts Banking Co. She became the wealthiest woman in Great Britain when, in 1837, she inherited her grandfather's fortune of nearly £2 million. She spent the majority of her wealth on endowments, scholarships and a wide range of philanthropic causes. These included the NSPCC (which she founded), and the RSPCA. She was also a benefactor of the Church of England. It is reported that she advanced £250,000 in 1880 for supplying seed to impoverished tenants in Ireland.

river. At that time he had been invited to Barrow-in-Furness to meet with Sir James Ramsden, following which they had unsuccessfully promoted a Cork to Fermoy connection.

Sir Benjamin Baker spoke of his connection with the harbour scheme at Rosslare and the railway thence to Wexford. He thought Rosslare was a good point for the construction of a harbour, although he had not been responsible for the plans either for it or the two river crossings, having been called in some three months before they were deposited. However, he was of opinion that the opening spans of the Barrow bridge might be made 80ft wide and the height of the bridge raised by 10ft, all within the 10% contingency allowed in the estimates. Furthermore, he would have gone about 1½ miles further upstream had he planned the crossing. A Lieut Alexander Boxer, ex Royal Navy and for many years in the employment of the Commissioners of Irish Lights (CIL), said he was fully acquainted with Rosslare and considered it would be very well adapted for cross-channel services. In fact, the Admiralty Surveyor, Capt Calver, had chosen it following an intensive survey of the southeast of Ireland in 1868.

Robert Worthington stated that the scheme had first been brought to his attention by a Mr Slattery, the Chairman of the National Bank and a Director of the CR, although he had previously considered it himself. He also stated that, apart from the CR, interest in the scheme had been shown by the Manchester, Sheffield & Lincolnshire Railway and the Furness Railway, each of which had subscribed £1,000 towards the promotion of the Bill. Worthington confirmed that the capital for the line was to be £1,425,000 and that he was prepared to construct the line for the Parliamentary estimate of £905,000 cash, without guarantees. This was to be a lump sum contract, with no claims to be made for extras or deductions made from the sum mentioned. Finally, he confirmed that he had had discussions with the Bristol Wagon Company regarding the supply of rolling stock, they having agreed to supply it for a sum of £70,000; his discussions with them had led him to assume that they would take shares for that amount at par.

Another important witness was Sir John Coode, an engineer of nearly 50 years standing. He had first become acquainted with Waterford as far back as 1858 when he was a member of a Royal Commission enquiring into harbours of refuge. He had also acted as Consulting Engineer to Waterford Harbour Commissioners for the previous 26 years. In 1867 he had inspected both banks of the River Suir to find the most suitable site for a graving dock, which was eventually located at Cromwell's Rock on the north bank. He thought that the proposed line would seriously interfere with the construction of the dry dock there. At this point Counsel intervened to point out that whilst the land for the dock had been purchased some 20 years previously, nothing had been done on the site; the Chairman of the Select Committee also made reference to this fact, expressing little sympathy with the Harbour Commissioners. Sir John had again inspected the port in 1874 at the behest of the GWR and the W&LR to see if the harbour and railway accommodation could be improved; this was also the period when various tramway schemes for Waterford were being put forward.

So as to connect the various railway systems in Waterford, Sir John Coode had in 1874 recommended a bridge across the River Suir in a similar position to that now being proposed. That scheme would have concentrated all of the lines on the south (city) side of the river. Sir John had nothing good to say about the ports of Aberdovey and Rosslare, stating they were so bad "that no one in their senses would use them." George Findlay, General Manager of the London & North Western Railway (L&NWR),[3] also put forward similar views regarding the former port as it was on an exposed coast with a bar at the entrance, and no lights for navigation. He was quite surprised to hear that the CR had successfully operated a steamer service to Waterford from Aberdovey for 20 months. Findlay also was of the view that the existing cross-channel services were more than adequate to cater for existing and anticipated future traffic, but then he would have been protecting the L&NWR's position.

James Otway, Engineer and Locomotive Superintendent of the WD&LR, was next examined.

---

3 The Select Committee Proceedings state that Findlay was previously also Manager of the Cambrian Railways. However, Christiansen & Miller's two-volume history (see Bibliography) makes no reference to this fact. He was in fact Manager of the Shrewsbury & Hereford.

He confirmed that he had approved the proposed junction between his line and the new line and also the new bridge at Waterford. Otway was, however, in a difficult position as he was also Engineer to the Waterford Harbour Commissioners. Wearing the latter hat, he was of opinion that the bridge across the Suir would be injurious to navigation. Due to the tidal conditions, a vessel going through the proposed bridge on an ebb tide would meet it on the skew; the new line would also take the entire north frontage of the river and would prevent future developments of the port. Once again, the Chairman stated that he had no sympathy with the Harbour Commissioners regarding the proposed bridge as they had, to use his words, "put up with the old wooden bridge for all these years and had not considered it a nuisance."

Capt Nicholas Parle, Harbour Master at Waterford for the previous 20 years, went into more detail in relation to the difficulties which would be encountered with the proposed new bridge. He maintained that it would not be possible to get a sailing vessel through both bridges on the same tide as by the time it reached the second bridge the tide would be too strong for any pilot to attempt to move further upstream. It would therefore be necessary for such vessels to remain between the two bridges for long periods of time, where they would not have sufficient room to swing. Parle was backed up in his comments by Capt Thomas Toole, the Mayor of Waterford and a nautical man for more than 30 years. Other discussions centred on the taking of roads on the north bank of the river, notably Salvation Lane and Murphy's Lane, with a necessity to provide level crossings. These were to figure in the Fishguard scheme some ten years later and received mention in that company's Act.

Turning to New Ross, John Redmond Colfer, the Solicitor acting on behalf of the New Ross Harbour Commissioners (NRHC) stated that the petition against the railway had been signed by virtually every trader and merchant in New Ross (214 signatures). The average number of vessels going up the River Barrow to New Ross in the previous 15 years was between 150 and 160, in addition to which there was a daily steamer service between that port and Waterford. The average width of the river between New Ross and the sea was about 300 yards, yet the promoters had chosen the widest possible point close to the confluence of the Barrow with the Suir. There would be no objection to a high-level bridge higher up the river. Furthermore, the present site was at the most exposed part of the river, very often with "puffy, squally and uncertain weather due to Snow Hill and high hills on the Kilkenny side."[4] In addition, Colfer, who had sailed up this stretch of river on many occasions himself, was of opinion that the tide at the point chosen ran very nearly parallel to the bridge; this would cause a vessel coming to anchor at a buoy just below the bridge to swing round almost parallel to the bridge and it would be virtually impossible to get her round at right angles. This was particularly so as many of the vessels using the river were crewed only by a master with two men and a boy.

The tidal conditions at that point on the river were attested to by a number of the New Ross pilots, but were disputed by Capt Boxer. He did, however, suggest that the bridge be shifted some 40 yards to the north close to the northern limits of deviation on the plans. He also suggested that the piers of the swivel spans should be placed at an angle to the tide so as to improve navigation through the bridge.

All the evidence having been heard by 6 June 1890, Mr Balfour Browne made a speech in which he attempted to explain why the proposed crossing of the Barrow was where it was. The explanation was simple, the company wished to keep as far as possible to the shore of the River Suir, so as to get land as cheaply as possible. In his view, the simpler, and cheaper, option would have been to extend the DW&WR line from New Ross to Waterford and construct a bridge across the River Suir at a cost of between £120,000 and £140,000; the present scheme was estimated to cost in the region of £385,000. The proposed line between Waterford and Wexford would not pass through a single village of any size, whereas the DW&WR served both New Ross and Wexford itself. In conclusion, he suggested that the C&F portion of the scheme should be passed this Session and the W&W section left for further consideration.

When the Select Committee reported, they considered the Preamble proved. However, they

---

4 The author can confirm that this stretch of river is liable to the onset of sudden squalls.

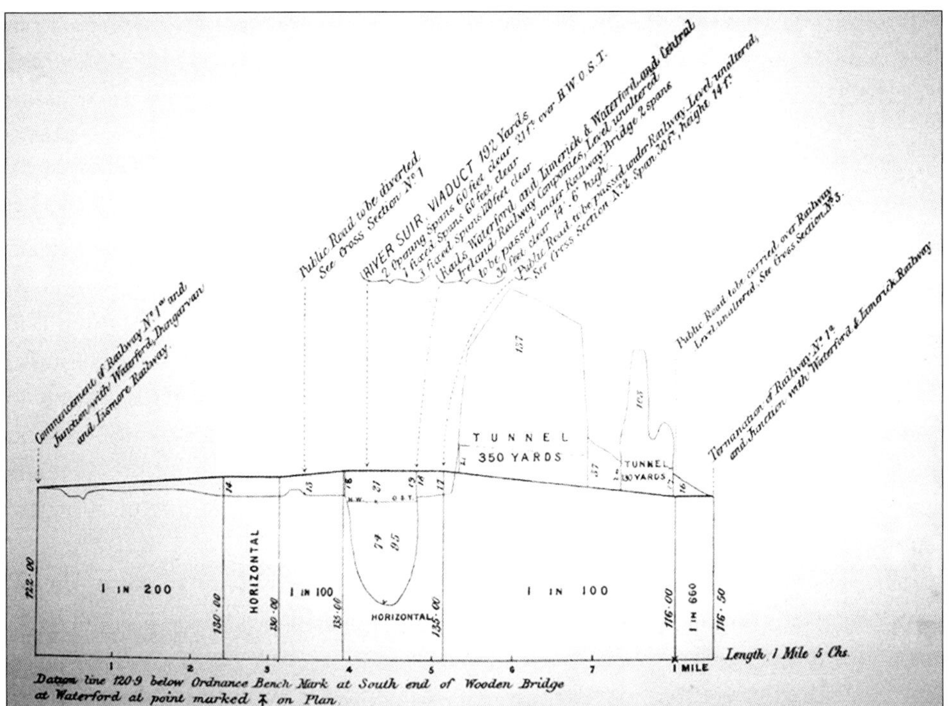

Part of parliamentary Plan relating to Railway No 1a as originally proposed under the C&F&W&WR scheme in 1891. Note there would have been two tunnels on the Waterford side. *(IRRS Archives)*

decided to reduce the company's capital from £950,000 to £750,000 with additional borrowing up to 50% of that figure. Following an intervention by Counsel on behalf of the promoters, it was agreed to increase the capital to £800,000 with 50% borrowing. It was stipulated that the promoters should consider the provision of a free footway alongside the bridge across the River Suir. In regard to the Barrow Bridge, it was agreed that it should be moved to the northern limit of deviation, that it should have a minimum height of 25ft above HWOST;[5] it was also stipulated that the suggestions of Sir Edward Harland[6] should be adopted, namely that the opening span of the bridge should open in line with the current and in square, and that there should be 70ft and not 60ft openings.

Considerable discussion took place regarding the taking of land alongside the river at Waterford, which might at some future date be required by the Waterford Harbour Commissioners for the development of the port, the railway company wanting to have the right to lay down sidings into existing works. The Chairman once again appeared to have some sympathy with the railway company's suggestions. Whilst the Committee

did not wish to give the company a monopoly of the frontage, it was wished to give them sufficient land to make sidings into existing and possible future industries there. They should also be able to purchase land from the Corporation to make a pier. The Chairman went so far as to refer to the attitude of both the Corporation and the Waterford Harbour Commissioners as a "dog-in-the-manger policy".

The Bill received Royal Assent on 18 August 1890. At the first meeting of the Directors held in the company's offices at No 134 Palmerston Buildings in Bishopsgate Street, London on 10 October, William Bailey-Hawkins was elected Chairman, while Thomas Hitchcock was appointed Secretary *pro tem*. It was resolved that Messrs Fowler, Baker and Fraser be appointed Engineers to the new company, but without liability to the company until the works were proceeded with and baronial guarantees obtained. At another meeting on 19 October, Worthington reported on correspondence between himself and Mr Mann, Engineer to the Waterford & Wexford Railway, regarding proposals for the latter company to be worked by the DW&WR. Worthington also reported on his interview with Mr Jackson, Secretary to the Treasury, regarding an application to that body for a grant of £150,000. In the following February a deputation led by the Marquess

---

5 High Water over Spring Tides.
6 Sir Edward Harland was one of the founders of Harland & Wolff shipyard in Belfast.

of Hartington met with Mr Jackson and put their case, based on the recommendations in the Allport Commission's report of January 1888.

In November 1890 notice of application was published for a Bill to enable and require the Grand Juries of the counties of Cork and Wexford to guarantee a fixed dividend. Power was also sought for the acquisition, by agreement, of the F&LR, WD&LR, W&WR and the Rosslare Harbour Commissioners, and the subsequent dissolution of those companies and Commissioners. The Preamble to the Bill, however, was not proved. A similar notice was published a year later seeking only a guarantee from the Grand Jury of Cork, but once again the Bill failed, there being strong opposition not only from the ratepayers of the baronies concerned, but also from the GS&WR. However, in June 1892 it was announced that a resolution had been passed by Cork Corporation and the Cork Poor Law Board of Guardians granting a guarantee of 4% on £50,000 for a period of 45 years from the date of opening for traffic of the line between Cork and Fermoy.

All ideas of acquiring other companies appear to eventually have been put aside as in June 1892 the Secretary was instructed to communicate with the WD&LR seeking terms for the working of the line by that company. This matter dragged on and it was not until 16 May 1893 that the Board had before them proposed terms for consideration. Basically, the WD&LR agreed to work the line at 55% of gross receipts so long as weekly receipts per mile did not exceed £17 or were between £17 and £17 10s 0d calculated on the year. Between £17 10s 0d and £18 the line was to be worked at 54%, dropping by 1% for every 10s increment on the weekly earnings for the year until the rate came down to 50%; whatever the receipts, it was not to fall below that percentage. Having considered the matter, the C&F&W&WR Board came to the conclusion that any such agreement must be subject to the approval of the BoW, who effectively held all of the company's debenture capital.

In June 1893 a deputation consisting of Sir James Ramsden, Francis E Currey, Mr Morley, Sir John Fowler, Robert Worthington, Mr O'Malley (the Secretary of the WD&LR) and Mr Hitchcock went to Paddington to make an application to the GWR for some form of rebate on through traffic. The result of the meeting was an offer from the GWR in July of a rebate of 25% for 15 years, Sir James being requested to try for a rebate of 30% for 30 years. This was optimistic and the company had in due course to be content with a figure of 27½% for 15 years.

Two Acts were passed in 1893 affecting the company. The Cork and Fermoy and Waterford and Wexford Railway (Guarantee) Act authorised that the undertaking should be divided into and constituted as three separate undertakings. This was to allow for the raising and borrowing of the capital in portions. The W&W section was to have a capital of £340,000 with borrowing of £172,500. This Act was clearly put forward to enable the second Act to be passed. This was the Cork and Fermoy Railway (Waterford and Wexford Section Abandonment) Act, which passed into law on 9 June 1893. Resulting from this Act, the name of the undertaking was altered to the Cork & Fermoy Railway Company. The capital was reduced from £800,000 to the sum of £455,000 with additional borrowing of £227,500. The company were given the option of raising this amount singly or in two separate amounts of £350,000 and £105,000 as provided for in the Guarantee Act.

The company's powers for the compulsory acquisition of land expired in August 1893 and the Board were informed that the Duke of Devonshire saw no good reason for keeping the powers alive. That said, Robert Worthington wrote to the Board in November asking that the question of publishing an abandonment notice be postponed; it was agreed to defer this for a further 12 months. Nothing further happened until October 1895 when it was finally decided that all powers be abandoned. Worthington was approached for a contribution of £100 towards the abandonment expenses, this being declined. Finally, in March 1896 the Secretary announced that the Parliamentary deposit had been released.

So came to an end, for the time being, the aspirations for a through route from Cork to Rosslare, but before we consider the Fishguard & Rosslare Railways & Harbours Company lines in Ireland, we must, however, return to Wales and look at events which were to bring about the formation of that company.

CHAPTER EIGHT

Narberth Road to Letterston & Goodwick

The county of Pembroke consists of two distinct parts, roughly divided by the large inlet of Milford Haven. To the south the land consists of fertile upland, whereas the land to the north is characterised by the Preseli hills (Mynydd Preseli).[1] They are frequently considered to be a southern extension of the Cambrian Mountains, and consist of open moorland with rocky outcrops similar to Dartmoor, rising steeply in places, the highest point being Presely Top (Foel Cwmcerwyn), about 2½ miles northeast of the village of Rosebush and at 1,760ft above sea level. From this vantage point on a clear day the hill walker can enjoy views to the north of Snowdonia, to the east the Brecon Beacons, to the south across the Bristol Channel to the West Country and to the west occasional glimpses of the Wicklow Mountains. The presence of many cromlechs provides evidence to suggest that Neolithic farmers lived in the area, while there is also a number of round cairns from the Bronze Age. What is of interest to the archaeologist is that the inner circle at Stonehenge, some 200 miles away to the south, consists of dolerite or blue stone, which is only found on the eastern edge of the Preseli Mountains. How these stones came to be at Stonehenge is something of a mystery, whether by human intervention or possibly the result of glacial movement.

Apart from the geological differences between the two halves of Pembrokeshire, there are other clear differences. At the time of the Norman invasion, a line of protective castles was constructed from Llansteffan on the west bank of the River Towy north-westwards to Roch, near St Bride's Bay. Known as the Landsker Line from the Norse word meaning frontier, in course of time it evolved into a cultural and linguistic divide, still evident to some extent today. To the north of this line, Welsh is more widely spoken, as witnessed by the many Welsh names for villages and towns; churches tend to be small in size and to have bellcotes and no towers. To the south of the line, English is the more widely spoken language while churches generally tend to be larger and clearly of Norman origin, and equipped with tall square towers, which served as lookouts. The area to the south was frequently referred to by the inhabitants of the northern half of the county as 'Down Below'.

The bay of Fishguard is some 3 miles wide between the headlands of Dinas to the east and Strumble Head to the west, and 1¾ miles from north to south. It has a depth of water varying from 30 to 70ft and is sheltered on three sides by hills rising to in excess of 400ft. At the south end of the bay lies the old port of Fishguard with its quay used by generations of herring fishermen. Samuel Lewis in his *Topographical Dictionary of Wales* published in 1833 describes Fishguard Bay as "affording good anchorage to ships of the largest size, which may ride in safety in all parts of the bay during the prevalence of gales from any point of the compass, except north and north-east". He quoted the dimensions as being 2400ft in length and about 1600ft wide at the entrance. The town of Fishguard (Abergwaun or the estuary of the River Gwaun) is divided in two by the river, Old Town nestling around the old port and New Town on higher ground to the west. The town derives its name from the Old Scandinavian word 'fiskgarðr', meaning an enclosure for catching or storing fish. The village of Goodwick (Wdig in the parish of Llanwnda) is situated on the western side of the bay about a mile from Fishguard. Goodwick derives its name from the stream Afon Wdig; prior to the coming of the railway, Goodwick was a scattered hamlet. Although separated physically, Fishguard and Goodwick are linked by The Parrog and are in effect 'twin' towns, having been administered

---

1 Various spellings are used for the North Pembrokeshire hills. The hotel at Rosebush used the spelling Precelly, and a locomotive was named *Prescelly*. The original spelling is Preseli.

for many years by the same Town Council. Although the modern port is always referred to as Fishguard, strictly speaking it should perhaps be more correctly known as Goodwick.

It is not clear when quarrying began at Rosebush, but it would appear that a Mr Hatton took rights to the Rosebush land in 1837 when he commenced work at the adjoining Bellstone Slate Quarry, although there is no proof that Hatton actually worked the Rosebush Quarry. Five years later the land was sold to a William Young; once again it is unclear if he worked the quarry before selling it on in 1862 to William Williams from nearby Narberth. Williams died in the summer of 1862 and his widow then let the lands to William Davies and William Keylock in the following year. It was from Mary Williams that the freehold was purchased on 29 May 1869 by Edward Cropper,[2] MP, and wealthy merchant banker from Penshurst in Kent, for £3,750 together with the plant for a sum of £800 from the Receivers of the Rosebush Slate Company. Exactly why Cropper, then aged 69 and reportedly in poor health, should take an interest in a slate quarry in rural Wales is unclear, but it is possible that his stepson, Joseph Babington Macaulay was already involved in the quarry.

Being a Director of the L&NWR it is perhaps not surprising that Cropper turned his attention to the construction of a railway for the transport of Rosebush slate.[3] At the time the nearest point on the GWR was at Narberth Road, some 8¼ miles away to the south; the latter station was located about 200ft above sea level whereas Rosebush was at 866ft. Despite the potential difficulties involved, notice was published in June 1871 of Cropper's intention to apply for a certificate from the BoT under the terms of the Railways Construction Facilities Act of 1864, as amended by the Railways (Powers and Construction) Act of 1870. Basically, this legislation had been introduced to allow individuals, or indeed railway companies, who had obtained the

Edward Cropper (1799-1877) was the power behind the NR&MR and the Rosebush Quarry. His son, Edward Denman Cropper, inherited the railway and quarry, but took little interest in their operation, preferring instead to pursue a military career. *(Cropper Family Archive)*

full consent of landowners and others to the taking of land for the railway, and had contracted for its purchase, to avoid the expense involved in going to Parliament for a separate Act. It was, however, still necessary to submit the usual plans and books of reference to the BoT for their approval, these being duly lodged in July 1871.

Capt HW Tyler, on behalf of the BoT, reported on the proposed Narberth Road & Maenclochog[4] Railway (NR&MR) line in the following October, which was to run from the GWR station at Narberth Road to Rosebush Slate Quarry, a distance of about 8 miles. The estimated cost of construction was shown as £43,000, of which £2,700 was to be paid to the GWR for the construction of an independent line of rails for 1m 10c[5] on their land. Tyler commented that the object of the new line was to convey slate and other produce from Rosebush to the GWR system and coals and lime in the opposite direction. Permanent way was to weigh about 60lb per yard, fished at the joints and secured to the sleepers by fang bolts. The sleepers themselves were to be laid transversely and it was expected that good ballast could be obtained

---

2 Edward Cropper, a Quaker, was born on 19 April 1799, the son of James and Mary Cropper of Dingle Bank near Liverpool. James was described as a merchant and philanthropist and was active in the anti-slavery movement. A branch of the family set up a very successful paper-making business in Kendal, still operational today.

3 Rosebush slate, although not regarded as being as good quality as that from North Wales, nevertheless had a claim to fame as the roofs of the Houses of Parliament were constructed of this material.

4 Maenclochog is Welsh for Ringing Rock or Bellstone. A second slate quarry at Rosebush owned by the local landowner, Sir Hugh Owen, was known as Bellstone Quarry. The line was generally referred to simply as the Maenclochog Railway, but to avoid confusion with the Midland Railway the full initials have been used in the present work.

5 There are slight discrepancies in distances quoted.

locally. Tyler also understood that the GWR lines would have been converted to the 4ft 8½in gauge by the time the Maenclochog line was completed. In fact the re-gauging of the entire South Wales main line from New Milford to Grange Court was completed by 22 May 1872. There were to be four bridges carrying roads over the railway as well as a viaduct over the River Cleddau; interestingly Tyler stated that there were to be no tunnels on the line; cuttings would be principally through rock. There were to be four intermediate stations on the line. In conclusion he stated that he saw no reason why a certificate should not be granted.

In the interim, following negotiations conducted by his step-son, Cropper concluded an agreement with the GWR for the use of facilities at Narberth Road Station for an annual rent of £500. This agreement, dated 3 July 1871, was incorporated as Part II of the Certificate. The latter, dated 24 June 1872, contains several interesting clauses which are worthy of mention. First of all, the length of the line authorised is shown as 7m 4f and was to commence in the parish of Maenclochog at the slate quarry in the occupation of Joseph Babington Macaulay[6]. Passing through Maenclochog and Llanycefn (Llan is a church or enclosed place and Cefn a back or ridge), following the valley of the Eastern Cleddau River (Cleddau, a sword) to a point about 67 yards west of the 265 milepost on the GWR line just over a mile west of Narberth Road.

Whilst the capital to be raised was set at £42,247, Cropper was authorised to borrow on mortgage on the security of the railway "any sum whatever". The line was to be built to standard gauge, although Cropper could lay down additional lines to any narrower gauge not less than 2ft, presumably quarry lines. Clause 21 stipulated that if the line was to remain unworked for a period of two years after its completion, the Bishop of St David's and the Ecclesiastical Commissioners should be at liberty to re-enter upon and take back lands given by them in the parish of Llanycefn. Clause 22 stipulated that Cropper was to arrange for one train

each way daily (except Sundays) to stop at or near the point where he had agreed with the Commissioners to erect a station. The final clause of interest stipulated that each station was to have a notice clearly visible stating the name and place of residence of the person currently in possession of and working the railway; in the event of the GWR taking over the working of the line, such notices were to be dispensed with. The agreement with the GWR made reference to the laying down of a third line of rails parallel to that Company's up main line, about 1m 1f in length; this line was to terminate at Narberth Road Station, where a bay was later provided at the east end of the up platform.

The contract for the construction of the single-track line was awarded to Messrs Jones & Jepson of Neath,[7] with a Mr Hurst acting as Resident Engineer and Mr J McDougall Smith as Consulting Engineer. The first sod was ceremonially turned by Macaulay's wife Eleanor on 15 April 1873, and she was presented with an inscribed spade made especially for the occasion. Construction work was commenced quickly, however, a number of difficulties were encountered, with the necessity for many cuttings and embankments and a tunnel through solid rock. The ruling gradient was 1 in 27 for almost two miles on the south side of Maenclochog. Despite these constraints, the line was completed within three years, but not without several accidents and the murder of a workman. With the line more or less completed by September 1875 a trial run was made by the contractors who allowed a group of people to travel over the line in connection with the annual hiring fair at Maenclochog. It would appear that slate traffic commenced in January 1876, and before long it was reported that the needs of the local farming community were being met.

Messrs Masterman, Hughes & Masterman, Solicitors to Mr Cropper, wrote to the BoT on 1 April 1876 advising of Cropper's intention to open the line for public traffic. Colonel CS Hutchinson was duly appointed to inspect the new line, this inspection taking place in May. Hutchinson quoted the total length of the line as 8m 50c, of which 1m 10c at the commencement was a line parallel to and alongside

---

6 Joseph Macaulay was the nephew of the celebrated poet and politician, Thomas Babington, First Baron Macaulay (1800–1859). He was later to be closely involved in the North Pembrokeshire & Fishguard Railway, described later.

---

7 Thomas Jepson, one of the firm's principals, was accidentally drowned on 30 April 1881 in the Ely mill race at Cardiff.

the GWR line with which it formed a junction at Clynderwen, nowadays generally spelt Clunderwen (Oak Meadow). When originally opened, Narberth Road Station was the nearest station to the village of Narberth. However, with the opening of the 16¼ mile long Tenby to Whitland extension of the Pembroke & Tenby Railway at the beginning of September 1866, a station was provided at the village itself. This led to confusion among travellers and, following the presentation of a petition from local people, including Edward Cropper, the GWR station was renamed Clynderwen as from 1 December 1875. The line abounded in steep gradients and sharp curves, some of the latter being of only 10 chains radius.

There were three stations, at Llanycefn, Maenclochog and Rosebush. At the latter point the line was extended for a short distance to the quarry, although this portion was not intended for passenger use. Permanent way on the first (GWR) section consisted of double-headed wrought iron rails weighing 80lb per yard on standard rectangular sleepers with broken stone ballast. The NR&MR proper had 72lb per yard flat-bottomed rail in 21ft lengths with broken stone ballast 15in deep. The tunnel near Maenclochog was 96 yards in length, a portion of which was lined. The signal arrangements had been carefully carried out, the signal boxes and equipment at Llanycefn, Maenclochog and Rosebush having been supplied by Messrs McKenzie & Holland of Worcester. Later, in 1895, a raised 6-lever frame was installed at Beag, possibly supplied by ST Dutton & Co, Worcester. It was intended to work the line on the one-engine-in-steam principle, the BoT requesting a certificate to this effect.

Hutchinson set out a number of requirements, pending the completion of which the line was not to be opened for passenger traffic. He had already inspected the arrangements at Clynderwen two months previously and had scathing comments to make in relation to the proposed working of the NR&MR traffic there. These were that up branch passenger trains should discharge their passengers on the up main platform, the train afterwards being shunted into a siding off the up line. Intending passengers for down branch trains were also to board at the up platform, the train then proceeding wrong road along

the up line for about 240 yards in the course of which it would pass over no less than five sets of facing points. This method of working he was not prepared to sanction, recommending instead the provision of a dock for branch trains. Having re-inspected the junction arrangements in September, Hutchinson commented that an entirely new arrangement of the junction had been made since the inspection on 3 May, the "objectionable mode of working the down branch traffic" having been altered. He still remarked that a dock had not been provided at the west end of the up platform, nevertheless he sanctioned the new arrangements.

The line was opened for passenger traffic on 19 September 1876 with free travel being provided on the opening day; the initial service consisted of four trains each way daily, journey time between Rosebush and Narberth Road being 35 minutes with 5 minutes extra allowed in the opposite direction. Apart from the stations referred to, which handled both goods and passenger traffic, there appears to have been a 'fare stop' at Beag, situated about 1¾ miles from Narberth Road, a short goods siding also being provided there. A public timetable for 1878 clearly shows Beag as being a 'fare station', with all trains stopping there on request to the Guard. Gale states that a platform was built there, yet none of the BoT reports in 1876, 1877 or 1895 make any reference to it, so it may have been short-lived. The new siding at Beag was inspected early in September 1877 by Major FA Marindin, who pointed out that the signals and points were worked from the aforementioned 6-lever frame, with three working and three spare levers. Only one signal was provided in each direction but as the line was single and was to be worked by one engine-in-steam and the siding connection was on a short piece of level with a steep ascent in each direction, he was happy to sanction its use.

Initially, traffic on the NR&MR was good, although the rent payable to the GWR for the use of Clynderwen Station absorbed any likely profit. Even at the opening day celebrations, there was talk of an extension of the railway from Rosebush to Fishguard, where a new port would be provided in direct opposition to the GWR's port at New Milford. There is no doubt but

Clynderwen station c1908, facing towards Fishguard Harbour. The coaches for the Maenclochog branch train can be seen standing in the bay behind the up platform. *(Photographer unknown, John Gale Collection)*

that Cropper was antagonistic towards the GWR, not least because of the rent for Clynderwen Station, but also, no doubt, because of his connections with the L&NWR. It was not long before a separate company, the Rosebush & Fishguard Railway (R&FR), was formed to further these aspirations and we shall shortly devote some time to that scheme.

Edward Cropper died on 23 May 1877 at the age of 78, leaving the NR&MR in the care of his son, Edward Denman Cropper.[8] In addition, Cropper's step-son, Joseph Macaulay, was not only the company's General Manager but was also in charge of the management of the Rosebush quarry. Later, Cropper's widow, Margaret,[9] married Colonel John Owen, son of Sir Hugh Owen Owen (1803–91), the local landowner, former MP for Pembroke, and also the owner of the Bellstone Quarry at Rosebush. Although the Rosebush slate was highly regarded, it was inferior to that from North Wales quarries and the business appears to have gone into decline, leading to the closure of the Maenclochog line as from 31 December 1882. It was about this time that Joseph Macaulay left Wales with his family and went to live in Paignton, Devon; that said, he continued to take a close interest in the R&FR's affairs. Almost unannounced, the NR&MR line was re-

opened for traffic on 15 December 1884, with a service of two passenger trains each way daily and a goods train operating as required, mainly to move slate from the quarry at Rosebush. The line was closed again by 1888 and was put up for sale by auction in London on 20 February 1889. The sale included the quarry and all of the rolling stock. However, the line remained unsold and lay derelict for many years; it would appear that at least some of the rolling stock might have been sold although the locomotives remained unsold. Whilst relations between the NR&MR and the R&FR were initially good, they quickly deteriorated, and we must now turn our attentions to the formation and early history of the latter company.

A prospectus had been published in July 1873 for the Rosebush, Fishguard & Goodwick Railway Company, nothing further being heard of this scheme. Four years later, the aforementioned Sir Hugh Owen Owen, had a survey conducted of a possible route for such a line, this resulting in an Act of Parliament receiving the Royal Assent on 8 August 1878 under the title of the Rosebush & Fishguard Railway Company. The Act authorised the construction of a line 13 miles 73 chains long from an end-on junction with the NR&MR at Rosebush, passing through Puncheston and Letterston to Fishguard. While the course of the line appeared to be circuitous, it was in fact the only one possible, bearing in mind the difficult topography of the Preseli hills. The Act also authorised running

---

8 Both Morris and Parker refer to the line being looked after by Edward's second son, James. The family has confirmed to the author that Edward Cropper had only the one son.

9 One of the locomotives in use on the line was named *Margaret*, after Cropper's widow.

powers over the Maenclochog Railway, but there was no mention of a possible purchase. Capital was £90,000, the first Chairman being Sir Hugh Owen Owen, with Joseph Macaulay as Deputy Chairman. HE Warren was appointed Secretary and James B Walton as Engineer.[10] The first sod was ceremonially cut at Rosebush on 28 August 1879 by the Hon Mrs Margaret Owen (the former Mrs Cropper) "in the presence of a large concourse of spectators from all parts of the County." The contractor, Frederick Appleby, presented Mrs Owen with a silver spade duly inscribed. Amidst much cheering, she turned the first sod, placed it in the barrow and then wheeled it over a plank "in true workmanlike fashion."

Subsequently a magnificent luncheon, prepared by Mr Burge of the Great Western Hotel in Fishguard, was held in an adjoining field. In the speeches that followed, great hopes were expressed for the future of the line which, it was suggested, would be completed within the five years allowed by the Act; during the course of the speeches some unsavoury remarks were made about the GWR. In the course of his speech, Colonel Owen referred to the efforts being made by the Rosslare Harbour & Railway Company (sic), which had been formed to develop Rosslare Harbour in the Bight of Balligeary (sic).[11] Reference was made to Capt Calver's survey of Ballygeary Bay in 1868 on behalf of the Admiralty, when he stated that a harbour constructed there would afford complete protection from the prevailing winds. Colonel Owen commented that Rosslare was the natural port for communication with South Wales, a view also expressed by Mr (later Sir) Alexander Rendell, a noted Civil Engineer, who had been involved in the harbour works at Milford. The construction of a harbour at Fishguard, capable of accommodating first-class passenger steamers and a short line of railway to connect that port with the GWR, would complete the arrangements.

Various meetings were held to further promote the Fishguard scheme. One such was held in the Town Hall at Fishguard on 5 December 1878, the attendance

including Sir Hugh and Colonel John Owen, Edward Denman Cropper, Robert William Broomfield and the Rev W Rowlands, Vicar of Fishguard, and as far as is known, no relation to Joseph Rowlands who later became involved with the F&RR&H Company. Broomfield was a Director of the NP&FR by 1894 and it may have been as a result of his contacts with Joseph Rowlands that the latter gentleman came to have a financial interest in the F&RR&H. The *Pembrokeshire Herald* referred in its issue of 21 November 1879 to a public meeting held in the new goods shed at Letterston for making arrangements to commence the Letterston section of the R&FR; Mr Walton stated that if the landowners were prepared to come forward in the right spirit, the line could reach the village within 12 months.

The contract for construction of the line was awarded to Messrs Appleby & Lawton of Milford Haven. Right from the beginning, however, financial difficulties beset the new company, particularly in relation to the raising of the necessary capital, much of which was held by the Directors and their families. Construction work soon started on the R&FR but progress was slow and it was necessary to obtain another Act in 1881 authorising a further three years for construction. By that time the line had only progressed to New Inn, only just over a mile from Rosebush; this was in part due to the boggy nature of the terrain through which the line was being built and also to difficulties with a landowner, a Mr Forde Hughes. However, by August of that year it was announced that Messrs Appleby & Lawton had ceased work due to non-payment for work completed.

As stated previously, relations were initially good between the two companies, agreement being reached for the use of NR&MR wagons. It is not clear exactly what transpired, but it was soon evident that relations between the two companies had soured. Edward Denman Cropper endeavoured to interest a London syndicate to purchase his line, but it appears they declined following consultations with the GWR. Although the R&FR had contemplated leasing Cropper's line, he refused, offering instead to sell it for a sum of £20,000, a figure which the R&FR refused to pay, and indeed could have ill-afforded in

---

10 Walton remained as Engineer until the line was taken over by the GWR.

11 Colonel Owen was friendly with George Le Hunte, who owned properties both in Wexford and Pembrokeshire, and was closely involved in the Rosslare scheme.

their straitened circumstances. Colonel Owen wrote to the L&NWR about this time suggesting that they might consider constructing a line to connect with the R&FR line. The response is unknown but was clearly unfavourable to the idea.

Another idea put forward in July 1882 was for a line from New Inn (west of Rosebush) running south to join the GWR line at Clarbeston Road. Whilst the matter was to be considered periodically for some three years, it is difficult to see exactly what the proposed line was likely to achieve, but in the event nothing further came of it. Meanwhile the R&FR had a mile of line constructed to the west of Rosebush. At one stage in 1883 abandonment of the entire project was being seriously considered. However, a timely injection of fresh capital saw a new Act in 1884 authorising yet more time for construction. When the Bill was in the process of being put together for submission to Parliament, the Parliamentary Agent, JC Rees, demanded an amount of £320 owing to him; the Bill was only saved as the result of JW Broomfield paying Rees an amount of £150 in cash. In addition, as if to signal a new start, the name of the company was altered to the North Pembrokeshire & Fishguard Railway (NP&FR). If this was intended to prevent Messrs Appleby & Lawton from taking legal proceedings against the company for a debt now amounting to £4,987, it did not succeed. Relations with Cropper deteriorated further, he refusing to allow plant or vehicles to pass over the, by now, unused NR&MR line. When the R&FR informed Cropper that they could enforce their running powers over his line, he appears to have decided to reluctantly assist his northern neighbour.

With little or no construction taking place, yet another Act was obtained in 1886 allowing further time. In the forlorn hope of getting their money back, Messrs Appleby & Lawton expressed their willingness to continue work, but failed to do so. Towards the end of 1891 the situation appeared to improve, when a Colonel Joseph Okell agreed to construct the remainder of the line, promising to have it open as far as Letterston by 1 September 1892; he duly employed a contractor, Henry Jackson, to carry out the work on his behalf. Once again, however, the Company was to be disappointed. Bad weather impeded progress, although by March 1893 the line had reached Puncheston, with earthworks completed almost into Letterston. Then, in January 1894 Colonel Okell was declared bankrupt and work ceased once again. Shortly after Colonel Okell initially became involved, two Birmingham gentlemen became interested, and were to shortly transform the scene and bring about major changes in the railway map of Pembrokeshire. These were Joseph Rowlands, a Birmingham Solicitor, and James Cartland, a brass-founder.[12] They acquired a large shareholding in the NP&FR, gradually building up a controlling interest.

It quickly became clear that Rowlands and Cartland had a vision for a new port at Fishguard and a breaking of the GWR stranglehold on the railways in the area. To this end they formed another company, the Fishguard Bay Railway & Pier Company (FBR&P). Incorporated by Act of Parliament dated 29 June 1893, the FBR&P Company was authorised to construct a line of railway 74 chains in length from the, as yet uncompleted, terminus of the NP&FR at Goodwick and terminating on the west side of Fishguard Bay at a point 100 yards northeast of the new (Cow & Calf)[13] lifeboat house at Goodwick. From the terminus of this railway a pier or breakwater was to be constructed, extending in a south-easterly direction for 350 yards into the bay. In addition, under Section 62 of the Act, the new company was empowered to take up to 20 acres of land for the purpose of erecting or building "an hotel and other necessary buildings or may purchase or acquire any houses or buildings for that purpose and may carry on the business of hotel keepers therein". Section 48 enabled running powers over the NP&FR. Capital was fixed at £120,000 with additional borrowing powers up to £40,000. Interestingly, the Act provided that shares could be divided into half-shares, respectively known as 'preferred half-shares' and 'deferred half-shares'. The former were to bear interest at a rate not exceeding 6 per cent per annum, the latter receiving the remainder, if any, of the profits. The first Directors named in the Act were Rowlands and Cartland along with Henry Partridge. All we know about Partridge is that he was born in Birmingham about 1829–30.

---

12 Further details of these two gentlemen are to be found in Appendix G.
13 Two rocky outcrops immediately north of Pen Cw.

Maenclochog Railway timetable poster for October 1880, re-dated by hand for March 1881. (*The National Archives, Kew*)

The Act stipulated that the company was to provide an archway or opening at least 12ft wide and 12ft high along with a suitable slipway for the launching of the life-boat in such a position as the Royal National Lifeboat Institution would approve; alternatively, the company might take down the existing life-boat house and rebuild it and provide a suitable slipway. The original life-boat house was situated on the Goodwick side of the Fishguard Harbour signal cabin. Finally, Section 34 of the Act empowered the company, subject to written consent from the BoT, to excavate, deepen and dredge such parts of Fishguard Bay and foreshore near the pier as might be necessary for securing convenient access for ships.

As related in Chapter Three, the Waterford & Wexford Railway (W&WR) had initially been worked by the DW&WR, but the latter company had ceased the working arrangements in May 1889 due to the W&WR's inability or refusal to pay the amount due for working the line. From evidence given by Rowlands before the Hybrid Committee of the House of Commons into the Fishguard & Rosslare Railways & Harbours Bill of 1898,[14] it is clear that negotiations for the transfer to the FBR&P of the pier at Rosslare and the railway thence to Wexford were opened in 1892, even before the FBR&P Company had become a reality. These negotiations culminated in agreements dated 27 and 29 July 1893 for the vesting respectively of the W&WR and the Rosslare Harbour Commissioners (RHC) in the new company; arising out of these agreements, the FBR&P returned to Parliament in 1894, the result of which was the Fishguard & Rosslare Railways & Harbours Act which received the Royal Assent on 31 July of that year. Of necessity, the aforementioned agreements also involved the Treasury and the Board of Works as mortgagees and debenture holders. The date of transfer in each instance was to be 1 August 1893.

Under Section 12 of the 1894 Act, the F&RR&H were authorised to retain so much of the receipts of the W&W section as shall be equivalent to £6 per mile per week. If the receipts exceeded this figure, the company were to retain 50% of the excess, the other moiety being paid to the BoW in relief of the debt owing to that body. If this latter situation pertained for seven consecutive years the company could then, on six months notice in writing to the BoW, purchase the incumbrancer's moiety of the surplus receipts at a price equal to 15 years purchase on the amount of

such moiety calculated on an average of the last three years of the seven year term, subject to a minimum payment of £10,000. In turn, the BoW had the right of repossessing the undertaking if the F&RR&H failed to perform any of the provisions of the Act. One of these was an agreement to repair the harbour works at Rosslare within six months, rendering them fit and safe to be used by shipping. The Act stipulated that all personal liabilities of Rowlands and Cartland under the agreements of July 1893 were to cease on the coming into effect of the Act.

Section 10 of the new Act was unusual, stating that the F&RR&H was to assume the responsibility for and continue the defence of "a certain action brought and now pending by the Wexford Harbour Commissioners against the Dublin Wicklow and Wexford Railway for an injunction in respect of that portion of the railways of the Wexford Railway undertaking which runs along the quay and piled wharf in Wexford Harbour." When the DW&WR agreed to work the W&WR, they automatically inherited the powers of working over the tramway along the quays at Wexford. However, the DW&WR continued to use the tramway after they ceased working the W&WR in May 1889; this was clearly in breach of the terms of user laid down in the W&WR 1871 Act. Bad as that was, they were also charging for goods being loaded into their wagons as if they were the owners of the harbour dues. It would appear that the WHC allowed this situation to continue for some time and it was not until April 1892 that they called on the DW&WR to discontinue using the railway along the quay. The railway company ignored this request and it became necessary to resort to a legal remedy.

When the case came before the Vice-Chancellor's Court in January 1893, the Vice-Chancellor said it was impossible for him to decide the matter, which depended on whether there had been a cesser of rights of the W&WR. To decide on this he requested that the W&WR should be added as defendants in the action. When the matter was finally decided in April 1894, it was in favour of the railway companies. Before that, however, the WHC had lodged a petition against the F&RR&H Bill, this only being withdrawn when Section 10 was included in the Bill.

While the parliamentary process was going on, Messrs Rowlands and Cartland arranged, on behalf of the NP&FR, to purchase the derelict Maenclochog Railway in 1894 for the sum of £50,000, this being approved at a shareholders' meeting of the former company held on 29 May. The NR&MR had lain derelict for the previous 12 years and was in a poor state of repair. With the line to Letterston approaching completion, urgent moves were made to carry out the necessary repairs. The NP&FR wrote to the BoT on 5 December 1894, stating that the stations on the Maenclochog line had been re-arranged and signalled, and would be ready for public traffic on 4 January 1895, the BoT, in reply, requesting drawings showing the various alterations. These were duly supplied on 18 January and it was intended to have a BoT inspection of the Letterston extension carried out on 29 and 30 January. However, Walton wrote to the BoT on 26 January from the Jubilee Hotel in Letterston informing them that there had been a very heavy fall of snow and there were drifts over 3ft deep on the line. Walton wrote again the following day advising that the snow fall had been the heaviest known for many years and that it would be at least a fortnight before repairs could be carried out.

The BoT inspection was eventually carried out on 12 March by Colonel Arthur Yorke.[15] In his report, Colonel Yorke stated that the new line was 8m 71c in length, single throughout although sufficient land had been purchased to enable the last two miles at the Letterston end to be doubled if required. Permanent way consisted of 75lb flat-bottomed steel rails, secured to standard 9ft long sleepers, not creosoted; ballast consisted of debris from the slate quarries at Rosebush. Gradients were reported to be severe, the steepest being at 1 in 40; only a small portion of the entire length of the line was level, while the sharpest curve was of 15 chains radius. Cuttings and embankments called for no special remark, nor did any of the 31 underbridges and 2 overbridges. There were only two stations on the new line, at Puncheston and Letterston. Both were described as 'single sided' stations, the former with a platform 200ft in length,

---

15 Colonel Yorke was later Chief Railway Inspecting Officer at the Board of Trade from 1900 to 1913.

while at Letterston it was 250ft. There was a siding at Puncheston, the points for which were locked and released by a key on the train staff. There was a loop at Letterston to enable locomotives to run round their trains, while there was also a goods yard with extensive siding accommodation. In addition to the two stations, there was a siding at New Inn, the points for which were released by a ground frame, the latter locked by a key on the train staff.

The signalling arrangements at Puncheston comprised a small signal box with four levers, all of which were in use; there were home and distant signals in each direction; Puncheston was not a block box or staff station. Letterston had a signal box containing six levers in use and nine spare. No turntable had been provided at Letterston, the Company informing the BoT that when the extension to Fishguard was complete, a turntable would be provided there. Colonel Yorke insisted on tank engines being provided pending the installation of the turntable; in addition he imposed a speed limit of 25mph. The BoT imposed further requirements, including the provision of an up advanced starting signal at Letterston, handrails to be provided on all underbridges; goods trains were to run direct into the goods yard at Letterston with an additional semaphore signal or else a disc signal to be provided for shunting into the yard.

Colonel Yorke also re-inspected the original line from Clynderwen to Rosebush. At Beag there was no passenger station and no place for crossing trains, but a block box had been constructed for the protection of the junction with the GWR at Clynderwen.[16] A separate ground frame was provided for working the siding points, released by a key on the train staff. This and a similar arrangement at Llanycefn would have been better worked from the signal boxes. Maenclochog was a block post staff station and crossing place, and had two platforms 250ft in length. Colonel Yorke reported that a considerable length of the line was insufficiently ballasted and some of the rails were in bad condition, matters which needed to be put right immediately; he also set out other requirements in relation to the signalling at stations. During his visit to the area,

Colonel Yorke also availed of the opportunity to inspect the arrangements at Clynderwen, again calling for some changes to the signalling. He also suggested the lowering of the branch line where it passed under the first overbridge west of Clynderwen so as to provide sufficient clearance. Finally, he suggested that a footbridge be provided there; this was to lead to a dispute as to which company should pay for it, the upshot being that the bridge was never constructed.

Goods traffic commenced running two days later, on 14 March. Passenger services began operating between Clynderwen and Letterston as from 11 April 1895, although it was not until July that the final BoT inspection was conducted, again by Colonel Yorke. The *Railway Times* referred to a service of five up and four down trains daily with a coach connection to and from Fishguard. Alan Nichols was appointed General Manager of the NP&FR, being based at Letterston in what had been intended to be a refreshment room; the local magistrates initially refused to licence such a venture, this being finally granted in August 1897 when first and third class refreshment facilities were provided.

A Bill was presented to Parliament in 1895 for extensions of the NP&F system, principally a line to Carmarthen, where it was to connect with the L&NWR. Rowlands had already made an approach to the latter company enquiring if they might extend their line from Abergwili Junction, near Carmarthen, to Clynderwen. This they declined to do, obviously not wishing to come into unnecessary conflict with the GWR; instead they suggested that if the NP&FR were to construct the line, then a working arrangement might be concluded. Under the same Bill powers were sought for a new loop line to bypass the difficult section near Maenclochog with its gradient of 1 in 27 and the tunnel. The proposed 5m 30c 'Llandilo loop' was to leave the existing line between Beag and Llanycefn and run further east, rejoining the original line at the south end of Maenclochog Station; it would still have had a ruling gradient of 1 in 50 for much of its length. Despite strenuous opposition from the GWR, the Company eventually acquired the various powers. Ambitious as the 1895 scheme was, Rowlands brought forward further expansion plans for the 1897 session and we shall look at these in a little more detail

---

16 At the request of the GWR; it was removed about 1899 after the GWR had taken over the working of the branch.

shortly. In addition, the contract for the extension of the NP&FR from Letterston to Goodwick was awarded to Messrs Holme & King of Liverpool, who undertook to have it ready for opening by 29 September 1897.

Also in 1895, the F&RR&H Company applied for powers to operate steam vessels between Fishguard and Rosslare, the relevant Act receiving Royal Assent on 30 May. Various other ports were included in the powers granted, including Aberdovey, Aberystwyth, Holyhead and Newport (Pembrokeshire), Wexford and Kingstown. The Company was also empowered to raise additional capital up to £50,000 and borrowing up to £12,500.

Reverting once again to the NP&FR, notice for a Bill for the Swansea Brynamman & Aberdare Extension Railways was published in November 1896, with very much more ambitious aspirations than hitherto put forward. The principal line was to run from Abergwili to meet the L&NWR south of Pontardulais, with branches to Gowerton and Morlais, making a junction with the GWR at the latter point; another line would make a connection with the Midland Railway at Brynamman, also providing a connection with the Neath & Brecon Railway. Yet another line was to run from Colbren Junction to a junction with the Taff Vale Railway at Aberdare, in turn connecting with the Vale of Neath line; in total the extensions amounted to almost 55 miles. In addition Rowlands came to the conclusion that the 'Llandilo loop', which would also have had steep gradients, would be of little advantage over the existing line, and now sought powers for a more direct line running northwest from Beag to connect with the existing line to the east of Letterston

Station. This line would have been 11m 78c in length and with a ruling gradient of 1 in 70. It is difficult to imagine what was in Rowlands' mind at this time. Was he genuinely proposing to construct all of these lines, or was it part of a grand plan to persuade the GWR to take over the NP&FR?

Certainly, the *Railway Times* had some interesting remarks to make on the proposed lines. In its issue for 5 December 1896, in a lengthy editorial, it commented *inter alia* that "Were it not that the NP&FR actually exists and is doing some work we might be excused for regarding the whole thing as a huge joke." It went on to remark that "We cannot forget that this part of wild Wales is not very far from another part of that beautiful country, to open up which the Manchester and Milford Railway Company was started some thirty years ago and has not yet succeeded in paying its way... We confess the whole scheme puzzles us, for with the exception of the opening up of a portion of Carmarthenshire for the benefit of the GWR and the LNWR, this proposed extension of the NP&FR can benefit no one – or at any rate no investors." It is hardly surprising that the GWR vigorously opposed the scheme, so much so that the only portion to receive Parliamentary sanction was the direct line from Beag to Letterston. If it was intended to serve as a wake-up call to the GWR it certainly succeeded, as we shall shortly see. The remaining history of the NP&FR including its takeover by the GWR and the abandonment of the various extensions proposed under the above Acts will be dealt with in Chapter Nine, which relates the history of the early years of the F&RR&H Company.

A New Company is Formed

In the previous chapter we dealt with the affairs of the NP&FR up to the obtaining of the Act of 1897 and also the formation of the F&RR&H Company. The original ideas for Ireland embraced a line from a new port at Rosslare via Waterford to Cork, involving the purchase of the WD&LR and the F&LR. Rowlands' original plan was to make use of the DW&WR line from Macmine Junction to New Ross and on to Waterford over that Company's proposed extension. Whilst this was far from ideal, due to the length of the route and the severe gradients and curves on that line, as well as the 5mph speed restriction along the Quay at Wexford, it was regarded in the short term as the best means of getting to Waterford. The ultimate plan was, of course, to construct a new line across South Wexford, an area said to be much in need of railway accommodation, although sparsely populated.

Various meetings took place between Joseph Rowlands and Colonel Tighe, Chairman of the DW&WR, the last of which was held in October 1896. It was initially suggested that the Waterford extension should be undertaken jointly, the DW&WR, F&RR&H and the WL&WR each contributing one-third of the cost. When the latter Company declined to become financially involved, Rowlands suggested that his Company should pay three-eighths and the DW&WR the balance, going as far as proposing that the F&RR&H themselves would promote the extension in Parliament with running powers being granted between Macmine Junction and New Ross. The response to the latter suggestion was that the F&RR&H should construct the line at their own expense and the DW&WR work it; this proposal was totally unacceptable to Rowlands. The final correspondence from the DW&WR on the subject was to the effect that they were preparing to go to Parliament for their own extension. With the negotiations at an end, and rather in haste – as was later admitted – the F&RR&H

gave notice on 12 November of a Bill to be lodged in the 1897 Session for a line from Rosslare to Waterford. This Bill was successfully opposed by the DW&WR and failed to gain the approval of the Examiner of the House.

The Times of London reported in September 1897 on the general dissatisfaction throughout the south and east of Ireland at the Treasury's decision to dispose of the WD&LR to the GWR/GS&WR alliance, as referred to in Chapter Six. The Fishguard scheme had been warmly supported, inasmuch as the Company had guaranteed, if declared the purchaser, to construct a direct railway from Cork to Fermoy and to make a connecting link from Waterford to Wexford, which would complete an alternative and cheaper route between Cork and Dublin via the DW&WR. The F&RR&H Syndicate (the appellation generally applied to the early company as formed by Joseph Rowlands and his associates) were at that time endeavouring to persuade the Duke of Devonshire not to dispose of his interest in the F&LR to the GS&WR unless the latter consented to provide running powers through to Cork. Indeed, the F&RR&H contemplated going back to Parliament in the next session for powers to construct the Cork and Fermoy and Waterford and Wexford lines, the success of which depended very largely on the co-operation of the Duke.

Meanwhile, at the invitation of the Chairman and Directors of the F&RR&H, a large party of important personalities from the south of Ireland visited Fishguard in October 1897 to view the works in progress. This invitation was undoubtedly made to persuade those with some influence in the south of Ireland to further the interests of the Fishguard Company. The Irish contingent included Maurice Healy, MP for Cork; Patrick H Meade, the Mayor of Cork; Edward A Neale, General Manager of the Waterford & Central Ireland Railway (W&CIR);

Sir Nugent Humble; Robert and John Worthington, Frederick Vaughan and James Tighe, respectively Manager and Engineer of the WL&WR. The attendance also included Frederick W Gelling, Manager of the F&RR&H in Ireland; Hubert Rowlands (Joseph's son and himself a Solicitor); James B Macaulay, Chairman of the NP&FR; along with Engineers Sir Benjamin Baker and Arthur E Joyce.

After an inspection of the works, luncheon was held in the Wyncliffe Hotel at Fishguard. In welcoming the visitors, Joseph Rowlands informed them that by connecting Cork and other parts of the south of Ireland with Fishguard, the Company would be doing a great deal to improve matters in Ireland. He went on to say that the F&RR&H had accepted terms laid down by the Treasury for the purchase of the WD&LR line but "influences which at the present time he would not attempt to describe prevailed, and the Great Southern & Western of Ireland and the Great Western of England were told that they could have the line." The F&RR&H did not mean to let them have it without a desperate struggle. He believed the Treasury should not have the final say but that the decision should be left to the representatives of the people in Ireland. The Mayor of Cork, in responding to the Chairman's speech, said he believed there was a great future in store for the Fishguard Company.

Reporting on the visit, *The Irish Times* informed its readers that the F&RR&H intended to employ a fleet of fast steamers to cover the journey from Fishguard to Rosslare in 2½ hours. Some 250 men were at that time employed in the construction of the pier at Fishguard. A gang of Welshmen had initially been engaged to carry out blasting operations on the cliff face, but on observing the extreme difficulties involved had declined the work. At that point a number of men who had been employed on the Rosslare Harbour works were brought over to Fishguard to do the work; on seeing them at work, the Welshmen had joined in and the works were now proceeding rapidly under the superintendence of Mr John Byrne of Rosslare. The NP&FR had secured powers to extend from Clynderwen Station to a junction with the L&NWR at Carmarthen, which would provide an alternative route to London. *The Irish Times* also noted that plans were

Workmen engaged on the cliff-face works at Fishguard on an unrecorded date. All without exception are wearing headgear. Looking at the loading of the wagon in the foreground it is hardly surprising that many of the men suffered injuries. (*Pembrokeshire Record Office*)

in hand for the construction of a line from Rosslare to connect at Waterford with the W&CIR, WL&WR and the WD&LR, and commented that this line was precisely the same as that promoted in 1890 by Robert Worthington, so powers being sought were practically a revival of the 1890 scheme.

On 4 November 1897 the Syndicate appointed Sir Benjamin Baker and Arthur Edward Joyce as Engineers to the Company. It was agreed that they be reimbursed their out-of-pocket expenses up to the date of either passing or rejection of the Bill, their fees for personal services in connection with the promotion of the Bill to be £1,000 if successful or £300 if rejected. In the event of the Act being passed, they were to act as Joint Engineers for the construction of the line to Waterford on a commission of 5 per cent based on the cost of construction; unsuccessful attempts were made to reduce the commission. It would appear that the GS&WR were not entirely satisfied with Joyce as, at their request, an arrangement was made for him to retire from the position of Joint Engineer on consideration of a payment of £3,000; he was replaced in December 1898 by the GS&WR's Chief Engineer, Kennett Bayley.[1]

Notices were published in November 1897 for two rival schemes for the 1898 Session of Parliament. The GWR and the GS&WR put forward a Bill for the joint acquisition of the WD&LR and the F&LR. The two companies agreed to repay the Treasury the £93,000 loaned to the WD&LR, none of which had to date been remitted; in addition, they agreed to pay £7 12s 6d for each £10 share in that Company. The purchase of the F&LR was dependent on the Duke of Devonshire who was still undecided whether to dispose of his interest in the Company to the GWR/GS&WR alliance or to the Fishguard Syndicate. The two companies also agreed to provide a reasonable through service of trains, the GWR agreeing to put on a faster train service to and from Milford in conjunction with an improved steamer service to Waterford. It was envisaged that the two Irish lines would be worked by a joint committee. The Bill also sought powers to provide a joint station at Waterford which would provide accommodation for all the lines serving the city on both sides of the river (with the exception of the isolated Waterford & Tramore line). The cross-river connection would be provided by the bridge authorised under the DW&WR Act of 1897 for its New Ross to Waterford extension. It should, however, be noted that there was no mention of a port at Rosslare as the GWR wished to maintain their monopoly of the shipping services at Waterford.

Reporting to his Board in November 1897, the Chairman of the GWR, Viscount Emelyn, confirmed that he had had an interview with Frederick Pim, Chairman of the DW&WR. Pim had requested the assistance of the GWR in raising capital for the construction of their New Ross and Waterford Extension Railway (NR&WER) and the bridge across the River Suir, powers for both of which had been

obtained in the Company's Act of 1897. He urged the importance to the GWR of the proposed line and bridge as being the best mode "of successfully opposing Rowlands' project for a line between Rosslare Harbour and Cork." The cost of the works was estimated at £200,000, towards which the WL&WR had agreed to guarantee interest to the amount of £2,000 per annum, the DW&WR shareholders would be requested to guarantee a sum of £4,000 per annum, and it was hoped the GWR would agree to guarantee a further annual sum of £2,000.

Viscount Emelyn told the GWR Board that he had asked Mr Pim whether, as an alternative, the DW&WR would be satisfied with a subscription from the GWR towards the necessary capital, Pim's response being that he would accept this, although preferring a guarantee. However, it was suggested that for the moment it would suffice to publish Parliamentary Notice, hopefully in the joint names of the GWR and the GS&WR. In the event, the GS&WR declined to join in the arrangement. So it was that in November 1897 the GWR published Notice of Intention to apply to Parliament, in the 1898 Session, for an Act to grant the Company powers to take over all the powers, rights and privileges conferred upon the DW&WR by their Act of 1897 with regard to the construction of the NR&WER, and to take shares and stock, including debentures, in the separate NR&WER undertaking. A figure of £60,000 was mentioned in relation to the GWR subscription to complete the Waterford extension, including the provision of the bridge across the River Suir. The GWR Chairman would later clarify matters by stating that they only wished to contribute financially to the bridge at Waterford, and not to the New Ross to Waterford extension. Despite the GS&WR's refusal to become involved at that stage, the Bill would allow them to become joint owners. Finally, at the suggestion of the WL&WR, it was envisaged that the various companies having termini in Waterford would enter into agreements regarding the construction of a joint station in that city, either new or by the enlargement of one of the existing stations. A second piece of proposed legislation, the GWR (New Works) Bill included, *inter alia*, powers for the construction of a branch line from the South

---

1 Kennett Bayley (October 1838–24 June 1911) was educated at Rugby and served a pupillage with Messrs Ransome of Ipswich. Following a period with the North Eastern Railway, Bayley was appointed Engineer to the GS&WR, retiring from the position in 1900.

Wales line near Clarbeston Road to a junction with the authorised NP&FR line near Letterston.

The rival scheme was of course put forward by the F&RR&H, which still sought to acquire the WD&LR, to construct a direct Cork to Fermoy link and a new railway from Rosslare to Waterford, including a crossing of the River Suir to make connection with the WD&LR. It also planned to provide connecting lines at Cork with the CB&SCR and the C&MDR, but apparently intending to make no connection with the GS&WR, a fact which was later to be disputed. Running powers were sought over various companies' lines, including the DW&WR, GS&WR and WL&WR. The *Railway Times*, reporting on the rival schemes, appeared to favour that of the alliance, although conceding that the Fishguard scheme had a considerable advantage with its short sea crossing. The F&RR&H also sought an extension of time under its Bill for the completion of works at Fishguard, originally authorised by the FBR&P Company Act of 1893. Finally, if the Act were obtained, the Company would have changed its title to the no less cumbersome Fishguard & South of Ireland Railways & Harbours Company.

The F&RR&H Bill came before the Examiner of the House of Commons at the end of January 1898 for proof of compliance with Standing Orders. The DW&WR opposed the proposed legislation, as did the Commissioners for improving the Port and Harbour of Waterford. The former's case seemed rather weak from the beginning. They argued that the notices published for the Bill made no mention of an intention to levy tolls and rates on certain railways over which running powers were sought. The promoters argued that the notices were quite sufficient as the intended tolls were already levied by the existing companies. Another argument was that the F&RR&H intended to erect a hotel at Rosslare on ground outside the limits of deviation, a matter disputed by Counsel for the promoters. The final argument from the DW&WR was that the estimates had not been deposited until 1 January, whereas they should have been in on the previous day. It transpired that the papers had in fact been in the Houses of Parliament at midnight but the Private Bill Office had been closed; the papers were handed into the care of a policeman and never left the House. The Examiner threw out all the objections and decided that the Bill had complied with Standing Orders.

With both schemes now in Parliament awaiting a decision from that august body on the merits of the two sets of proposals, a surprise announcement appeared in *The Times* of 24 February to the effect that the F&RR&H Syndicate had withdrawn from the promotion of their railway scheme and had disposed of their rights to the GWR. Two days later, the *Railway Times* reported that the F&RR&H, in the absence of the co-operation they had expected from the Treasury and the Duke of Devonshire, had decided to throw in their lot with the GWR. The GWR/GS&WR Bill was also withdrawn as were the NP&FR plans for extensions in Wales. It went on to report that the GWR had agreed to the establishment of a through service from South Wales to the south of Ireland via the short sea crossing. Needless to say the GWR (DW&WR) Bill was also withdrawn. So what had happened to bring about this seismic shift?

The official line put forward by the GWR was that they had become aware that certain shareholders in the F&RR&H had taken the decision not to invest any further in the scheme. This information was apparently passed on to Alexander Henderson, MP, a member of Greenwood & Company, a firm that had from time to time had business relationships with the GWR. Henderson himself was a Director of the Great Central Railway and had advised the GWR on financial matters over the previous 25 years. He claimed that he had not come to any agreement with the GWR in relation to the F&RR&H, although he had been informed that "it would suit the GWR Company to have that interest (the F&RR&H) in friendly hands". If the Bill failed to pass through Parliament he would remain as the sole holder of the Fishguard shares; in that event he might consider raising further capital himself. The whole interest amounted to a figure in excess of £300,000, of which £150,000 related to the F&RR&H, the balance to the NP&FR. It seems highly unlikely that a gentleman of Henderson's business acumen would have left himself exposed to such a liability without some guarantees.

In June, Joseph Rowlands, giving evidence before the Hybrid Committee of the House of Commons considering the Fishguard Bill, said the first inkling he had of difficulties was around 9 or 10 February when it was intimated to him that certain of his friends and colleagues were not disposed to go any further with the scheme and intended selling their shares. This left him in a position of great difficulty and ultimately he had to sell his own shares. He confirmed that he personally had invested between £60,000 and £70,000 of his own money in the undertaking and would have been prepared to invest more. Further reference is made to the sale of the line at the end of this chapter.

Whatever the circumstances, what we do know is that a Memorandum of Agreement was signed on 15 February 1898 between Alexander Henderson of 28 Austin Friars in the City of London and Messrs Cartland, Rowlands, Remnant, Walker and Combe, the proprietors of the F&RR&H Company, for the purchase by the former for the sum of £150,000 of the whole undertaking of the F&RR&H Company, including the railway in Fishguard Bay with all plant and materials, the land for the harbour works, engines, rolling stock, the harbour and works at Rosslare, and the railway from Rosslare to Wexford. Included in the sale were the Wyncliffe Hotel and the steamer, SS *Voltaic*. A similar agreement was signed on the same day for the purchase of the NP&FR for a sum of £157,500. In the House of Commons, the WD&LR and F&LR (Vesting) Bill and the GWR (DW&WR) Bill were withdrawn at the end of March 1898, followed in May by the withdrawal of the Bill of the NP&FR for powers of extension in Wales. This now left only the Fishguard Bill to be considered, apart from the GWR (New Works) Bill. When it came up for its second reading in the House of Commons at the beginning of May 1898, some doubts were expressed as to how far the GWR and the GS&WR were working together, and in the circumstances it was agreed that the Bill should be read a second time and then referred to a Hybrid Committee; that was the only way in which full light could be thrown on the intentions of the promoters. So it was that a Hybrid Committee was set up under the chairmanship of Sir Ughtred Kay-Shuttleworth, meeting for the first time on Wednesday

8 June. Other members of the Committee included Sir William Arrol, Maurice Healy, MP for Cork, and John Redmond, MP for Waterford City. By that time some amendments had already been made to the Bill, the most notable being the striking out of the powers for connecting the railways south of the River Lee in Cork.

Addressing the Committee, Mr Pope, QC for the promoters, stated that the GWR, through their friendship with Mr Henderson, had a preponderating influence in the affairs of the NP&FR. They had approached the GS&WR, who had "become alive to the fact that if they were to serve the south of Ireland they must throw in their lot bona fide with the GWR and must be parties to the promotion of such a scheme as is now before the Committee." In relation to the Bill the GWR had accepted it in its entirety with the exception of the line from Cork to Fermoy, for which they did not intend to seek powers as it was adequately served, in their view, by the GS&WR line via Mallow. It had been agreed that the latter Company would charge the same rates and fares as would have applied by the direct line proposed in 1890, some 14 miles shorter. It was confirmed that the capital of the F&RR&H was to be guaranteed by both companies, the GS&WR taking responsibility for the works on the Irish side and the GWR those in Wales. The figures put forward for these works, in excess of £1 million, indicated clearly why the original promoters felt unable to continue with the project. The GS&WR had agreed to provide an efficient daily service of passenger and goods trains, at least up to their standards on their own lines, the GWR providing a similar service on the Welsh side; whilst the GWR had agreed to take over the NP&FR it was unsuitable for the running of express traffic and a new line would be required from Clarbeston Road to Letterston, a line following very much the original route laid down over 60 years previously by Brunel. The Earl of Cawdor, the GWR Chairman, confirmed also that the Company intended from the outset to promote American liner traffic at Fishguard.

Initially, the intention had been for three Directors from each of the companies to serve on the board of the F&RR&H, with Alexander Henderson representing the Fishguard Company. However, a brief statement was read to the Committee on 13 June from the GS&WR to the effect that whilst they felt it would have been equitable to have had equal representation on the Board of the new Company with an independent Chairman, they were desirous of showing that they did not wish to be obstructive or appear to be creating a block, and therefore assented to a modification of Clause 55 to allow four GWR Directors and three from the GS&WR.

Some discussion had taken place as to the GS&WR taking over the W&CIR and the WL&WR, the Earl of Cawdor refusing to be drawn on the matter, while the GS&WR suggested that it had nothing whatsoever to do with the Fishguard Bill. Later, Joseph Wilkinson, General Manager of the GWR, reluctantly accepted that WL&WR officials attending a meeting at Paddington had been reminded that the GWR rebates were due to expire in 1899. It was suggested to him that this was a very diplomatic way of telling them that if the amalgamation with the GS&WR did not go through, then the rebates would cease. Furthermore, probably unknown to the Hybrid Committee, the Earl of Cawdor had informed his fellow Directors on 24 February (the exact same day that the surprise announcement by the F&RR&H appeared in *The Times*) that he had decided that there should be no further capital expenditure in Ireland, and that the Company should ultimately, if not immediately, withdraw any rebate arrangements with Irish companies. The Committee strongly recommended that the proposed amalgamation with the WL&WR be reconsidered, but the GS&WR refused to concede anything in this regard and the matter had to be dropped.

As would have been expected, the DW&WR petitioned against the Bill on the grounds that the proposed new line across the south of Wexford was very costly, unnecessary, would serve no towns of any importance and would seriously interfere with traffic on their Waterford extension. Other petitions came from the New Ross Harbour Commissioners and the Waterford Harbour Commissioners, in relation to the proposed river crossings which would obstruct navigation; these objections were largely overruled. The Hybrid Committee concluded its deliberations on 1 July and the Bill went before the House of Lords a

fortnight later, that body deciding not to give running powers to the DW&WR as sought between Waterford and Cork.

The F&RR&H Bill duly received Royal Assent on 12 August 1898. It is worth spending a little time looking at some of the relevant clauses in the Act. As both the DW&WR and the F&RR&H had obtained powers for the construction of a bridge across the River Suir in Waterford, it was agreed that the bridge should be constructed by the latter Company so as to be capable of accommodating a double line of rails, should the DW&WR decide to avail of the facility. That Company were also given the option, under Section 12 of the Act, of becoming joint owners of a stretch of line a little over 2 furlongs in length from a point where it connected end-on with the WL&WR goods extension at Salvation Lane to the point where their line to New Ross would deviate from the Fishguard line (later known as Abbey Junction). Section 68 (8) required the F&RR&H (in effect the GWR who agreed to provide the service) to put on an efficient daily service of fast steamers for passengers and coaching traffic between Fishguard and Rosslare; furthermore, as soon as the traffic required, they were also to provide a reasonable service for goods and livestock. Under Section 70 the GWR were to maintain their daily service between Waterford and either Milford or Fishguard. This service was to remain until determined by Parliament.

With the Act passed and the takeover by the new Company, the Earl of Cawdor, Chairman of the GWR, was elected to a similar position on the F&RR&H with Joshua Pim, Chairman of the GS&WR, as his deputy. At the first board meeting held at Paddington on 26 October 1898, Alexander Henderson announced his resignation, which was accepted with much regret. At the same meeting two payments were made, one to Robert Worthington in an amount of £10,500, the other a payment of £1,000 to Wexford Harbour Commissioners (WHC). In regard to the former, Worthington had been retained to advise the Fishguard Syndicate in relation to the 1897 and 1898 Bills. Arising out of this and for his perceived failure to be awarded the contract for construction of the Company's lines in Ireland, he had lodged a substantial claim, reported to be in the region of £50,000, against the Company. Following lengthy negotiations Worthington agreed to accept a sum of £11,000 in full settlement of his claim. It was agreed that an amount of £500 would be held back until the Bills promoted by the GS&WR for the absorption of the W&CIR and the WL&WR passed through Parliament; the remaining amount was in fact paid over in January 1901, the old F&RR&H Syndicate agreeing to contribute £5,500 towards the total payment.

The payment to the WHC was the balance due to that body under Section 5 (2) of the Rosslare Pilotage Order Confirmation Act of 1897 and Section 68 (10) of the F&RR&H Act of 1898. The Rosslare Act, which initially was promoted by Joseph Rowlands, was passed to compensate the Wexford Harbour Commissioners (WHC) and the Wexford pilots for the loss of dues at Rosslare Harbour. When the new harbour first opened, the WHC maintained the right to provide pilots for vessels entering and leaving Rosslare. This was strongly contested and in fact two summonses had been issued against Capt Robert Keown, master of the Company's steamer *Voltaic* for his refusal to pay pilotage charges. Under the Act two payments, each of £1,000, were to be handed over by the F&RR&H, the sums to be divided between the Commissioners and the pilots.

At the same meeting the Secretary reported that although arrangements had been made between the two guaranteeing companies, for the GS&WR, as agents of the F&RR&H, to take over the W&WR as from 12 February 1898, yet it was still being managed by Mr Gelling, the local Traffic Officer and the expenses paid and receipts collected by the F&RR&H. It was resolved that the line be placed under the control of the GS&WR as from 1 November. Previous researchers have made reference to the fact that the W&WR was worked by the DW&WR between February and October 1898. This assumption most likely arose from the delay in the taking over of the working of the line by the GS&WR as referred to previously. The present author has found no evidence to suggest that the DW&WR worked the line for 8 months during 1898, neither company's records making any reference to it. In fact, at the F&RR&H Board meeting on 13 December 1898 the GS&WR representatives present stated that owing to the W&WR being so far removed from their system, it was expensive to work, and asked whether there would be any objection on behalf of the F&RR&H to their making a temporary arrangement with the DW&WR for working of the line until the Rosslare to Waterford line was opened for traffic. The F&RR&H Board approved the principle of this arrangement on the understanding that it would not relieve the GS&WR from the responsibility of bearing any deficiency that might arise in the working. A working agreement with the F&RR&H had in fact been mentioned in August 1897, when reference was made to a payment of £250 per annum for the use of Wexford Station. The agreement was approved in principle in February 1898 but the author believes that this referred solely to the use of the DW&WR station at Wexford rather than the working of the Rosslare line.

The DW&WR board minutes indicate that their Mr Coghlan had spoken to Mr Colhoun of the GS&WR at the beginning of December in this context, the result of which was that Samuel J Shannon, the DW&WR Engineer, was ordered to inspect the Wexford to Rosslare line as soon as possible; this would hardly have been necessary if they had worked it up until a month before. Shannon reported back to his Board on 15 December and there the matter rested for a year, the GS&WR advising in November of the following year that they would prefer to work their own line. They had requested permission in February 1899 to transfer an engine from Ballywilliam to Wexford as a spare for the Rosslare line. Shannon submitted plans on 21 December 1899 of a proposed new platform, siding and dock for the accommodation of the F&RR&H at Wexford, these plans being approved; reference was made to the necessity for a new agreement and a minimum annual payment of £500 for the use of facilities in addition to the cost of the alterations. As we know, these alterations were never carried out, although the GS&WR did shed their locomotives at Wexford. A DW&WR board minute of 9 November 1899[2] clearly states that the GS&WR "would prefer for the present to keep the working of the Rosslare line in their own hands."

2 Board Minute No 5818

Likewise, although the WD&LR and the F&LR had been vested in the Fishguard Company as from 1 July 1898, the working was still being carried out by the WD&LR. The formal transfer of these lines also occurred on 1 November, on which date the locomotives and rolling stock were removed to Inchicore and replaced by GS&WR stock. Gelling and JC Hughes, the Secretary, both resigned their positions with the coming of the new order. Hughes was replaced by George Whitelaw, a GWR man. Reporting to the Board in December 1898, Whitelaw stated that on his appointment to the F&RR&H he found the accounts of the Syndicate in a very confused condition and had been compelled to re-model them entirely from the beginning of the year. To effect this he had found it necessary to engage some GWR clerks to work outside normal office hours and had paid them £35, a figure which was approved.

Still smarting from their perceived defeat at the hands of the GWR, Henry Burgess, Irish Manager of the L&NWR, visited Waterford early in December 1898 and interviewed various businessmen regarding his Company's position in relation to cross-channel trade. Whilst the L&NWR had no desire to interfere in the arrangements of Irish companies, they planned to go to Parliament seeking powers to run over the GWR line between Carmarthen and Fishguard so as to provide traders in the south of Ireland with a shorter route to Lancashire and other manufacturing centres in the north of England generally when the Rosslare route was opened.

Reference has been made earlier in the chapter to the fact that Rowlands only allegedly became aware of financial difficulties days before he himself was forced to sell his shares. Two legal cases show that there was some acrimony among the Partners. The *Railway Times* reported in February 1899 on a legal case brought against Rowlands and Cartland by some of their erstwhile colleagues, Messrs Combe[3] and Walker, seeking to appoint a Receiver in respect of the partnership and for the possession of the partnership's books of account.[4] It was contended that "the whole thing had practically been done in Mr. Rowlands' office, and there the books had been. The costs for Parliamentary Agents had been enormous and the plaintiffs had no right to retain anything in the nature of a secret profit." An accountant had seen the books but there were a large number of matters requiring further investigation. The usual judgment in a partnership action was then made, with cross-orders for discovery.

The second case came before the Chancery Division of the High Court in the following December. On this occasion Rowlands took a case against two of the Syndicate's members, George Watkins Yardley, a London stockbroker, and James Farquharson Remnant, Secretary to the brewing firm of Messrs Combe & Co. Ltd, of which the principal was R.H. Combe. In this instance the evidence was that the GWR had approached Rowlands making an offer for the purchase of the F&RR&H, but he had declined to continue, whereupon Remnant and Yardley on behalf of the Syndicate had entered negotiations which led to the sale of the line and its assets to the GWR. When the purchase moneys were handed over, the defendants retained a sum of £16,000 odd as compensation and remuneration, with a further sum of £4,000 claimed by another Syndicate member. Rowlands took the action to recover the amount of £16,800. When the case came before the Judge, it was reported that an agreement had been reached whereby Yardley and Remnant were to respectively receive £5,000 and £2,000, the balance being lodged in Court. What the actual sequence of events leading up to the sale of the F&RR&H were may never be known for sure, but we come to the conclusion of this phase in the history of the F&RR&H company, and in the next chapter we will take a look at the construction works during the period up to the opening of the new route in August 1906.

---

3 R.H. Combe was a member of a brewing family with headquarters at Castle Street Brewery in Longacre.

4 Perhaps this is why the Minute Books are no longer extant.

CHAPTER TEN

Construction Commences on the Welsh Side

Although the harbour works at Fishguard had been commenced some years previously, it is clear that progress had been slow. With the GWR in effect taking over responsibility for the works in 1898, Isaac J Mann,[1] who had been in charge of the harbour works at Rosslare, was appointed as Resident Engineer under James (later Sir James) Inglis, the GWR's Chief Engineer. The *Pembroke County Guardian* reported in February 1896 that Mann had in fact been brought over to Fishguard towards the end of 1895 and had carried out a detailed survey of the harbour. "Short of diving", he had expressed himself quite satisfied both as regards the shelter which would be provided and the fact that there was likely to be little or no scouring due to tidal conditions. By that time the small boat quay had been completed and the breakwater commenced. The principal difficulty had been the sheer cliff, a large part of which had to be removed in order to construct the quay for the proposed steamer berths. The problem was that there was virtually no level ground for the workmen employed in making bore holes for the explosives; initially it became necessary to let the men down on ropes from the top of the cliff, which in places was up to 200ft high. So dangerous was the work considered to be that the Welsh men initially engaged refused to work, only agreeing to resume after a group of men were brought over from the harbour works at Rosslare; an Irishman, John Byrne, aged 47, was appointed Manager of the harbour works.

Prior to the GWR involvement there was, however, another matter that had caused some delay. A small quay had existed at Goodwick for a considerable length of time and had been used for many years by local inhabitants and fishermen. It was feared that the construction of the proposed railway works would cut off all access to the quay. The owners of the quay sought compensation of £1,000 to hand over the property. Rowlands, as Solicitor for the Syndicate, served Notice to Treat and this was to lead to an inquiry being set up by the BoT to consider the situation. The inquiry was conducted by Vice-Admiral Sir George S Nares, KCB, FRS, at the Wyncliffe Hotel in Goodwick on 10 June 1897. The inquiry was attended by Joseph Rowlands and Isaac Mann on behalf of the F&RR&H and by Mr William Winterbotham, of the London firm of Solicitors, Waterhouse, Winterbotham, Harrison & Harper on his own behalf and on behalf of the inhabitants of Goodwick. Part of the difficulty appeared to be that the Company had not finally decided on the exact course of the line, although they appeared to be leaning towards running it entirely on the foreshore below high water mark, about 15 or 20ft outside the existing quay. Rowlands confirmed that the Company had no desire to deprive the local people of the facilities which they had enjoyed for so long, but was not prepared to expend an estimated £2,000 on a bridge under the line. Eventually, a new quay was constructed by the F&RR&H under powers granted under an Act of 1899, further referred to below.

The GWR wrote to the Fisheries & Harbours Department of the BoT on 16 January 1899 informing them that the Fishguard Company had been reconstituted, Mr Rowlands having no further involvement with the scheme. This letter apparently followed previous correspondence between the Syndicate and the BoT as a note on the front of the file in part states "Now that the Officers of the Fishguard Company are GWR Officers, and the old Fishguard Directors are out of it, I think matters are very materially altered for the better." It would appear from this remark that the BoT had either also experienced

---

1 Isaac John Mann, MICE, was born in Dublin on 26 January 1836. After being educated at Trinity College Dublin, he was involved in railway construction works in Ireland and Wales, later becoming Assistant Engineer to the Dublin Port & Docks Board. He was the inventor of a machine for testing Portland cement. Mann retired in 1901 and died at Orford, Suffolk on 13 January 1917. His son, HC (Harry), was also involved as an Assistant Engineer in the works at Fishguard.

The result of an explosion at the rock face. In this view there appear to be two or three members of the gentler sex evident on right hand side. Dinas Head is in background. *(The National Archives, Kew)*

difficulties with Mr Rowlands and his colleagues or had lacked confidence in their ability to deliver such a grand scheme. The reason for the correspondence was to ask the BoT to recommend to Government a grant in aid for construction of what was regarded by the Company as a harbour of refuge. Statistics were quoted to show the large number of shipping casualties which had occurred for the year ended 30 June 1899 in the adjacent portion of the Irish Sea. The application was declined on the grounds of the proximity of both Milford Haven and the Pembroke Docks and Dockyard.

Reporting to the F&RR&H Board on 6 June 1899, Inglis confirmed that about 90,000 tons of rock had been excavated since the beginning of the year and that the railway embankment had been extended along the foreshore; it was hoped that an early connection would be made with the NP&FR line at Goodwick. This would enable more machinery to be brought in, as up until this point the railhead was at Letterston with haulage over the intervening distance on poor roads with animal power. The Admiralty requested that a footbridge be provided across the lines at Fishguard to provide a temporary approach to the main road; a plan of the proposed bridge, estimated to cost £200, was approved.

The Company had given notice in November 1898 that they would seek Parliamentary powers in the 1899 Session for further harbour works at Fishguard. These were incorporated in the Company's Act that received Royal Assent on 1 August 1899. They included an extension of 350 yards to the breakwater originally authorised under the FBR&P Act of 1893, bringing the total length to 700 yards. The Act also authorised a second breakwater commencing on the shore near Penryhn House, extending east for 31 chains and then northeast for a further 29 chains. Close by there was to be a jetty or landing place, some 20 chains in length; this was in substitution for the old quay at Goodwick referred to previously. From this jetty a wharf wall or embankment was to extend along the shoreline to the breakwater, this providing the actual quay on which the station would be constructed. Later, in October 1899, the Board decided that the minimum depth below low water at this quay should be not less than 20ft. It was also agreed that repairs would be carried out to two cottages in Goodwick, recently vacated by the Coast Guard, and then to be tenanted by men employed on the harbour works. Other properties purchased about that time included the Rose & Crown public house, Ivy Cottage and gardens and Rock House. The latter was described as being an integral part of the Wyncliffe Hotel, which had formed part of the agreement between Alexander Henderson and the Syndicate in February 1898, while Ivy Cottage adjoined the hotel. Matters in relation to the hotel and other properties are dealt with in Chapter Twenty-three.

In what was to be a change to a more mechanised approach to the harbour works, in October 1899 the first of a number of Ingersoll steam rock drills was acquired at a cost of £80; also in October, Inglis was authorised to purchase from the GWR 37 tipping wagons at £36 each for the harbour works. Further reference is made to these wagons in Chapter Nineteen. October 1901 saw the beginning of a greater push to have the works completed; it had at one stage been anticipated that staff from Milford would be moved to Fishguard during 1902 although this was to prove extremely optimistic. At the board meeting on 10 October 1901, approval was given for the purchase of 12 steam drills and associated machinery for £2,328, two 15-ton steam travelling cranes for £3,850, a second-hand Titan crane for £1,806, plus £700 for dismantling and re-erecting it; it was also reported that an 0-4-0ST locomotive had been ordered from Manning Wardle & Company for £825. Difficulties were being encountered in employing men on the works due to a shortage of lodging accommodation and it was agreed that huts be provided for about 75 men at an estimated cost of £800.

Also in October 1901 an agreement was entered into with Messrs Hill & Company for the hire of a dredger for the harbour works at a cost of £125 per month; in addition the Company agreed to pay the working expenses for the dredger, including wages. Inglis further proposed that a contract be entered into with Alfred Maine Treglown[2] of 114a Queen Victoria Street, London, for blasting and throwing down rock in accordance with a specification and tender submitted, this also being sanctioned. Under the contract, Treglown was to provide all labour, while the Company agreed to provide all plant, including rock drills, air compressors and the like. As

2 Alfred M Treglown was born in Camborne, Cornwall about 1849. He and his brother, William Maine, spent some time in the USA as miners, both appearing in the UK 1911 Census as citizens of the USA. Alfred's wife, Flora, was in fact born in the United States.

and when required by the Engineer, the contractor was to break up any masses of rock into such sizes as could be handled by cranes. In addition to other conditions, no work, except such as in the opinion of the Engineer was absolutely unavoidable, should be carried out on Sundays; this clause was clearly inserted in keeping with the sensitivities of the local inhabitants. The contract was to run for two years from 1 December 1901, payment for the first year to be at the rate of 9½d per ton and 8½d per ton for the second year. The contractor was obliged to give prior notice to the Engineer of blasting so that the necessary arrangements might be made for the protection of the railway sidings and other works of the Company. The contract was later extended, first to 31 December 1904 and finally to 30 June 1905.

On the recommendation of Inglis, it was agreed in June 1902 that the Company should obtain a stone crushing plant for crushing the smaller sizes of the excavated rock at Goodwick for various purposes. These included stone for making concrete blocks, first class ballast for supply to the GWR, the substitution of finely crushed stone in lieu of large quantities of sand then currently being used, and for obtaining a superior class of road metalling. Inglis advised the Board that a suitable crusher could be supplied by Messrs Gates & Company at an approximate cost of £1,600, while foundations and the requisite sheds for the machinery, as well as laying down additional sidings were estimated at a further £1,900; this latter work was to be carried out by the Company's workmen. The total expenditure of approximately £3,500 was approved by the Board, subject to the consent of the GWR Board being obtained to the purchase of ballast and road metal by that company.

Thus the scene had been set for a significant change in the pace and nature of the work. In future two methods of bringing down the cliff face were to be employed. The first involved boring holes up to 20ft in depth and 2½in in diameter, into which gelignite charges of between 20 and 50lb were placed and then fired electrically. The second method involved the driving of a tunnel 40ft into the cliff face; from the inner end of such tunnels two branches, each 40ft in length, were driven, forming a 'T'. Small chambers were then made at the inner ends of the T-pieces, into which were placed boxes containing seven tons of gunpowder. The tunnels were then packed with rock and the charges electrically fired. By this method, known as 'mine firing', it was possible on more than one occasion to bring down well in excess of 40,000 tons of rock in one firing. George Lambert Gibson, who was Mann's successor, later described these events, stating that they caused very little noise or vibration; indeed, local residents were on occasions reported to have been unaware that one had been set off. This was in sharp contrast to the first such explosion, which occurred on 23 August 1902, when people apparently walked several miles into the countryside to be out of harm's way.

The blasted rock was loaded into wagons by the travelling steam cranes, eventually numbering 14. Stones between 3 and 15 tons in weight were tipped on the sea side of the breakwater, those between 1 cwt and 3 tons being used to form the harbour side and also as filling for the quays and sidings. Those weighing less than 1 cwt were sent to the ballast crusher, believed to be the first of its type to be used on a British railway. Known as a gyratory crusher, it was described by Gibson as being similar to a coffee mill, except that it wobbled rather than rotated. The rock was tipped into a large hopper and then through a set of jaws, which reduced it to 2in size before being dropped into a 70ft elevator, which in turn carried it to a large rotary screen. The screen removed ¾in chippings and sand, allowing them to fall either into a concrete mixer or a reserve bin. The 2in stones were dropped into large bins of 400 tons capacity, under which empty ballast wagons were placed; it was then possible to place 90 tons of ballast into the wagons within 20 minutes, this ballast being distributed over the GWR. The small screenings from the ballast hopper were mixed with Portland cement in a cement mixer working in conjunction with the crusher. From the mixer the soft concrete dropped into small tipping wagons, which were run into the block yard opposite where the mixture was tipped into casings, large stones being added. The blocks thus formed were left for a week, at which point the casings were removed. The blocks were then moved by means of a travelling gantry into a stack, where they were left to mature for three months; at the end of that period the blocks were ready for setting in the quay wall.

A report from Mr Inglis in October 1901 suggested the retirement of Isaac Mann on account of his age

The crushing plant on the site of the Marsh sidings, with rather crude looking ballast wagons in evidence. Judging by the proximity of the house behind, it is hardly surprising that complaints were made of the noise from this plant. *(The National Archives, Kew)*

and indifferent health. It was agreed that Mann, who was then approaching 66 years of age, should retire at the end of December 1901, and that he be paid his full salary for six months, at the end of which he would receive a pension of £200 per annum for three years. George Lambert Gibson, who had been the GWR Resident Engineer in connection with dock works at Plymouth, was appointed to succeed Mann at a salary of £350 per annum.

By July 1902, Inglis was able to report that the north breakwater had been tipped to a length of 500ft with the deposit of 232,000 tons of rock. Three months later Messrs Treglown had excavated 213,000 tons of rock, the breakwater was now 628ft long, and 231 concrete blocks had been made, the latter totalling 2,501 by the end of June 1903. At this latter date, plans were submitted of the works required for the accommodation of both the trains and the steamers, the Board authorising the expenditure of a further £100,000. It was also decided to purchase a steam hopper suction dredger named *Porteur* at a cost of £2,500, which would be capable of dredging material from the bottom of the harbour. This was in addition to a 6-ton steam crane purchased from Messrs Grafton & Company for £510, which was used to fill trucks; up until then such work had been largely done by hand.

The GWR announced in November 1902 that they would require to enlarge the facilities at their Goodwick Station and to lay out the yard there. Some of the materials blasted from the cliff, which would otherwise have been tipped into the sea, proved ideal for filling up ground. The GWR consented to this material being deposited on their ground at Goodwick, paying the cost of this work. About that time complaints were received from residents of the Wyncliffe Hotel and houses on the cliff at Goodwick referring to the noise caused by the working of the stone crusher. As the Company would soon require accommodation for the station and port staff when the harbour was opened for traffic, it was decided that the properties of those residents should, if reasonably possible, be acquired. Authority was given by the Board to negotiate for the purchase of properties along the Hotel road between the post office and Colonel Porter's house, including those of the 12 or 13 complainants, together with land behind them.

The GWR advised the BoT on 3 September 1903 that a temporary connection was about to be laid down on the down side at the Letterston end of Goodwick Station. Passing through the area later occupied by the engine shed, this connection was put in to provide rail access to the new works. This was duly inspected by Colonel Yorke who reported that the points for the new connection were worked by a ground frame

Looking in towards the harbour at Fishguard during construction. The block ground on left will later be occupied by the Marsh Sidings. The Fishermen's Quay is visible on the right hand side, with the Wyncliffe Hotel on the hill to the left. *(The National Archives, Kew)*

containing two levers, these being unlocked by a key on the train staff. The connection remained in use until 8 July 1906.

With the time for the opening of the port approaching, attention was given to the provision of a lighthouse, Mr Inglis suggesting that it should be placed on one of the promontories on the southwest side of the entrance to the harbour, and Strumble Head was suggested as the most suitable location. An application was lodged with the Elder Brethren of Trinity House so that allowance might be made in the budget for 1904. It was not, however, until August 1905, following further correspondence with Trinity House and the Board of Trade, that the former body agreed to locate a lighthouse on Strumble Head at a cost of £12,000, provided the Company contributed £2,000 toward the expense. In a bid to make the port safer, it was agreed in November 1906 to erect a lighthouse at the outer end of the north breakwater at a cost of £1,450 17s 8d. The question of providing steamers was first raised in November 1903, orders being placed in May 1905; these and other maritime matters are dealt with in Chapter Twenty-Two.

By June 1904, the north breakwater extended 1,112ft, a total of 563,232 tons of rock having been deposited. It was decided to enter into a contract with Messrs Howell & McGahan of Pembroke for the fixing of the concrete blocks under water. As the loading of rock was not keeping pace with the remainder of the work, arrangements were made to obtain two or three additional travelling cranes. On the subject of cranes, Mr Inglis suggested that nine 30 cwt and one 21-ton crane be procured for the loading and unloading of vessels, motive power for these cranes being electric motors. Messrs Stothert & Pitt of Bath[3] was one of nine firms who tendered for the supply of these cranes, others including Messrs Cowan Sheldon & Co and Messrs Crompton; tenders varied from £8,940 to £16,435. These were considered at the board meeting on 3 November 1904, that of Messrs Stothert & Pitt Ltd at £9,361 being accepted; this figure was made up as follows: nine 30cwt electric cranes at £775

each, a 21-ton electric crane at £1,756 and three 1-ton capstans at £210 each.

The large crane was described as a coaling crane and was fitted with a cradle capable of lifting and tipping railway wagons up to 21 tons gross weight at a radius of 35ft 9in; it was intended for use in connection with the coaling of the steamers via a lighter and was fixed in position at the north end of the quay. The smaller cranes were capable of lifting their maximum load at a radius of 35ft. Separate motors were provided for lifting and slewing, all being supplied by Messrs Siemens.

The last major contract to be awarded was that for the complete installation of an electricity supply, not only for the harbour facilities, including the cranes, but also to the Wyncliffe Hotel, Harbour Village, the marine workshops, floating dock and the station, yard, engine and carriage sheds at Goodwick. Tenders were opened at the board meeting on 2 August 1905, these ranging from £11,057 from Siemens Bros & Co Ltd to £14,971 15s 0d from the British Thomson-Houston Co Ltd. On the recommendation of Mr Inglis, the Board agreed to accept the Siemens tender.

Writing to the Company in June 1905, Messrs Siemens pointed out that the generators they proposed to supply for the power house were each capable of a continuous output of 120kW, two of these in conjunction with the batteries being capable of providing an output of 300kW, 10 per cent in excess of the 270kW estimated requirements. The steam boilers, three in number, were to be supplied by Messrs Babcock & Wilcox. Each boiler was to consist of nine sections, each section comprised of ten best quality steel tubes 18ft long and 4in diameter; grate area was to be 27sq ft and heating surface 1,330sq ft. The generators were to be Siemens patent standard base type, shunt wound, with an output of 120kW, 480 volts at 350rpm. The batteries, to be manufactured by the Electrical Storage Co Ltd, were to consist of 266 thin CH15 cells in glass boxes.

Meanwhile, the Directors and officers of the GWR and the GS&WR paid a visit to Fishguard to inspect the works in progress. On completion of their tour the party was taken from the boat quay by steam launch to the GWR steamer *Ibex* for a short trip, this vessel

---

3 The firm was originally founded in 1785 by George Stothert, Robert Pitt joining the company early in the twentieth century. It is today part of the Clarke Chapman Group, which also incorporates the other well-known travelling crane manufacturer, Messrs Cowan Sheldon.

A view taken in 1909 showing the Ocean Pier under construction on the inner end and side of the North Breakwater, with the Titan crane to the right. The three chimneys of the power station can be seen on the left at the inner end of the breakwater. *(The National Archives, Kew)*

having earlier in the day steamed round from Milford.

The tender of the Horsehay Company Limited was accepted for the supply of steel flooring and other steelwork at the harbour in an amount of £336 11s 9d. It was reported in January 1905 that extensive repairs were required to the Company's dredger *Porteur*, amounting to £642 15s 8d. As the repairs were considered urgent, it was decided to send the vessel to the Jersey Dry Dock Company in Swansea. Pending repairs, the Company hired the grab dredger *Samphire* from the Milford Docks Company, so as to continue the work of clearing a trench to enable the foundations of the quay wall to be laid.

With work on the breakwater and the quay approaching completion, attention turned in May 1905 to the provision of station facilities. It was decided to install two sets of electric traversers between the platforms in lieu of a second subway as originally intended, and it was agreed that these should be supplied by Messrs Stothert & Pitt at a cost of £1,692. Correspondence with Messrs Stothert & Pitt in February 1905 indicates that four traversers were to be supplied, two for a double line of rails and two for a single line. They were designed so that they could be entirely withdrawn under the platforms when not in use, leaving the lines clear for traffic; they were electrically interlocked with the signalling, no train movements being possible at the relevant platforms unless the traversers were fully retracted. They were electrically operated, there being two motors, each rated at 3bhp, in each traverser. The larger ones ran on 16 wheels, the smaller on 8 wheels. The manufacturers quoted £461 each for the former and £385 for the latter, inclusive of erection. Terms of payment were 65% on delivery, 20% when erected and the balance when the work was approved by the Company's Engineer. In October 1907 it was decided that as a precaution against power failure, four sets of hand gearing be provided, these being supplied by Stothert & Pitt at a cost of £230.

Further steelwork was obtained from Messrs John Lysaght & Company for £3,709 15s 10d for the station roof and £1,706 0s 6d for the roof over the goods platform, making a total of £5,415 16s 4d. The contract for its erection was awarded on 3 October 1905 to William Richard Howell; there is no mention of the amount involved on the contract. The Company agreed to prepare the concrete bases for the columns and to insert the necessary securing bolts. Provision was also made for signalling (£1,606) and the supply of water for locomotives (£1,000). By the time these contracts were being awarded in August 1905, some 1,606ft of the breakwater had been completed and the quay wall completed to a length of 850ft, leaving

The steelwork for the overall roof of the passenger station is taking shape with the cattle pens in the foreground. This photograph also gives a good idea of the difficulties encountered in blasting rock from the cliff face. *(The National Archives, Kew)*

a further 250ft to be built. Also, by that time, Messrs Treglown had removed 1,181,552 tons of rock from the cliff, of which a little over half had been used as filling for the quay. The workforce numbered 531, of whom 463 were employed by the Company, a further 54 by Messrs Treglown, and the remaining 42 by Messrs Howell & McGahan.

It had been clear for some time that the NP&FR route was not suitable for the passage of express passenger trains and the GWR turned their attentions to an alternative. It should be remembered that earthworks in connection with Brunel's original line had been commenced over a distance of about seven miles west of Clarbeston Road. The GWR (New Works) Act of 1898 gave powers to the GWR for the construction of a new line 10 miles 5 furlongs and 5.05 chains in length from Clarbeston Road to form a junction with the NP&FR line near Letterston, the new line being referred to as the Clarbeston Road & Letterston Railway (CR&LR). As this line was to be on easier gradients it was to entail heavy excavations in Treffgarne Gorge, at a point where work had ceased in the 1840s as a result of the extremely hard rock formations encountered. However, it was decided to hold off on construction of the new line until the harbour works were further advanced. Perhaps this was just as well as a fresh survey led to a deviation

being proposed at Treffgarne Gorge, powers for which were taken in the GWR (New Works) Act of 1903. Tenders for construction were duly sought in November 1903. Five months later, the tender of Messrs Joseph T Firbank & Company of London was accepted in an amount of £125,857 13s 10d, two years being allowed for completion of the line.

Initially there was considerable activity although difficulties were encountered with the excavation of the 243-yard long Spittal tunnel, the rock of which consisted of soft shale. It was reported that the Navvy Missionary Society[4] soon established a mission to look after the men's spiritual welfare, the GWR agreeing to make a grant of £25 a year for two years. Temporary works were established, including four signal boxes. One of these, originally in use at Truro viaduct, was opened in the second half of 1904 at what became known as Goodwick Junction (281.50); this 9-lever box was closed on 15 January 1906. There were also temporary boxes on the up side at Wolf's Castle, just to the east of Spittal tunnel and at Treffgarne, all opened on 29 August 1906.

The work on the CR&LR was not without its

---

4 The Navvy Missionary Society was founded in 1877 by a Yorkshire vicar, the Revd Lewis Moule Evans to campaign against what were referred to as 'the three great evils', namely desecration of the Sabbath Day, immorality, and drunkenness. It had been preceded by the Christian Excavators' Union formed by Mrs Elizabeth Garnett in 1870, with similar aims.

An early view of Fishguard Harbour. The nine electric cranes can be seen along the quay as well as the larger 'coaling crane' on the left. It would appear that the cattle pens have not yet seen occupation and, in addition, laden ballast wagons can be seen on the extreme right-hand line. *(Great Western Trust)*

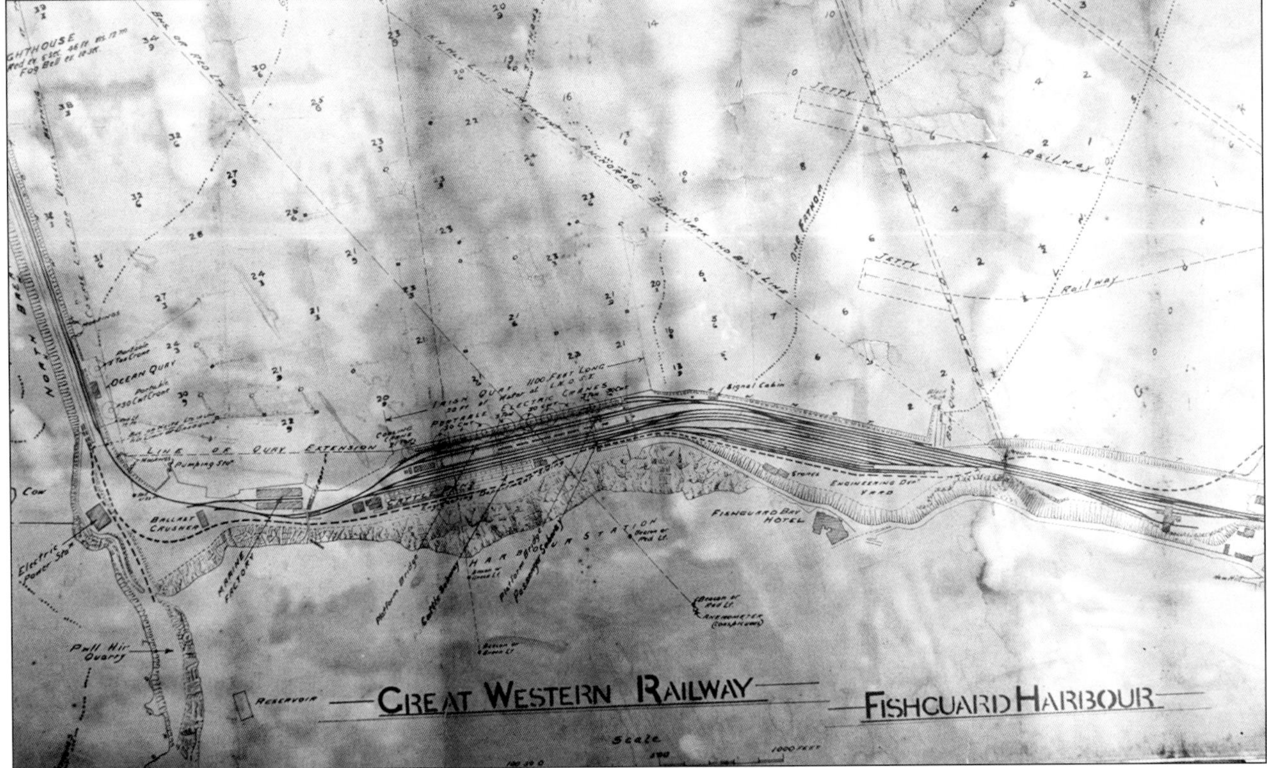

Although of poor quality, this diagram gives a good overall impression of the track layout at Fishguard Harbour. It is of particular interest in that it also shows two of the proposed lines intended to run on to new jetties as envisaged by the GWR (New Works) Act of 1903. *(Ernie Shepherd)*

difficulties. Two explosions occurred in February 1906, one of which was fatal. A report by Capt MB Lloyd of the Explosives Inspectorate sheds an interesting light on the use of explosives at that time. As it was wintertime, the cartridges tended to be congealed when removed for use in the morning. The chargeman rose at 2.30am on the morning of the second explosion and prepared the cartridges for use by placing some of them in two warming pans containing hot water; only having two warming pans at his disposal, he placed a further 18 cartridges in a bucket of hot water. Having subsequently removed the cartridges from the warming pans, the chargeman was in the course of pouring more hot water into them (sufficiently cool so that he could put his hand in the water), when an explosion occurred knocking him to the ground. In his evidence to the inquiry, he said he had heard a fizzing sound just before the explosion. Following lengthy and exhaustive tests, it transpired that mercury had been added to the explosives as a masking agent to conceal the instability of the explosive in question. The manufacturer was subsequently convicted of the offence.

Ballast materials for the line were brought from the GWR quarry at Tenby, being worked over the NP&F line from Clynderwen, where three ballast sidings were installed in July 1903; later, as the cliff was excavated at Fishguard, ballast was obtained from that source. Probably arising from the difficulties associated with the works at Treffgarne and Spittal, Messrs Firbank were declared bankrupt, the GWR then taking over the works themselves.

CHAPTER ELEVEN

Progress on the Irish Side

It was reported in October 1898 that powers had lapsed for the extension of the pier at Rosslare, the Board ordering that such powers be obtained in the Company's Bill for the coming Session. It quickly became clear, however, that there was insufficient time to prepare the necessary plans and it was not until 27 October of the following year that approval was given to amended plans, which had been vetted by Captain AF Boxer, a retired Inspector of Irish Lights. Orders were then given for soundings to be taken, this leading to a request from Kennett Bayley for the provision of a boat and diving apparatus at a combined cost of £110. The F&RR&H gave their approval to this expenditure only after enquiring whether it would be charged to revenue or capital. Bayley announced his resignation as Joint Engineer in the following June, being replaced by James Otway,[1] who had been the WD&LR Engineer. Mr Colhoun confirmed in early May 1900 that new whistling and lighting buoys had been installed at the harbour along with an occulting light

The powers for the extension of the harbour were contained in the Company's Act, which received Royal Assent on 30 July 1900. First was an extension of the existing pier or breakwater for a distance of about 337 yards, in addition to which was a wharf wall or embankment so as to reclaim portions of the foreshore at the shore end of the viaduct leading to the existing pier. Finally, a new road was to be constructed in substitution for the existing road from Ballygillane

Little to the beach. To carry out these works, the Company were granted powers to acquire additional lands from Messrs George Nolan and William Goff Davis Goff.[2] Importantly, the Act gave the Company powers to dredge and deepen the harbour, and, if thought necessary, to build or purchase their own steam dredgers. As we shall shortly see, the Act also gave powers for two deviations in respect of the line from Rosslare to Waterford as had been previously authorised under the Company's Act of 1898.

Otway wrote to the GS&WR Board in November 1900 suggesting that Messrs Coode, Son & Matthews should be consulted as to the plans for the harbour; also suggesting that work on the block ground should be commenced at once. Messrs Coode informed the F&RR&H in the following March that they were not disposed to carry out the inspection. As a consequence, Captain Frederick W Jarrad, RN, reported on the harbour plans, suggesting some small modifications. If these were carried out, Captain Jarrad believed that the extended harbour would secure complete shelter to vessels berthed in the harbour and that there would be no difficulties in entering or leaving the harbour.

The first contract to be awarded in connection with the extension of the pier at Rosslare went to Messrs Robert McAlpine & Sons under an agreement dated 26 March 1900. The work was to consist of the construction of a rubble concrete wall 750ft in length, the trimming, dressing and drainage of the cliff face overlooking the harbour, the material so removed to be used in the formation of a block ground, and finally a new road along the cliff itself, 900ft in length and 20ft wide. The tender was for £8,049 5s 6d and the work was to be completed on or before 1 August 1901. McAlpines wrote to the Company on 8 December to the effect that they had only sufficient land in their

---

1 James Otway had been Engineer WD&LR from 1878, a position that embraced the role of Locomotive Superintendent from 1880 until July 1898, and Engineer of the Waterford Harbour Board until 1899. He had subsequently been appointed the Assistant Engineer of the GS&WR, but on 1 June 1900 he was relieved of that position on his appointment by the F&RR&H as Joint Engineer with Sir Benjamin Baker for the construction of the Rosslare & Waterford Railway and as Engineer for the Rosslare Harbour works in succession to K Bayley. Following the death of Sir Benjamin Baker on 19 May 1907, he continued to execute his responsibility for the Rosslare & Waterford Railway jointly with AC Hurtzig. He resigned his positions with the F&RR&H on 31 December 1907.

2 George Nolan was later awarded contracts in connection with the line to Waterford.

An interesting view of Rosslare Harbour during the period of construction. In the foreground is the block ground. These large concrete blocks were used on the new pier extension. (*Philip Quigley Postcard Collection*)

possession on the South Wexford line to keep their workmen employed for a further three weeks, at which point they would be faced with laying off men. In addition, and obviously anticipating that they might not gain the contract for the extension works at the pier, they pointed out that they had found it necessary to erect two huts at Rosslare, each capable of holding 60 men, at a cost of £100 per hut. They therefore requested that whoever was the successful bidder for the harbour works should be obliged to take over these huts, paying McAlpines £50 each for them. The Engineers reported in October 1902 that 305 blocks had been constructed and that a suction dredger, capable of pumping about 2,500 tons per week to the block ground, was in use. The work of erecting staging and of block setting was severely delayed during the winter of 1902 due to heavy seas and strong winds.

Tenders were received on 17 October 1901 in respect of the extension of the pier, ranging from that of Messrs Charles Brand & Son of 172 Buchanan Street, Glasgow at £138,642 8s 0d to £222,367 14s 4d from the Cleveland Bridge Company of Darlington.[3] A contract was duly signed on 14 February 1902 between the F&RR&H and Messrs Brand & Son for

the works in connection with the extension of the pier at Rosslare at the tendered amount. The new works were described as being the extension of the existing pier in a northwest direction for a length of 965ft and a width of 110ft, and an extension landward of the southeast end of the existing pier for about 95ft in length and 58ft wide. On the sea and harbour sides, and at the end of each extension, the space between the walls was to be filled in with rubble hearting. At the point where the old and new sections met, the former was to be taken down and stepped back so that a new connection might be made in mass concrete. The walls were to be placed on a level bed excavated to the depths shown on the drawings, the excavated material not to be used as filling between the new pier walls, but to be deposited at sea. Permission was granted for the Contractor to fill in hollows in the sea bed by means of concrete in the proportion of six to one and laid in bags about the size of ordinary cement bags, three-quarters filled.

A cattle creep was to be constructed from near the southern end of the back extension along the existing pier, part of which was to be raised, and under the goods platform. Portion of the creep was to be covered with 5in Baltic redwood planks as per drawings, the planks to be securely spiked with 8in galvanised iron spikes to pitch pine longitudinals, which in turn were to be laid in the concrete side walls. The floor

3 The Cleveland Bridge Company built many notable bridges, including the Sydney Harbour Bridge, the Zambezi Bridge and, in more recent times, the Forth and Severn road bridges. They also supplied the lifting bridges for the Cork City Railways.

Group of Rosslare pier extension divers photographed in 1904. (*J Moloney Collection*)

of the cattle creep was to have V-shaped grooves 9in apart so as to prevent animals slipping.

In regard to the concrete blocks, these were to be made in the 'Block Ground' located on the east side of the approach viaduct to the existing pier. The blocks themselves were to be made in strong wooden boxes, with the inside face of the timber planed so as to provide a smooth surface on the blocks. Any block which twisted, even to the slightest extent, was to be rejected, removed and broken up. Casings could be removed after 36 hours, subject to the approval of the Resident Engineer. Blocks were only to be used after lying for a month to cure, the date of completion to be legibly marked on each block. The contractors were to be allowed to move the blocks along the existing line of rails to where they were to be laid, subject to the contractor satisfying himself that the existing viaduct was strong enough to support their weight. Finally, the contractor was to provide and keep in proper repair, a diving dress and apparatus for the use of the Company's Resident Engineer, with proper boat and suitable attendance. In this context Otway had written to the F&RR&H in the previous June stating that the underwater inspections should, as far as possible, be undertaken by AD Delap[4] and recommending that an additional

allowance be made to him for that work; this was approved, Delap's salary to be increased accordingly from £250 to £300 per annum. It was stipulated in the contract that the works were to be completed on or before 1 November 1904 under a penalty of £100 sterling per week.

Mr Whitelaw wrote to the GS&WR in November 1901 asking if Messrs Brand might be let off port dues at Rosslare Pier; this was agreed to, provided that they agreed to handle all their own materials and bore the risk involved. A further letter early in January of the following year approved of the appointment of Messrs Delap and Griffiths as Resident Engineers at Rosslare Harbour.

A letter was received in June 1903 from Messrs Charles Brand & Company suggesting that, since they were already engaged in the substructure works for the new viaduct, they be allowed to quote for the supply and erection of the superstructure. Albert Gordon, Kennett Bayley's successor as Chief Engineer of the GS&WR, who acted as Consulting Engineer to Otway on the Rosslare Harbour Works

---

4 Arthur Dover Delap (1871–1943), the third son of Canon Alexander Delap, was educated at Trinity College Dublin and then served as assistant for two years to SG Fraser before spending some time in the USA. On his return to Ireland, Delap joined the GS&WR and was appointed Engineer-in-charge of the construction works at Rosslare

Harbour. In 1911 he went into partnership with James Waller to found the consultancy firm of Delap & Waller, still in business today with offices in Ireland, the UK and Romania. In a tribute published in the *Irish Builder*, a friend described Delap as a man of "rare intellectual honesty, high moral courage, and exceptionally broad sympathies."

from October 1901, was authorised to obtain an offer from the contractors, although it was to be referred to the Directors before any further action was taken; this tender, in an amount of £22,693 10s 0d, was put to the Board on 5 November 1903 and was approved. At the same meeting it was stated that the arbitrator had ordered that an approach road to the beach be constructed with a level crossing over the railway; Gordon expressed his reservations in view of the difficult nature of the cliff face and the slippery clay, it being suggested that a bridge be substituted for the crossing.

By the following June the east wall had been extended beyond the second bend and up to the level where the parapet wall was to be erected; likewise the west wall had progressed about 188ft beyond the bend. Up to that time, 2,540 blocks had been constructed, of which 2,150 had been set in place. Due to bad weather much difficulty had been encountered with the dredger in supplying gravel; the suction dredger suffered a number of breakdowns in the ensuing year due to gravel fouling the blades of the pump. As a result the contractor sought, and received, permission to substitute sand for gravel. By May 1905 all of the piers had been completed to bed-plate level, in addition to which eight of the main girders were in position on their piers. At about that time plans were prepared showing the proposed position and accommodation of the houses for staff; also Messrs Stothert & Pitt wrote offering to supply electric cranes for Rosslare.

March 1906 saw the completion of all concrete work on the east and west walls, all steelwork for the new viaduct, the completion of the cattle creep and work well advanced on the passenger footway. The old viaduct had by then been removed and the old piers taken down to water level. Arrangements were to be made for the erection of an engine shed, retort house and power house, a contract for these being made with George Nolan in an amount of £2,472. The firm of Messrs Morton of Liverpool was engaged to erect a roof over the passenger station. All of these works were completed in time for the opening of the new facilities in August 1906.

Waterford to Rosslare

As far as the Rosslare & Waterford line was concerned, the Company's Act of 1898 authorised no less than seven railways, of which Railway No 14 was independent of the remainder. It was to be a short line, 2f 3c in length, commencing by a junction with the WD&LR at Grace Dieu, crossing the River Suir by an opening bridge and terminating by a junction with the Limerick to Waterford line of the WL&WR in the townland of Newrath. The bridge was to be located just to the west of that authorised by the

Valentine series postcard of Rosslare Harbour in 1904. The Pier Signal Cabin can be seen as well as the lighthouse at the outer end. *(Philip Quigley Postcard Collection)*

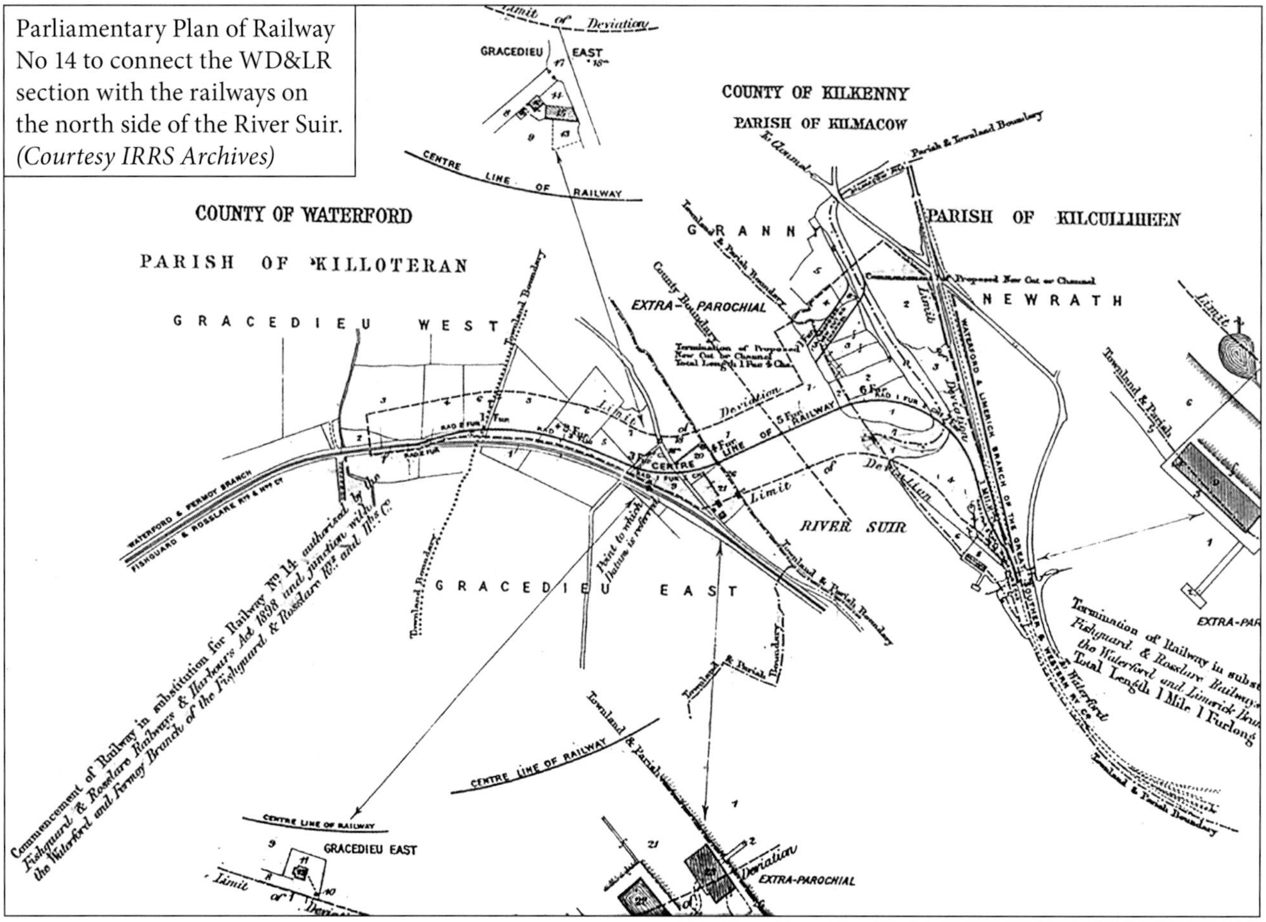

Parliamentary Plan of Railway No 14 to connect the WD&LR section with the railways on the north side of the River Suir. *(Courtesy IRRS Archives)*

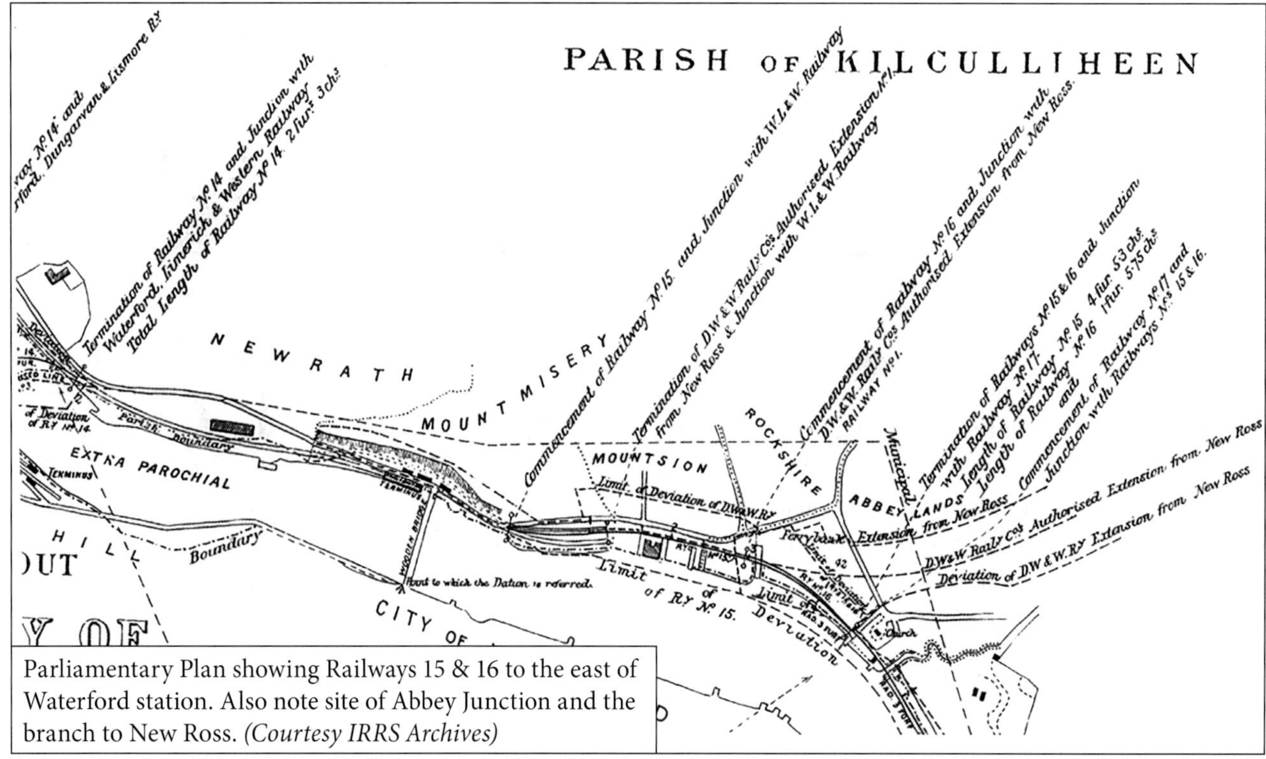

Parliamentary Plan showing Railways 15 & 16 to the east of Waterford station. Also note site of Abbey Junction and the branch to New Ross. *(Courtesy IRRS Archives)*

DW&WR Act of 1897. Section 10 of the 1898 Act, in acknowledging that powers had been granted for two adjacent bridges, made provisions for the F&RR&H bridge to be made so as to accommodate a double line of rails and for the Wicklow Company to be given the option of becoming joint owners, paying one-third of the cost of construction. The DW&WR were then to have equal rights in working over the bridge. Running powers were to be exercised from the junction with the WL&WR through that Company's station. Railways 15 & 16, as authorised under the F&RR&H Act of 1898, were to basically occupy the same narrow strip of land alongside the River Suir at the east end of Waterford Station from the toll bridge to Abbeylands.

A portion of the line between Waterford goods yard and Abbey Junction was to be the joint property of the F&RR&H and the DW&WR. We shall shortly take a closer look at this section of line as it was to be the cause of some dispute at a later date. Meanwhile, the DW&WR entered into two contracts on 21 June 1899 with Messrs S Pearson & Son of 10 Victoria Street, Westminster. Contract 'A', in an amount of £92,565, was in respect of a line about 13½ miles long from Rosbercon (New Ross) "to a point 35 feet beyond peg 713 in the townland of Abbeylands." Contract 'B' in an amount of £4,935 was in respect of a line 3f 95y in length from the termination of the line referred to in Contract 'A' to a junction with the WL&WR in the townland of Mountmisery. Railway No 17 was to commence at the termination of Railways 15 and 16 at Abbeylands (almost directly behind Abbey Church) and run for a distance of 7m 3f 1c and to terminate some 227 yards east of the northeast corner of Dunbrody Abbey and 220 yards south of the centre of the public road bridge over the Canpile River. In the meantime, the Engineers reported at the board meeting on 27 October 1899 regarding progress with the preparation of the plans for the construction of the line to Waterford, it being agreed that tenders be invited for the construction of about 29 miles of line from Rosslare to a point near the Wexford end of the bridge over the River Barrow (Railways 18, 19 & 20). On 9 February it was announced that five tenders had been received from the following parties:

Messrs Fisher & Le Fanu	Kilkeel, Co Down	£162,753 10s 10d
Charles Brand & Company	172 Buchanan Street, Glasgow	£229,463 0s 5d
J Strachan	50 Charles Street, Cardiff	£152,500 0s 0d
S Pearson & Son	10 Victoria Street, London SW	£185,661 0s 0d
R McAlpine & Sons	188 St Vincent Street, Glasgow	£144,423 9s 5d

It was decided to accept Messrs McAlpine's tender, the line to be completed on or before 1 July 1903. Sir Benjamin Baker reported that he had had discussions with the contractors regarding some additional works, which would have the effect of increasing the contract figure by about £2,000; it was also decided to set security at £6,000 and it was ordered that a contract deed be prepared. The contract for Railways 18, 19 and 20 was in fact signed on 26 May 1900 in a revised figure of £150,308 12s 1d. The contract included the laying of permanent way, platforms, cattle banks, fencing and gates for six stations at Campile,[5] Ballycullane, Wellington Bridge, Duncormick, Bridgetown and Killinick, the latter situated at the junction of Railways 18, 19 and 20.

The GS&WR representatives notified the board meeting on 18 May of the appointment of James Otway to succeed Kennett Bayley. The F&RR&H Board agreed that he should act in conjunction with Sir Benjamin Baker and James Inglis in the construction of the R&WR and the harbour works at Rosslare. A little over a month later, Sir Benjamin Baker informed the Board that work had been commenced on 19 June at Wellington Bridge, at which time the Company was in possession of four miles of land along the railway. Sir Benjamin suggested that Messrs McAlpine should be allowed to complete the line from the commencement of Railway No 17 into Waterford on the same schedule of prices as the existing contract, other than the deep cutting to the

---

5 Spelt as Canpile in the Contract and also on the Parliamentary Plans. The modern OS map shows Ceann Poill as the Irish spelling for both the village and the river; Billy Colfer defines it as Cam=winding and Poll= a small tidal estuary.

east of the Barrow Bridge and Snow Hill tunnel. He also suggested to the Board that the time had come to make contact with the DW&WR regarding the joint line at Waterford. Having considered the matter, both suggestions were approved. A formal agreement was signed with Messrs McAlpine on 20 November 1900 for the completion of the line into Waterford on or before 1 July 1903.

Reference has been made to the question of the joint lines at Waterford and we must now take a closer look at the short section of line between Waterford Station and Abbey Junction. The F&RR&H had written to the DW&WR in July 1900 enquiring if that Company wished to exercise their option under Section 12 (2) of the Fishguard Act to become joint owners of the section of line from the point of junction at Abbeylands (Abbey Junction) to the connection with the goods extension of the GS&WR (ex WL&WR). The DW&WR Board decided to defer consideration of the matter, instead writing to protest at any likely delay in arranging a meeting of the companies' Engineers to discuss plans for the joint line. Later in the same month it was reported that Sir Benjamin Baker had recommended that the F&RR&H should exercise their powers under the 1898 Act and themselves construct the railway. To give effect to this a meeting was held on 19 July in Sir Benjamin's offices between representatives of the two companies.

The DW&WR representatives present confirmed that the Company already held a contract with Messrs Pearson for the construction of works at Waterford (Contract 'B') and they had negotiated the option of accepting or declining this prior to 1 September. As the prices in that contract were quite likely to be lower than would now pertain, it was argued in the joint interest of both companies, that a decision should be arrived at allowing that contract to stand. The upshot of the meeting was that SJ Shannon, the DW&WR Engineer, was requested to send copies of the relevant plans and contract to his opposite number, James Otway. Pending a decision on the matter, the DW&WR negotiated an extension to January 1901 on their option to accept or decline the contract.

The F&RR&H wrote again in September, calling on the DW&WR to remove a fence which had been erected in Hurley's field at Ferrybank, which was allegedly encroaching on land authorised by the F&RR&H Act of 1898; the DW&WR agreed that the fence should be removed, again requesting a meeting between the officers of the two companies to agree on the position of the joint lines. Such a meeting eventually took place towards the end of November 1900. It was also about this time that Alexander Gordon suggested to the GS&WR Board that they should consider the question of how traffic at Waterford Station might be worked when the two new lines were opened. This was to lead to the drawing up of plans and the obtaining of an Act in 1903 providing powers for the construction of a new station.

In January 1901, Sir Benjamin Baker recommended that the contract for the additional track of the joint lines at Waterford should be given to Messrs S Pearson & Son at cost price, as determined by the Engineers, with 10% profit, this recommendation being accepted. The plan showing the proposed junction was submitted to the GS&WR Board on 7 March 1902, approved and ordered to be sent to the F&RR&H; it was approved by the latter Company's Board on 11 March and in turn passed to the GWR for final approval. The contract was in fact signed on 10 March 1902, with the work to be completed not later than 1 January of the following year. Far from completing the work by January 1903, Messrs Pearson complained in November of that year that they were still awaiting plans of the junction with the GS&WR although they had requested this in writing on no less than six occasions during the year; these were finally provided in December. In due course the DW&WR were informed that the joint lines were complete; they advised, however, that as Their Majesties the King and Queen were scheduled to visit Waterford on 2 May 1904, they would prefer a BoT inspection to be carried out early enough to enable their New Ross to Waterford extension to be opened some days prior to that date. Colonel von Donop duly carried out his inspection on 25 April and passenger services commenced two days later.

Another problem came to light in December 1900. The F&RR&H notified the DW&WR that it had been discovered that it would not be possible to lay out the line in accordance with the plan signed by

King Edward VII arrives at Waterford North station in 1904. He later travelled over the WD&LR as far as Lismore to stay with the Duke of Devonshire. *(Photographer unknown)*

Lord Camperdown and at the same time to permit of the centre line being set out at the distance from the Waterford Gas Company's gas holder tank as required in both companies' Acts. It was decided to approach the latter body and see if they would permit the distance being reduced to 30 or 35 feet. The gas company's works were located close to the proposed junction of the two lines at Abbeylands. Under Section 31 (1) of the DW&WR Act and Section 8 (1) of the F&RR&H Act the companies were required to maintain a distance of at least 50ft between the nearest rail and the edge of the gas holder tank. Following correspondence with the Gas Company, an agreement was reached reducing the clearance to 35ft, subject to a sum of £1,000 being lodged with the Gas Company, to be returned at the end of ten years provided no injury was caused to the tank.

The plans for the connection with the North Wharf were, in accordance with Section 14 (1) of the 1898 Act, referred to the Borough Surveyor, who expressed himself satisfied with them, but when they were referred on to the Waterford Corporation, the latter body decided not to approve them. The matter was then referred to the BoT to arbitrate, as provided for in the Company's Act, Maj Gen Hutchinson being duly appointed. Hutchinson met the parties involved at the Town Hall in Waterford on Friday 20 June, deciding that the works should be carried out more or less in accordance with the Company's plans. The only requirements were that the width of Salvation Lane should be increased from 20 to 28ft, and that a footbridge should be provided over the line.

The F&RR&H wrote to the DW&WR in November 1902 undertaking to have the joint lines ready for traffic by the time the latter Company's Waterford extension was completed, and also consenting to the DW&WR acquiring the 'yellow land' provided that Company agreed to proposed alterations regarding the site and construction of the Suir viaduct; the DW&WR agreed to these suggestions. The 'yellow land' was one of three parcels of land shown on Lord Camperdown's plan mentioned previously and referred to in Section 12 of the 1898 Act. In due course, the F&RR&H in fact purchased virtually all of this yellow land except for a narrow strip about 20 feet wide next to the river. The strip in question was at the time in the possession of Messrs AE Graves and WGD Goff. Graves proposed the construction of a wharf on his (western) portion for the discharge of timber from vessels; he confirmed that he was prepared to lay a siding on the wharf, giving the DW&WR free use of it. The DW&WR decided to maintain their option on this strip of land until they saw how the GS&WR were prepared to treat them as regards station accommodation. This land, along with other land, which the Company held on the north side of their line, might have proved extremely useful for providing goods and wharf accommodation. In due course the DW&WR decided not to exercise their option.

It was not until June 1906, with the F&RR&H almost ready to open their new South Wexford line, that the question of where the point of junction between the joint lines and the GS&WR was to be delineated was finally discussed in any detail. A memorandum dated 7 June 1906 from MF Keogh, the DW&WR Secretary, to his General Manager, AG Reid, attempts to set out the situation as the DW&WR saw it. Keogh stated that the original point of junction defined in Section 6 of the Company's Act of 1897 was with the goods extension lines of the then WL&WR at Salvation Lane. Section 30 (2) of the same Act stated that the junction should be at a point 30 feet or thereabouts south of the face of the eastern end of the WL&WR goods platform, going on to state that "additional rails between such junction and the rails of the Limerick Company at a convenient place shall be laid down." Keogh then goes on to point out that the "convenient place" selected by James Tighe, the WL&WR Engineer, was near the overbridge carrying the Waterford to New Ross road over the railway.

The DW&WR had contended that the effect of Section 30 (2) was not to shift the point of junction up to that place, but to practically retain it at Salvation Lane, but imposing on the DW&WR the obligation to lay rails through the WL&WR yard, which would become the latter Company's property. When the F&RR&H lodged their plans in the following year, Section 7 of their 1898 Act referred to Railway No 15 commencing (at its western end) at a point immediately under the easternmost face of the bridge carrying the mail-coach road from Waterford to New Ross at a point 202 yards east of the easternmost corner of the toll bridge house. On the other hand, Section 9 (1) showed the junction of Railway No 15 with the WL&WR as being at a point on the west side of Salvation Lane, not less than 25 feet south of the eastern end of the goods loading platform, more or less conforming with the location in the DW&WR Act.

There is yet a further complication in that Section 12 (1) of the 1898 Act provides for the construction of the joint lines in accordance with Plan 'A' signed by the Earl of Camperdown. This plan had a note appended, which is here quoted in full, viz:

"The Joint Line from point near Salvation Lane to be carried on through the Waterford Limerick & Western Railway Yard and premises either by a single line or double line as may be arranged up to a junction to be formed with the WL&W Railway at or near the Overbridge approach carrying the Dock Road (The Waterford to New Ross road) over the Railway and to be used jointly by the two Companies, viz the Dublin Wicklow and Wexford Railway Company and the Fishguard and Rosslare Railways and Harbours Company."

The note, if binding, would have tended to confirm the DW&WR Company's views on the matter, but the likelihood was that it would be argued that it could not over-ride the provisions of the two Acts. The plan in question did not in fact show any connections between Salvation Lane and the rails of the GS&WR near the overbridge.

Both the GS&WR and the F&RR&H, as expected, strongly contended that the point of junction was at Salvation Lane and that the note referred to could not over-ride the definite sections of the two Acts, even though, as pointed out by the DW&WR, a plan dated 1903 emanating from Mr Gordon's office showed a continuation of the joint lines up to the overbridge. The DW&WR offered to withdraw their objections in exchange for a payment equivalent to the sum, which they would have had to pay in respect of the construction and working of a connection to Messrs Hall's milling premises adjoining the joint line; this suggestion was rejected outright. The GS&WR objected to the idea of another company having ownership of lines through a large yard, and foresaw difficulties in identifying the limits of the joint ownership and in determining the joint expense of maintenance. These objections were perhaps well founded when the Company concerned was the DW&WR, who tended to raise objections in an attempt to limit their financial exposure.

While these machinations were going on in relation to the joint lines, there had been developments in other directions. Sir Benjamin Baker reported in March 1902 that some 204,000 cubic yards of excavations and 10,900 cubic yards of concrete for use in bridges had been completed; three steam navvies, three locomotives and about 600 men were reported to be at work. By June of the following year there were almost 1,000 men at work, with five steam navvies and ten locomotives in use. The joint lines, on which work had been started on 13 October 1902, were making good progress and were in fact completed by November 1903. It was hoped by year's end to have about 20 miles formed and ready for ballasting. It was agreed that the

GS&WR would supply the necessary permanent way for laying. It was also reported in June that Wexford County Council had instituted proceedings against the Company for neglecting to repair the public roads that had been cut up by the contractors. In due course Wexford magistrates made an order for the repair of the roads within three months, the contractors agreeing to complete this work.

Albert Gordon submitted plans to the GS&WR Board on 17 April 1903 for the intermediate stations on the Rosslare & Waterford (R&WR) line, which had been prepared by the GS&WR Architect, JC Dewhurst. These were approved in principle, but the question of the buildings was to be carefully considered before a final decision was made. This led to a report to the Board on 7 August from Charles H Dent recommending some reductions in the cost of the stations, this being approved and referred to the F&RR&H for a final decision. Amended plans were submitted in November. These provided that the whole of the contemplated works were not initially to be carried out, the platforms being made shorter, approach roads narrower and the centre siding loops omitted. They were, however, arranged such that the original plans might be carried out at any future time; the saving to be effected by the amended plans,

which were approved, was estimated at £3,220. A memorandum was received on 31 March 1904 from the inhabitants of Great Island and Cheek Point asking that a station be erected at the east end of the new Barrow Bridge, this request being declined. As recorded later, a halt was subsequently opened at this location in 1966 in connection with the construction of an electric power station at Great Island. Final working plans for the intermediate stations were approved in October 1904.

June 1904 saw the tunnel at Snow Hill driven through with the side walls lined. A total of 8 miles of permanent way had been laid, 3 miles of these west of the Barrow Bridge, and 5 eastwards from the deep cutting at Great Island. The total of permanent way laid down had increased to 17 miles by November 1904, at which time plans for the junctions of Railways 19 and 20 with the existing W&WR had been approved. It was ordered that tenders be obtained from four or five contractors for the construction of intermediate station buildings as well as signal cabins, the latter to the GS&WR Company's standard plans. It was further agreed that the latter Company should be responsible for providing the signalling installations for the new line.

The GS&WR Board considered four tenders for the construction of the station buildings and goods stores at their meeting on 24 March 1905, that of Messrs A & J Main in an amount of £5,380 being accepted. The previous month, they had accepted Mr George Nolan's tender for £1,399 for the erection of the necessary signal cabins; Gordon enclosed plans in May showing the position of the proposed signal cabins on the platforms at the various stations. The Commissioners of Irish Lights wrote to the GS&WR in December 1905 sanctioning a 4,500 candle-power

Reconstruction works at Waterford in connection with the F&RR&H extension c1904. *(Photographer unknown, IRRS Collection)*

lighthouse at the end of Rosslare Pier, to be positioned 35 feet above high water. In addition they approved of one whistling and three gas lit buoys, the former in the fairway, the latter to mark Splaugh Rock, South Long Bank and Calamieres Rock. Mr Gordon was ordered to obtain tenders for the pier-head light. In due course an order was placed with WT Douglas of Victoria Street, Westminster, who undertook to have the work completed in the following June.

The BoT received a letter dated 30 April 1906 from the F&RR&H proposing the immediate opening of the new line between Waterford and Wexford for goods traffic and requesting an early inspection of the new junction at Felthouse, where it joined up with the W&WR, already open for passenger traffic. From the tracing supplied, the BoT sought the early provision of trap points on both the up and down lines at the junction. Colonel von Donop was appointed to inspect the new works, which he duly carried out on 17 May. He confirmed that the points and signals were to be worked from a new signal cabin with a 26-lever frame, of which 12 were spare. As the interlocking and all other arrangements were deemed to be in order, BoT sanction was given for the new works to be brought into use.

With the works on both sides of the Irish Sea approaching completion, a meeting was arranged at Paddington towards the end of May to discuss arrangements in connection with the opening of the

new route; the GS&WR attendance included Messrs EA Neale and JH Bell. Mr Morris, for the GWR, said that, according to the information then available, it was unlikely that everything would be in place by the proposed opening date of 1 August; Neale, however, thought that the works on the Irish side would be ready. The times of the connecting rail services in Ireland and England had already been circulated and, with minor exceptions, had been agreed. It was agreed that conditional stops would be allowed at intermediate stations between Rosslare and Waterford, as there was sufficient slack in the proposed schedules to allow this.

A lengthy discussion took place regarding the provision of goods services, the GWR stating that it was proposed to start the cargo boat from Fishguard at 20.35, but this appeared to be too late for the GS&WR as it would not fit in with their existing services. Neale stated that he could not agree to the running of additional trains and could only improve the service by tweaking of the existing service. The GWR urged the necessity of introducing a convenient and reasonable service, even if this involved additional mileage on the part of the GS&WR. With a view to meeting the GS&WR, it was agreed to depart Fishguard at 14.00 and arrive at Rosslare at 19.00 (18.35 Irish Time), which would enable a train to leave Rosslare at 21.00, arriving Waterford at 22.30. From the latter point, trains were to run over the ex-WL&W line to Limerick, Tralee and Sligo, over the ex-WD&L to Mallow and Cork, and via Kilkenny to Dublin. In the opposite direction some difficulties were encountered as the GS&WR complained that the proposed departure of the steamer from Rosslare at 06.30 was too early, Neale suggesting a departure at 10.00. At a subsequent meeting on 30 May, Neale handed in details of what he claimed was the best he could arrange, viz a train leaving Waterford at 06.00 and arriving at Rosslare at 07.30; reluctantly, Neale agreed to a vessel departing at 09.30.

The GWR advised that they intended to operate a passenger, cargo and cattle service between Fishguard and Waterford, calling at Rosslare only on the eastbound journey as per the undernoted timetable. This latter stop was intended to accommodate the export of cattle, traffic which it was anticipated would go via Rosslare. It is not known whether the Rosslare stopover ever operated, but if it did it must have been short-lived.

Waterford	Dep 17.00	Fishguard	Dep 23.45
Rosslare	Arr 21.00	Waterford	Arr 07.35 (Irish Time)[6]
Rosslare	Dep 23.30		
Fishguard	Arr 04.00		

The GS&WR informed the meeting that trains in connection with the boat services would be made up of first and third class only between Rosslare and Waterford, with the provision of luncheon and dining cars. The GWR had written to the GS&WR in January 1906 reporting that they were willing to restrict bookings on the F&RR&H route to first and third classes if the GS&WR were prepared to do the same, this being accepted. Neale stated that the Company were about to construct some 12-wheeled bogie carriages 67ft long, but that there might not be sufficient available to form all the trains on the route; the boat trains would, however, be formed of the best stock available. In response to a query, Neale undertook to consider whether the Company would provide travelling conductors on the Cork to Rosslare boat trains; it was reported that travelling ticket checkers would operate between Paddington and Fishguard. Neale also confirmed the GS&WR intention to close Waterford South Station once the new service was inaugurated. The GWR suggested that a couple of cargoes should be diverted to Fishguard from New Milford in advance of the opening to test the new facilities. This was considered unnecessary by the GS&WR, as was a suggested trial passenger trip.

Considerable time was given to a discussion of the proposed fares on the new route, the GWR proposing single fares between Paddington and both Rosslare and Waterford of 50s first and 22s third class, with respective return fares of 82s and 36s. Mr Neale objected, claiming that the Rosslare figures should not be more than the Waterford direct fare, considering the journey was shorter by 52 miles. This was countered by Mr Morris who stated that the current Waterford fares were too low. The GWR also contended that fares to intermediate stations should be the same as to Waterford, a suggestion which the GS&WR considered to be unreasonable. Fares to other destinations such as Limerick and particularly Dublin had to be considered in the light of those charged via the L&NWR and Holyhead. Finally, it was agreed to charge 10s saloon and 7s steerage between Fishguard and Rosslare, with return fares set at 15s and 10s; third class train passengers wishing to transfer to saloon on the boat were to pay a supplement of 3s single and 4s 6d return, the same as via Holyhead.

At a further meeting held at Paddington on 15 and 16 May, and attended only by GWR officials, some consideration was given to staffing and other requirements at New Milford and Fishguard. It was believed that a total of 130 men would be required at Fishguard, including 55 porters and either 24 or 30 coaling men. It was considered that certain of the goods and passenger trains would require banking assistance as far as Manorowen. In order to avoid the necessity of stopping passenger trains at the latter point, it was decided that the banker should be placed behind and coupled to the train by a loose coupling. The Locomotive Department were requested to report

6 At the time of the opening, Irish Time was 25 minutes earlier than in London, a situation which remained until the outbreak of War in 1914.

back with their recommendations for putting this into operation and also as to whether the shunting engines proposed to be employed at Fishguard would be sufficiently powerful for the task. Some consideration was also given to the employment of signalmen, it being agreed that three would be needed at Fishguard, and two each at Manorowen, Letterston Junction and Wolf's Castle, with an additional two at Spittal on a temporary basis until the line was doubled.

The coaling of vessels at Fishguard as compared with New Milford was considered to be a totally different operation. For a start only 48 tons of coal was required daily at the latter port, whereas the figure for Fishguard was calculated at 220 tons. The Traffic Department took responsibility for this task at New Milford, but it was felt that the magnitude of the work at the new port would require the undivided services of a large gang of men, hence the need for up to 30 coaling men referred to above; it was considered that they should be put under the charge of the Locomotive Department.

The F&RR&H wrote to the BoT on 5 July 1906 enclosing a signalling plan for Rosslare Pier passenger station and Ballygeary (Locomotive depot) Junction, the relevant inspection being carried out exactly a week later. Colonel PG von Donop confirmed that the pier at Rosslare had been lengthened by about 350 yards and a new station had been constructed, consisting of a platform 550ft long and of ample height and width. The station was provided with adequate shelter, and it was reported that all necessary accommodation for passengers was being provided; however, on account of special arrangements, which had been made for the opening of the line by the Lord Lieutenant, the accommodation had not been completed. Points and signals were worked from a new 24-lever signal cabin, 4 of which were spare. At Ballygeary Junction two new connections, facing to down trains, had been added on the single passenger line. Here a new signal cabin had also been provided, this one containing 16 levers, 4 of which were spare. Interlocking at both cabins was correct and, subject to Nos 15 & 16 trap points being brought nearer to the passenger line, Colonel von Donop confirmed that the line could be opened for passenger traffic.

The BoT inspections of the principal works associated with the South Wexford line were carried out during the month of July, the entire line from Waterford to Rosslare Junction being inspected by Colonel von Donop on 13 July. He confirmed that the line was single throughout, except at the double line junctions and at each of the intermediate stations where passing loops were provided. Steel rails, 45ft long and weighing 87lb per yard, were secured in 50lb cast-iron chairs to standard-sized Baltic timber sleepers, with broken stone ballast 12in deep below the sleepers. Traffic was to be worked by the electric tablet system. The ruling gradient was 1 in 71 for 128 chains and the sharpest curve on the running lines was of 21 chains radius. The deepest cutting, at Great Island, was 81ft deep and the highest embankment 30ft high. In total there were 62 underbridges, 42 of which were of steel troughing and varying from 8 to 20ft in span; there were 11 steel-girder bridges on concrete abutments with spans of between 20 and 58ft and 9 consisting of brick arches. There were in addition 21 overbridges and 2 viaducts. Taylorstown viaduct consisted of seven circular brick arches, each of 44ft span, while there was one tunnel at Snow Hill, 197 yards long, lined with a brick arch. There were no less than 98 level crossings on the line, 11 of which crossed public roads.

Stations were located at Campile, Ballycullane, Wellington Bridge, Duncormick, Bridgetown, Killinick Junction and Rosslare Junction (otherwise known as Rosslare Strand); all stations had signal cabins, the interlocking of which were correct. At all the stations loops were provided, there being a running line on each side of the island platform; siding accommodation was also provided. At Rosslare Junction, which was an existing station on the W&WR line, a loop was provided on the up side with an additional platform 270ft in length.

Colonel von Donop specified a number of requirements as follows:

[1] the gates at all accommodation level crossings to have a permanent arrangement to prevent them opening inwards

[2] targets and lamps to be provided on all public road level crossing gates

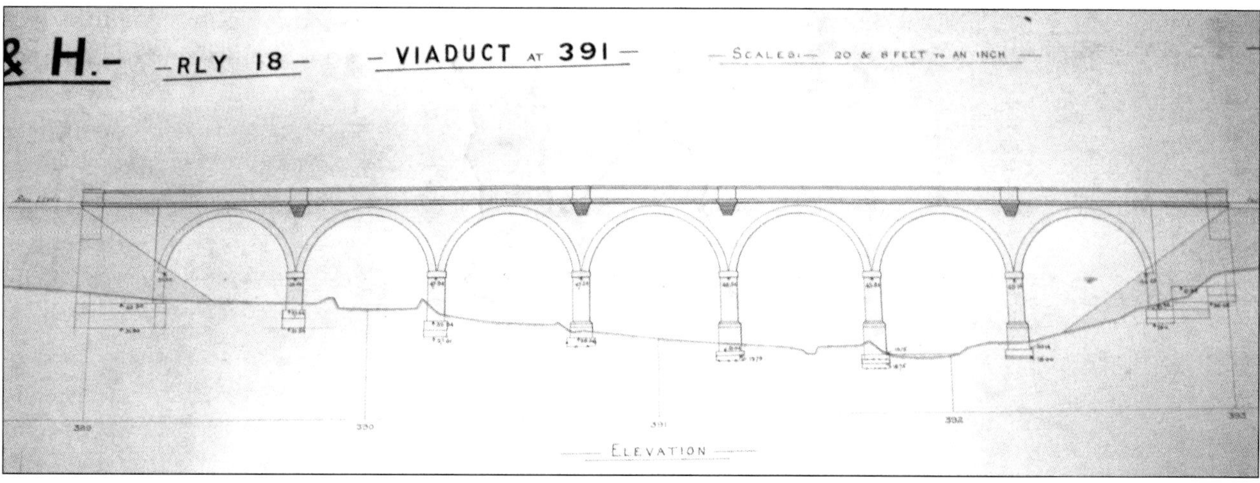

A F&RR&H elevation drawing of Taylorstown viaduct. *(Irish Rail)*

[3] at an overbridge at 29m 78c, additional clearance was to be provided between the abutment on the down side and the rails

[4] at Bridgetown Station a tree was required to be trimmed back to allow better sighting of No 17 signal

[5] at all stations, lamps with station names were to be provided on the platforms as well as requisite furniture provided in waiting rooms

[6] on account of the exposed location of the Barrow Viaduct, wind screens were to be provided on each side of the viaduct, extending to a height of 4ft above rail level

[7] the electrical interlocking at the Barrow Viaduct to be completed

[8] all points to be properly connected up

At all island platforms the only means of approach for passengers to the platforms was by means of a level crossing across one of the running lines at one end of each station. As the Cork Express was timed to run through these stations without stopping, this arrangement was deemed unacceptable and the early provision of footbridges was made a further requirement. The Company gave an undertaking to the BoT that until the footbridges were completed a man would be stationed at the crossings whenever a train was running past them. Tenders had already been obtained in December 1905 for footbridges at Ferryslip (Salvation Lane), Wellington Bridge and Bridgetown, that of Messrs Manisty of Dundalk being

accepted at £708. At the F&RR&H board meeting on 1 November 1906 it was reported that the GS&WR had accepted the tender of Messrs Manisty at £1,410 for the erection of six footbridges, the foundations to be provided by the Company at an additional £25 each. It was not until June 1907 that the Company was able to confirm to the BoT that the footbridges had all been completed.

A second notice in respect of Railway No 14, the short line connecting the WD&LR system to the WL&WR section via the Suir Viaduct, was given to the BoT on 21 July 1906, but only ten days later the Company advised that the works would not be ready in time for the inspection, and it was not until 10 August that an amended notice was issued. Colonel von Donop duly inspected the works at the beginning of October. The line commenced and terminated by double junctions, otherwise it was single and 1m 38.53c in length. The BoT report wrongly states that it terminated at Grace Dieu "by a double junction with the existing line from Waterford South to Mullingar."(sic). The ruling gradient was shown as 1 in 76 and the sharpest curve was 10.6c radius. There were only two requirements, namely that fencing was required at one spot adjacent to an underbridge, and that the points required to be correctly connected up and bars provided at all facing points. When the line at Rosslare was re-inspected early in March of the following year, it was confirmed that all facilities had been provided for passenger accommodation at the station.

CHAPTER TWELVE

The Barrow and Suir Bridges

The two most important engineering structures on the new line were the bridges across the Barrow and Suir rivers. Indeed, the Barrow Bridge is, at 2,131ft, the longest rail bridge spanning entirely across water in Ireland and, at the time of its completion, ranked as the third longest such structure in Britain and Ireland after the Forth and Tay bridges in Scotland. In this context, therefore, it is worth spending a little time reviewing the factors involved in their design, construction and operation. As already noted, both of these river crossings had been envisaged in plans for the C&F&W&WR scheme of 1890, and they were the subject of some debate during the hearings before the Select Committee of the House of Commons.

The principal objectors to the Barrow Bridge were the New Ross Harbour Commissioners. These objections have already been referred to in Chapter Nine and need not be repeated here. However, in May 1899 a lengthy report from Sir Benjamin Baker and Kennett Bayley, the GS&WR Engineer, was placed before the F&RR&H Board in respect of a possible alternative location for the river crossing. This was in fact towards the northern limit of deviation allowed under the 1898 Act, to the north of a small quay. The major advantage was that the bridge would be altogether on the straight and would cross the river at right angles to both the river itself and the set of the current. Furthermore, for two-thirds of its length it would be in shoal water; this, and the fact that the currents were more predictable than at the original location, would lessen the risk of injury to the bridge from vessels navigating to New Ross although, as we shall see later, collisions were not entirely prevented.

The F&RR&H Act of 1900, which received Royal Assent on 30 July, took account of the report from Baker and Bayley by authorising a deviation of 4 miles 2 furlongs and 7½ chains from Drumdowney to Carrowanree in the parish of Killesk. At the same time

In this excellent view of the Barrow Bridge, an eight-piece 29000 class crosses on Saturday 5 November 2011. The line had been closed to traffic in September 2010. However, due to severe flooding in late October 2011 IE expressed concerns about possible damage to the bridge carrying the Dublin to Rosslare line over the River Dodder at Lansdowne Road, leading to the line's closure between 27 October and 8 November. The closure trapped two railcar sets away from their maintenance depot and two empty stock workings were carried out over the South Wexford line. *(Finbarr O'Neill)*

Portion of Parliamentary Plan for the 1898 Session showing the originally proposed course of the line at Kilmokea. Under this plan the line would have approached the River Barrow rather further south than later constructed. There would have been no tunnel at Snowhill. (*Courtesy IRRS Archives*)

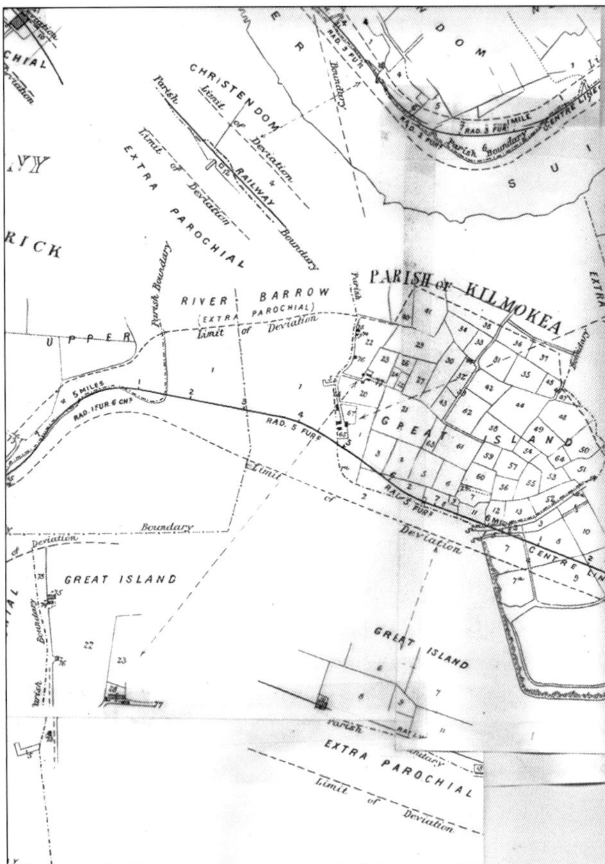

an alteration almost 7 miles in length was authorised further east in Co Wexford. The 1898 Act had proposed that Railway No 17, the line from Waterford towards Wexford, would cross the River Barrow near to Drumdowney Point at the confluence of the Barrow and the Suir rivers.[1] The earlier plans do not show any tunnel at Snow Hill, the line at that point passing much closer to the River Suir, and the Barrow Bridge commencing from the Kilkenny shore somewhat south of its present location. At the Wexford end, the bridge was to curve to the right on a 50 chain radius, passing to the south of a small quay (still there), and running along the southern side of Great Island to cross the Campile River to the south of Dunbrody. The various provisions laid down in Section 15 of the 1898 Act in relation to the Barrow Bridge were reinforced in the 1900 Act. This stipulated that there were to be two opening spans of 80ft clear over the main channel, the headway under the opening spans and under the two adjoining spans to be 25ft clear above high water of ordinary spring tides. It was also stipulated that the piers were, as far as possible, to be set parallel to the course of the current.

The principal objections to the Suir Bridge came from the Waterford Harbour Commissioners and the Waterford Bridge Commissioners (WBC). The bridge, as envisaged in 1890, was to be located about 1,300ft above the then existing wooden toll bridge, and nearly square to the course of the river. In particular, Capt Nicholas Parle, the Waterford Harbour Master, confirmed that there was a large trade above the existing bridge. He maintained that it would not be possible to get a sailing vessel through both bridges on the same tide, thus causing considerable delays. The 1898 plans for the Suir Bridge were submitted to William Friel, who had succeeded Otway as Engineer

to the Waterford Harbour Commissioners. Similar objections to this scheme were put forward, until Counsel for the F&RR&H pointed out that a bridge in an identical position had already been authorised under the DW&WR's Act of 1897. The DW&WR's New Ross & Waterford Extension Act of 1897 had, as referred to in Chapter Nine, authorised a second crossing of the River Suir, by a swing or opening bridge, which was to be immediately adjacent to the F&RR&H bridge.

The foregoing proposal led to a suggestion that some arrangements should be made with the DW&WR for a single bridge with a double line of rails. As we have already noted in Chapter Nine, this suggestion was in fact incorporated in Section 10 of the Fishguard Act. The DW&WR were granted the facility to become joint owners on payment of one-third of the cost of construction, including land; they were also to be responsible for the future maintenance of the bridge in proportion to the traffic carried by the two companies. Friel also objected to the fact that on

---

1 It is of interest to note that all of the railways authorised under the 1898 Act took the same numbers as those incorporated in the C&F&W&WR Act of 1890.

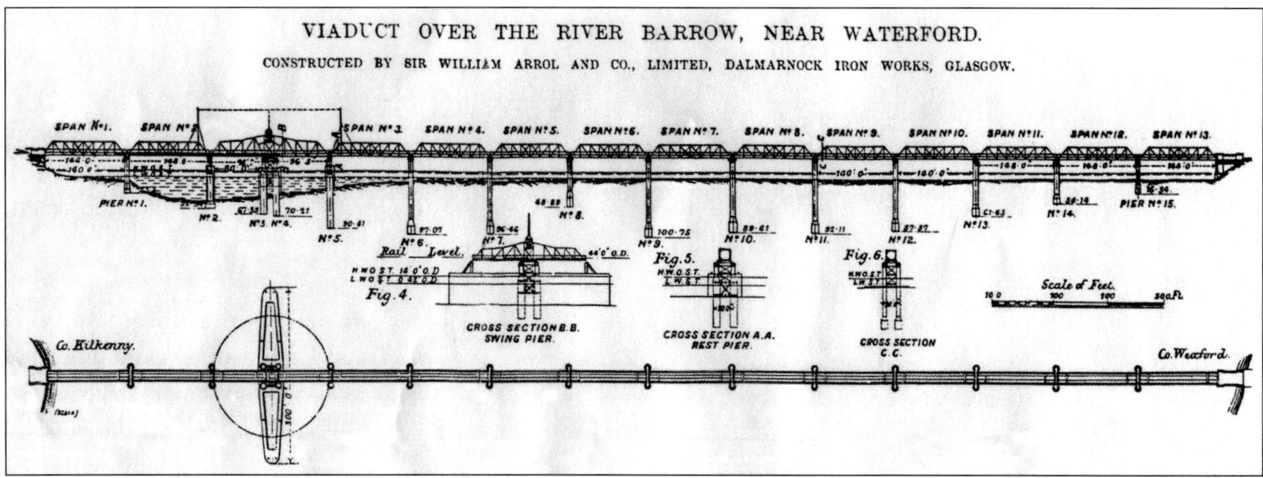

A fine drawing of the Barrow Bridge. The reason for locating the opening span close to the Kilkenny shore of the river was because deepest water was found at this point. *(Courtesy Irish Rail)*

the Kilkenny side of the river the end of the bridge would materially augment the deposit of silt at the upper berths at the railway wharf. He suggested the provision of an additional short span in substitution for the proposed solid work, this being agreed to by the F&RR&H. However, as we shall shortly see, the location of the bridge was again altered, being moved further up river to Granagh (sometimes referred to as Granny) about 1½ miles above the city.

The F&RR&H Act of 1898 authorised a crossing of the River Suir by a line (Railway No 14) 2 furlongs and 3 chains in length. It was to commence by a junction with the existing WD&LR, 300 yards to the east of the first road bridge over the line adjoining the WD&LR station at Waterford and terminate in the townland of Newrath by a junction with the existing line of the WL&WR, at a point 50 yards from the east corner of the junction signal cabin and some 280 yards from the south corner of Newrath House.

Another question raised during the Parliamentary debate was the provision of a footway alongside the railway bridge for the convenience of the public, an issue that had first been raised during the 1890 debate by John Redmond, MP. Section 17 of the 1898 Act required the Company to seek powers in their Bill for the 1899 Session and indeed this matter was specifically referred to in a special report published by the Hybrid Committee in June 1898. Section 53 of the 1899 Act authorised the F&RR&H to affix a footway 6ft in width

to the railway bridge. However, just before the 1899 Act became law on 1 August, it was announced that an arrangement had been made with the Waterford Harbour Commissioners and the Corporation of Waterford under which the Company was relieved of the obligation to provide the footway. Instead, they were to contribute a sum of £5,000 towards any scheme for purchasing and freeing the existing toll bridge; this resulted in the powers being removed under Section 49 of the Company's Act of 1900.

In June 1899 it was decided to employ a contractor to make borings in connection with both bridges to ascertain the nature of the foundations. A letter from the GS&WR in June 1901 in relation to the proposed subscription towards freeing the toll bridge suggested postponement of advertisements seeking tenders for the construction of the Suir Bridge. Sir Benjamin Baker produced detailed plans of the two bridges in October 1901, which he estimated would cost in the region of £230,000, as against the parliamentary estimate of £198,000, the excess being due to the borings having shown the necessity for carrying the piers down much deeper than initially anticipated. With these figures to hand, it was decided to seek tenders for the construction of the Barrow Bridge and leave the Suir Bridge on hold *pro tem*.

It was in March 1902 that consideration was first given to an alternative location farther up river for the Suir Bridge, which might effect a substantial saving, although further borings would then be required. Whilst the Company's officers were of opinion that a single line bridge would be adequate, Sir William Goulding was asked to enquire if the DW&WR would agree to this alteration. It was suggested that they could be persuaded to agree to the proposal if the Fishguard Company agreed to complete the joint line at Waterford to coincide with the completion of the DW&WR's New Ross and Waterford extension to the point of junction at Ferrybank. As a consequence of agreement on these arrangements, it was decided in October to publish notice of the Company's intention to apply for powers in 1903 for a single line bridge with a single opening span farther upstream.

Tenders for the Barrow Bridge were received in December 1901 from ten contractors and that of Sir William Arrol & Company Limited of Glasgow, being the lowest at £109,347, was accepted in March of the following year; on the recommendation of the Engineers it was agreed to dispense with sureties. In March 1903 it had been found necessary to obtain land for a spoil bank on the shore of the river just to the north of the bridge. Following considerable negotiation, arrangements were made and compensation of £50 paid to a Mr James Fleming; an additional £1 was paid to the BoT who gave formal consent for the use of the river bank. Reporting at the end of June on the progress to date, the Engineers stated that the Wexford abutment of the bridge had been erected to bed stone level, while the southern cylinder of No 8 pier had been 'severely tested' to ascertain if the sand in the bed of the river was sufficiently good to build, the result being found satisfactory.

By November 1904 the cylinders for the piers on the east side of the opening span had been sunk to their final depths, some of them reportedly down to 108ft below mean water level; the extra depth required to found the piers on bedrock increased the cost of the works by an estimated £12,000. The only cylinders remaining to be sunk at that stage were those of No 2 pier near the Kilkenny shore. The steel work of the six spans next to the Wexford shore was then practically complete with the erection of the remaining spans in progress.

In the report of his inspection of the line, Colonel von Donop described the Barrow Bridge as being 739 yards in length, this figure being 81ft in excess of the generally accepted figure of 2,131ft or 710 yards; the figure quoted in the contract document with Messrs Arrol Brothers. The 13 fixed spans, constructed in mild steel, are Pratt-type trusses comprising latticed side girders with cross girders to support the railway

Fishguard and Rosslare Railways and Harbours Company.

BARROW VIADUCT.

CERTIFICATE FOR CONTRACT WORK.   No. _25_

_5th_ day of _October_ 1904

THE FISHGUARD & ROSSLARE RAILWAYS & HARBOURS COMPANY,   To SIR WILLIAM ARROL & CO., Dr.

	Now to be Paid.			Previously Paid.			Total to Date.		
GROSS AMOUNTS ... ... £	3,508	18	6	86,209	15	4	89,718	13	10
Less 10 per cent., as per Agreement	350	17	10	8,620	19	6	8,971	17	4
NETT AMOUNTS ... ... £	3,158	0	8	77,588	15	10	80,746	16	6

We hereby certify that the Sum of £ 3,158..0..8 is due to the Contractors on account of the above Contract.

Dated this _5th_ day of _October_ 1904.

B. Baker } Engineers.
James Otway }

RECEIVED from the FISHGUARD AND ROSSLARE RAILWAYS AND HARBOURS COMPANY the Sum of ______ being the Amount, less per-centage reserved in accordance with conditions of Contract, due to us under above Certificate.

Dated this ______ day of ______ 190 ______ Contractors.

Left: Certificate in respect of the 'Barrow Viaduct' dated 5 October 1904. Note signatures of Sir Benjamin Baker and James Otway. _(Author's Collection)_

The Barrow Bridge approaching completion on 27 April 1905, with the opening span, apparently with the skeleton of the signal cabin, in place. *(Royal Commission on the Ancient & Historical Monuments of Scotland, Sir William Arrol Collection)*

track and overhead cross bracing between the main girders. The two end spans adjacent to the opening span are 144ft long, the 11 other fixed spans being 148ft each. Apart from the masonry abutments on each shore, the ends of the spans are supported on piers, each comprising two 8ft diameter, cast iron cylinders, in-filled with concrete and founded on the underlying rock with cross bracing between the cylinders. The clear waterway under the 148ft spans is 140ft, but at the two spans adjacent to the opening span, where dolphins are provided to protect the piers against ship impacts, the clear waterway is reduced to 121ft 6in on the Kilkenny side and 136ft on the midstream side. The opening span is of the usual swing type, 215ft in overall length, the central pivot being supported on a steel deck constructed on the top of four cylinders, which are braced together. It is located at the deep-water point in the river and is therefore much closer to one shore than the other, with only two fixed spans between the Kilkenny shore and the opening span. When the span is swung open for shipping traffic there is 80ft of clear waterway on each side of the central pier.

Special arrangements had to be provided for the control of the bridge to prevent any danger occurring to trains. Saxby and Farmer, Ltd of Kilburn, London, supplied the signalling and interlocking equipment to control the working of the bridge. As Tyer's tablet instruments were used to authorise train movements on the line between Abbey Junction, Waterford, and Rosslare Strand, the signalling arrangements had to ensure that no tablet could be withdrawn if the bridge was open or was being opened and, conversely, the bridge could not be opened if any tablet had been withdrawn from an instrument. In the signal cabin on the bridge a 3-lever locking frame was provided to control home signals in each direction and, owing to the intervention of Snow Hill tunnel, the lever for that from Waterford simultaneously operated an outer home signal. The third lever in the locking frame was the key (or king) lever, which provided an interlock between the bridge controls and the railway signalling. To the right of the signal locking frame six levers were provided for bridge operating purposes, including control of the electrical machinery for rotating the opening span. Levers 1 and 1a operated the bolts that locked the bridge in the closed position; Lever 2 controlled the vertical movement of the opening span, which was necessary to enable withdrawal of the levelling blocks and lowering of the span; Lever 3 was for withdrawing the blocks to allow the ends of the opening span to be lowered clear of the fixed spans; Lever 4 initiated rotation of the opening span; and Lever 5 provided latching of the span in the open position.

Block instruments were provided to control the working of the section to Campile on the east side of the bridge and to Abbey Junction, Waterford, on the west side. Lever C in the locking frame is the king lever, and this was controlled from both Campile and Abbey Junction signal cabins. The starting signals for the direction leading to the bridge at those locations could not be pulled off unless electrically released from the bridge cabin. Similarly, the king lever, which is interlocked with the fixed signals at the bridge, could not be pulled over unless it was electrically released by both Campile and Abbey Junction signal cabins. This back-to-back interlocking ensured that operations were efficiently protected insofar as the fixed signals were concerned. In addition, any move of the king lever, once it was unlocked, would cut off the tablet wire current by the action of an electric circuit breaker, thus ensuring that no tablets could be withdrawn. However, if a tablet had already been withdrawn the king lever was locked and could not be pulled.

When the Signalman at the bridge wished to open the bridge he would pull Lever C (the king lever) halfway over, this action locking his home signals at danger. He could not do so if a train was already in the section between Abbey Junction and Campile, or if a tablet had been withdrawn for one. Having got the lever halfway over he would request both Campile and Abbey Junction for permission to turn the bridge. The granting of this permission locked their starter signals for the direction to the bridge, cut the tablet line, and unlocked Lever C so that it could be pulled fully over. An indicator was provided in the bridge cabin to show when this permission had been received. Levers 1 and 1a, the levers that control the locking bolts, stood normally in the pulled-over position when the bridge was locked for railway traffic. They were interlocked

with Lever C so that, when the latter was pulled fully over, they could be put back to unlock the bridge. Withdrawal of the locking bolts in turn freed Lever 2 (the lifting lever) so that the ends of the opening span could be lifted. An electrical lock on Lever 3 (the blocking lever), operated by the lifting mechanism, ensured that the blocks could not be withdrawn until the ends of the opening span had been fully lifted. The complete withdrawal of the blocks enabled Lever 2 to be reversed and thus lower the bridge clear of the fixed spans. In turn, this action unlocked Lever 4 so that it could be pulled to open the bridge. When

An interesting, if somewhat unusual, view of the central portion of the opening span of the Barrow Bridge. This view clearly shows the teeth associated with the turning mechanism. It also shows the ladder situated on the outside of the span which provided access to the signal cabin located on top of the span. *(Ernie Shepherd)*

Right: The Suir Bridge under construction. *(IRRS Collection)*

the bridge was fully open it was latched in position by Lever 5, which also locked Lever 4, so that closing of the bridge could not commence until it was again unlatched from the open position. To close the bridge the order of the movements was reversed, but the king lever could not be restored to its normal position until electrical contacts proved that the locking bolts worked by Levers 1 and 1a were fully home.

As noted in the previous chapter, the BoT inspection of the principal works associated with the South Wexford line were carried out during the month of July 1906. Arising from his inspection, Colonel von Donop required the electrical interlocking at the Barrow Bridge to be completed and specified that, on account of the exposed location of the bridge, wind screens were to be provided on each side, extending to a height of 4ft above rail level. Messrs Arrol agreed to provide the wind screens at an estimated cost of £912.

Even before parliamentary approval had been given for the single line Suir Bridge, Sir Benjamin Baker was instructed to prepare contract plans for the new bridge and to make contact with the Scherzer Bridge Company of Chicago for details of their rolling lift opening span, which it had been decided to employ in the bridge.[2] Section 4 of the F&RR&H Act of 1903,

which received Royal Assent on 21 July, authorised a railway 1 mile 1 furlong 1½ chains long in substitution for Railway No 14 of the 1898 Act. It was to commence in the townland of Grace Dieu and parish of Killoteran, by a junction with the WD&LR and terminate by a junction with the WL&WR section of the GS&WR in the townland of Newrath. In addition to the new line, the Company were obliged to provide a new cut or channel on the Kilkenny side of the river, along with a wharf or embankment.

In June 1904, Sir Benjamin Baker suggested the desirability of entrusting the entire bridge works and approach railways on both sides of the River Suir to the same contractor as the Barrow Bridge, and he confirmed that Sir William Arrol & Company would be prepared to tender. This they did, offering to undertake the works at £58,408 5s 3d for the bridge and £11,759 for the approach railways; the provision of permanent way and junctions at both ends of the new line bringing the total cost up to about £75,000. Mr Whitelaw confirmed that Messrs Mitchell Brothers of Glasgow had been appointed as sub-contractor for the approach railways.

---

2 The Scherzer rolling lift bascule bridge was a novel concept in movable bridges designed and patented just before his death by William Donald Scherzer (1858–93), an American engineer. The design combines the balanced counterweight of a conventional bascule bridge, with a unique rolling lift motion that all but eliminates friction. The Scherzer Rolling Lift Bridge Company was founded in 1898 by his brother, Albert H Scherzer.

Left and below: Two views from a series of photographs taken during construction of the Suir Bridge. *(Royal Commission on the Ancient & Historical Monuments of Scotland)*

The exact date that work commenced on the Suir viaduct is not known but it must have been about August 1904, as we do know that an order was given in June 1904 for the contract deed to be prepared. Reporting to the F&RR&H Board on 3 November 1904, the Engineers stated that the staging was well advanced and that piers 1 & 2 were being got ready for sinking in place. A report in the *Irish Times* for 26 January 1906 makes reference to a fatal accident that had occurred on the previous day at the bridge works; further details of this accident are to be found in Chapter Twenty-One. Reporting at the beginning of March 1906, Sir Benjamin confirmed that 15 out of the 18 cylinders composing the 9 piers had been sunk to foundation level. In addition, a large cutting on the south side of the river for the approach railway had been completed. Some difficulties were faced on the north side due to a soft peaty substance being encountered, this causing continuous slips for a time. It was expected that the entire works would be completed by the end of July. The final certificate for the Suir Bridge contract showed the total cost at £73,250 11s 8d, the increase over the tender price being in part due to a BoT requirement to provide wind screens, as had been stipulated for the Barrow Bridge.

A second notice was given to the BoT on 21 July 1906 in respect of inspection of Railway No 14, the short line connecting the WD&LR system to the WL&WR section via the Suir Bridge, but only ten days later the Company advised that the works would not be ready in time for the inspection and it was not until 10 August that an amended notice was issued. Colonel von Donop duly inspected the works at the end of August, giving permission to the line being opened subject to several requirements; he carried out a final inspection at the beginning of October when everything was deemed satisfactory. The Suir Viaduct was described in the inspection report as consisting of eight fixed spans varying from 103 to 140ft and one lifting span of 50ft. The eight fixed spans were of exactly the same Pratt-type latticed girder design as those constructed for the Barrow Bridge, seven of them also being 148ft long. The exception was a short span at the Co Waterford end, which was just 102ft 9in. The spans were supported over the river on

The opening span of the Suir Bridge showing the signal cabin above. Also note the ball on right which was raised to advise the ship's pilot/captain that the bridge had been successfully opened. *(IRRS Collection)*

the same design of piers as used for the Barrow Bridge and on similar masonry abutments on each shore. The clear waterway under five of the 148ft spans is 140ft, but at the two spans adjacent to the opening span, it is reduced to 128ft on the Co Waterford side and 136ft 6in on the Co Kilkenny side. This was mainly due to the arrangement for support of the fixed girders in conjunction with the lifting span, but also partly due to the dolphins that were provided to protect the piers.

As previously mentioned, the opening span on the Suir Bridge was of the Scherzer rolling-lift type. The rolling end of the lifting span was contained within the last fixed span on the Co Waterford side of the opening. This span actually overhung the pier on which it sat, the positioning accounting for much of the reduced clearance in the waterway that was referred to previously. When the nose end was down it sat inside the first fixed span on the Co Kilkenny side of the opening. The actual waterway that was available between the dolphins for shipping was a clear 50ft, despite the lifting span actually having an overall length of 80ft.

Saxby and Farmer again supplied the signalling and interlocking equipment to control the working of the bridge. The arrangements at the Suir Bridge were practically the same as those for the Barrow Bridge except that they were modified for controlling a rolling-lift bridge, operated by hand instead of by electric power. As the section of line between the signal cabins at Grace Dieu Junction and Waterford 'C' was worked by the electrical train staff, the arrangements had also to be modified in that respect. In this case the bridge cabin had only six levers: two levers for controlling the signals, one for each of the up and down homes; one lever as key (or king) lever for interlocking signals and bridge controls; a lever for locking bolts and pawls at the nose end of bridge; a lever for locking bolts and pawls at the rear end of bridge; and one lever for the sliding bars for keeping rails level and in line. An additional feature at both bridges was the provision of a ball signal, which was raised when the bridge was about to be opened and lowered when it was about to be closed. The winch for working the ball signal was located in the bridge cabin and interlocked with the operating levers so that it could not be raised until all the necessary opening operations had been completed. This was to ensure that river craft could not be misled. The method for operating the bridge was the same as that already described for the Barrow Bridge.

CHAPTER THIRTEEN

Opening of the New Line

Saturday 21 July 1906 was an auspicious day for the SF&RR&H Company as the ceremony of officially inaugurating the new South Wexford line and Rosslare Pier extension was performed by the Lord Lieutenant, Lord Aberdeen, accompanied by his Private Secretary, Lord Herschell, and his Aide-de-Camp, Lord Anson. They had travelled from Kingsbridge, Dublin, on a special train laid on by the GS&WR, the formation of which included the newly built GS&WR Royal Saloon. Also travelling on the train were Sir William Goulding and Francis B Ormsby, respectively Chairman and Secretary of the GS&WR. Having left Kingsbridge at 09.00, the train arrived at Rosslare just after 12.45, having travelled via Kilkenny and Waterford; at the latter station a number of carriages conveying dignitaries from Cork were attached to the special. *The Irish Times* reported that the guests, numbering altogether about 500, were entertained to a luncheon in the train shed, which was tastefully decorated; the guests included the Marquis of Waterford, the Earl of Bessborough, the Earl of Westmeath, Lord Ardilaun, Earl Cawdor, the Earl of Kenmare, Sir William Arrol, Sir Benjamin Baker, Sir Ralph Cusack, and many other political, religious and military dignitaries. Some small embarrassment arose when the GWR steamer SS *Pembroke* bringing guests from England ran aground on Holden's Bed sandbank off Rosslare Harbour and had to await the rising tide to refloat her.

Sir William Goulding thanked the Lord Lieutenant for the honour he had done "in taking this long journey in the midst of all his multitudinous engagements to open this harbour and line." In reply, His Excellency said he was very much impressed with the notable undertaking which was the outcome of far-seeing energy, enterprise and skill. The scheme was not to be regarded as depending for its success on the diversion of existing traffic, but on the creation of new sources of activity. His Excellency went on to refer to the scheme to connect the railways in Cork, which would assist considerably the transport of fish from West Cork ports and also to the export of flowers, a subject dear to the heart of Lady Aberdeen. On the conclusion of the main speeches, Sir William Goulding presented the Lord Lieutenant with a cup of old Cork silver, bearing the inscription "Rosslare Harbour and Railway. Opened by His Excellency the

The Lord Lieutenant, Lord Aberdeen, arrives at Rosslare Harbour in July 1906 for the official opening of the new route. *(Philip Quigley Postcard Collection)*

Earl of Aberdeen, GCMO, 21 July, 1906. From the Great Southern and Western Railway."

In the past it has been generally accepted that the section between Waterford and Felthouse Junction was opened for traffic on 1 August 1906, followed on 30 August by the short stretch of line between Killinick Junction and Rosslare Strand. However, recent research has cast some doubts on the former date. A GS&WR notice in the *Irish Independent* for 25 June 1906 announced that the railway between Waterford, Rosslare (via Wexford rather than from Killinick to Rosslare Strand) and Wexford would be opened for goods and livestock traffic as from Monday 2 July. Particulars of rates and train services could be obtained from local Station Masters, the District Manager in Waterford and the Traffic Manager at Kingsbridge. In the latter context, GS&WR staff registers show the appointment as from 25 June of Station Masters to the various new stations, with a note at the top of each relevant page reading as follows: "Opened for Goods 25 June 1906 and for Passengers 1 August 1906."

However, only Station Masters were appointed on 25 June, most of the signalmen not being put in place until 24 July; this would not have been a problem if only one train was operating on the line at the time. Finally, an article in the *Waterford News* for 6 July 1906 records that the line was opened "unostentatiously" on the previous Monday (2 July) with the running of a train at 5am from Waterford to Wellington Bridge in connection with the cattle and sheep fair at Taghmon. Relevant to this is the appointment as from that date of Patrick Tynan as a porter at Wellington Bridge. It is now certain that the line was opened between Waterford and Felthouse Junction, albeit on a limited basis for goods and livestock traffic, to provide a service between Waterford and Wexford as from 2 July 1906. It appears that it was local passenger services between Waterford and Wexford that commenced on 1 August 1906, and that the boat train services from Cork via Waterford to Rosslare Harbour followed on 30 August 1906 when the Killinick to Rosslare Strand section was brought into use.

Three vessels were ordered for the new service, two from the John Brown Yard on Clydeside and one from Cammell Laird in Birkenhead, two of them being launched in January 1906 and the third in the following month. Full details of the ordering of the vessels and their descriptions are to be found in Chapter Twenty-Two. Everything was now ready for the official opening of the new port at Fishguard, which took place on Thursday 23 August. Approximately 100 guests were taken to Rosslare Harbour on the SS *St Patrick*, and then by train to Waterford so that they could inspect the new line, returning to Fishguard the same evening. As some of the guests had arrived from London on the previous day, they slept on board the new steamer SS *St David*, while a contingent from Glasgow came on the SS *St Patrick*, which only arrived at Fishguard at about 09.00 that morning on her maiden voyage. A correspondent for *The Irish Times*, who travelled on the SS *St Patrick*, waxed lyrical not only about the boats but the entire service:

> "which is no small enterprise launched in a timid or tentative way and waiting on success for development, but a large undertaking carried out on a grand scale and complete from the outset... equipped to compete in every respect with the very best existing cross-Channel services."

The Times of London, in its issue for 23 August, gave over more than a column to a description of the new route. More importantly, it gave details of the timetable to come into force with the opening of the new service to the public due to take place on 30 August. Details of this timetable are to be found in Chapter Fifteen, but suffice to mention that it was based on two sailings daily, one day and one night time sailing in each direction. A similar notice appeared in *The Irish Times* for 25 August giving details of the connecting train service between Rosslare and Cork via Waterford and Mallow. The first commercial sailings took place on 30 August, the westbound service being operated by the SS *St David*, under the command of Captain Davies, and which for the record left Fishguard 5 minutes late with 231 passengers, and lost a further 10 minutes en route. Meanwhile, the SS *St Patrick* had travelled empty to Rosslare the previous evening to inaugurate the eastbound service, leaving Rosslare at 13.05 under the command of Captain Bournand, with 112 passengers on board.

During the course of the author's research at The National Archives in Kew, an interesting file came to light headed 'Opening of Rosslare–Fishguard route (an account by a 'spy' of the L&NWR)'. The spy in question was WA Ree, the Goods Manager at Swansea. The correspondence opens with a letter dated 18 December 1906 from Frank Ree,[1] the Chief Goods Manager of the L&NWR at Euston, and most likely a relation of WA Ree, which opened with the following sentence, viz:

"You have heard what Mr Burgess said at the Goods Conference as to the GWR, when the wind is in a certain direction, using boxes or baskets for landing passengers arriving by the boat at Fishguard."

The letter went on to ask WA Ree to send some reliable person to Fishguard to find out whether it was really a fact that passengers had been landed in such a manner, and if so, how frequently, commenting that it would be advisable not to let the GWR know that the L&NWR were making such enquiries.

Possibly for the latter reason, WA Ree decided to conduct the enquiry himself, travelling over early in January 1907 to Rosslare by the night boat and returning on the day boat. Apart from answering the all-important question, the report gives us some insight into the facilities available at the two ports and on the new vessels, so is worthy of some consideration. Ree confirmed that there was only one train run in connection with the day sailing, conveying first and third class passengers. On the day of travel, there were only 2 first and 21 third class passengers when the train left Landore; the train was comprised of a 50ft third, a third diner, a first diner, a composite and a third brake. Ree understood that the train set in use had been downgraded from the Cornish Riviera service. Arrival at Fishguard was on schedule at 14.20, the boat departing from the quay only 8 minutes later.

Apart from the platform facilities at Fishguard, there was a small booking office, with a single window opening directly on to the platform, no booking hall being provided. The first and second class waiting room was very small, with neither carpet nor fireplace, the intention being to heat it by means of electric radiators; it contained six chairs upholstered in leather but there was no table, the general appearance being described as dismal. As regards third class, it contained two wooden benches and a small round table, once again devoid of carpet and heat. The gentleman's lavatory was noticeable for having the appearance of what might be found at a small station, and was already dirty in its appearance. The first and second class refreshment room was small, incapable of holding more than about 12 people, yet again unheated as was that for third class which was slightly larger. There was a separate first class dining room which could only be accessed through the third class refreshment room and with accommodation for no more than six to eight people. It seemed that the GWR had opted to provided the minimum of accommodation commensurate with short transfer times between the arrival of the trains and departure of the boats, and vice versa.

As regards the staffing level at Fishguard, Ree found the Station Master reluctant to provide the information and did not therefore press the matter. Ree did, however, comment that every second day was known as 'two boat day', when the Waterford boat also arrived and departed. The staffing level appeared to have been decided on the basis of two boats, and on alternative days the staff were quite definitely underworked. Ree also made reference to the Wyncliffe Hotel, formerly a private residence, and still furnished as such. As with the station, there were no fires lit and the general appearance was described as being "rather cheerless." Ree had admiration for the steamers, which he referred to as fine, exceedingly comfortable boats. Accommodation generally was excellent, cabins were very comfortable and the catering on board well done.

As we know from the BoT report, the accommodation at Rosslare was by no means completed, the rooms which were to be turned into waiting rooms being then occupied by the office clerks. The booking office was similar to that at Fishguard, the first and second class waiting room containing only a few chairs. Staff chiefly comprised GS&WR porters who had been drafted in from all parts of

---

1 Frank Ree later became General Manager of the L&NWR on 1 February 1909, on the retirement of Sir Frederick Harrison.

the system with a few local inhabitants, although the GWR separately provided a staff of checkers.

The report then dealt with the specific question which had led to Ree's visit in the first instance, had passengers been slung to or from the ships at Fishguard in windy weather? This appeared to be no more than a rumour, which had arisen from one occasion when the boat had swung away from the quay and it was discovered that two passengers had been left on the quay. Due to the adverse weather conditions, the ship's Captain was reluctant to come along side again, and, at their own request, the passengers were slung onto the boat, the hawsers not having been slipped; Ree commented that he personally had also seen this done at Holyhead. There was no question but that in certain wind conditions vessels had difficulties in coming alongside, one ship having been engaged in this operation for at least three hours after rounding the breakwater, despite the assistance of tugs. It had in fact been found necessary to lengthen gangways due to the difficulties in bad weather. It must be remembered that at this period the northern breakwater had not been lengthened.

The final word on the 'spy' papers must go to a note attached to the file, dated 26 April 1951, when Mr F Gibbs in Room 303 at Euston House wrote to a Mr Campbell commenting "You may like to file these old papers for record. The rumour that passengers were slung ashore in a basket at Fishguard must have caused a stir!"

As mentioned previously, the facilities at Rosslare Harbour were incomplete when the new service commenced. Early in September, Dent reported to the Board on the necessity to provide additional siding accommodation at once, lodging accommodation for men working specials to Rosslare, additional cottages and at least one 30cwt capacity crane. It was ordered that two 'plain' sidings be put in alongside the cattle sidings, that estimates be obtained for 12 additional cottages, each containing one more room than the present batch. Estimates and drawings were to be obtained for a 10 ton crane. Finally, Mr Coey, the Locomotive Superintendent of the GS&WR, was requested to obtain plans and estimates for a sea-water supply in case of fire.

Ever since the opening of the WD&LR, there had been sporadic complaints made in relation to the crossing of the Causeway at Dungarvan. This came to a head in February 1906 when Dungarvan Urban District Council (UDC) wrote to the BoT complaining of the great inconvenience caused to the public by the crossing. Enclosed with the letter was a plan showing a simple diversion, which the UDC officials believed might relieve the congestion at modest cost. The BoT duly forwarded a copy of the correspondence to the GS&WR for their observations. In reply, it was

An early photograph of a train crossing The Causeway at Dungarvan. The locomotive is in the ownership of the WD&LR. (*Waterford County Museum*)

pointed out that the line was single between Fermoy and Waterford, apart from crossing places at stations, and that five trains each way daily in each direction passed through the offending crossing, four passenger and one goods. They went on to say that there were five level crossings in the Dungarvan area, two of which were situated on the Causeway.

The situation was that the gates were only closed across the public road when trains were in the Dungarvan to Durrow section, the average length of closure being seven or eight minutes, not an unreasonable delay in the Company's view. These comments were passed to the UDC who refused to accept the arguments put forward. While advising the Dungarvan UDC that they had no statutory powers to insist on the GS&WR to either divert the line or erect a bridge, the BoT agreed that Colonel von Donop would be requested to inspect and report on the matter when he was next in the area. This he did on 15 May 1906 when he agreed with the Company's views; they were requested to make a return of delays encountered by road traffic at Causeway crossing over a period of two weeks and submit this to the BoT. During the course of his visit, Colonel von Donop called on the Company to provide a distant signal at one of the other crossings in the area, this being brought into use on 8 October.

Meanwhile, the GS&WR submitted their return on 7 June in respect of the two weeks ending 31 May, figures being supplied as follows:

Delay encountered	2m	3m	4m	5m	6m	7m	8m	9m	10m	11m	Total
Passenger	47	2	2	24	10	11	4	2	1	1	104
Goods	9	2		2		1	4	1	3		22
Special	2	1		2					1		6
Ballast	1	2					1				4
Pay	1			1							2
	60	7	2	27	10	12	9	3	5	1	136

As noted, most of the closures occupied between two and five minutes, although some passenger and most goods trains from Durrow did result in delays of over seven minutes.

In the interim, JJ O'Shee, an ex Director of the WD&LR and MP for Waterford, had become involved and had written to Lloyd George, then President of the BoT, seeking a copy of the Inspector's report, which was sent to him and Dungarvan UDC. Still unhappy with the delays, the UDC wrote again on 11 July to the BoT with further proposals and plans. The GS&WR, obviously emboldened by Colonel von Donop's report, considered that the proposed works were quite unnecessary and would cost considerably more than the estimate being put forward by the UDC. As late as 25 September 1906 the Dungarvan UDC, still with backing from Mr O'Shee, once again requested that Colonel von Donop should again visit Dungarvan. He declined the request as he was disposed to agree with the GS&WR as regards the likely cost of the alterations. There the matter rested and the status quo remained until the eventual closure of the line in March 1967.

A letter was received on 2 February 1906 from the Secretary of the County Wexford Committee of the Gaelic League asking that the names of stations on the new South Wexford line be put in Irish as well as English, thus anticipating by some 18 years the provisions of Section 68 of the Railways Act of 1924. The request was declined, as was a further request from the same body in June.

The Earl Cawdor had resigned as Chairman of the GWR Board in March 1905, having accepted the office of First Lord of the Admiralty in Mr Balfour's Government, a post he was only to hold until the following December when there was a change of Government. He was replaced as Chairman by Alfred Baldwin, head of an iron and steel manufacturing firm in Bewdley, Worcestershire.[2] It quickly became clear that relations between Sir William Goulding and the new Chairman were becoming strained. The two men met in London in the spring of 1906, Baldwin suggesting the creation of additional Ordinary Stock by the F&RR&H Company in connection with the Cork City Railway scheme. This was at odds with Sir William's views, a letter from him dated 30 March 1906 attempting to put the record straight. Sir William pointed out that as Baldwin had not been on the Board

<hr>

2 Alfred Baldwin was MP for Bewdley from 1892 until his death in 1908. He was succeeded by his son Stanley, who subsequently served as Prime Minister of Great Britain (1924–1929 & 1935–1937), the only Prime Minister to serve under three Monarchs.

of the F&RR&H in the past, he was patently unaware that the recent proposals by the GWR indicated "a total change of policy", as in Earl Cawdor's time it had been agreed that the two companies were to be partners in the undertaking, with equal voting power, and no suggestion was ever made that any further Ordinary Stock was to be created. His letter went on to state that the GS&WR must retain equal control over the Fishguard Company and would never consent to any creation of Stock, or other course which would tend to alter their position.

It was also suggested that the GWR rather than the F&RR&H should subscribe to the Cork City Railways project. Furthermore, there was a veiled threat that the Irish members of the F&RR&H Board would be present in the House, "with ample powers from their colleagues here to deal with any emergency." Baldwin responded to this letter in December pointing out that the proposed Bill for additional works at Fishguard could properly only be promoted by the Company in whose favour the powers for the works were granted (the F&RR&H). It was also made abundantly clear that the GWR must retain a preponderating influence over decisions regarding the Fishguard Company. Complaints also came to light at that time regarding the poor timekeeping of the cross-channel steamers, in particular the night boats. It was reported that in December 1906 on average they were arriving 64 minutes late; the GWR, however, refused to give any extension of time in the timetable.

A plan was submitted in October 1907 for extending the platforms at Dungarvan Station at a cost of £225, this being approved. This work was duly carried out, being inspected in August of the following year by Colonel von Donop on behalf of the BoT; he confirmed that both platforms had been lengthened by about 150ft, the extensions being at the Waterford end; in addition, the loop was also extended by some 90 yards. The opportunity was taken to provide the facing points at each end of the loop with a more modern locking arrangement, with all points and signals worked from the signal cabin. As everything was deemed to be in order, Colonel von Donop recommended that the BoT should sanction the use of the new works. At 451ft and 439ft long, the up and

down platforms were the third longest on the line between Mallow and Rosslare, only being exceeded by those at Fermoy and Rosslare Harbour.

It was reported in October 1909 that an independent supply of water for railway purposes at Dungarvan could be obtained from the River Colligan. Expenditure of £1,000 was approved by the F&RR&H Board, which was to include the erection of a tank and two standard water columns; a hydraulic ram would pump the water from the river through 4in diameter pipes. At the same board meeting, held on 15 October 1909, two further matters relating to Dungarvan were approved. Firstly, it was agreed to extend the roadway alongside the cattle bank siding. The second matter was the approval of an additional £248 over that previously agreed for the provision of a turntable. Initially it had been hoped to utilise a second-hand table at Waterford South, but this was found to be unsuitable and so a new one of 44ft 9in diameter was provided at a total cost of £870. Expenditure of £320 was approved in July 1912 for the construction of a footbridge at Dungarvan. The only other expenditure appears to have been a sum of £3,900 approved in January 1947 for the provision of additional loading accommodation.

Initially, road access had not been provided to the cattle and other facilities at Rosslare Pier Station. Several suggestions were put to the board in November 1907 for the provision of such a road, including one from a William Murphy who offered to hand over the necessary land where the road would pass through his property; this road was intended to commence near the station at Kilrane. He stated that he had already approached the Wexford District Council for a contribution of say £200, and, if the Company would subscribe a similar amount, he would pay the balance. An alternative suggestion was to run from Kilrane village; once again the District Council had been approached for a contribution. After considering the matter in some detail, the Company agreed to subscribe a sum of £200, provided that whichever road was constructed it was to their Engineer's satisfaction. Both schemes came before the Wexford District Council at their meeting on 10 November, but both were rejected and it was agreed that no further action should be taken pending a further approach to the Council.

It was reported in April 1907 that local residents again intended to apply to the District Council to pass a presentment for a public road leading to the harbour. As a result Sir William Goulding and other Directors visited the spot and, having considered both of the proposed schemes, agreed to support Murphy's proposals for a road from Kilrane Station to the Company's premises at Ballygillane Big, also agreeing to increase the Company's contribution to £500. The Council in fact approved this scheme on 13 April and, in connection with it an application that had been made to the F&RR&H to construct a connecting roadway with a bridge over the railway to provide the necessary access to the cattle bank, was also approved. This scheme resulted in the construction of the familiar reinforced-concrete bridge at Rosslare which, at the time of its building, was the longest span concrete structure in Ireland. It remained in use carrying all traffic into and out of the port until recent times. It was demolished when the port was modernised during the 1970s, as it suffered from being too narrow and was approached by dangerous bends.

As early as November 1904, the Engineer had reported difficulties in providing an adequate water supply at Rosslare. At that time experiments had been carried out with boring, but to no avail. Water from a bore hole sunk near the block ground proved to be unsuitable for either domestic use or the steamers. The Engineers found it necessary to go further afield and looked at a spring situated about 1½ miles away at Churchtown. This supply was found to be satisfactory and so arrangements were made with the landowner, James Furlong, to purchase the necessary rights and sufficient land to sink a well and erect a pumping station. The intention was to pump the water from the well to a reservoir and water tower to be erected at Rosslare. It was reported in May 1908 that the well had been completed and a 5in pipe laid to bring the supply to a reservoir with a capacity of 100,000 gallons located on the Company's land overlooking the harbour. A water tower was also erected for supplying the Company's houses at Rosslare village, this tower being a familiar landmark in the area. The reservoir was filled for the first time on 29 February 1908. Resulting from this work, the Resident Engineer, AD Delap, was granted an increase in salary from £300 to £350 per annum. To guard against a possible failure, a second pump was provided at Churchtown in October 1909 at a cost of £160. The Company also supplied water to local residents at Ballygeary at a charge of 2s 6d per 1,000 gallons.

Similar problems to those encountered at Rosslare with the provision of an adequate water supply were also experienced at Fishguard, particularly in relation to the steamers. Mr Inglis recommended that as a considerable volume of water came down the valley

Rosslare Harbour (note misspelling, which also appears on other postcards) with the new concrete road bridge dwarfing Ballygeary signal cabin. On right can be seen different capacity GS&WR locomotive coal wagons. *(Philip Quigley Postcard Collection)*

Rosslare Harbour village. These houses were similar to those provided for the Company's workers at Goodwick. *(Philip Quigley Postcard Collection)*

from Pen Cw it should be tapped and a main laid to the harbour, the cost of which was estimated at £700; this was approved by the Board in January 1907. However, due to the turbidity of the stream in question, further tests were carried out and in due course a supply was found close to the 286 milepost. Some two years later, in October 1909, Inglis reported that future developments at Fishguard Harbour were likely to make this source insufficient for the Company's requirements and it was decided to tap an additional source four miles further to the south, at milepost 282. In July 1914 it was reported that the supply of treated water was inadequate, which had led to the use of untreated water, this latter injuriously affecting the boilers of the steamers. This led to increased storage and treatment accommodation being installed. Water supply to the Fishguard Bay Hotel also proved to be a problem about that time, leading to the North Pembrokeshire Water Company supplying both it and the Harbour Village via a new 6in main. This in turn proved to be inadequate on occasions and as a consequence it was agreed in July 1917 to provide a 20,000 gallon storage tank close to the hotel.

The GS&WR agreed to erect a club and a shop for the employees at Rosslare Harbour, a tender from George Nolan in an amount of £1,599 being approved at a board meeting on 25 January 1907. The shop was run on a co-operative basis, with the employees taking shares in it; the shop remained in use until closed in 1965, while the club is still in existence in the village. A gas main was laid down from the gas works early in 1908 so as to provide lighting not only for the club but also the Station Master's house, the Company's cottages and the enginemen's dormitories. A handball alley and a coal yard were later provided in 1909 respectively in connection with the Social Club and the Co-operative.

The facilities as finalised at Rosslare Harbour included a refreshment room, it being agreed that this be let to Mr FJH Koenigs, who rented all the GS&WR Company's refreshment rooms; the arrangement with Koenigs came to an end on the last day of 1915 when his contract expired, the Company taking over the working of the restaurant. In some quarters it was suggested that his German sounding name had a bearing on the matter, and in October 1917 it was reported that Koenigs had issued a writ for specific performance of an alleged contract to renew his agreements, this being vigorously defended by the Company.

The GS&WR advised the Board in October 1907 that it was considered advisable to build a larger house than originally intended for the Felthouse Junction Signalman at Drinagh level crossing in order to accommodate another of the Company's men. This was approved at an estimated cost of £337 7s 1d.

The section of line between Killinick and Felthouse Junctions was closed to passenger traffic as from 1 July 1910. Proposals were put forward in March 1911 to close the signal cabin at Felthouse Junction and the portion of line between there and Killinick to all traffic. It was decided, however, that the signal cabin and the line should be maintained in such a condition as to admit of their being used for traffic if required, at short notice. The saving in maintenance would amount to £152 per annum and in the signalmen's wages a further £100 per annum.

The line was closed completely as from 28 May 1911, but was in fact re-opened for about three months in 1913 while the Coal Channel bridge was being rebuilt. Later still, towards the end of World War I, the GS&WR decided to construct a branch line to serve the Castlecomer Collieries in Co Kilkenny. Work was held up for a time through being unable to obtain two girder bridges and the suggestion was made that two bridges on the line between Felthouse and Killinick Junctions would answer the purpose. Approval was granted by the F&RR&H Board and the bridges were then removed to Co Kilkenny, which spelt the end for the line.

It will be recalled that suggestions were made on several occasions during the planning period for the W&WR for the closing up of the Crescent in Wexford. This matter was raised once again in December 1911 when the Wexford Harbour Commissioners wrote asking the Company to consider the advisability of filling up the Crescent Quay. Mr Gordon pointed out that the Crescent Bridge was seldom opened and was not currently in need of renewal; if and when it did, a wall could be built across the opening of the Crescent for a sum of about £5,000. The bridge was subsequently rebuilt in 1933 and has since been fixed in position. The bridge was once again completely rebuilt in the spring of 1980. To enable the necessary work to be carried out the line was diverted over the former siding, connections to which were by reverse curves at either side of the bridge. Following this, seven concrete piles were driven to support the new structure. The old girder structure was then removed and 48 concrete spans placed in position in March 1980 by the Inchicore 35-ton crane. The final work involved pouring concrete between the inverted T-shaped spans in order to restore the public right-of-way along the quay. This new bridge still provides access to the sea.

Inglis reported to the Board in January 1907 that since the opening of the new steamer route, considerable inconvenience had been experienced consequent on the inadequate telegraph facilities existing at Rosslare, vessels sometimes arriving before messages relating to them were received. He suggested that a trial be carried out of a wireless system between the two ports as well as its introduction on the steamers; it was agreed that a contract for the

Rosslare Strand in 1913. An excursion train, well filled, has arrived from Wexford. Many Wexford people, and indeed many from further afield, availed of these Sunday excursions to the seaside. There is a line of wagons on the up side of the station. Virtually everyone is wearing head gear. *(Philip Quigley Postcard Collection)*

Wexford Crescent Bridge on Sunday 24 August 1980. No 027 works a Shelton Abbey to Waterford train. Behind the locomotive can be seen the 'new' road bridge spanning the River Slaney. *(Barry Carse)*

temporary provision of the necessary apparatus for experimental purposes be finalised with the owners of the Lodge-Muirhead system free of charge, apart from the cost of hotel accommodation for the Wireless Company's Engineer. If satisfied with the trials, the cost of installation at £350 for each steamer and £350 for the land installation was also approved. The system in due course proved successful and a second land station was provided near the Harbour Village in Fishguard.

An accidental fire on 9 July 1907 destroyed the station buildings on the up side at Clarbeston Road Station. To the annoyance and inconvenience of passengers, no immediate moves were made to rebuild the station. However, on 23 April 1913 a contract was entered into with Messrs S Robertson Ltd of Pennywell Road, Bristol in an amount of £4,555 14s 0d for the construction of new buildings on a site on the Fishguard side of the road bridge. This site provided sufficient room to construct a bay platform 368ft in length behind the up platform; at the same time the two main line platforms were lengthened to 502ft. The contract stipulated that the works were to be completed within nine months of their commencement, subject to a penalty of £20 per week for non-completion. The work was finally completed in July 1914. As part of the war effort to provide rails for export to France, the line between Clarbeston Road and Neyland was

singled in 1917, necessitating the provision of a new Clarbeston Road West signal box (six working & two spare levers). The new facilities were inspected and passed by Maj GL Hall on 16 July 1919 on behalf of the BoT.

Hardly had the new service commenced when inadequacies of the facilities at Fishguard were being highlighted. As early as 1 November 1906, Inglis was authorised to lay down two additional sidings of sufficient length to accommodate 129 wagons, along with a new connection from the cattle pen siding at the London end of the station. In the following January, authority was granted to add an additional storey onto the Marine Factory to provide office accommodation for Marine Department staff; a small shelter was also approved for the use of off-duty firemen from the steamers. These works were completed by the following October, along with an additional 74 cottages for various staff. Two 3-ton cranes were installed on the quay side, one opposite to the Waterford berth, the second opposite the turbine steamer berth.

In the previous July a new down platform was provided at Fishguard & Goodwick Station, the goods loop being extended to become part of the down main line. As the signal box was located on the proposed site of the new platform, the latter was built around the box. Following an inspection of the new works by Colonel Yorke on behalf of the BoT, a set of catch points was deemed necessary at the London end to prevent runaways towards the harbour. At about the same time as these works were being undertaken, a trailing siding was installed on the down side, adjacent to a level crossing at the 287¼mp, to provide access to the Fishguard Harbour Brickworks Co Ltd. Under an agreement dated 13 December 1907 the Brickworks Co agreed to pay a sum, estimated at £312, for the works provided by the GWR, along with an annual rent of 10s. The title of the company was altered to the Goodwick Brickworks Co Ltd in November 1910. Apart from the standard gauge sidings, there was a 2ft gauge railway for internal transport on the brickworks site. During the 1920s, production reached 75,000 bricks per week, peak production of 120,000 per week being achieved during World War II. Following the war, road transport largely took over for the removal of the products. The works were taken over in 1946 by the British Anthracite Co Ltd, and with production gradually falling off, closure came in 1969.

Right: Harbour Village at Goodwick. Some of the houses appear to be occupied while others await completion. The road has also to be finalised. *(The National Archives, Kew)*

Left: An interesting view of Fishguard & Goodwick station showing two signal boxes, the larger one apparently just completed, so dating this photograph from early 1906. The smaller box with 17 levers was opened on 1 July 1899 and was officially closed on 29 June 1906, although the new box did not apparently come into use until 29 July. When the second platform was provided the water tank was removed and the platform was constructed around the new signal box. *(Martin Lewis Postcard Collection)*

CHAPTER FOURTEEN

Post Opening, Two World Wars & Nationalisation

Under the F&RR&H Company's Act of 1899 a second pier or breakwater at Fishguard had been authorised. This was to have commenced some 3 chains east of Penrhyn House and extended into the sea for 31 chains in an easterly direction, with the remaining 29 chains in a northeasterly direction. Neither this breakwater or a short jetty or landing place also authorised under the provisions of the 1899 Act were constructed. Inglis prepared a report in October 1907 for submission to the Board, in which he outlined additional works he considered necessary to afford protection to vessels using the harbour from the effects of northeasterly gales. These included a mole starting from the beach at Goodwick which would enclose a water area of 150 acres. The area to be enclosed under this new plan represented nearly double that authorised by the 1899 Act. Between the railway and the new breakwater the foreshore down to low-water level was to be filled in and a new quay constructed; two jetties jutting out from this would be connected by two railways, with an additional new line from the breakwater to the new up line. Following considerable discussion, the Board approved of the scheme and ordered that steps be taken to obtain the necessary parliamentary approval in the ensuing Session. At the same board meeting, Inglis also suggested the necessity of providing a barge to enable the steamers' boilers to be filled with water; experience during the previous year of operation had shown the difficulties of bringing vessels alongside the quay in heavy seas. The Board authorised the purchase of a suitable tender from the Dublin Dockyard Co for a sum of £1,997.

The F&RR&H Act duly received Royal Assent on 18 June 1908 and granted powers for, *inter alia*, the following works, viz a pier or breakwater commencing at a point 18 chains to the southeast of the bridge carrying the A40 road over the railway line at Goodwick Station, and extending into the sea for a total distance of a little over a mile; an embankment for reclaiming portion of the foreshore, two jetties and a boat slip; and three short lengths of railway, two of which were to be laid on the two new jetties. With their Act obtained, Inglis was instructed to proceed with the works as soon as possible. The material required would be obtained from a cutting near Goodwick Station on the site of the proposed new up line authorised in the GWR Company's New Works Act of 1903.

Work on the new line was making satisfactory progress by July 1909, this work being initially confined to the Goodwick end; work was expected to shortly commence on the tipping of material for the new breakwater and its approach embankment. A temporary connection was made from sidings at Goodwick Station to enable the contractors, Messrs Topham, Jones & Railton,[1] to bring in their plant. Basically the new line was to run to the east of the existing line, crossing under it north of Manorowen by means of a 235 yard long tunnel, and again running to the east in a longer tunnel (2,163 yards) before rejoining the existing line at Letterston Junction. At a point where the line entered a cutting just outside Goodwick, a stone road over-bridge was built, which today remains as a testimony to the proposed new line. A short branch was to deviate from the new line by a facing junction on the up side and serve the new eastern breakwater. However, only three months later, in October 1909, Inglis informed the Board of difficulties in obtaining rock arising from the inefficiency of the drilling equipment in use; he recommended removing the air compressing plant then in use below the Fishguard Bay Hotel, which was

---

1 Although this firm was based in London, at least two of the principals, Messrs Jones and Railton were of Welsh birth. Sir Evan Davies Jones was at one time Lord Lieutenant of Pembrokeshire; his second wife was Lily Ann, daughter of James Railton of Monmouthshire, a successful contractor.

The Irish Quay Extension works as at September 1915. The area now enclosed by this extension is today the RNLI lifeboat base. Work also continues on the extension of the North Breakwater, although restricted by the War in Europe. *(The National Archives, Kew)*

creating a noise nuisance to residents, and re-erecting it at the cutting.

In order to improve passenger facilities it was decided in December 1909 to make the No 3 goods line platform available for passenger working; to effect this the BoT requested the installation of a set of catch points and facing point locking. It had also been decided to extend the Irish Quay as, with steamers operating to Rosslare, Waterford and Cork, it was necessary to provide additional quay space. To facilitate the laying down of the foundation work, a diving bell barge was hired from Messrs Hill & Co at a rate of £25 per week, along with the purchase of a Goliath crane from Messrs Walker & Co, the latter to assist in lifting and stacking the blocks. A condition of the barge's hire was that it be returned in the same state of repair as it was at the beginning of the hire. When the hiring came to an end in October 1913, the estimated cost of putting the barge back in original condition was estimated at up to £900, so it was arranged that the contractors purchase it.

Sir William Matthews of Messrs Coode, Son & Matthews,[2] was requested in June 1912 to report on

major improvements in the port facilities. His report, submitted to the Board on 19 July, recommended the completion, in a stable form, of the seaward side of the Northern Breakwater and the provision of a round-head, the completion of the Irish Quay extension so as to provide an additional turbine berth and the provision of a round-head to the Eastern Breakwater. Estimated to cost £264,000, the work was approved and it was decided to appoint Sir William to supervise the work at a remuneration of 5 per cent on the outlay. To enable the works to be carried out it was necessary to seek parliamentary approval to raise additional capital.

When the Bill came up for its second reading in the Commons on 10 April 1913, an Irish MP, Mr Delaney, moved the rejection of the Bill, being supported by a number of Irish and Labour members. The grievances centred around the GS&WR's working of the line from Rosslare and its treatment of its employees, particularly in relation to the payment of low wages and the Company's refusal to re-employ some staff who had taken part in a strike in 1911. At one stage in the dispute, reference was made to remarks made by the GS&WR Chairman, Sir William Goulding, as to his apparent inability to recruit proper men, it being

---

2 Sir William Matthews, KCMG, was born in Penzance in 1844, and after spending time with his father, who was the County Surveyor, he began work as Chief Assistant to John Coode, later becoming a Partner in the business. He undertook works on Dover, Singapore and Valetta harbours.

suggested that there was religious bias involved.[3] In addition, the fact that Cunard had ceased to call at Queenstown and terms of Section 32 of the Bill were believed to play a part in the opposition. Section 32 had been inserted so as to make both the GWR and the GS&WR liable for the guarantee of interest on issued capital. Despite pleas from other MPs to support the Bill on the grounds that its provisions related solely to works at Fishguard, when the vote was taken, due to a poor attendance in the House, the Bill was rejected by 133 votes to 95. This caused the *Railway Times* to refer to the general hostility and obstruction towards railway bills in the House of Commons, such attacks having nothing to do with any proposals in the bills.

Despite this setback, tenders for the work were considered at the board meeting on 11 July 1913. The lowest of these tenders was well in excess of the estimated cost of the works, largely accounted for by additional work necessary in consequence of severe storm damage to the breakwater in the previous winter; in addition, the Board of Agriculture called for additional pens for cattle arriving from Ireland at a cost of £11,370. In view of the urgent necessity of strengthening the Northern Breakwater, Sir William Matthews strongly recommended that that work be put in hand without delay, and so a contract was entered into with Messrs Topham, Jones & Railton of London in an amount of £365,222, the work to be completed in 3½ years. Work actually commenced on 1 September and was reported to be well in hand by mid-October.

The F&RR&H returned to Parliament in 1914, all references to the GS&WR being removed from the Bill. The Act received Royal Assent on 8 July 1914, giving the necessary powers for the works at Fishguard. The Act also enabled the Company to abandon part of the Eastern Breakwater, two of the railway lines and jetties or landing stages authorised under the 1908 Act. Periodic reports from the Engineer detailed the progress of the work; for example by July 1915 good progress had been made with widening the outer slope of the Northern Breakwater, about 225,000 tons of rubble having been deposited. The laying of concrete blocks forming the berm had been completed for a length of 955ft and the pell-mell wave breaker blocks

had been set for a total length of 880ft. A caisson had been placed so as to form the round-head at the end of the Eastern Breakwater, this having been filled with concrete. Likewise, on the Irish Quay extension about 209ft of wall had been built on foundations previously prepared. Work on the east breakwater was suspended in October as a result of a shortage of men due to the war, the workforce being down to only 340 by March of the following year.

With the works approaching completion, consideration was given in December 1918 to providing a system of lighting for the new lighthouses on the two breakwaters; that on the Northern Breakwater was brought into use on 13 November 1919. The works were finally completed in December, Sir William Matthews commenting most favourably on the work carried out by the contractors, particularly having regard to the shortage of both materials and labour during the war. With the work completed, Mr G Lambert Gibson, the Resident Engineer, who had been seconded on temporary loan from the GWR, returned to his former employer. It was reported that the bridge over Sands Road, leading from Goodwick to Fishguard, built to allow rail access to the Eastern Breakwater, and by then no longer required as the rail connection had not been made, was required by the GWR. They were prepared to credit the F&RR&H with the value of the materials, this being approved by the F&RR&H Board.

With the coming of ocean liners to the port in 1909, severe congestion occurred at the quay wall and station, and so a timber 'Ocean Quay' was constructed on the inside of the Northern Breakwater. Customs facilities were provided along with a crane and a bonded store. It was intended that ocean mails would be unloaded here and trains worked round the sharp curve and behind the station through the cattle pen sidings without interfering with passenger traffic. Ocean liners ceased to call at Fishguard at the outbreak of World War I and the traffic never resumed. As the timber works associated with the Ocean Quay were found to be in urgent need of repair and, as the cost of repairs was not financially viable, it was decided that the Ocean Quay should be removed and any good timber used in the renewal of the piling at the Irish

---

3 Sir William Goulding was heavily involved in the Masonic Movement.

Quay, which in turn was in bad need of replacement. It was announced at the board meeting on 6 July 1917 that the Admiralty had taken over the site of the Irish Quay Extension for an air station as from the previous 24 February, thus necessitating the stoppage of all contract work for the time being.

Matters appear to have moved fairly quickly as the first Royal Naval Air Station (RNAS) personnel had arrived by 4 March, with the new station under the charge of Squadron Commander John T Cull, DSO, RN. By that time, ground had been cleared and levelled to the north of the railway station by Messrs Topham, Jones & Railton. A hangar of wood and canvas had also been erected, this being later supplemented by a more permanent structure of wood. Further work included the completion of a runway from the hangar to the Quay and the installation of an aviation fuel store in the former GWR garage. A slipway and launching crane were also provided while a 35ft motor launch was brought from Pembroke Dock.

The first recorded aircraft delivery was a Short Type 184, which arrived at Fishguard on 13 April 1917, although other aircraft might have been previously transferred from Milford Haven. Officers were quartered in the Fishguard Bay Hotel, while ratings were billeted in Goodwick village; there was also tented accommodation. It would appear that around 35 ratings were initially drafted to the new station. By the end of 1918 there were 233 personnel, including 30 officers; this total figure included 35 WRNS and 19 women domestics.

Three main types of aircraft operated from RNAS Fishguard, the Short Type 184 Seaplane already referred to, the Sopwith Baby and the Fairey Hamble Baby. At least two aircraft were delivered to Fishguard by rail, a Short 184 Seaplane No 9086 on 13 April 1917 and a Sopwith Baby N9033 on the same day, presumably in parts for assembly. It is not known exactly how many aircraft were delivered to and operated by RNAS Fishguard, although 33 have been identified, of which 7 are reported to have crashed. Operations from RNAS Fishguard mainly took the form of anti-submarine patrols. The first fatal accident occurred on 22 April 1917 when Sopwith Baby N1033 crashed on take-off, killing Lieut RE Bush. His aircraft caught fire after striking the rocks behind the station, the spot still being visible to this day. Lieut Bush's coffin was taken from the Fishguard Bay Hotel to Fishguard & Goodwick Station with a military escort. The last recorded action occurred on 3 September 1918, when a Short 184 bombed a suspected U-boat.

Meanwhile, on 1 April 1918 the assets and personnel were transferred to the newly formed Royal Air Force as No 245 Squadron, when it became part of No 14 Coastal Operations Group with its headquarters at Haverfordwest. The Squadron was disbanded on 14 May 1919, with the station being closed five days later.

Although not of good quality this photograph illustrates a Short 184 Biplane N1683 about to be recovered from Fishguard Harbour, with the Ocean Quay in the background. Note the interesting steam powered crane in use. *(Martin Hale via Roy Lewis)*

A sports and social club was formed known as the Fishplane; regular cricket matches were played against local teams, while concerts were held in the YMCA hut in Goodwick and the Temperance Hall in Fishguard. The aviators appear to have been well received in Fishguard during their stay. Following the ending of the war, the *County Echo* mentioned talk of Fishguard Harbour becoming a terminal for trans-atlantic air services, but this came to nothing. This was hardly surprising in the then state of aviation. With the departure of the naval personnel, arrangements could be made for a resumption of work on the Irish Quay. However, it was agreed that the rates that had obtained in early 1917 could not be enforced as costs had escalated considerably in the intervening period. It was, therefore, decided that the work should be carried out by the GWR's own men.

With the end of World War I, the railways of Great Britain and Ireland were in poor financial state due to large increases in wages and other operating costs resulting from wartime conditions. The respective Governments decided to bring about an amalgamation in the hope of improving matters. In Britain the newly formed Ministry of Transport had been looking at some radical reforms since 1919, the result of which was the passing of the Railways Act of 1921, the opening paragraph of which stated:

> "With a view to the reorganisation and more efficient and economical working of the railway system of Great Britain railways shall be formed into groups in accordance with the provisions of this Act, and the principal railway companies in each group shall be amalgamated, and other companies absorbed in manner provided by this Act."

The Act took effect on 1 January 1923, by which date some mergers had already taken place, some from the previous year. Of the four big companies created, only the GWR retained its title and the legislation had little or no effect on the F&RR&H.

In Ireland railway employees refused to accept the recommendations of the Carrigan Tribunal,[4] which

had been established to deal with standardisation of salaries and wages, and also the question of the eight-hour working day. The GS&WR announced its intention to withdraw all services as from 8 January 1923 due to its deteriorating financial position. The Government, however, stepped in and confirmed that it would be prepared to maintain services operated by any company that was unable to provide them on financial grounds, including the GS&WR. The Provisional Government appointed a Railway Commission at the end of April 1922 to review the position of the Irish railways and where they should go for the future. The report of the Commission indicated that there were no less than 46 different railway companies in Ireland, which were operated by 28 working companies. The railways generally had performed well prior to the outbreak of war, but subsequent Government control had permanently worsened the position as regards shareholders. It was pointed out that pre-war, shareholders had received dividends due to companies paying low wages to their men; this situation could not continue into the future.

Two reports were in fact issued by the Commission. The majority report suggested that the railways should be brought into State ownership under an independent Railway Board. The minority report, whilst agreeing with many of the salient points of the majority report, was not in favour of a State takeover and recommended instead the unification of the railways in the Irish Free State, but with Governmental control for three years. The fledgling Government was clearly not in a financial position to invest in the railway system. The Government had announced in December 1922 that it would not sanction any scheme for the State purchase of the railways although it did favour centralisation of management.

The Minister for Industry & Commerce announced in January 1923 that in the absence of any agreement to bring about a scheme for grouping by 1 March, he would introduce legislation to bring about unification by 1 July of that year. The GS&WR and the CB&SCR had already agreed to an amalgamation of the two companies, further provisional agreements between the GS&WR, MGWR, C&MDR and CB&PR being subsequently made. The D&SER refused to become

---

4 This Tribunal was set up in August 1921 under the chairmanship of William Carrigan KC.

involved with the GS&WR, largely because of the L&NWR's financial involvement in the Company, suggesting instead an amalgamation with the Great Northern Railway (Ireland); this latter would not have been countenanced as the GNR(I) was by then operating in two states and was in due course left out of the amalgamation arrangements. Eventually the Railways Act of 1924 became law on 23 July 1924, bringing about the amalgamation of the railways operating wholly in the Irish Free State, with one or two minor exceptions, and the formation of the Great Southern Railways (GSR). As far as the F&RR&H was concerned it was to be business as usual. As referred to in Chapter Seventeen, the CCR was later absorbed into the GSR.

Apart from the financial difficulties being encountered by the Irish companies, they had to cope with political unrest, which caused severe disruption to rail transport, first by the so-called Munitions Strike of 1919 and later in 1922/23 by the Civil War. The Civil War in Ireland effectively began on 1 July 1922 with the siege of the Four Courts in Dublin and ended on 24 May of the following year. As far as the southeast of the country was concerned, a South Eastern Division of the Irish Republican Army (IRA) was formed. The town of Wexford was held throughout the period of the civil war by the Free State Army, while the city of Waterford was held for a time by the IRA. Early on in the campaign there was a strategic plan to isolate Waterford from attack, taking the form of assaults on the railways surrounding the city. Thus we find serious damage being caused to the D&SER, WL&WR, W&CIR, the ex-WD&LR and the South Wexford line.

As regards the F&RR&H system, all of the signal cabins on the South Wexford line were damaged or destroyed by fire between July and December 1922, along with five cabins on the line between Grace Dieu Junction and Ballyduff. One of the earliest occurrences was the destruction on 25 August 1922 of the Coal Channel Bridge near Drinagh, the Irregulars returning to carry out a further attack on 17 October. One arch of Taylorstown Viaduct was destroyed by explosives in July 1922, resulting in the collapse of three further arches, thus closing the line until the viaduct was finally re-opened on 29 December of the following year. It was reported at the F&RR&H board meeting on 10 November 1922 that the D&SER (as the DW&WR had become in January 1907) had offered to afford the GS&WR access to Waterford via the Macmine Junction to New Ross route, the F&RR&H Board being of the view that circumstances did not warrant taking advantage of the offer. However, with the situation unresolved, an agreement was concluded on 3 December 1923 between the two companies,

Taylorstown viaduct as damaged during the Civil War. Note track is still in situ although the top of the arch has been destroyed. *(Photographer unknown, Courtesy Horeswood Historical Society)*

Ballyvoyle Viaduct partially destroyed in August 1922 with the local Keohane family. *(Sean Murphy, Mahon Bridge, Co. Waterford, via Waterford County Museum)*

allowing the GS&WR to run their passenger and goods trains over the D&SER between Wexford North and Waterford North. The GS&WR agreed to pay 5s per train mile, the distance for ascertaining charges being agreed at 41m 63c.

Despite having effectively closed the South Wexford line, local trains had been running east as far as Ballycullane and so the insurgents also decided in February 1923 to target the Barrow Bridge. On this occasion they did not resort to explosives, but to the very simple expedient of opening the bridge and then removing a crown-pinion wheel associated with the opening mechanism and dropping it into the river below. This was carried out by one of the insurgents, one Peader Sinnott, who borrowed a salmon cot and rowed out to the bridge by himself; despite the fact that the bridge was guarded by a detachment of troops, Sinnott appears to have carried out his mission unobserved.

The other major act of destruction was the blowing up of Ballyvoyle Viaduct, this severing the Dungarvan line until 1925. Not content with destroying the viaduct, a ballast train was subsequently run into the gap, destroying '101' class 0-6-0 No 189. It was not just bridges and signal cabins that were targeted, as for example the goods store at Durrow Station was burned down on 18 December 1922; the joint D&SER/GS&WR goods shed at Waterford was also destroyed by fire on 10 December 1922. Some trains were also involved, the 17.05 from Waterford being derailed at the 55mp on 7 December, the same train being again derailed 3 miles further west on 29 December.

The GS&WR announced in November 1923 that all underbridges, with the exception of those at Taylorstown and Ballyvoyle, had been repaired, either temporarily or permanently. Taylorstown Viaduct was finally re-opened at the beginning of December 1923, Ballyvoyle on 19 June 1924. Compensation amounting to £9,776 2s 7d was paid up to the end of October 1925 by the Free State Government, work carried out up to that time amounting to £12,642 10s 0d. These figures did not refer to the above viaducts, repair

Left: Ballyvoyle Viaduct following its destruction on 31 January 1923; it had been partially damaged in the previous August. On the second occasion a ballast train was intended to be run to its destruction. Surprisingly, the coupling on the first wagon held and prevented it from meeting its destruction. *(Sean Murphy, Mahon Bridge, Co Waterford, via Waterford County Museum)*

Right: Waterford goods store was destroyed by fire in January 1923 during the Civil War. *(Photographer unknown, IRRS Collection)*

work on which was undertaken by the Government. An amount of £704 10s 4d compensation was belatedly awarded in July 1931 for the malicious destruction of Abbey Junction signal cabin on 13 November 1922. The GS&WR decided not to rebuild the cabin on its original site in the 'V' of the junction, but to erect a new one adjacent to the Pier Head crossing at an estimated cost of £800. The F&RR&H Board agreed to pay over the compensation against the cost of its construction. Meanwhile, in response to the unrest, the GWR took the decision in July 1922 to suspend the steamer service between Fishguard and Rosslare, this taking effect as from 14 July.[5] Corresponding with this, rail services to and from Fishguard were curtailed. The steamer service was reinstated as from 17 September 1923, along with the relevant rail services.

At the meeting of the Board of the F&RR&H on 30 October 1925, reference was made to the death on 12 July of the Deputy Chairman, the Rt Hon Sir William Goulding. Sir William had been a member of the F&RR&H Board since the incorporation of the new Company in October 1898. During this long period he had rendered very valuable service to the Company, both in relation to its establishment and the conduct of its affairs generally. He was succeeded as Deputy Chairman by Sir Walter Nugent, Bart, who had previously been Chairman of the Midland Great Western Railway and had also succeeded Sir William as Chairman of the Great Southern Railways At the same meeting, John F Sides, the Engineer, informed the Directors that the Free State Government had awarded an amount of £9,796 2s 7d against claims of

---

5 The services between Fishguard and Waterford and Cork were maintained.

£12,642 10s 0d in respect of damage incurred during the Civil War.

In October of the following year the F&RR&H Board expressed some concerns regarding the train service being provided by the GSR, the service from London by the longer LMS route via Holyhead being faster to and from the majority of stations in the south and southwest of Ireland. They urged that the service should be improved so as to be at least equal to that provided prior to the war. The GSR representatives present agreed and suggested that the Traffic Officers of both companies should confer immediately with a view to determining ways of improving the service.

Some matters relating to Fishguard require brief mention. A new siding was laid down in March 1928 for Messrs Bryant & Langford Quarries at the outer end of the harbour at Pen Cw. In January of the following year one of the two subways was removed along with five sets of catch points. The generating station at the landward end of the Northern Breakwater was closed down in October 1933, and an arrangement made with the West Cambrian Power Company for the supply of electricity to the harbour and the tenants in the Harbour Village.

Dredging of Rosslare Harbour, and indeed that at Fishguard, became a regular occurrence down the years. As an example, in April 1927 a contract was awarded to the Fowey Harbour Commissioners in Cornwall in an amount of £6,562 10s 0d, this work being completed by the time of the following board meeting in October. Again, in May 1930, a further contract was awarded for the dredging of approximately 100,000cu yd of material, based on the hire of the Fowey Commissioners' dredging plant at the rate of £1,650 per month, a monthly output of 25,000cu yd being guaranteed. In fact the total quantity dredged was 138,475cu yd at a cost of £9,139 7s 0d. The Fowey Harbour Commissioners were reported to be still involved in dredging at Rosslare Harbour as late as 1951.

It was decided to carry out lifting capacity tests on the Company's 5-ton steam crane at Rosslare in 1929. However, during the course of the tests the crane toppled over into the sea, luckily without injury to the operator; it was subsequently lifted from the sea bed and scrapped. In January 1932 the GSR recommended that a 50-cwt steam crane, then out of commission at Rosslare, should be replaced by a 5-ton electric crane at an estimated cost of £2,000, this expenditure being approved. This crane was supplied by Messrs Thomas Smith (Rodley) Ltd at an actual cost of £1,599 3s 4d. In the following July the three 30-cwt cranes at Rosslare Harbour were found to be unsuitable for use with the new *Saints* and it was agreed to provide a suitable undercarriage for each at a cost of £410, this expenditure also being approved by the F&RR&H Board; this proved necessary to improve the crane operator's visibility when placing and removing loads from within the ship's hold. Two of these cranes were converted back to their original configuration in 1956, one of these then being scrapped in 1965. An additional crane of 2½ tons capacity was provided by Smiths in 1936 at a cost of £1,400.

It was also in 1936 that electric power was first obtained from the Electricity Supply Board. Prior to that time, power for the harbour had been provided from the Company's own facilities. In 1906 the F&RR&H had installed two 40hp Crossley gas engines in the gas house adjoining the locomotive shed for generating current, which remained in use until 1936. As the latter supplied alternating current, it was then necessary to install a mercury-arc rectifier to convert to direct current for use by the cranes. As the rectifiers deteriorated when lying unused for lengthy periods, there were occasions between 1950 and 1964 when CIÉ brought one of their 'D' class diesel-electric shunters to Rosslare[6] and placed it in a siding beside the power house to supply direct current power to the cranes. A second rectifier was installed in 1964, having previously been in use on the Hill of Howth Tramway system, the two rectifiers then being used on alternate weeks. On the subject of cranes, a 7½-ton crane was supplied by Smiths in 1957.

The Company's generating station at Fishguard Harbour was closed down in October 1933, power thereafter being supplied by the West Cambrian Power Company. It was arranged to sell to them the poles and cables previously used to supply power to the

---

6 This was brought from Inchicore by a Dublin driver as the Rosslare and Wexford drivers were unfamiliar with the 'D' class.

No 44 preparing to leave Rosslare Harbour on the 06:30 to Wexford on 28 June 1938. *(HC Casserley)*

Company's houses in the Harbour Village, along with the right to supply their tenants as from 16 November 1933 for a once-off payment of £1,000. Some minor changes occurred at Fishguard Harbour in 1928. A new siding was provided at the Pen Cw end of the station for Messrs Bryant & Langford Quarries Ltd. The City of Cork Steam Packet Company agreed to contribute £250 towards the cost of providing a fog signal on Pen Anglas – the point of land immediately north of Fishguard Harbour – and also to contribute to its future maintenance. At about the same time the Company came to an agreement whereby Goodwick Urban District Council took over and agreed to maintain certain roads in the Harbour Village which had been constructed by the Company. In July 1928 a lease was approved in connection with the provision of a new lifeboat house and slipway for the Royal National Lifeboat Institution, for a period of 21 years at a nominal annual rent of 10s. A brief history of the lifeboat stations at both Fishguard and Rosslare can be found as Appendix H.

The Irish Government decided in the 1930s to set up a number of factories for the production of sugar from home-grown sugar beet. One of these was located at Carlow, to which produce from the growing areas in South Wexford was transported by rail. This brought about a necessity for improvements at most of the stations on the South Wexford line.

Improved siding and loading bank accommodation were provided at Campile, Bridgetown, Duncormick, Wellington Bridge, Ballycullane, Killinick and Kilrane. These, together with similar facilities at Cappagh and Tallow Road on the former WD&LR line, cost a total of £1,309 5s 10d, this expenditure being approved at a F&RR&H Board meeting in January 1935. A new loading bank was installed at Campile early in 1937 for the use of the Shelburne Co-Operative Agricultural Society, the cost of which was paid by the Society. Arising from complaints from the Department of Agriculture in July 1939, the GSR reported that it had been found necessary to provide additional cattle pens along with additional hay racks and drinking troughs at Rosslare Harbour for cattle passing through the port.

Shortly after the outbreak of World War II, the British Government introduced the Fishguard & Rosslare Railways & Harbours Act, 1898, Relaxation Order[7] to take effect from 23 January 1940. This short piece of legislation suspended the obligation under Sections 68 and 70 of the 1898 Act to provide a daily service of steamers respectively between Fishguard and Rosslare and Waterford; the suspension was to remain in force until the Order was revoked. The Order was in fact revoked in May 1940 and replaced

---

7 Statutory Rules and Orders 1940 No 4, Emergency Powers (Defence) Railways (Steamship Services), dated 23 January 1940.

by SR&O No 809 of 1940, effective from 18 May, which was issued to remove any doubts as to the meaning of the previous Order.

In the interim, correspondence between the Ministry of Shipping and JE Stevenson, the High Commissioner for Ireland, referred to the possible implications of the suspension of services. In February 1940 the cross-channel service was operating three times a week on each route. If either of the remaining vessels should be requisitioned, there would be adverse effects both on local employment and on port revenues. More importantly, however, such a suspension would lead to a curtailment of supplies of essential commodities. It was pointed out that, even with a reduced schedule, more traffic than normal was going by the Rosslare route. Consideration was given to chartering Irish-registered vessels. These would most likely have been operated by Irish crews; in any event, serious difficulties would have resulted if British crews were put on these ships as compensation for death or injury only applied to crews on ships registered in Britain, not to mention political sensitivities. Another point was that there would be possible difficulties with Irish vessels complying with special war time restrictions imposed by the Admiralty regarding the use of navigation lights and other matters. In the event, it was not found necessary to charter in Irish vessels.

Around lunchtime on the 26 August 1940, two German bombers were spotted crossing the Wexford coast in the region of Carnsore Point and then flying over Johnstown Castle and Taghmon before going their separate ways at Clongeen. One of the aircraft continued in a westerly direction until it reached Duncannon; it then flew up the estuary over Passage East where it turned northwards to approach Campile from the direction of Ramsgrange. It continued over the village of Campile towards Kilmannock before turning back towards the village at about 13.30. Witnesses reported that as it approached Campile it went into a dive, and at a height estimated at between 300 and 400ft dropped three bombs over the Shelburne Co-Operative Agricultural Society's premises adjacent to the railway station. One of these penetrated the creamery and restaurant, more or less reducing the building to rubble and tragically killing three of the employees, Kathleen Hurley and sisters Catherine and Mary Ellen Kent, and injuring a number of others, including the Station Master's two children. It was lucky that many of the Co-Op's employees were on their lunch break when the raid took place or the casualty list would have been higher. Another of the bombs, which came down adjacent to the petrol pumps, failed to explode. The aircraft, a Heinkel He111, then made a further bombing run, dropping a fourth bomb, which exploded in a nearby field. Apart from the damage to the Co-Op, the railway

Left: On 26 August 1940 two Luftwaffe Heinkel III aircraft dropped bombs over South Wexford, killing three workers in the Shelburne Co-Operative Society's premises adjacent to Campile station. In this view the Shelburne Co-Op premises is on the right and the damage to the station master's house can be seen. (*Irma Nix*)

Opposite: Here can be seen the result of the third bomb dropped at Campile, which badly damaged the siding leading into the Co-Op premises. (*Author's Collection*)

siding was destroyed and considerable damage done to the Station Master's house.

The second aircraft, meanwhile, had flown south as far as Cullenstown before turning back towards the railway line. Four bombs were dropped adjacent to the Ambrosetown viaduct (more generally known as Mill of Rags), all four falling in a field and damaging an adjoining house. Both aircraft then headed back to sea, passing over the coast in the region of Dunmore East. It was believed that the bombing was deliberate and may have been carried out as a deterrent to the Co-Op who had been supplying butter and poultry products to Britain; they also used the railway to transport some of the goods, hence the second attack. Initially the German Government denied any involvement in the bombing despite strenuous protests by the Irish Government. Eventually, in October 1940 the Germans expressed regret and agreed to pay compensation. A claim for £15,000 was in due course lodged, a settlement figure of £12,000 being paid in 1946.

The tunnel at Castell Forlan near Maenclochog Station on the North Pembrokeshire branch was the scene of a bombing raid on 6 October 1943 by a RAF Mosquito. This was to test the new 'Highball' bombs designed by Sir Barnes Wallis, the inventor of the famous dam busting 'bouncing bombs', and intended for use against railway tunnels in Northern Italy. The devices used were dummies but the experiment was adjudged to be a success. It was reported that two of the bombs dropped actually went straight through the tunnel.

The GWR gave some consideration in November 1945 to the transfer of the Rosslare passenger service to Waterford. As already mentioned, under Section 70 of the F&RR&H Act of 1898, the GWR were obliged to operate a daily service of steamers between either New Milford or Fishguard and Waterford. The Relaxation Order had not been rescinded at that time, and indeed has not been as this is written in 2015. The cost of transferring the Rosslare service to Waterford was estimated at £60,000, made up of £39,000 for additional fuel and £21,000 for harbour dues, which incidentally were not payable at Rosslare, although CIÉ at one stage sought unsuccessfully to have such a charge levied. Figures taken out by the GWR Accountant indicated that annual net revenue over the period 1928 to 1939 had only been £340; this certainly left no margin for the payment of harbour dues at Rosslare.

The formation of CIÉ in 1945 and the subsequent nationalisation of the railways in Britain and Ireland, respectively in 1948 and 1950, brought little change to the operations of the F&RR&H. However, it was announced in June 1948 that CIÉ had commenced legal proceedings against the F&RR&H seeking an injunction on two grounds, firstly that the serving English Directors had not been validly appointed, and secondly that the Company had no powers to divert its vessels to other services operated by the Railway Executive. In regard to the first point, under the provisions of the Transport Act of 1947, the British Transport Commission (BTC) had nominated former officers of the Western Region (basically the old GWR) to act as Directors in place of the previous GWR Directors on the Board. In this context the BTC had no doubts regarding the validity of their appointments.

Regarding the second matter, the Railway Executive had found it necessary to provide a spare steamer to operate the Harwich to Hook of Holland service as from the beginning of April 1948, while the

Train from Cork arriving at Rosslare Harbour on 26 April 1955 in charge of a Woolwich 2-6-0 No 384. *(HC Casserley)*

SS *Arnhem* was undergoing overhaul; her sister ship, the SS *Prague* had been burned out and sunk during the course of her refit in 1947. The SS *St Andrew* had been considered suitable as a replacement, and, not then being required for the F&RR&H service, was loaned on a charter basis to the Railway Executive on 2 March. Apparently having some doubts as to the legal position regarding charters, it was decided, pending the hearing of the case, to keep the *St Andrew* lying up, unused, at Fishguard Harbour. The Railway Executive was of opinion that this was really no concern of CIÉ as the BTC, as successors to the GWR, were entitled to all the profits derived from the steamer service.

With the cessation of hostilities it was arranged that the cross-channel service would re-open on 23 May 1947, with sailings from Fishguard on Mondays, Wednesdays and Fridays, and in the return direction on the other weekdays. Although the Company had sufficient vessels to operate a daily service in 1948, the traffic was deemed insufficient, apart from the summer months. It was, therefore, decided to maintain a thrice-weekly service in each direction until mid-July, and from 17 July to 6 September it was to be operated daily, with sailing tickets required on Fridays.

The South Wexford line was closed for several days in late March 1946 due to the discovery of a floating wartime mine close to the Barrow Bridge. The mine was eventually lassoed by two fishermen from nearby Cheekpoint and dismantled by the army. Following the publication of the Milne Report in 1949 into the future direction of the railways, Waterford Harbour Commissioners made a strong case for the diversion of cross-channel traffic from Rosslare to Waterford. The Commissioners contended that the railway line between Waterford and Rosslare Harbour was "uneconomic and unnecessary" and that Rosslare was taking traffic for which Waterford was the natural port. They went on to say that they had come to an agreement with CIÉ for a general re-organisation of the facilities at Waterford. The Rosslare Harbour Development Association challenged the facts put forward and protested against the "continued interference by Waterford Harbour Commissioners in the affairs of Rosslare port." Not only was the port of Waterford almost double the distance by sea from Fishguard, but it was also some 16 miles from the sea up a narrow and tortuous and on occasions a fog-bound river." Representation was made, with the support of both Wexford County Council and Wexford Corporation, to British Railways Western Region. As we now know, the Rosslare authorities eventually won out in the argument.

Under the Transport Act of 1947, the railways in Britain were nationalised from 1 January 1948, the BTC being set up to take responsibility for the main line railways, including the Great Western Railway. In

Ireland, the Transport Act of 1944 had brought about the amalgamation of the Dublin United Transport Company and the Great Southern Railways to form Córas Iompair Éireann (CIÉ) or the Irish Transport Company from 1 January 1945. In June 1950 CIÉ and the Grand Canal Company were amalgamated and became a nationalised body under a Transport Act of that year. These legislative changes had little if any effect on the F&RR&H and its cross-channel operations.

CHAPTER FIFTEEN

Under New Management

In January 1961, on the recommendation of CIÉ, the F&RR&H Board approved the inclusion in a forthcoming Bill of the proposed sale to the Waterford Harbour Commissioners of the North Wharf at Waterford, including part of the Company's undertaking, consisting of the portion of Salvation Lane connecting the southeast portion of the North Wharf with the public road leading from Waterford to New Ross. The sale of the land in question was completed later in the year, resulting in a credit to capital account of £4,000. In Britain the Transport Act of 1962 dissolved the British Transport Commission and set up the British Railways Board (BRB) to take over the railway undertakings, excluding the London underground system, which became the responsibility of the London Passenger Transport Board. Once again, such legislative changes had no effect on F&RR&H operations.

As late as August 1963, the *Irish Times* quoted Frank Lemass, General Manager of CIÉ, as saying that despite meetings in Dublin with senior officials of British Railways (BR), there were no plans for any major improvements at Rosslare Harbour. However, with passenger traffic showing a considerable increase during 1963, thoughts turned to how improvements could be made in the handling of vehicles at both ports. The practice of craning cars on and off vessels was clearly no longer viable with increasing volumes of vehicular traffic and some alternative scheme was called for. A decision was taken to request Messrs Coode & Partners to prepare a report on the likely alterations necessary to cater for the increased traffic. Before dealing with their report we must, however, make reference to a working group that was set up as a result of a meeting of the parties involved held in Dublin on 21 April 1964.

That meeting, between representatives of CIÉ, BR (Western Region) and the F&RR&H Board, reviewed the shipping services based on Fishguard. Arising from this meeting, the grandiosely titled Traffic Potential & Operating Plans Working Party was established to look into the likely substantial increase in cross-channel traffic, both private car and freight, from which it was felt the two railway companies should benefit. The guidelines for the group included looking at the economics and other implications of four systems of working, viz:

(a) operating exclusively through Rosslare

(b) operating exclusively through Waterford

(c) operating seasonally for passengers and cars via Rosslare, with all-year-round services through Waterford

(d) continuing the current pattern of operations through both ports.

It was decided quite early on in their deliberations that stern-loading vessels would be superior to conventional types. However, because of limitations due to swell at Fishguard and siltation at Rosslare, and the lack of experience at both ports with stern-loading activities, it was felt that a Consulting Engineer of international repute should be appointed to advise the F&RR&H. As a result, Messrs Coode & Partners of London were engaged by the F&RR&H to report on the feasibility of providing a stern-loading system for the two ports. Before looking at the reports presented by the consultants, we must first look at the findings of the Working Party.

Certain economic assumptions were made, including the expectation that both Britain and the Republic would join the European Economic Community (EEC), which would see tariff barriers lowered. During the previous decade, passenger traffic by sea and air had grown by approximately 50%, those travelling by air rising spectacularly from some 300,000 to 950,000 per annum in the ten-year period, whereas passengers (including motor car traffic) using

Loading cars on to one of the Saints at Fishguard Harbour. *(Great Western Trust)*

sea routes had only grown from about 1,350,000 to 1,550,000 per annum, at which point it had more or less stabilised. It was admitted that there had been no fundamental changes in the service offered to sea passengers or to the ships since before World War II, whereas air services had seen vast improvements in speed, carrying capacity and the opening of new routes. Interestingly, the Working Party concluded that air traffic would continue to grow but not at the same spectacular pace that had been the feature of the previous few years – how wrong they were to be!

A decision had been taken in 1963 to increase the car carrying capacity of the *St David* with side-loading drive-on/drive-off facilities at Fishguard. Daylight sailings were increased in 1964 to once daily each way, Sundays excepted, between June and September, with corresponding improvements in rail connections. The resultant figures speak for themselves as per the table below:

Passengers	Day	Day	Night	Night	Total	Total
	1964	1963	1964	1963	1964	1963
Rail/Sea	41,696	9,364	60,115	76,388	101,811	85,752
Motorists	27,339	11,597	28,018	20,451	55,357	32,048
Total	69,035	20,961	88,133	96,839	157,168	117,800
Increase	48,074				39,368	
Decrease			8,706			

It was believed by the Working Party that rail/sea passenger traffic would continue to respond to improved daylight services, due to the fact that travel by surface routes was appreciably cheaper than by air, and it was more attractive to potential passengers who did not live close to an airport. Bórd Fáilte, the Irish Tourist Board, estimated that, given adequate car ferry services, it could be expected that about 75,000 cars would move between Great Britain and Ireland in 1964, rising in 1974 to 170,000. On the other hand, Science in General Management Limited, who had been engaged by the BRB, came up with figures of 95,000 in 1965 and 180,000 by 1970. Despite the differences, there was clearly scope for a very great increase in accompanied motor car traffic, given adequate facilities. The Working Party optimistically considered that with end-loading facilities at the two ports and the introduction of new ships on the route, the total number of passengers, both rail/sea and motor, could rise to 380,000.

On the Fishguard to Waterford route, gross receipts from general freight and livestock accounted for nearly half the total gross receipts earned by the Rosslare and Waterford ships, amounting in 1963 to £339,000 for freight and £37,000 for livestock. The only vessel equipped to handle livestock was the *Great Western* and this traffic was exclusive to the Waterford route. This traffic had declined, due in part to bovine tuberculosis, despite which the Working Party foresaw the receipts rising to £50,000 per annum. Consideration had to be given to whether this traffic should continue through Waterford or be transferred to Rosslare; it was feared that if the service was withdrawn from Waterford, another carrier would most likely take the traffic. Waterford already had strong competition in the form of J&A Lines, operating from that port to Preston, their success being due to the widespread use of containers.

Having considered the traffic, both current and anticipated, the Working Party then turned their attentions to how a future service might be operated. Intensive use of shipping was required in the summer period to deal with the demand for passenger and motor car accommodation. If for no other reason, Rosslare was the obvious choice of destination, at least for the summer months; it would be impossible to make two round trips in 24 hours using Waterford as the Irish destination, whereas with drive-on/drive-off facilities such an operating pattern was possible through Rosslare. As regards freight and livestock, it was considered that there should be a year-round service from Waterford. The choice therefore came down to options (b) and (c) as outlined earlier. If, however, Rosslare was to be closed for several months of the year there would be severe manpower and social problems, and the final decision was therefore to leave the status quo stand.

Turning to the provision of a new vessel for the Rosslare route, it was considered that this should be a car carrying passenger and cargo ship, with passenger accommodation under cover for 900 passengers, and with limited cabin accommodation. The car deck would have a capacity for about 160 cars when used exclusively by cars. However, the car deck should be made high enough to accommodate 20 large containers, leaving space for approximately 120 cars. All cargo would be either containerised or palletised. In addition, a new cargo and livestock vessel was required as a replacement for the *Great Western* on the Waterford route. It was the opinion that any new vessel should be able to take 400 head of cattle and 35 large containers or commercial vehicles on the main

deck. This ship should also be stern-loading so that it could supplement the Rosslare route by carrying cars. However, it was proposed that motorists would not be allowed to accompany their cars on this new vessel, which would have to sail in parallel with the passenger vessel.

Finally, in relation to the summer timetable for 1964, the Working Party suggested that the new car carrier should depart Fishguard at 07.00 and 17.00, corresponding departures from Rosslare being at 12.00 and 22.45. In addition, the *St David* would leave Fishguard at 01.45 and 14.30, and Rosslare at 09.00 and 19.30. The cargo ship, carrying cars only when required, would leave Fishguard at 06.30 and depart Rosslare at 12.15; it would have a journey time of 4 hours each way, as opposed to 3¼ for the other two vessels. The basic winter service would see the ship leaving Fishguard at 07.00 and returning from Rosslare at 22.45 on Tuesdays, Thursdays and Saturdays.

Turning now to Messrs Coode & Partners, Mr DC Coode visited Fishguard on 11 May 1964 and had fruitful discussions with various officials, including EC Cookson, the Western Region Assistant Civil Engineer, as well as the Harbour Master and the Quay Superintendent. This was followed by a visit two days later to Rosslare, where he was met by various officials of CIÉ. The F&RR&H had initially indicated that the proposed stern-loading vessel would be 355ft in length with a draft of 13ft 6in. Subsequent correspondence had suggested lengths of 375ft and 400ft and a 14ft 6in draft.

At Fishguard the most suitable site for any additional ferry berth was considered to be at the southern (inner) end, although there was insufficient depth of water. Any car ferry berth would have to be sited alongside the existing quay or parallel to the north breakwater. Two items militated against the existing Rosslare berth, namely a ferry berthing there would preclude the use of one of the adjoining Waterford and Cork berths, and, the side-loading facility at the Rosslare berth would need to be retained for use until the new stern-loading facilities were completed and ready for use.

Two schemes were proposed, one sited beyond the station and right at the northern end of the Irish

Quay; it would essentially be of solid construction so as to provide protection from the swell entering the harbour, while to assist in berthing the car ferry it was to be angled slightly from the line of the Irish Quay. One drawback to this site was the narrow section of the quay, which would suffer damage from a vessel coming astern onto the berth, even at 2 knots, quite possible in rough weather conditions. The second scheme was for a berth parallel to the north breakwater more or less where the original Ocean Quay had been located. This scheme would necessitate the construction of a wharf alongside the breakwater to allow for passengers embarking and disembarking by rail.

At Rosslare the consultants initially considered the use of Berth No 4 as being the most suitable site but once again it had disadvantages, not least the necessity of maintaining the railway tracks, allied to the narrowness of the pier. These two factors would make it virtually impossible to provide the necessary road facilities. It was therefore decided to locate the berth at the extreme southern end of Berth No 3, partly taking in Berth No 2. By 1964 these two berths were seldom used, and then only as shelter for small fishing boats in severe weather conditions. In order to provide additional space for the road approach to the car ferry berth, Messrs Coode proposed carrying the road on two rows of sheet steel piling, some 21ft apart, in front of Berths 1 & 2, the space between the piles being filled with sand.

Reference has already been made to sand accretion, which had been an ongoing problem at Rosslare since the opening of the port; as already mentioned, maintenance dredging had to be undertaken every four years at a cost of about £40,000. By the 1960s the inshore end of the viaduct was virtually blocked by sand. To accommodate a car ferry at Berth No 3 it would be necessary to maintain a depth of 18ft at all states of the tide, not only at the berth but also on the approach and in manoeuvring areas. As the littoral drift in the Rosslare area was from south to north, Messrs Coode considered that the viaduct could be blocked up, allowing sand to accumulate outside the harbour; this would still require periodic dredging to prevent silting up at the harbour entrance. However, they suggested that a sand tracer test should be carried out by the Hydraulics Research Station at Wallingford. This was agreed to, although subsequent tests proved somewhat inconclusive.

Before Messrs Coode produced their second report in October 1964, separate reports were submitted to the F&RR&H Board by EC Cookson on the facilities at Fishguard, and by JJ Meleady, the CIÉ Engineer, for Rosslare Harbour. Mr Cookson reported that there was a proposal in hand to single the line between Clarbeston Road and Fishguard, which would enable the abandonment of some siding accommodation at the south end of Fishguard Station. This led to a scheme being drawn up, incorporating part of the Rosslare berth and the provision of a new approach road from the A40, made possible by the removal of sidings. This scheme would also allow the abandonment of the existing road access to the port past the Fishguard Bay

Rosslare Harbour in 1950 with three vessels alongside, including one of the Saints. The level of sand accretion at the inshore end of the viaduct can also be witnessed. In the foreground we can see a number of laden coal wagons. *(Philip Quigley Postcard Collection)*

Hotel. The total cost of the scheme was estimated at £289,100; included in this figure was a sum of £40,000 in respect of signalling, including the provision of a new signal box as the existing one would require to be removed.

Mr Meleady's scheme for Rosslare also allowed for the construction of a new single lane road 10ft 6in wide from Ballygeary across the steel viaduct, and along the pier to serve the end-loading portal for the new stern-loading ship, and also the entrance to the side-loading ship, the latter by means of a tunnel under the pier platform. To construct the road it would be necessary to remove one of the existing rail lines to the pier. Separate car parks for incoming and outgoing vehicles would be provided at Ballygeary, along with a customs examination building, offices, waiting room and toilet accommodation. To replace the bay platform, which had to be removed to allow the road to be built, a new covered platform was to be constructed alongside the storm wall. The estimate for the Rosslare Harbour works was £361,300.

Messrs Coode's second report, dated 13 October 1964, was based on the deliberations of the Working Party and the two Engineers' reports. In the interim, it had been decided that it was no longer of paramount importance to maintain access for vessels to both the Cork and Waterford berths at Fishguard, thus removing the main objection to the use of the Rosslare berth for the car ferry terminal. In addition, the removal of rail sidings on the mainland at Ballygeary made available an area for a car park and customs facilities, thus freeing up space on the pier itself. Some doubts had been expressed as to the construction works impeding the use of the Rosslare Berth for the side-loading *St David*. Further investigation, however, showed that the terminal abutment carrying the portal, would be sited some 70ft to the stern of the *St David* when using the side-loading facilities.

Under the new arrangements, the Rosslare scheme was to consist of an outer arm to provide protection to the ferry from swell, this arm being 340ft in length, at the north end of which would be a roundhead of 35ft diameter, in which would be set a bollard for hauling off the vessel when leaving the berth. At the south end of the berth would be an abutment shaped to accommodate the stern of the vessel. Based on the revised proposals, the consultants estimated the works at Fishguard at £461,397 and at Rosslare £112,707. It was suggested that the electrical installation work at both ports should be carried out by the respective railway companies themselves.

Work commenced at Rosslare on 9 November 1964 with the demolition of the goods line on the landward side of the viaduct, and the moving closer together of two sidings on the pier to make room for the new platform along the back wall of the pier. The new

St David at Rosslare Harbour in 1954. *(Philip Quigley Postcard Collection)*

roadway across the viaduct consisted of large sections of pre-cast concrete placed on the cross members of the viaduct. These sections were cast at CIÉ's Inchicore Works and were brought by rail to Rosslare on Sundays 7 and 21 March 1965. As the loads were 'out-of-gauge', special precautions were necessary for the journey, the second line between Inchicore and Bray being kept clear of traffic, while strict speed restrictions were imposed for the trains' passage through the various tunnels on the line. Access to the new road over the railway line was by means of a new manually-operated barrier-protected level crossing. The tunnel giving access to the side-loading car ferry had to be excavated in a cut-and-cover method by hand, as machinery could not be used under the station roof. The tunnel was formed of mass concrete with an adjustable ramp so as to connect with the ship at all states of the tide. The ramp was also designed and fabricated at Inchicore Works.

History was made on 23 May 1965, 18 years to the day since the resumption of services after the War, when the *St David* docked and for the first time all 63 cars and a motor cycle aboard were driven off through a door in the vessel's side, onto a movable ramp, and from there through a subway under the pier. Prior to this a 'Motor Train' had been used to transport cars between Ballygeary and the Pier and vice versa. This originally consisted of four-wheeled wagons but in 1936 these were replaced by the chassis of six-wheeled coaches 1M and 44M (both ex Midland Great Western), each taking two cars. They were later supplemented until by 1964 ten were available. The wagons from the 'Motor Train' were now redundant and were removed to Bridgetown for storage. The new drive-on/drive-off facilities were officially opened on 11 June 1965 by Erskine Childers, the Minister for Transport & Power. As part of the ceremony, the Minister, accompanied by Dr CS Andrews, Chairman of CIÉ, was driven on and off the *St David*. Afterwards, invited guests were provided with lunch, courtesy of CIÉ, at the Talbot Hotel in Wexford. The new 7-lever signal cabin at Rosslare had been brought into use on the previous day.

Such was the success of the new service, that the *Irish Times* announced in October 1965 that a new car-carrying rail service provided between London and Fishguard, combined with the improved service and facilities, had seen an increase of 45% in car traffic on the route during the first nine months of the year. The 'motorail' service commenced running between Kensington Olympia and Fishguard on 18 June 1965. It was the first such service to use carflats instead of covered vans, a standard fare of £18 per vehicle being charged irrespective of the number of passengers. The car train was reported to have carried 2,900 cars and 10,000 passengers in its first season, representing over 70% of its total capacity, a not-inconsiderable achievement, and the hope was expressed that a second car ferry would soon be provided.

A problem soon manifested itself with the loading ramp at Rosslare. As originally built the ramp was 7ft wide between kerbs at its narrowest point, co-incidentally just where cars entered the ship. It was discovered that about 25% of drivers were unable to negotiate this without fouling the kerbs, frequently causing delay and in a number of instances damaging their cars. As a result the width was soon altered to 7ft 7in, which appeared to resolve the problem. However, at the end of 1965, British Railways announced that they proposed to transfer the cargo ship *Slieve Donard* from Holyhead as a relief vessel for car traffic during the summer of 1966. This vessel would simply carry cars, their drivers and passengers being required to travel separately on the *St Andrew*. This would require the two vessels to sail at about the same time, with allowance being made for the difference in transit times, viz 3½ and 4¼ hours. The *St Andrew* would still accommodate up to 60 cars, which would still require to be loaded and unloaded by crane. These vessels operated in addition to the *St David*.

CIÉ officials drew the attention of the British Railways authorities to the fact that as the cattle doors on the *Slieve Donard* were only 6ft 11in wide, this would lead to problems at Rosslare. In berthing, the vessel would have to be so positioned that virtually no fore and aft movement could be accommodated, whereas the *St David* could range fore and aft by as much as 11in each way; this alone would mean that the berthing manoeuvre would take considerably longer than heretofore. The problem at Rosslare was due to the peculiar construction of the ramp, and did not apply at Fishguard as there was a 50ft long straight gangway, which was flexible enough to accommodate ship movements. Two further potential problems were raised in connection with the *Slieve Donard*. It was pointed out that immediately inside the car deck were two vertical columns, which would require drivers to make a sharp turn as they entered the vessel. The second issue related to the extra height of the car deck above the waterline as compared with the *St David*, which CIÉ officials felt might result in a suspension of loading operations for up to an hour at spring tides. While British Railways conceded that berthing times might be longer, they refused to make any alterations to the ship, not only on the grounds of cost but also they could not spare the time to carry out renovations. They anticipated no problems with spring tides, claiming that this problem could be overcome by ballast adjustment.

The summer of 1966 was unique in that it was the first time since the service began in 1906 in which three large vessels were in Rosslare Harbour at the same time. As can be seen from the proposed British Railways timetable as given below, the port must have been a hive of activity on summer mornings:

05.30	*St Andrew* arrive at No 3 Berth to discharge passengers and cars (by crane).
05.45	*Slieve Donard* arrive at No 4 (ramp berth). Discharge cars. Drivers only going from *St Andrew* to *Slieve Donard* to drive cars off.
08.30	*St Andrew* shifts to Nos 2/3 Berth.
09.00	*Slieve Donard* shift to No 3. Load cars from 09.30 by crane.
09.15	*Slieve Donard* to No 4 to discharge cars and passengers and load cars and passengers.
10.15	*St David* depart.
10.30	*Slieve Donard* shift to No 4 ramp berth. *St Andrew* to load cars and passengers in Nos 2/3 (aft only) if possible to do so, otherwise it would be necessary to shift back to No 3 and load.
11.30	*Slieve Donard* to depart from No 4.
11.45	*St Andrew* to depart from Nos 2/3.

Proposed closure

CIÉ intimated to the F&RR&H in March 1964 its desire to terminate all services on the line between Mallow and Waterford as part of the Company's moves to improve its financial position. To enable the closure of the line between Waterford and Fermoy the formal consent of the F&RR&H Board would be required. The F&RR&H agreed to obtain the opinion of the BRB's Solicitor as, whilst under Irish legislation CIÉ could be empowered to withdraw the service, the legal position of the Fishguard Company was not clear. However, it was felt that legislation might be required in both jurisdictions. In due course the Transport Act 1966 was enacted, amending, where necessary, the Transport Acts of 1950 and 1958;[1] basically, this allowed the Board of CIÉ to terminate services on the lines of the F&RR&H within the Republic.

In accordance with its statutory obligations, CIÉ gave notice in *Iris Oifigiúil*, the official State Gazette (which replaced the old *Dublin Gazette* in January 1922), of its intention to close three lines after the last trains of 25 March 1967, including the Mallow to Waterford line. Even before the announcement was made it was clear that CIÉ intended to close the line. An off-the-cuff remark in the summer of 1966 from the Waterford Area Manager, that the future of the line was under review, led to confirmation from the Minister for Transport & Power that the line was in fact to be closed, quoting the usual statistics indicating the low degree of use by traders and passengers. Soon after this announcement various works were commenced on the Limerick Junction to Waterford line to better equip it for the running of the Rosslare Express. These included the extension of the loops and platforms at Carrick-on-Suir and Kilsheelan to allow the crossing of longer trains at those stations; two-way signalling was also provided at these and a number of other stations. Mechanical staff exchanging apparatus was also provided at Grange, Fiddown and Kilsheelan so that trains could run through at higher speeds.

The Rosslare Express would continue to run, going via Limerick Junction to Waterford and Rosslare Harbour, with 20 minutes added to its schedule. It was

---

1 The two Acts only legislated specifically for CIÉ lines and not those of the F&RR&H in Ireland.

also announced that the cross-channel service for the summer of 1967 would consist of up to four sailings each way on weekdays at its peak, to be worked by the *St David* and the *Duke of Rothesay*, the latter vessel being chartered from British Rail for a period of five years from 12 May 1967. In the interim she was to be converted to a side-loading vessel. It was announced in February 1967 that the *St David's* sister ship, the *St Andrew*, had been withdrawn and sold to Joseph de Smedt of Antwerp for £35,017 for demolition. Other rail services would be replaced by road services; as regards passenger traffic the new bus routes would not serve Clondulane or Durrow Stations, while on the freight side, road services would radiate from Mallow to Cappoquin and from Waterford to Cappagh.

In the event, the section of line between Waterford via the Suir Bridge and Grace Dieu Junction to the premises of Waterford Ironfounders Ltd, located at the old Waterford South Station, was to be retained "for the foreseeable future." It is interesting to note that the matter of the lease of the old station premises was raised in February 1972 when it came to light that the GSR had granted the lease for 99 years from 1 December 1935 at an annual rent of £75. However, the property in question was owned by the F&RR&H and it was necessary to apply for a Deed of Rectification.

Up until the closure, this section of line had been worked by means of a subsidiary instrument in the Waterford West to Kilmeaden staff section. This was replaced by an ordinary ETS instrument, with a second one provided at Suir Bridge cabin. Two such instruments were installed in Waterford West cabin, linked to, but normally out of phase with those at Suir Bridge and Grace Dieu. For the four instruments there were three staffs, one locked in Suir Bridge cabin, one locked in Waterford West and one held 'free' at Waterford West. The two locked staffs were lettered 'Suir Bridge Control', the free one 'Waterford West/Grace Dieu'. This latter was used as a manual staff for the section, except that it was inserted in the Grace Dieu instrument on arrival of a train or light engine there, so that the Signalman could withdraw the staff for the matching instrument in West cabin. This was then held free in case the bridge had to be opened before the 'factory shunt' returned to Grace

Dieu. Each of the three staffs had a key to release the Suir Bridge control lever. To open the bridge, the 'free' staff in Waterford West was inserted in the instrument linked to the Suir Bridge cabin, enabling the person in charge of opening the bridge to withdraw the staff in the Bridge cabin and to unlock the control with it.

The last train to run on Saturday 25 March 1967 was the Rosslare Express, which consisted of General Motors locomotive B121, heating van, a composite, buffet car 170N, three standards and a brake van. It reportedly received a rousing send-off from Mallow with an elongated fusillade of detonators. Considering the occasion, time keeping was excellent with an arrival at Waterford only eight minutes late. Changes to the timetable from Monday 27 March meant that the railcar which had previously worked the two return trips to Kilmokea Halt was not available. To operate the service railcar 2509, ex Sligo Leitrim & Northern Counties Railway 'B', was sent down from Dublin; however, it failed in May and was initially replaced by ex GNR BUT railcar 716N, and later again by a locomotive with a single coach, which continued to Campile so as to run round.

The Mallow to Fermoy section was formally abandoned by CIÉ within months of the closure, with lifting expected to commence in October or November 1967. However, barely six months after the closure of the line it was announced that a processing plant was to be established by Quigley Magnesite Ltd near Clonea, Dungarvan for 'washing' of dolomite. This material, used in the manufacture of firebrick lining for the iron smelting industry, had been discovered at Bennett's Bridge in County Kilkenny. It was expected that CIÉ would handle the traffic by rail over the 52 miles from Bennett's Bridge to Dungarvan via Waterford, in special vacuum-braked block trains, which would necessitate the re-opening of the ex WD&LR line as far as Dungarvan and the construction of a new line nearly two miles in length to serve the new plant. The intention was that the line from Grace Dieu Junction would be worked as a siding, possibly with an intermediate block post at Kilmacthomas.

Formal application was made by CIÉ on 4 September 1968 to the Minister for Transport & Power for a Railway Works Order under the provisions of the

Kilmokea Halt on 29 August 1970 with Railcar 2509 on an IRRS tour. This railcar, originally owned by the SL&NCR, provided a service between Waterford and Kilmokea in the late 1960s in connection with the construction of the Great Island power station. *(Barry Carse)*

Transport Act 1963 for the construction of a new line of railway. The necessary Order was granted on 9 December 1968[2] giving powers to CIÉ for the compulsory acquisition of land and the construction of a single line of railway approximately 1½ miles in total length, and forming a junction with the ex WD&LR line at or near a point 49m 910y and terminating "on the southern side of the road … near to the entrance of the approach road to Ballynacourty lighthouse;" the junction faced towards Waterford.

In the interim a temporary lifting headquarters had been established on 11 January 1968 at Dungarvan and actual lifting commenced, not as anticipated on the Mallow to Fermoy section, but from a point east of Lismore Station at 32m 790y; by 11 March rails had been removed to a point a few hundred yards short of Ballyhane No 1 level crossing at the 38¼ milepost. The gang used ex camping coach HC7[3] as accommodation. The lifting train was mainly worked by Metrovick Bo-Bo C208 and included bogie rail wagons 8229 and 1107M along with winch wagon 504A. An extraordinary general meeting of the F&RR&H was held at Paddington Station on 4 April to approve resolutions for the Abandonment Order for the section of line from the point of junction with

the ex GS&WR line at Fermoy to the 45¾mp (about 1,060 yards west of Dungarvan signal cabin), and to appoint CIÉ as agents in respect of its implementation, and the winding up of the portion of the undertaking involved.

Construction work on the new branch commenced in the spring of 1969, progress being such that rails were reportedly being laid by June of that year, the track-work being that removed from the line between Dungarvan and Lismore. It was reported that the construction of the new factory at Ballinacourty was expected to be completed by the end of 1969. The junction for the branch was laid down in May.

Meanwhile, adjacent to the Barrow Bridge on the South Wexford line, the Electricity Supply Board (ESB) began the construction during 1966 of a large generating station at Great Island. Since many of the men employed on the scheme came from the Waterford area, and with the nearest road crossing of the Barrow some 15 miles distant at New Ross, CIÉ agreed to open a short-platformed halt at Kilmokea, immediately to the east of the bridge. To serve this a special passenger train departed Waterford daily from Monday to Friday at 08.10, arriving Kilmokea at 08.20; a return service left Kilmokea at 18.10. The halt was subsequently briefly re-opened in 1970 in connection with the construction of an extension to the power station.

---

2 SI 252 of 1968.
3 Ex GS&WR 50ft bogie third No 832 of 1902 and latterly Departmental Vehicle 529A.

CHAPTER SIXTEEN

Dissolution Plans

Consideration was given in 1966/67 to the dissolution of the F&RR&H, which by then had become something of an anachronism. The Company's capital included £1,237,664 of 3½% New Guaranteed Preference Stock, which had been raised to finance assets solely in Ireland, CIÉ being responsible for payment of the interest on that stock. CIÉ in fact paid the BRB a sufficient amount to pay the interest on the stock, but as this represented income as far as that Company was concerned it was deemed to be liable for corporation tax under the UK Finance Act of 1965. The effect was that the Company was left with insufficient funds to pay both the full 3½% interest and corporation tax; the shortfall amounted to some £29,000 annually. A solution to this inequitable situation could be found by promoting a Bill in Parliament to vest the assets of the Fishguard Company in England in the BRB, including the ships, and to transfer the Company's shipping powers to the BR Board. In addition, the F&RR&H stocks and shares held by the BR Board should be cancelled and the joint guarantee on the stock should be repealed as far as the BRB was concerned.

The effect of this would be to leave the Company in existence exclusively with Irish interests, with all its ordinary shares held by CIÉ, thus in effect becoming an Irish subsidiary of CIÉ. This would in turn have led to further tax problems, as dividends would then be treated as overseas income. In view of the possibility of applying for an Act, it became necessary to consult with CIÉ on the matter. Initially CIÉ expressed an interest in acquiring a 50-50 share in the venture, with equal representation in the management of the services. Subject to the agreement of the BRB to this proposal, CIÉ would then have to seek Irish Government approval.

The next move was that the BRB wrote to their shareholders in November 1966 giving details of the proposed British Railways Board (Fishguard Harbour etc Vesting) Bill to be introduced in the following Session of Parliament. The primary purpose of the Bill was to enable the BRB to withdraw from the Fishguard Company. It was suggested that CIÉ should move the principal office of the F&RR&H from London to Ireland. Legal advice to the BRB seemed to indicate that if the Bill was enacted, there would still remain a liability on the part of the F&RR&H to pay the interest and also to provide a cross-channel shipping service. However, as the provisions of the Bill included transfer of all vessels to British Railways, the F&RR&H would then have no ships.

It was about this time that tri-partite negotiations were taking place between the BRB, CIÉ and the British & Irish Steampacket Company (B&I) with a view to rationalising the southern Irish Sea shipping services by some form of pooling arrangement. If this were to come to fruition, any argument for the enforcement of the F&RR&H obligation to provide a shipping service would most likely have been removed.

Perhaps the most important point in relation to the new Bill was that the F&RR&H had originally been created by statute and its status could therefore only be changed by statute. It would appear, at least in the understanding of CIÉ's legal advisers, to be a "wholly anomalous and ridiculous situation if the powers created could be changed at will by either Parliament without at least the appearance of consistency by complementary legislation by the other." It is difficult to understand why CIÉ wanted to take over all responsibility for the F&RR&H and to transfer its offices to Ireland, particularly as a decision had already been taken in principle to close the Mallow–Waterford section, which included the F&RR&H line between Fermoy and Waterford. CIÉ informed the BRB in January 1967 that if a scheme could be devised for the dissolution of the F&RR&H, which met with the Board's approval, the Minister for Transport & Power would be asked to introduce appropriate legislation. The Minister had already indicated that, subject to provision satisfactory to him, for the maintenance of shipping services and safeguarding CIÉ against any financial liability beyond that already in existence, he would agree, in principle, to introduce such legislation. That said, the CIÉ Solicitor informed the BRB that he had been directed to lodge a petition against the BRB Bill.

It later transpired that two of the holders of the New Guaranteed 3½% Preference Stock, the Prudential Assurance Company and Lord Faringdon's Trustees[1] had also lodged petitions against the Bill. The opposition, apart from that of CIÉ, was chiefly directed to the proposal to relieve the BRB from their liability under the joint guarantee with CIÉ, of the interest on the New Stock. Despite CIÉ's petition against the Bill, there was a broad measure of agreement between the two companies on the fundamentals; in view of this, the BRB agreed to withdraw the Bill and to further pursue the scheme for dissolution of the F&RR&H. Despite this, the matter was dropped and was not raised again for nearly ten years.

Correspondence between the Department of Transport & Power and CIÉ in September 1967 indicates that the Department was in favour of the development of Rosslare Harbour for use by stern-loading vessels, particularly since there was a distinct prospect of a new service being introduced in the summer of 1968 by Irish Shipping. The provision of a new berth was estimated to cost £80,000, the Department agreeing to provide this amount as a repayable capital advance. So anxious was the Minister to see this work carried out that CIÉ were urged to press ahead with the preparation of plans for the new berth. Initially it was proposed to make the link span at the berth suitable only for cars and caravans unless calculations showed that little extra cost would be incurred in providing for commercial vehicles and buses. Yet again Messrs Coode & Partners were called in to carry out the design work. The estimate for the work was later altered to £68,000, this figure being approved by the F&RR&H Board.

Another player entered the scene in July 1968 when it was announced that B&I Line had expressed an interest in using Rosslare Harbour as a base for a service to Swansea, the new service to commence on 23 May 1969 and run through to the end of September. Various objections were listed regarding the use of the stern-loading ramp at the south end of No 3 berth due to the type of ship's ramp in use. Also, adverse comment was made regarding the road access to the two berths, insufficiency of car marshalling areas and customs facilities, poor signposting in the Rosslare area, and the fact that foot passengers would have to embark and disembark by means of the ship's stern door. William Mulligan, General Manager of B&I, met with Mr Harrington, the General Manager, Shipping & International Services Division of the BRB, to further discuss the matter. Mr Mulligan was left in no doubt that the BRB regarded the entry of the B&I as an unfriendly act and was particularly disappointing in view of the discussions that had already taken place regarding closer co-operation on the Irish Sea routes. The BRB also considered themselves free to vary rates and charges on the Rosslare service.

It was obvious by the end of the 1960s that the facilities at Fishguard were by then totally inadequate for even current traffic demand, including larger vehicles. The F&RR&H Board therefore developed a plan to provide an end-loading ramp and enlarged handling facilities as well as improving amenities for foot passengers. All this was to be provided by early 1972. It should be remembered that the F&RR&H still provided the ships for the Rosslare route, at that time by chartering them from the BRB. The latter, under statutory agreement, worked and managed Fishguard Harbour and the shipping services. The proposals included the provision of the end-loading ramp at the southern end of the quay, the removal of surplus track to provide a circulating area for cars, a new customs hall for cars with a separate customs clearance shed for commercial vehicles, a new access road, modernisation of foot passenger facilities and the provision of an end-loading door in the *Duke of Rothesay*.

The report recognised that future growth was subject to the influence of the political troubles in

---

1 Alexander Henderson had been appointed the First Baronet Faringdon in 1902, being raised to the peerage as Baron Faringdon in 1916.

Aerial view of Fishguard Harbour showing the much reduced facilities of recent years. Going up the centre of the picture can be seen the lifeboat pen, beside which are the two marine workshops. Beyond these is the two-storey administration building. In the centre is the linkspan used by the *Stena Europe*, beyond which (beside the white building) is Goodwick Quay. Top centre, the railway begins its climb towards Manorowen. The eastern breakwater on the left hand side, runs out from The Parrog, the road connecting Goodwick and Fishguard. *(Stena Line)*

Northern Ireland, and to the rising level of prices in Ireland. It was also obvious that air travel would continue to expand, but it was felt that increases in airport charges, maintenance and re-equipment costs would bring about substantial fare increases and thus divert traffic back to sea routes. The provision of an end-loading ramp at Fishguard would also allow the carriage of commercial vehicles and coaches. A survey of businessmen had shown very favourable interest in the short Rosslare sea route and it was anticipated that commercial vehicle carryings for 1972 would total 1,400, rising to 2,500 four years later; it was then expected to remain at the latter figure for at least another six years.

The total estimated outlay at Fishguard was £604,000, to which was added a sum of £20,000 for the conversion of the *Duke of Rothesay*. However, although the completion of the work was important, it was also essential to provide matching facilities at Rosslare and to consider likely traffic growth levels over, say, the ensuing ten years. A new vessel was expected to enter service in 1974 and this would provide for about 230 cars, and would enable the Company to match demand until the end of the decade. An overriding factor causing some concern for the BRB was the

change of Government in June 1970, when the Tories came to power under the leadership of Edward Heath; it was felt that this change might bring about limitations on capital availability.

At a F&RR&H Board meeting in February 1970 it was suggested, in view of the increasing volume of movements in and out of Rosslare Harbour, that there was a growing need for the appointment of a Harbour Master with previous sea-going experience. In writing to CIÉ, it was pointed out that there was no other harbour of comparable size which did not have such a person in charge. It was stated that it was only due to the skill and experience of the ships' captains and their training at Fishguard which had prevented any serious incidents occurring at Rosslare. Despite this request it was to be 1 January 1973 before Captain MC Holden was duly appointed to the post.

A management conference was held in October 1970 to consider the construction of an end-loading ferry ramp and associated shore works at Fishguard, the objective being to earn increased revenue on the route. It was intended to construct such a ramp to allow vehicles with a headroom of up to 14ft 6in to be loaded through the stern door of the *Caledonian Princess*. In addition, it was proposed to cut a similar door in the stern of the *Duke of Rothesay*. A new customs baggage hall would be required. The sale in 1968 of the Fishguard Bay Hotel included the access road to the station and harbour. As part of the agreement for the purchase of the hotel, British Railways were to provide an alternative access to the port as the existing road was quite unsuitable for heavy vehicles and was regarded as unsafe for use; a new road was also therefore included in the proposals which were estimated to cost £583,000. Similar facilities would, of course, be required at Rosslare Harbour.

The Fishguard scheme and expenditure were approved at a board meeting on 11 December, subject to an examination of the possibility of bringing about an end to the Waterford service, having regard to the provision of ro-ro services and evidence that further ship capacity would be required at Fishguard in the not too distant future; ongoing talks with B&I Line were also expected to be taken into account. It was agreed that platforms 2 & 3 should be removed at Fishguard to make way for the new road facilities. The contract for the work at Fishguard Harbour was awarded to Messrs John Mowlam & Company at a figure of £218,118.84.

The facilities at Fishguard were not as extensive as those at Rosslare, the new loading ramp being an extension of a converted cross-platform subway (the old cattle creep), and had a major disadvantage for future expansion in that it was only suitable for side-loading; furthermore, headroom was restricted to 6ft 3in, meaning that only cars could be transhipped. The entrance to the subway involved difficult and complex manoeuvres, including crossing the main railway track to reach the vessel. The car hall was a conversion of one of the old cattle sheds and was situated in an awkward location adjacent to the entrance to the subway. The main drawback at Fishguard, however, was the approach from the main A40 road as it passed over part of the property of the Fishguard Bay Hotel, as already stated, by then no longer in railway ownership. Many complaints had been received from the hotel authorities and the local authority had agreed to its use being continued until the end of 1971, when a new road approach would become necessary.

Following the official opening of the new stern-loading ramp at Fishguard on 6 July 1972 by Richard Marsh, Chairman of the BRB, the cross-channel service was operated solely by the *Caledonian Princess*. The *Duke of Rothesay*, although allocated to the route, was not used owing to a reduced demand for accompanied cars, due in part to the increased terrorist activity following 'Bloody Sunday',[2] including the burning of the British Embassy in Dublin on 3 February and the Aldershot bombing on 22 February. However, with the introduction of daily sailings off-peak, the substantial increase in commercial vehicles would require additional freight capacity, particularly in the summer months. It was expected that accompanied car figures would reach 36,000 in 1973, and it would be necessary to install the mezzanine deck on the *Caledonian Princess*, so as to increase the car carrying capacity on each crossing.

The CIÉ Board at its meeting on 15 April 1971 approved expenditure of £76,100 for further improvements at Rosslare Harbour. It was announced that a deal had been concluded with Motor Distributors Ltd of Dublin, under which fully assembled German motor vehicles would be imported in full charter shiploads through Rosslare; expected figures for 1973 were 4,000 to 5,000 vehicles involving about 18 shipments, while it was anticipated that the number might well rise to 10,000 a year by 1984. BRB's forecast of freight vehicles on the route was 700 units in 1972, rising to 2,500 units by 1976. In the event, the number of vehicles carried handsomely exceeded all expectations; during the 24-week period from 3 July to 16 December 1972 more than 2,500 freight units had been carried, causing BRB to revise their forecasts to 10,000 for 1973, rising to 25,000 by 1977. To cater for the summer 1973 traffic, it was proposed to provide a freight-only vessel, freight-only sailings being all year round from 1974 onwards. Despite earlier reservations about the use of foreign flag ships, negotiations were opened for a short-term charter during the peak summer months of a vessel at a cost of about £900 per day. Ships considered included the MV *Isartal*, the SNCF's *Capitaine le Goff*, the *Stena*

---

2 On 30 January 1972, 26 people were shot dead by the British Army in Derry.

Trailer or a shared charter with Irish Shipping Ltd of the MV *Greymaster*, none of which materialised. Reference is made later to the new continental service opened up by Irish Shipping Ltd in 1969. The service only lasted for three years but Irish Continental Lines Ltd[3] commenced a new service to Le Havre on 2 June 1973.

It had become obvious that these various developments necessitated the provision of further improvements at Rosslare. The port depended entirely on a single ro-ro ramp; if that ramp should suffer damage, the port would be effectively closed to that type of traffic. Irish Continental reported that their vessel *St Patrick* was unable to put to sea in strong winds without hauling-off assistance, and they suggested that a tug be procured. The cost of providing a full-time tug would have been prohibitive, and BR would certainly refuse to contribute to the cost since they and their predecessors had been managing quite well for nearly 70 years. One possible alternative was the provision of hauling-off wires on the bed of the harbour; however, with the depth of water available within the harbour, these would present a serious hazard to ships.

A fresh report on the future development of Rosslare Harbour was presented in March 1974 by Messrs Coode & Partners. They suggested that two additional berths for stern loading vessels should be provided by means of a new pier about 550ft to the west of the existing pier with new car parking and customs facilities adjacent. They also recommended that a berth should be provided for the servicing of oil rigs, as it seemed likely that oil would be discovered in the Irish Sea. Messrs Coode considered that the existing viaduct should be blocked off, which would result in a build-up of sand to the east of the harbour. The material dredged from east of the harbour should then be deposited on the beach at Rosslare Strand; it was felt that if properly controlled the sand deposited there would not cause extra siltation at the entrance to Wexford Harbour.[4] The works were estimated to cost in the region of £1,866,000 and would take approximately

18 months from the date the contractors came on site.

Following receipt of the report, CIÉ looked at the likely traffic projections up to 1980, these being based on figures supplied by British Rail and Irish Continental Lines. Passenger numbers were expected to rise from 387,000 in 1974 to 551,000 in 1980, while cars would increase from 82,000 to about 130,000 in the same period. Freight units would increase from 17,000 to 40,000 while port revenue would go from £383,000 to about £719,000; the revenue figures were in respect of port working only and did not include indirect business accruing to CIÉ. Various public bodies expressed an interest in giving assistance in connection with the development of the port. In particular, Bórd Fáilte and the Electricity Supply Board were mentioned, the latter in connection with their proposal to build a nuclear power station at Carnsore Point, just to the south of Rosslare.

The new West Pier was finally commenced in 1978 and was completed two years later, but with only one stern-loading ramp on the east side of the new pier; a third ramp was later provided in 1991, while a fourth ramp was constructed at the outer end of the original pier in 1995/96. With the construction of the West Pier it became necessary to provide alternative accommodation for fishing vessels, which had traditionally used the harbour as shelter in bad weather, so a new harbour was constructed further to the west near to Kilrane.

British Railways set up a new shipping division as from 1 January 1968, known as the Shipping & International Services Division; this had little if any effect on the F&RR&H. However, British Railways began using a new brand name in 1971, Sealink, this being applied to the ships in the following year. It was not until January 1979 that a new BR subsidiary, Sealink UK Limited, was officially established, the F&RR&H becoming a subsidiary of Sealink UK. It was announced in the House of Commons in July 1984 that Sealink UK Limited was to be sold for £66 million to Sea Containers Limited, a Company based in Bermuda, the sale being completed on 27 July; the Company then became known as Sealink British Ferries. The Company was sold again in 1991 to the Swedish firm Stena Line, already one of the

---

3 Owned jointly by Irish Shipping (50%), Fearnley & Eager of Oslo (25%) & Lion Ferry of Sweden (25%).

4 Sand accretion along the coast to the north of Rosslare Harbour has been an on-going problem for many years, this sometimes being blamed on the provision of the various facilities at Rosslare.

The F&RR&H Board at the 111th AGM at Fishguard in 2006. Back row left to right:- Michael Murphy, Richard O'Farrell (deputy Chairman), Ian Jamieson, Vic Goodwin; front row Les Stracey (Secretary), Gareth Williams (Chairman) and John Keenan. *(Stena Line)*

largest ferry operators in the world.[5] The new Company became known as Sealink Stena and later still Stena Sealink. The Sealink brand name finally disappeared in 1996 when it became simply Stena Line. Stena took over the role of joint owner with IÉ of the F&RR&H Company; today IÉ's Partner in the enterprise is Stena Line Ports Limited. Shareholders' annual meetings are still held, the current directorship consisting of four representatives from Stena and three from IÉ, thus continuing the preponderating influence originally granted to the GWR. The question of who should take responsibility for the administration and operation of Rosslare Harbour still remained to be resolved. Should it be transferred to CIÉ who operated it, or to Wexford County Council, or perhaps to a newly-established Port Authority? However, it was not until 1984 that the creation of a new Port Authority was finally announced under the Government's New National Plan.

Reference has been made to earlier negotiations between B&I and the F&RR&H regarding the use of Rosslare Harbour for a cross-channel service. This became a reality in 1980 when the B&I commenced a service to Pembroke with the *Viking III*. Later, in 1986, B&I suspended the Pembroke service and began operating a joint service to Fishguard with Sealink. This was to be short-lived and B&I reverted to Pembroke in 1987. Plans by CIÉ for Rosslare Harbour were discussed at a F&RR&H Board meeting on 29 August 1984, these including the provision of a main terminal building, customs vehicle examination shed, and additional station platform and track alterations at Ballygeary. In addition, an elevated walkway was to be provided from No 2 Berth to the main building; the total cost of this major development was estimated at £3.5 million. Major reclamation work was carried out during the late 1980s and the new terminal building was provided on a 6½ acre site in 1988, by which time the cost had risen to £5.5 million. The terminal consisted of a two-storey building having a concourse area, departure lounge, restaurant and bar, customs and emigration zone, and office accommodation, with a total floor area of 3,500 sq m. Site clearance began in April 1987, and the official opening of the new station and passenger terminal was carried out on 14 September 1988, the ceremony being performed by the Minister for Transport & Tourism, Seamus Brennan, TD, with various CIÉ and Iarnród Éireann (IÉ) officials in attendance.

The first phase of a new £18.8 million development plan for the harbour commenced in 1992 with the award of a contract to the Finnish firm Haka Limited. An area was surrounded by sea walls and then pumped dry to allow blasting operations so as to deepen the port to 7.2m to cater for larger ferries. It was announced that IÉ would finance the project with grant aid from the EEC. Berth No 1 link span was to be replaced while No 3 was to have a new link span to

---

5 Stena Line had originally been founded in 1962 by Sten A Olsson.

facilitate the Stena Sealink ship *Felicity*; in addition the West Pier was to be extended by 50m. It was reported that the Minister for Transport & Tourism travelled on the Executive train to Rosslare Harbour on 28 October 1992 to start the first phase of the new development. The Minister detonated an underwater blast of 400kg of commercial explosive to remove 2,000 tonne of rock; dredged material was to be used to reclaim about 30 acres of land. Additional vehicle standing was also to be provided at Fishguard Harbour at an estimated cost of £5 million, subject to the approval of the Stena Sealink Board. The latter alterations were inaugurated on 13 July 1994 by the Rt Hon John Redwood MP, Secretary of State for Wales, the same day as the new fast ferry service began operating with the Stena *Sea Lynx I*.

During the course of discussions on the proposed dissolution of the F&RR&H Company, another subject had been discussed. Whilst not of direct concern to the F&RR&H, the question of the service between Fishguard and Waterford was interlinked in that Section 70 of the 1898 Act obliged the GWR to provide a daily steamer service from either New Milford or Fishguard to the Irish port. This service was to remain in operation until determined by Parliament. However, by an agreement dated 18 March 1939 between the GWR, the Waterford Harbour Commissioners and the Borough of Waterford, it had been agreed that the Company should provide a minimum of three sailings weekly on alternate days in each direction, in return for which the various bodies in Waterford would not seek to enforce Section 70. A further agreement was made between the parties in June 1959. It should be remembered here that Section 70 of the Act did not apply in Britain at this stage, following its suspension in 1940, although it continued to apply in Ireland; Counsel in Ireland had advised in 1966 that there was little prospect of Section 70 of the 1898 Act being repealed because of likely opposition in Waterford.

It is not clear why discussions between CIÉ and the BRB came to an end in 1967, but it was to be another nine years before the whole question of dissolving the F&RR&H came to prominence again. In July 1976 the BRB Legal Department submitted a lengthy report for the consideration of the Board, suggesting that the same procedure be followed as had been put forward in 1967. It was considered that the harbour part of the Irish side of the operation, namely Rosslare Harbour, should be put in charge of a new Irish port authority and of the railways in Ireland to CIÉ. However, it was important that Rosslare Harbour should not be passed to a body with power to operate competing shipping services. CIÉ advised that they were unhappy at becoming involved financially in plans being discussed for the enlargement of Rosslare port at a cost of some £2–£3million. Their legal advice was that the existence of the F&RR&H might make it more difficult for the work to be financed from outside, possibly the EEC. CIÉ's view was that Rosslare Port should be transferred to a body other than themselves. The BRB legal people also considered it essential that the statutory obligations to operate shipping services between Fishguard and Rosslare and Waterford should be repealed. It was reported that negotiations had already commenced with the Waterford interests to ascertain the terms under which they would agree not to oppose the repeal of Section 70 of the Act of 1898.

The CIÉ Board at its meeting held on 11 March 1976, in considering future developments at Rosslare Harbour, agreed to write to the Minister for Transport & Power pointing out that the F&RR&H Company was an anachronism and should be dissolved. Later, in January 1977, the CIÉ Chairman, Liam St Devlin, suggested that the Company's assets in Ireland, including the port at Rosslare, should be transferred to Irish interests. To enable CIÉ to transfer the interest in the F&RR&H, it would be necessary to buy-out the holders of £1,237,664 of 3½% Guaranteed Preference stock; this would most likely necessitate the registration of the Fishguard Company under the Companies Act of 1963 in Ireland. Legal opinion was sought both in Britain and Ireland, the consensus being that legislation would be required in both jurisdictions. Bearing in mind the difficulties and expenses involved, it was suggested that 'if it works, don't fix it'. As a consequence the F&RR&H Company is still in existence in 2015, the statutory annual general meetings being held to comply with Company law.

With Liam St Devlin's retirement as Chairman of

CIÉ at the end of 1983, the Government appointed GT Paul Conlon,[6] as Executive Chairman, his appointment taking effect as from 1 January 1984. Four years prior to this appointment, Messrs McKinsey International, who had previously reported on the state of CIÉ in 1971, were again commissioned in September 1979 by the Department of Tourism and Transport to "examine reasons for the deterioration in the financial position of CIÉ and to recommend such corrective measures as may be possible to bring about an improvement in the position." The report was submitted to Government in December 1980; this is not the place to go into any detail of the report's findings but suffice to say that the main thrust was that CIÉ should be broken up and replaced by three operating companies. The *Irish Times* commented that the report cast a "consistently weary look at the railway system", not thinking much of its future, "if it had one at all." Seen by some as a 'hatchet-man', Conlon was asked to report on McKinsey's findings. Generally he was in favour of setting up three operating companies, but with the proviso that CIÉ should remain as a holding company. Meanwhile, in October 1984 the Government published its National Development plan under the title of *Building on Reality 1985–1987*. As regards transport, the plan adopted much of McKinsey's findings. Included in the plan was the setting up of a port authority to oversee Rosslare Harbour.

The Transport (Re-Organisation of Córas Iompair Éireann) Act passed successfully through the Dáil on 11 December 1986, enabling CIÉ to form three subsidiary companies, which came into operation on 2 February 1987. These included Iarnród Éireann or Irish Rail (IÉ), which was tasked with operating both the rail system and the road freight business. Section 8(4) of the new Act made provision for each operating company to include additional functions subject to the approval of the CIÉ Board and the Ministers for Transport & Power and Finance. It was therefore decided to include the Board's catering activities and Rosslare Harbour in IÉ's brief. The question of setting up a port authority for Rosslare was left in abeyance,

prompting local TD (Member of the Dáil) Hugh Byrne to enquire of the Minister for Communications on 18 December 1985 when he proposed setting up the authority. Minister Jim Mitchell's reply referred to the fact that the harbour was technically owned by the F&RR&H Company and it would therefore require the passing of legislation both in the UK and Ireland to effect a change. Some concern was expressed regarding the fact that one of the joint owners of the F&RR&H, Sealink British Ferries Ltd (as successor to British Railways), was a private company. Mrs Avril Doyle, another local Wexford TD, raised the question of a port authority again in February 1988, this time of the Minister for the Marine, who was about to take responsibility for Rosslare Harbour. Once again, he referred to the complex legal issues which were then under consideration; 20 years later, little has changed.

On the freight side, sugar beet had been a good source of income, albeit restricted to a season of about 16 weeks annually. The Irish Sugar Manufacturing Company was established in 1926 in Carlow. Under the provisions of the Sugar Manufacture Act of 1933, the Irish Free State Government brought into being Cómhlucht Siúicre Éireann Teoranta, the Irish Sugar Company, (CSÉ) to help make Ireland self-sufficient as regards sugar supplies. The new Company took over the Carlow factory and constructed new facilities at Mallow, Thurles and Tuam. The latter two factories were closed during the early 1980s, with production being concentrated at Mallow and Carlow. The South Wexford area was one of the principal beet growing regions in the country. As an example, in the 1950s, Campile dispatched 25 wagons daily, Ballycullane 21, Bridgetown 18, Wellington Bridge 17, Duncormick 11, Killinick 9, Kilrane 6 and Rosslare Strand 3; on the Dungarvan line, Dungarvan sent out 23 wagons daily. By the mid-1990s the two remaining factories were receiving about 1.5 million tonnes of beet and producing 220,000 tonnes of sugar, with a turnover of £128 million.

In the interim, under the CIÉ Rail Development Plan of the 1970s the conveyance of beet was given special consideration. As already stated, the season lasted for only 16 weeks annually and required some 1,000 wagons to be kept in reserve. The concept

---

6 Conlon was an accountant by profession and had, prior to his appointment to CIÉ, been Managing Director of Nitrigin Éireann Teoranta (Irish Fertiliser Industries)

Left: Wellington Bridge on 3 November 1984. Co-Co No 052 with 30 laden wagons and goods van awaits departure on the 13.30 to Campile. Laden trains were restricted to 30 wagons as far as Campile where they were re-marshalled into 43 wagon trains for their onward journey. *(Barry Carse)*

Right: Another view at Wellington Bridge showing to good effect the beet loader with a trailer of beet awaiting unloading. Bulleid designed corrugated wagons are evident. Later, these wagons were rebuilt at Limerick wagon works with two bodies mounted on one underframe to increase capacity. The date is 29 December 1979. *(Barry Carse)*

of a central beet loading station somewhere on the South Wexford line was put to CSÉ and received approval. In due course it was decided to develop suitable facilities at Wellington Bridge, as it was in the centre of an intensive beet-growing area. The necessary land was purchased at the north side of the station, where the land was at a sufficient height over rail level to allow the loading of wagons. Work commenced in the summer of 1979 and was completed in record time to allow the first load of the season to be sent away on 25 September of that year. The beet loading and sampling facilities were provided by CSÉ, with the necessary track-work being installed by CIÉ.

The new depot was equipped with a reception office, flanked by two weighbridges, one for fully laden vehicles, the other for the same vehicles when empty, thus enabling the tare weight to be easily ascertained.

After being weighed, the vehicles then moved to a sampling plant, where the incoming beet was quality tested to establish the sugar content. On the basis of this test, the farmer was paid for his produce. From the sampling point the beet was discharged into a giant hopper and beet elevator. The latter, of German design, was built on wheels and was capable of loading a 40-wagon train within 70 minutes. The wagons were moved along the loading siding and beneath the loading arm by means of an electrically-powered capstan operated from the cab of the elevator. Some idea of the overall efficiency of this arrangement can be gained from the fact that a total of 260 wagons were loaded in a day. During the 1980/81 season, 15,040 wagon loads of beet were moved by rail from Wellington Bridge to the Thurles factory; at an average of 11½ tons per wagon, this equated to 167,640 tons.

Under the Sugar Act of 1991 CSÉ was privatised, becoming known as the Greencore Group. The Carlow factory was closed down on 11 March 2005, all sugar beet thenceforth going to Mallow. However, following a decision of a meeting on 24 November 2005 of the Council of Ministers of the European Union, it was announced that the Mallow factory was also to close with the loss of 300 jobs, this taking effect as from 12 May 2006. This effectively brought about an end to the growing and processing of sugar beet in Ireland, and the consequent loss of this traffic to Irish Rail, a factor which ultimately saw the closure of the South Wexford line.

Improvements at Waterford

A decision was made in 1966 to modernise Waterford Station, work in this regard commencing in February of the following year with the demolition of the fine terminal building erected by the Waterford & Limerick Railway in 1864. This was replaced by a modern three-storey building of reinforced-concrete frame construction. It is worth mentioning that the enlargement of the old station facilities in 1906 to accommodate the F&RR&H, involved the first large-scale use of this material in Ireland, closely followed by the road bridge giving access to Rosslare pier at Ballygeary. In addition to work on the new station building, the locomotive maintenance facilities at Waterford were closed on 25 March 1967, apart from fuelling and watering facilities for diesel railcars. A new staff dormitory was built on the north side of the line at Sion Row, opposite to Waterford East signal cabin; the dormitory was brought into use on 9 August 1968. The new station was finally brought into limited use on 15 December 1968. The new booking office and concourse presented a modern appearance with a ceiling to floor glass wall facing out towards the river. Additional car parking facilities were provided by removing the east-facing bay platforms Nos 1 & 2. The new facilities were officially opened on 3 March 1969 by the Minister for Transport & Power.

The west-facing bay platforms, Nos 7 & 8, were removed in 1982 to provide space for bus parking, these facilities remaining in use until the opening of the new Bus Éireann bus station on Merchants' Quay in March 2000. Waterford East signal cabin was closed in July 1985, the section then becoming Waterford Central to Abbey Junction.

At the same time as the improvements were being carried out at Waterford Station, the Harbour Commissioners were constructing a depot and wharf close to Abbey Junction for Messrs Bell Ferry. Initially it was not intended to avail of rail transport, but certain difficulties with road transport soon came to light and a siding was laid in, this coming into use for the first time on 1 July 1969. The connection to the F&RR&H Rosslare line was made inside the up home signal, 825 yards east of Abbey Junction. Traffic quickly developed and proved to be lucrative for CIÉ. Moving ahead some years, a new port terminal, known as Belview Container Terminal, was constructed some 3½ miles to the east of the existing Bell Ferry terminal. The new facilities, commissioned on 16 August 1993, necessitated the provision of a new level crossing – Belview – at 79m 1505y in the Abbey Junction to Wellington Bridge section. The new freight yard, consisting of four sidings, each 590 yards in length between fouling points and with a head shunt of 50 yards at the east end, opened for traffic on 22 August 1993. The original Bell Ferry terminal was then closed. The turnout for the Ballinacourty branch at Waterford West was scotched and clipped early in 1994, with the relevant crossover disconnected and all signals for the branch removed. One of the Suir Viaduct spans was removed over the weekend of 27/28 May 1995 and placed on the north side of the river, where it remains to this day.

Major signalling alterations were carried out at Waterford in 1994/95. Track circuiting was extended out to Barrow Bridge signal cabin, including Belview sidings. This enabled Wellington Bridge signal cabin to be switched out when the section between Waterford and Belview was occupied. Abbey Junction was also included in the track circuiting, resulting in the elimination of the signal cabin there, although it still remains in situ adjacent to Pier Head level crossing.

The various alterations included the previous up line between Abbey Junction and Waterford Central becoming a siding, movements in both directions henceforth being made over the down line. The new signalling was fully commissioned on 14 May 1995. These various alterations also saw a new level crossing being provided at Belview, located at 79m 1329y and known as Belview No 2, the earlier Belview crossing being renamed Belview No 1. The Barrow Bridge was in future to be electrically released from Waterford Central. The current semaphore signals protecting the bridge were removed and replaced by electric colour-lights WD359 and WD361, and a set of trap points on either side, the Bridge Signalman having a facility to replace these to danger in an emergency. Under the new arrangements, a train could leave Waterford or Wellington Bridge even though the bridge might be open. The New Ross branch, which had been disconnected during the signalling works, was reconnected on 29 May; it will in future be operated on the manual Token Staff principle, with no reversion to ETS working. It should be mentioned that although the northern half of the ex D&SER line between Macmine Junction and New Ross was closed to all traffic in 1963, the portion between the latter and Waterford had been retained although unused for many years.

Early in 1998 it was reported that six shipping companies were regularly serving Belview. However, Bell Ferry was not one of these as the company had gone into liquidation in July of the previous year. As a result there was virtually no rail borne traffic out of the terminal. In recent years, Irish Rail have been importing new rolling stock through Belview, a situation brought about by the loss of rail facilities at Dublin Port. It has recently been announced that Irish Rail intend to build a new, modernised, station at Waterford; whether this will go ahead in the present economic climate remains to be seen.

The WD&LR line between Waterford and Kilmeaden has in recent years seen a new lease of life. This followed on a meeting of a group of interested people in 1997 in Waterford with a view to setting up a company to construct a 3ft gauge line on portion of the old WD&LR track bed. The group reported in 1998 that grant aid had been received from Waterford City and County Enterprise Boards towards the commissioning of a locomotive and two carriages. An operating company, the Waterford & Suir Valley Railway Co Ltd was duly set up in 1999 with track laying commencing in 2000, aided by the donation by Iarnród Éireann of track panels. Good progress was made and by 2001 approximately 3.75km of track had been laid down between Kilmeaden and the Mount

Waterford and Suir Valley heritage railway. *(Waterford and Suir Valley Railway)*

A 2800 class Railcar set passes along the Quays at Wexford in 2010 en route for Rosslare. Note the proximity to the parked cars. By the time this photograph was taken the Quays had been extensively reconstructed in connection with the town's main drainage, removing the rustic charm of the earlier wooden works. *(Ernie Shepherd)*

Congreve Estate. The line was extended a further 2.25km to Carriganore in 2002, 4km to the site of Grace Dieu Junction in 2003 and the final 2km to Bilberry in 2004.

Meanwhile, on 25 August 2001 the Simplex locomotive and two carriages made four round trips for invited guests, with the line being opened to the public as far as Carriganore on Monday 6 August 2002. Currently (in 2011) the line is open to Grace Dieu Junction between April and September, with trains departing each hour on the hour between 11.00 and 16.00 on Mondays to Saturdays (15.00 in April and September); there is also a Sunday service. Ample car parking is provided at Kilmeaden and for those without their own transport a bus service is operated from Waterford in conjunction with Suirway Bus & Coach Services. The booking office and souvenir shop at Kilmeaden are housed in an ex IÉ Mark II carriage located on the platform. Some 16,000 passengers were carried in the first year, this figure having risen to 29,000 in 2010.

As part of IÉ's ongoing programme of signalling upgrading, the line between Dublin and Rosslare Harbour was modified in 2008, with CTC installed with a corresponding cessation of ETS working. Thus for normal operation between Wexford and Rosslare Harbour there was no necessity for a Signalman at Rosslare Strand. However, to cater for trains to and from Wellington Bridge the necessary ETS instrument was moved from the signal cabin into the old parcels/goods area adjacent to the booking office in the station building. When a train required to proceed towards Wellington Bridge, the Rosslare Strand Signalman obtained a staff with the permission of Wellington Bridge, this withdrawal releasing a starting signal control key from the ETS instrument. This key was then placed in the starting signal control lock and turned to operate an electronic switch, which in turn allowed a signal designated RS2 to be cleared. The Signalman then requested RS3 and RS2 signals. The former, also known as RL568, could only be cleared to a proceed aspect if both the Rosslare line Signalman at Greystones had requested the route to Wellington Bridge and the Strand Signalman had requested clearance of the signal. Before RS2 could show a green aspect, the level crossing gates at Grange Big had to be closed across the road. Similar arrangements applied to trains approaching from the Waterford direction.

The withdrawal of the sugar beet traffic referred to earlier in the chapter really spelt the end for the South Wexford line, as the admittedly totally inadequate passenger service was unable to make any meaningful monetary contribution. The CIÉ Chairman, Dr John Lynch, reportedly stated that revenue from the two trains per day only approximated some 2% of the annual outlay on the line,[7] apart from the high maintenance and operating cost of the Barrow Bridge,[8] there were in addition no less than 11 manned level crossings. The much altered financial climate in which the Company was operating had seen several reductions in the Government subvention, with pressure to apply considerable savings.

It was in the above scenario that CIÉ lodged an application with the National Transport Authority (NTA) on 26 March 2010 seeking approval to terminate services. The Company published notice on 21 May informing the public that all passenger services between Waterford and Rosslare would be terminated as from 21 July. However, the NTA withheld their decision pending receipt of a report from the Southern & Eastern Regional Authority. Approval was finally given by the NTA on 3 September 2010.

The last trains therefore ran on Saturday 18 September 2010, the last service train being the 17.20 service from Waterford, comprised of a four-car railcar set, Nos 2711/12 and 2714/13; this set returned to Waterford with invited guests, arriving there at 20.12. This closure saw the F&RR&H operating system in Ireland reduced to two short lengths of line, viz Wexford to Rosslare and Waterford to Belview (still open for freight traffic).

In giving approval for the closure, the NTA made it clear that the "suspension of rail passenger services does not equate to line closure." The approval stipulated that IÉ were obliged to maintain the line so as to enable a reinstatement of the service if considered desirable. At the time of closure, some 6¼ miles of the 30¾ miles between Belview and Rosslare Strand consisted of continuously welded track, the remainder being 87lb bull head rail, much of which was still in situ from the time of the line's opening. Closure saw the line become an Engineer's siding, with a reduced speed limit of 25mph and worked when necessary by manual token. The Company are obliged to inspect the line once a year by engineer's inspection car and also to carry out annual weed spraying. Signals remain in place, the distant showing caution and all semaphore home signals taken out of use with an 'X' on the arms. So comes to an end the fascinating history of the F&RR&H.

---

7 The author can confirm, having travelled over the line on a number of occasions in the six months prior to closure, that the average number of passengers per day was about 25, principally students travelling to and Waterford.

8 The Barrow Bridge was manned by signalmen 24 hours a day, 365 days a year for river traffic to and from New Ross. This involved three signalmen who, because of the isolated and potentially dangerous location, were paid more than their counterparts in adjoining signal cabins. To reach the bridge cabin it was necessary to walk across the bridge from the Kilmokea (Wexford) side, this being the only convenient road access, and climb a vertical ladder to the cabin high up on the bridge structure.

CHAPTER SEVENTEEN

Cork Connections

One of the earliest schemes for connecting the railways in Cork city is referred to by Colm Creedon in his three-volume CB&SCR history, now out of print. In 1861 plans were drawn up for a line running from the GS&WR terminus at Penrose Quay to Victoria Road; this rather strange scheme envisaged running across the retaining wall of a proposed floating dock, with an opening bridge across the sluice gates. These proposals were stillborn. Eleven years later, on 12 September 1872, the Cork Tramways Company Limited began operating what were referred to as 'Train Cars', not because they operated on rails but because the idea of a tramway system in Cork city was put forward by an eccentric American, George Francis Train. The tramway ran from Victoria Road along Albert Quay, across Anglesea Bridge, along South Mall, Grand Parade, Patrick Street, St Patrick's Bridge, Bridge Street, what is now MacCurtain Street (then known as King Street) to a terminus at Alfred Street, close to the present Railway Street. The purpose of the tramway, which was laid to 5ft 3in gauge, was to link the main railway termini in the city, it being intended to install suitable sidings for this purpose; however, the system was short-lived, closing down after three years.

Two schemes were proposed in 1888, both involving the Cork Bandon & South Coast Railway (CB&SCR). One was to have left the CB&SCR at Waterfall and run via Carrigrohane to Blarney and then to a junction with the GS&WR at Waterloo. A third rail would have been laid between Carrigrohane and Blarney to accommodate the line on the track of the Cork & Muskerry Light Railway, which was constructed to a gauge of 3ft. A second scheme envisaged a line from Chetwynd, crossing the city at high level, and tunnelling under Patrick's Hill to connect with the GS&WR at Blackpool. The scheme would have included a second line, also partly in tunnel, to join up with both the Cork Blackrock & Passage Railway (CB&PR) and the Cobh branch of the GS&WR. Once again, neither of these schemes progressed any further. The C&F&W&WR scheme of 1890 has already been described in some detail in Chapter Seven and will not be repeated here.

Following on from the C&F&W&WR Act of 1890, the F&RR&H 1898 scheme envisaged Railways 1 to 11 around the city of Cork. Railway No 12 was originally intended to commence close to the premises of the Watercourse Distillery in the street of the same name, and to terminate by a junction with the F&LR at Fermoy at a point 373 yards from the centre of a bridge carrying that line over the Fermoy to Clonmel coach road; these lines were in effect a re-submission of Worthington's proposals of 1890. However, when the Company's Act was obtained in 1898, the line as authorised was shortened by some five miles at the Cork end, commencing instead in the townland of Sarsfield's Court and parish of Templeusque. The Select Committee considering the Bill were so concerned about certain aspects of it that they published a special report on 1 July 1898 outlining a number of important points. The Committee expressed their dissatisfaction with the Company's plans to terminate their line at Fermoy or availing of running powers via Mallow to Cork as had been suggested. Under pressure from the Committee the promoters agreed to extend their system by a more direct route from Fermoy to Cork via Dunkettle, from which point running powers might be exercised over the GS&WR.

As a result, Section 68 (11) of the Act obliged the Company to apply to Parliament in the 1899 Session for powers to construct a line from or near Dunkettle on the C&YR line to Fermoy, incorporating so much of Railway No 12 as might not be altered by Parliament in the new Session – the Cork & Fermoy Direct Railway (C&FDR). This obligation had its origins in an agreement dated 21 July 1898 between the Lords Commissioners of Her Majesty's Treasury and the F&RR&H. In addition to the C&FDR line the Company agreed to the construction of connecting lines in Cork; this latter arrangement was incorporated in Section 68 (12) of the Act. This arose from strenuous opposition from the Cork Harbour Commissioners (CHC) who saw the GS&WR as the only outlet from the city and harbour of Cork, and they were, therefore, solely dependent on that Company for traffic facilities. Passing of the Bill in its original form would have resulted in conferring even greater power on the GS&WR and the GWR.

To focus minds, the agreement stipulated that the return of the sum of £93,000 to be paid to the Treasury against the mortgage of the WD&LR was to be contingent on the completion of the lines between Rosslare and Waterford and between Fermoy and Dunkettle. The sum of £50,000 was to be repaid to the F&RR&H when half of the two lines was completed, the balance to be handed over when the works were completed in their entirety. Reference was also made to the fact that rates and fares between Cork and Fermoy would be calculated on the direct mileage rather than via Mallow, a reduction of 14 miles.

Section 30 of the F&RR&H Act of 1899 authorised a line 22m 1f 3.9c in length from a junction with the C&Y line of the GS&WR in the townland of Lotamore near to Dunkettle Station and terminating by a junction with the GS&WR line just west of Fermoy Station. This line was in substitution for that authorised under Section 68 of the previous year's Act, although the course of the new line differed in part. Leaving aside the obvious difference at the Cork end, the 1899 scheme saw the line run further north just past the village of Glenville, there turning northeast to pass just to the north of Rathcormack, from whence it was to follow a more or less northerly course to terminate close to the junction with the Fermoy to Mitchelstown branch. The 1898 line would have passed to the east of Rathcormack, turning north to terminate to the east of Fermoy Station, a location which would have necessitated a reversal to reach the station.

It soon became clear that there was little appetite for the construction of the C&FDR, despite the potential financial loss to the Company. Whilst Kennett Bayley was ordered by the GS&WR Board in August 1898 to carry out a preliminary survey, and a letter of guarantee was issued in July 1900 confirming that the line would be started within a year, no construction was undertaken. In what appeared to be some softening of their attitude on the part of the Treasury, Mr Hanbury wrote to Mr Whitelaw on 11 July 1900 advising that unless the Board could assure the Treasury that arrangements had been made for the execution of a scheme for connecting the two sides of the River Lee they would be unable to postpone the payment of the £93,000 due by the F&RR&H. The Treasury did in fact agree in January 1901 to the postponement of the date of repayment until June 1903, subject to the half-yearly interest thereon being increased from 2½% to 3¼%; it was also stated that the Treasury expected the construction of the C&FDR to be proceeded with as soon as possible. The GS&WR expressed the view that the latter line was not required and, even if constructed, it would not pay its way. They urged the F&RR&H to press ahead with the cross-city connection and endeavour to relieve themselves of the obligation to construct the Fermoy line, this suggestion being approved by the F&RR&H Board.

In a follow-up to the GS&WR suggestion a meeting was arranged in Dublin for 1 May with Mr Wyndham, the Chief Secretary for Ireland, and the Chancellor of the Exchequer, Mr Austin Chamberlain, when the Company's case was fully laid before them. Mr Wyndham expressed himself in favour of the Company's representations and promised the deputation's views would have very favourable consideration. In the event it was reported in October that the Treasury had declined to agree to the suggested course of action. It was then agreed that the £93,000 should be paid to the Treasury on 1 November along with interest accrued up to that date.

Although the connecting railway was not proceeded with at that time, it is worth making some further mention of it. When the plans were first referred to the CB&SCR, it was made clear that the F&RR&H Company initially envisaged the new line being paid for jointly not only by the CB&SCR and the C&MDR, but also by Cork Corporation and the

CHC. If, however, the F&RR&H were relieved of their obligation to construct the proposed Fermoy connection then they would be prepared to bear the entire cost of the connecting lines in the city, a suggestion understandably agreed to by the Bandon Company.

In his plans, Albert Gordon proposed to cross the north and south channels of the river by swing bridges at quay level. He also envisaged making the bridges wide enough to accommodate both road traffic and pedestrians, anticipating by some years the actual Cork City Railways scheme as built. Gordon's figure for construction was rather optimistically estimated at £70,000, a figure that was to include all land, buildings and signalling, but excluding the electrical equipment both for the line itself and the operation of the bridges. The estimate was based on figures supplied by the Dublin United Tramways Company and it was expected that the electrical supply could be obtained from the recently opened Cork Electric Tramways & Lighting Company Limited (CET).

Another, apparently unconnected, matter was discussed at the GS&WR board meeting on 18 October 1901, namely the question of the proposed free bridge at Waterford. The existing toll bridge across the Suir close to the W&L station had for many years been a matter of dispute between both the GWR, who had their shipping facilities on the south (city) side of the river, the GS&WR, and the relevant authorities. In the event of the F&RR&H being relieved of their obligation to provide a footway alongside the Suir viaduct, they had agreed to contribute a sum of £10,000 towards the free bridge. They now went further. If Parliament authorised the connecting line at Cork in lieu of the Fermoy line, they would, subject to being allowed free use of the quays at Waterford, increase their contribution to £50,000!

To give effect to these various matters it was decided to promote a Bill in the 1902 Session. The Bill sought powers for a railway connecting the GS&WR at Glanmire Road with the CB&SCR at Albert Quay, along with a number of sidings on various quays. The Company sought powers to work the lines by electrical power, which was to be obtained from the CET. Section 11 of the proposed Bill sought powers

to abandon and relinquish the construction of the C&FDR, the Cork connecting line to be substituted therefor. Section 8 intended that the agreement between the Company and the Treasury regarding the sum of £93,000 should be retained and was to apply to the railways and sidings under the Bill. Finally, it sought powers to subscribe to the new road bridge in Waterford, and to repeal the provision in Section 53 of the 1899 Act in relation to the footway over the Suir Viaduct. Included in the proposed Bill was provision for granting contingent running powers to the DW&WR to Cork via Mallow in lieu of those which had been granted over the proposed C&FDR line.

In fact the DW&WR petitioned against the Bill on the grounds that certain railways included were not railways in the true sense, but more correctly tramways as they were to be laid on public streets; in addition there was no reference to which side of certain streets these lines were to be laid on, or to what gauge they were to be constructed, or even what motive power was intended to be employed. The point being made by the DW&WR was that tramways required the approval of the local authorities, which had not been obtained. When the matter came before the Standing Orders Committee in the House of Commons on 11 February 1902 the DW&WR objections were upheld and the Bill was thrown out as not having complied with Standing Orders. It is interesting to record that a notice appeared in *The Irish Times*, about the time these objections were being raised, to the effect that the L&NWR intended to go to Parliament to include in their Bill, already in the Commons, clauses empowering the Company to subscribe to the DW&WR and to appoint a Director or Directors to the Board of the Wicklow Company. The L&NWR confirmed that they did not intend to purchase or even take a controlling interest in the DW&WR, but were anxious to counter any attempt to divert traffic from the port of Dublin in which, of course, they had a considerable stake.

The Cork Harbour Commissioners wrote to the F&RR&H in March 1902 pointing out that they would not consider any scheme for connecting railways in the city put forward as an alternative to the construction of the C&FDR. The Board decided to take no immediate decision on the latter. It was also mentioned that Youghal UDC had written suggesting the construction of a direct line from Youghal to Dungarvan in lieu of the Fermoy line, a scheme which had first been put forward two years previously.

With no further progress, and pressure being applied for the construction of the Fermoy line, the Company again communicated with Mr Wyndham in June and November 1903 seeking to overturn the requirement for that line to be built. While Wyndham had some sympathy with the Company's views he mentioned that, in return for his assistance, he trusted the F&RR&H might persuade the GS&WR to aid him with two other matters[1]. Wyndham wrote again in November 1903 advising that due to a change of Government, he had not been able to push matters on, but he was still hopeful of overcoming opposition to the release of the Company from its obligation in relation to the Fermoy line. He went on to say that he believed that an application to the Treasury for the transfer of the £93,000 to the connecting lines would be successful. With the powers for construction of the C&FDR under the Act of 1899 about to expire on 1 August 1904, the Company decided to take no further action in the matter, this effectively being the end of the C&FDR scheme.

We must now turn our attentions to the various proposals for connecting the railway systems to the west of the city of Cork with the GS&WR. One of these, the GS&WR Company's own scheme of 1901, led to the F&RR&H bringing their Bill before Parliament in the 1902 Session, which has already been described. A new Bill was lodged in Parliament in the 1905 Session under the title of the Cork Junction Railways in respect of two lines in Cork; this scheme was promoted by Messrs RM Sanders and SG Fraser. Railway No 1 was to connect the GS&WR and CB&SCR termini; it was very different to the 1902 Bill in that it was to run on a viaduct 20–25ft high for much of its length, including the crossings of the river. Railway No 2 was to make a connection between the CB&SCR and the Cork & Macroom Direct Railway

(C&MDR) at Ballyphehane. Once again, the line was to be worked by electrical power, supplied by the CET Company. Powers were sought for a number of companies to subscribe to the undertaking, including the CB&PR, CB&SCR, C&MDR, F&RR&H, GS&WR, GWR and the L&NWR; it was also anticipated that the Treasury would provide a grant, most likely from the £93,000 paid for the WD&LR.

SG Fraser, the Engineer for the scheme, wrote to the CB&SCR in March 1905 requesting that the Directors hold a Wharncliffe Meeting of shareholders to approve of the scheme. The CJR Bill came before a Committee of the House of Commons in May 1905 under the chairmanship of the Hon Alan De Tatton Egerton, being opposed by the Cork Harbour Commissioners (CHC) on the basis of obstruction to navigation. While most steamers would be able to travel under the proposed viaduct, this would not be the case for sailing vessels. Fraser reported that finances for the proposed line included a guarantee of £50,000 from Cork County Council, in addition to which they hoped to get some £65,000 to £70,000 out of the WD&LR payout.

Lord Barrymore, a Director of both the F&RR&H and the GWR, confirmed that the former Company had carefully considered the scheme and considered it would be of advantage to that Company. However, the GS&WR members on the F&RR&H Board had pledged to their (GS&WR) shareholders that they would not spend any further money at that time, although they were in favour of the scheme. Lord Barrymore went on to say that provided the County Council granted the sum of £50,000 and a further £60,000 came from the Treasury, the GWR would be prepared, on behalf of the F&RR&H, to find the necessary funds to complete the finance of the line and its subsequent working. The scheme was considered at a specially convened meeting of the F&RR&H Board on 6 June, resulting from which it was resolved that if the GWR, as the GWR proper, wished to undertake to financially support the CJR, and to afford the F&RR&H the option of taking it over at some future date when the GS&WR was in a financial position to do so, the latter Company would give their assent. It was also suggested in June 1905 that Fraser should be

---

1 Although unspecified, one of these related to the Tralee & Dingle narrow-gauge line, which was at the time in financial difficulties, Wyndham urging strongly in June 1904 that the GS&WR should take over the working of that line.

appointed as Construction Engineer under Mr Inglis with Walter Scott & Middleton[2] as contractors. The whole question proved to be academic as the Bill was rejected in July.

Three further schemes for connecting railways in Cork came before Parliament in the 1906 Session, namely the Cork & Waterford Railway (C&WR), Cork Link Railways (CLR) and the Cork City Railways (CCR). The C&WR was rather more than a scheme to simply connect the railways in the city as it also proposed extensions to connect with the Mallow to Waterford line. Railway No 5 of that scheme, commencing at Youghal, was to make a junction with the Dungarvan line about 700 yards to the east of Cappagh Station, while Railway No 8 was to be a short branch from No 5 to serve the Castle Brickworks near Kinsalebeg. The Engineer for the CLR route was John William Dorman,[3] a scheme referred to by the *Railway Times* as being similar to the Cork City Railways & Works proposals. There the similarity ended as the Link line was intended to be built at high-level, the railway crossing the River Lee on the upper deck of two-level bridges. Mr Barrington, the GS&WR Solicitor, informed the GS&WR Board on 19 January 1906 that notice had been published of intention to submit the C&WR Bill for the approval of Cork County Council regarding a guarantee of 4% on £100,000. However, neither the C&WR nor the CLR passed Standing Orders and so we are left with the CCR to consider.

It is clear that the F&RR&H were taking an interest in the Cork City Railway scheme at least as early as June 1905, when it was confirmed that the GS&WR representatives on the F&RR&H Board reported to the main GS&WR Board the details of a special meeting recently held in London. At that meeting the GWR members had proposed that the Fishguard Company should come to the support of the CCR Bill, the GWR agreeing to guarantee 3½% on £30,000 and suggesting that the GS&WR should do likewise; it was expected that the CB&SCR would guarantee a

similar percentage on £10,000, while the Treasury was expected to put up a sum of £60,000 and Cork County Council £50,000. The GS&WR, however, "absolutely refuse(d)" to contribute 1d to any scheme until the F&RR&H route was open and working satisfactorily. They did agree that if the GWR, as the GWR proper, wished to undertake financial support for the CCR, the F&RR&H should have the option of taking it over at some future date, when the GS&WR might be in a better financial position and wished then to become involved. Writing to the GS&WR in August, Alfred Baldwin, the GWR Chairman, whilst agreeing with the undesirability of any such new scheme being proposed by the F&RR&H, was clearly unhappy that the DW&WR might step in and propose a line to Cork, which would include the city connections.

By November it was stated that the GWR were supporting the "high-level scheme for a connecting line in Cork" but reserving liberty to consider the low-level (CCR) scheme. In December the GS&WR agreed that a watching petition should be lodged against the Cork City Railways & Works Bill. The lines for the most part were to run on streets and along the quays with merchandise traffic only being contemplated. The promoters were Joseph Barrett, Sir Edward Fitzgerald (the Lord Mayor of Cork), James Long (a leading member of Cork County Council & Chairman of both the CHC and the CB&SCR), James Ogilvie, William McDonald, Joseph Pike and John Collins. The length of the lines proposed, eight in number, was 1m 20c, with a proposed capital of £150,000 and borrowing of £75,000. The total estimated cost of the works was £98,000.

The F&RR&H wrote to the GS&WR in January 1906 suggesting that the CCR Bill should be submitted to a Wharncliffe meeting for approval, it being also suggested that the three companies should petition against the other connecting schemes, this course of action being approved. In the following month it was confirmed that Cork County Council had decided that no guarantee should be given to any of the three connecting railways, including the CCR. In March Mr Barrington informed the GS&WR that a deputation representing the county and city of Cork had waited upon Mr McKenna, the Secretary to the

---

2 Walter Scott & Middleton of Westminster were responsible for the construction of a new graving dock at Belfast, first used in April 1911 by the *Olympic*. They also constructed a foot tunnel at Woolwich. The Company was finally dissolved in 1966.
3 Formerly Engineer to the Cork & Bandon Railway (1873–84)

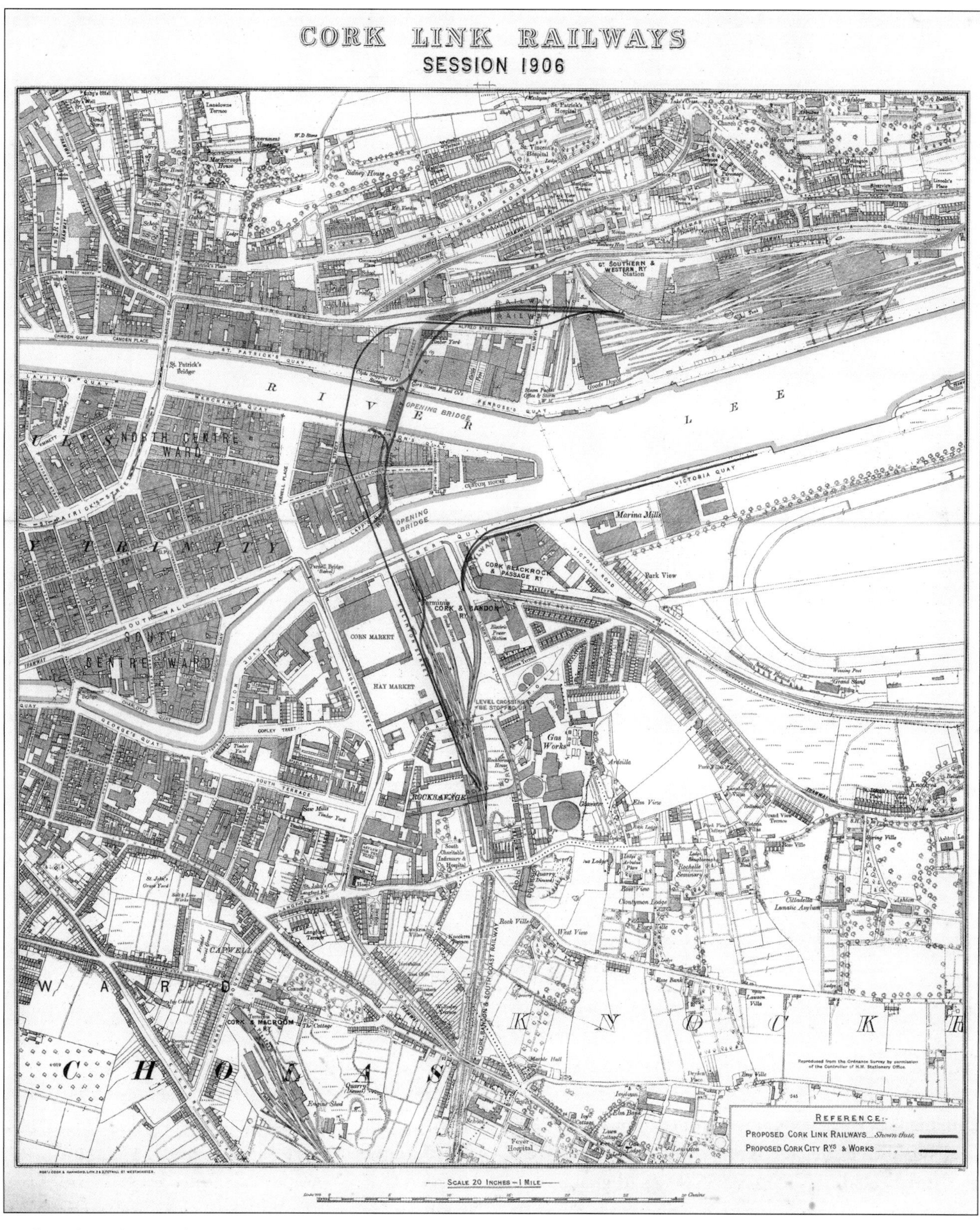

Cork Link Railways scheme as proposed to Parliament in 1906. Parliament favoured the low-level Cork City Railways scheme. *(Gerald Beesley Collection)*

Treasury, and had obtained from him an assurance that of the sum of £93,000 held by the Government, £60,000 would be applied towards the connecting railways in Cork, the balance of £33,000 for the new road bridge at Waterford. This assurance was to lead to questions being raised by JJ O'Shee, MP for Waterford West, on 22 May in the House of Commons that the local authorities had now refused to contribute to the scheme. Mr McKenna, in reply, stated that it was true that one of the conditions on which the Treasury had agreed to contribute the £60,000 was that a sum of £50,000 would be forthcoming locally. He went on to say that the pledge had now been withdrawn; this did not prevent McKenna and Mr Power, MP for Waterford East, making some adverse comments regarding the GWR and its failure to carry out its promises in Ireland.

Colonel Yorke of the BoT came over to Cork in April 1906 to inspect the plans and the proposed route of the CCR, expressing himself generally satisfied with his inspection. Colonel Yorke saw no objections to a street-level line, the only point on which he commented was that some additional precautions might be necessary for the protection of road traffic at crossings. When the Bill came before the House of Commons Select Committee in May, it was clear that petitions had been lodged against the Bill by a number of parties. These included the Clyde Shipping Company, Cork Gas Consumers' Company, City of Cork Steampacket Company, Cork Corporation, Cork County Council, Cork Electric Tramways & Lighting Company, and the promoters of the Cork Link Railway. James Price, Engineer to the CHC, was called to give evidence and stated that 73% of the gross traffic that could be accommodated by the railway would emanate from the deep-water quays, amounting annually to about 90,000 tons. Price confirmed that he had prepared three plans, one of them virtually identical to JW Dorman's Cork Link Railway scheme. Inglis, the General Manager of the GWR, informed the Committee that he had always been interested in a low-level scheme and intimated that the GWR would "be prepared to see the scheme through" provided the CB&SCR contributed £10,000.

At a meeting of the CB&SCR Board held on 21 May it was unanimously resolved that the Company would recommend to the proprietors making a subscription of £15,000 to the CCR, provided the Treasury gave a substantial amount. Only two days later it was announced that the Treasury had decided to only contribute £25,000 towards the scheme, the GWR expressing their dissatisfaction at the amount offered. Despite the considerable opposition to the scheme, the Cork City Railways Act received Royal Assent on 4 August 1906. The longest of the railways authorised was No 1, 3f 8.35c long, commencing by a junction with the CB&SCR in Cork (Albert Quay) station yard and terminating in the parish of St Anne's on the south side of King Street. Railways 2 and 3 were to make the all-important connection with the GS&WR by a junction with that Company's avoiding line opposite the west end of the signal cabin in Glanmire Road Station. Railway No 4 was to run from a junction with the CB&SCR cattle pen siding in Albert Quay yard and terminate on the roadway of Albert Quay itself. Railway No 5, basically an extension of Railway No 4, represented lines along Albert and Victoria Quays, Nos 6 & 7 similar lines on Lapp's and Anderson's Quays, No 8 on St Patrick's Quay. The construction of three new roads was also authorised. Capital, originally envisaged at £150,000, was set at £100,000 in £10 shares with borrowing powers up to £50,000, subject to the usual provisions. Section 46 of the Act stated that there were to be five Directors, three of whom were to be appointed by the GWR, one by the CB&SCR and one by the promoters. The GWR duly nominated Alfred Baldwin, Lord Barrymore and Viscount Churchill, the CB&SCR nominee being Joseph Pike.

A major advantage bestowed on the CB&SCR by the Act was the closing up of the level crossing at Gasworks Road adjacent to the terminus and its replacement by Hibernian Road bridge; the level crossing had been the subject of many complaints of delays and accidents down the years and it was inevitable that the Company would have had to replace it at some point. Section 67 of the Act gave power to the Company to work the traffic on the railway by electric power, such power to be obtained from the CET. Section 84 authorised the GWR, GS&WR, CB&SCR and the F&RR&H to subscribe to the undertaking, not exceeding in the

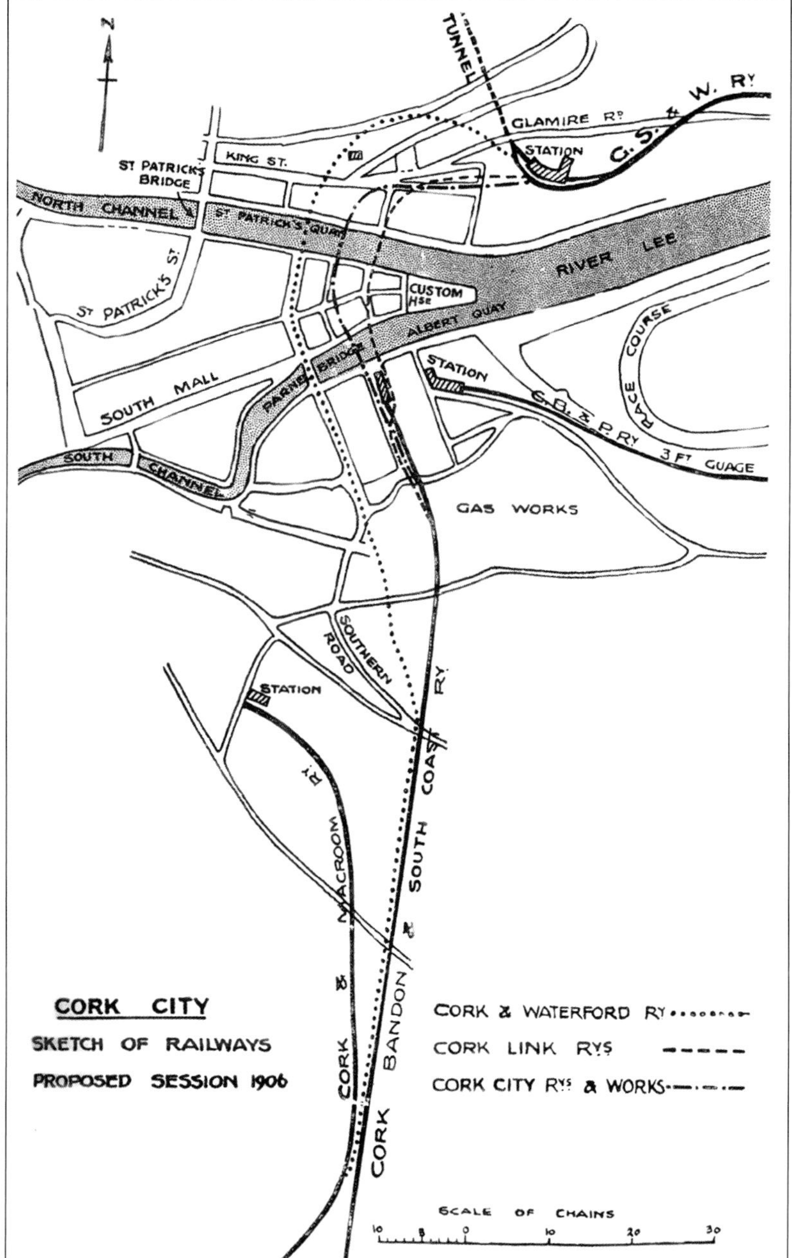

Plan of 3 railways proposed for the 1906 Parliamentary Session to connect the CB&SCR with the GS&WR systems in Cork. The successful scheme was the Cork City Railways & Works. *(Author's Collection)*

to carry out the construction of the railways under the direction of JC Inglis at a commission similar to that which had previously been arranged with Mr Fraser in respect of the proposed CJR. The promoters informed the GWR that they were prepared to forego their right to select an engineer if an increased payment of £400 was made to them, this being approved by the GWR Board. On 15 February 1907 the GWR shareholders formally authorised a subscription of £85,000 towards the CCR, this amount later proving to be insufficient. The contract for the railway and road works was awarded to Messrs W Muirhead & Company of London, while that for the two river bridges went to Sir William Arrol of Glasgow. The bridges themselves were supplied by the Cleveland Bridge & Engineering Company.[5] The supervision of the bridge construction was placed in the hands of William Burnside, AMICE.

Reporting on 2 December 1911, the *Weekly Irish Times* referred to the completion of the CCR, an event which "marks a noteworthy railway development in the South of Ireland." The principal works on the new line were of course the two rolling lift bridges carrying the line over the two river channels. That over the north channel measured 231ft 1in and that over the south channel 196ft 10in. The bridges were of steel construction

whole £100,000. It had, however, been agreed that the GWR would subscribe the moneys necessary for the carrying out of the works to completion, subject to subscriptions of £15,000 from the CB&SCR, £10,000 from the CHC and £25,000 from the Treasury.

Under an agreement dated 1 December 1906 it was arranged that if either CS Meik[4] or James Price was elected by the promoters, he should be appointed

---

4 CS Meik is mentioned in the Agreement, but it appears to have been his brother PW Meik who jointly drew up the plans with James Price, Engineer of the CHC.

5 The Cleveland Bridge & Engineering Company was founded in 1877 and built a number of spectacular bridges, including the Victoria Falls Bridge, King Edward VII Bridge in Newcastle, the original Severn Bridge (1966), Auckland Harbour Bridge (1959), Forth Road Bridge, Chiswick Bridge. In 2002 it was awarded the contract for the roof of Wembley Stadium.

One of the two opening bridges across the River Lee. To avoid disruption to navigation the bridges were erected in the open position. In view of the dignitaries visible on the right, this view may show the bridge down for the first time. *(Author's Collection)*

carrying a single line of rails, a public carriageway and two footpaths, giving a width overall of 48ft between the parapets. Each bridge was supported by masonry abutments and three intermediate piers dividing them into four spans – an approach span at each end, an opening span in the centre of the channel to facilitate the passage of vessels, and a back span next to the opening span. The abutments were built of Mount Charles stone on a concrete foundation contained behind a close-piled dam of 12in Jarrah wood.[6] Each pier consisted of a pair of steel cylinders braced together, filled in solid with Portland cement concrete. Unusually, the bridges were constructed in the upright position so as not to interfere with navigation in the river.

The opening spans, which had a clear length of 62ft, were of the Scherzer rolling lift type. At the tail ends of the main girders quadrants were formed, which were made to roll on straight fixed tracks of somewhat similar construction. Projections on the tracks fitted into corresponding spaces in the quadrants, and kept the bridge in position while moving. The opening spans were operated by electricity, with motors geared to a double train of cog wheels, and placed on a platform immediately behind the opening spans. The

great advantage of the rolling lift bridge was that it was self contained, whereas a swing bridge required almost its own area again in the open position.

The new railway lines were duly inspected on 30 December 1911 by Colonel von Donop on behalf of the BoT. He arranged for the bridges to be tested by running two GS&WR locomotives coupled together over them, along with a steam road roller and a petrol lorry. Colonel von Donop found everything to his satisfaction and the line was opened for traffic on the following Monday, 1 January 1912, being worked from the outset by the GS&WR. However, as it was rather isolated from the main system, the Victoria Quay siding was worked by the CB&SCR. The line was used for freight only, apart from the summer months of 1914 when a passenger service briefly operated. In later years, occasional through working of special trains took place between Albert Quay and Glanmire Road Stations for sporting events and the like.

It was reported in May 1911 that expenditure up to that point amounted to £108,522 with estimated further expenditure of £54,316, making a total of £162,838 against the original estimate of £98,000. By that time the whole of the CCR capital had been issued, although they had borrowing powers of £50,000. The GWR Board approved additional expenditure

---

6 Eucalyptus wood from Western Australia. Jarrah derives from the Aboriginal name for the eucalyptus tree. Also sometimes known as Swan River Mahogany.

to complete the line. The GWR intimated to the CCR in July 1924 that they were no longer prepared to financially assist the CCR. The latter Company opened discussions with the Irish Government, the GS&WR and the CB&SCR, informing them that without financial assistance from the GWR they might be forced to close the system down. Further discussions with the GS&WR led to arrangements being made for that Company to take over and assume all responsibility for the CCR, the GWR agreeing to transfer their holding to the GS&WR for a nominal consideration. Arrangements were then made for the CCR to be absorbed into the new Great Southern Railways; this was given effect to by SI No 6 of 1925, The GSR Absorption (No 2) Scheme. In total the GWR had subscribed £124,500 to the CCR, receiving in exchange £39,300 4% Debentures and £84,950 Ordinary Shares.

There is little to record post-1925 as the line had a fairly quiet existence. Approaches were made by the GSR in 1927 to the Cork Harbour Commissioners intimating an intention to apply for powers to enable the closure of the CCR as the line was operating at a loss, a situation which was unlikely to improve. As an example the annual report for 1923 shows revenue receipts of £1,371 4s 9d against expenditure of £6,036 12s 5d. West Cork fish traffic had proved disappointing, yielding an average of about 2,500 tons per annum, much less than had been anticipated. Likewise, livestock traffic only produced a maximum of about 1,200 wagons annually. However, following a public outcry the Company decided not to proceed with their plans. The Bandon section of CIÉ was closed as from 31 March 1961 but Albert Quay was retained as a goods depot, thus guaranteeing the continued existence of the City Railway for a little longer. It was in fact not until April 1976 that the final chapter was written in the CCR story, with the closure of Albert Quay.

CHAPTER EIGHTEEN

Description of Lines

This chapter describes the route as may have been observed by a cross-channel traveller proceeding towards Fishguard and, after crossing, to Rosslare, travelling onwards to Mallow for Cork. Although this presents the route on the Irish side counter to the normal manner of following the down direction of the line, it is felt that in this case it is appropriate for the description of the F&RR&H route as a whole. The Maenclochog line is also described, as but for its existence the railway might never have reached Fishguard and, of course, the new line from Clarbeston Road was provided as an alternative to the heavily graded NP&FR line, which was totally unsuited to the running of express trains. Although the F&RR&H lines in Wales, consisting of up and down main and goods lines, ended 3 chains short of the overbridge carrying the A40 road over the line at Goodwick, we shall commence our journey at Clynderwen.

Two routes to Fishguard

Originally known as Narberth Road, Clynderwen (264:22 from London, Paddington) had two staggered platforms with that on the down side being located nearer to Fishguard. The station buildings were on the up platform and, behind this platform at the Paddington end there was a bay which was used by the Maenclochog branch trains. Sidings were provided on both sides of the line, although the goods shed, coal yard and cattle pens were on the up side opposite the down platform. The original signal box, a timber one erected in 1876, was replaced in 1895 by a standard GWR brick built box containing 41 levers. When the branch line was closed, the number of levers was reduced to 19, the signal box finally closing on 3 October 1966 following the removal of all sidings and points at the station. A feature of Clynderwen was the down home signal, which was on a 60ft high post to aid sighting by approaching down trains.

To accommodate the Maenclochog line as it headed west, the main line tracks were realigned to allow the branch to run alongside the up main line. At a point where the cutting through which the lines ran, at Gelli, the branch curved sharply northwards onto an embankment which brought the line to a deep cutting in which Beag Halt (266:02) was located. This halt was never of much importance to the branch, although traffic in rabbits was of some value! A short siding was installed on the down side, facing to down trains. A 6-lever signal box was provided in 1895 at the request of the GWR for the protection of the main line; it was closed by 1907. This box was supplied by McKenzie & Holland, who provided all of the signal boxes on the branch. On leaving Beag, the line dropped into the valley of the Eastern Cleddau River, which it followed for several miles before reaching Llanycefn (268:04). This station had a single platform overlooking the river on the up side and a level crossing; beyond which, also on the up side, there was a small siding faced to up trains. The level crossing was operated from a 6-lever signal box on the down side, but strangely the siding points were hand-operated from a ground frame released by the staff for the section to Maenclochog.

After Llanycefn the line began climbing on steep gradients to pass through the 100 yard Maenclochog tunnel (270:02), on leaving which the gradient steepened for a short stretch at 1 in 27 where the line was carved out of the hill side. It then entered a short cutting before arriving at Maenclochog Station (270:74), the second largest on the line and the recognised crossing point for passenger trains. There were two passenger platforms with the station building on the down side, and three goods sidings were located behind the up platform, behind which was also situated the goods store. At the down end there was a level crossing beyond which was a water tank. A 14-lever signal box was provided at the rear of the down platform in 1876 for the opening of the line, this remaining in use until about 1923.

From Llanycefn to Rosebush, the gradient eased somewhat but on the approach to the latter station it reverted to 1 in 50. Rosebush Station (272:42) was the highest point on the branch at 866ft above sea level, having left Clynderwen at 200ft; this fact alone will give the reader an idea of why the branch would have been totally unsuited to express traffic to and from Fishguard. Originally the terminus of the line, Rosebush had a single passenger platform on the up side of the line. There were three sidings and a loop with a small goods shed on the up side. A timber signal box was provided for the opening of the line in 1876, this being closed on 31 December 1882. A new box of brick construction, and containing 11 levers, was built in March 1895 on the up side at the Letterston end of the station. The Precelly Hotel was located in the grounds of Sir Hugh Owen's estate, behind the platform. Cropper's quarry was situated just beyond the station and had a connection on the up side facing to down trains. The quarry siding was quite long with a

short spur serving a small locomotive shed. It appears that there was some form of internal tramway as there is evidence of a bridge near the entrance to the quarry itself.

Leaving Rosebush, the line curved away sharply over marshy ground towards New Inn Halt (273:69) which was situated in a shallow cutting. The line then turned south and ran downhill on gradients of 1 in 50 and 1 in 41 to Puncheston Station (276:52). Situated at 540ft above sea level, this station had a single platform on the up side and also a siding serving a goods store. Whilst a small signal box with four levers was provided at the Letterston end, the siding points were operated from a ground frame as at Llanycefn. The ruling gradient in the section between Puncheston and Letterston was 1 in 50, with a rise at 1 in 60 for the last mile. There were three halts in this section at Castlebythe (277:47), Martell (278:42) and Beulah (279:37). Letterston (281:34) was the most impressive station on the branch, being the headquarters of the line for some years. It initially had only a single platform on which the main station building was

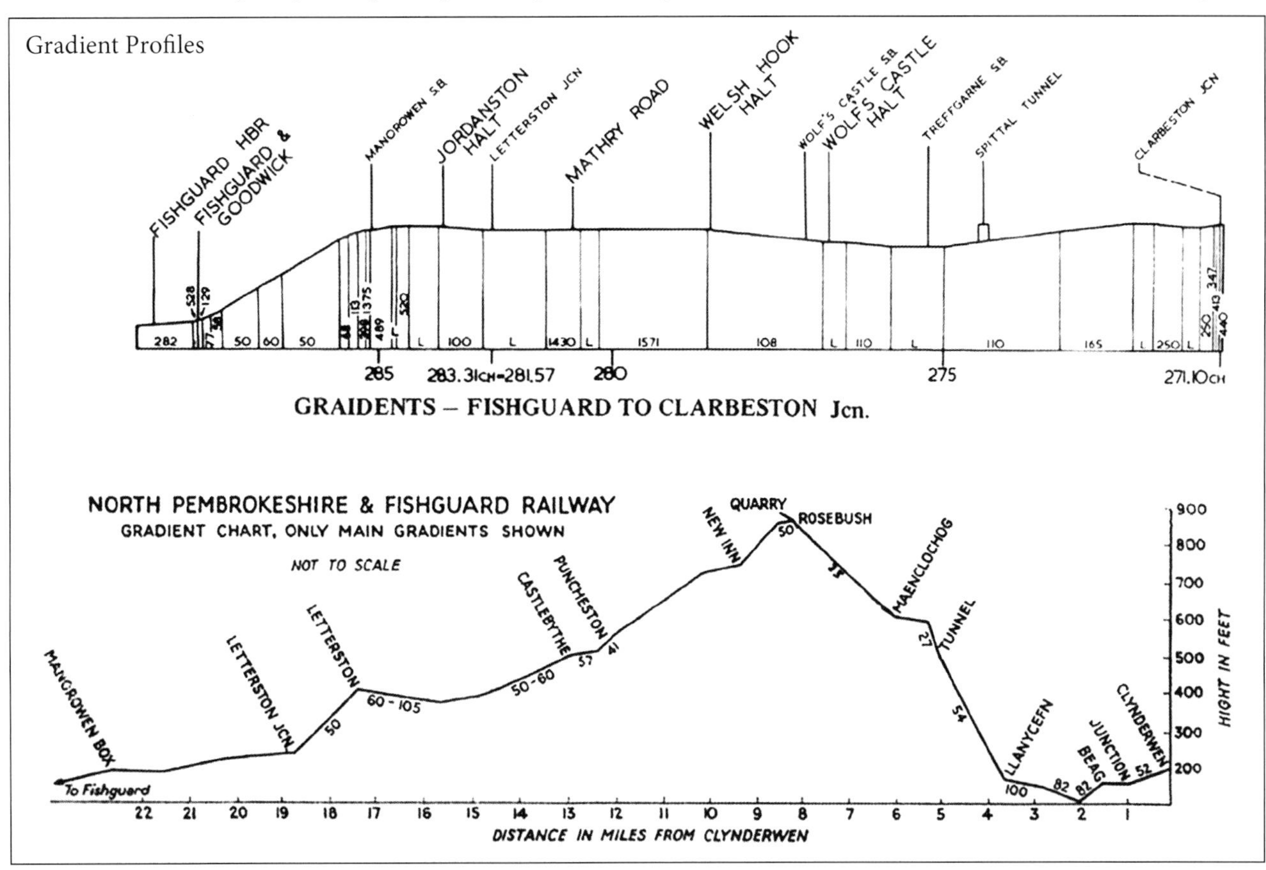

located, but a second one was provided on the down side for the opening of the extension to Fishguard. Siding accommodation on the down side served a large goods shed and cattle pens; there was also a small locomotive shed at the Puncheston end of the station. A 15-lever signal box located on the up platform was in use from March 1895 until September 1926.

As the branch proceeded from Letterston Station it ran through a cutting to meet the main line from Clarbeston Road at Letterston Junction (283:31). However, before moving along the line to Fishguard we need to return to the mainline at the point where the NP&FR diverged 11 chains to the west of Clynderwen Station. At this point the mainline began a descent at 1 in 82 towards the 241½ milepost before commencing a climb on gradients that varied from 1 in 303 to 1 in 107 to reach Clarbeston Road Station (270:71). This station served as the junction between the main line to Fishguard and the branch through Haverfordwest to Neyland; the actual junction was situated 19 chains west of the station, the Neyland line diverging on the down side. Clarbeston Road Station had two platforms with the main station building located on the down platform and a bay behind the up platform. There was a loop and a long siding on the up side, and goods facilities, including a store, were provided on the down side at the Fishguard end of the station.

The station at this location dated only from 1914, the original station, located 7½ chains to the east, had its up side buildings destroyed by fire on 9 June 1907. Much to the annoyance and inconvenience of local residents, nothing was done to quickly replace this and it was not until April 1913 that a tender was accepted for a new station.

On departing from Clarbeston Road the line ran downhill at 1 in 165 before steepening to 1 in 110 for almost two miles; entering the 243 yard long Spittal tunnel (274:46) the line emerged into Treffgarne Gorge, a section of line which caused great construction difficulties for the contractors. A temporary signal box containing six levers was opened there on 29 August 1906 but was closed on 17 December of the same year on the introduction of full double-track working. In connection with the installation of a siding to serve a

granite quarry on the down side at 275:35, to which the connection was from the up line, a new signal box was opened there on 1 July 1925. This was accidentally burnt down and was replaced in its turn by a ground level box; this latter caused some amusement with the signalmen on either side who referred to it as a glorified ground frame (all three boxes had six levers). It lasted until 17 August 1958.

From Treffgarne Gorge the line continues to rise at 1 in 110 for a short distance and runs into Wolf's Castle Halt (276:70), at which the name boards proclaimed that the station was 'Wolf's Castle Halt for Treffgarne Rocks.' Opened on 1 October 1913, it was unusual for a GWR halt; the 115ft up platform and 155ft down platform, and the passenger shelters were built of brick rather than timber. A small 9-lever, timber signal box of GWR design, measuring 15ft 6in by 10ft 7in, remained in use from August 1906 until February 1925. A climb at 1 in 108 brought the line into Welsh Hook Halt (278:49), opened on 5 May 1924, From Welsh Hook Halt the line was level for a distance of almost three miles. Mathry Road Station (280:46), originally called Mathry (for St David's) when it was opened on 1 August 1923, was several miles from the village of its title, so the GWR decided to rename it Mathry Road (for St David's). It had two short platforms with a basic timber building, and on the up side there was a siding capable of holding 15 wagons, a second siding being added later. The signal box, in use between November 1925 and September 1965, was situated on the up side at the Fishguard end of the station and contained 14 levers.

Letterston Junction (283:31 & 281:50)[1] originally had quite a small layout, but with the opening of the Royal Navy armaments depot at Trecwn in 1938 three additional loops were laid in. The depot was mothballed in the early 1990s and subsequently much of the equipment from the extensive internal narrow gauge railway system was removed to preserved lines such as the Talyllyn Railway. There were loops on either side of the main line as it approached the junction from the Mathry Road direction with the NP&FR line swinging in from the right. The connection to the armaments depot trailed in on the up side of the NP&FR line just

---

1 Mileages beyond Letterston Junction were shown as via the NP&FR route, representing a difference of almost two miles.

Letterston Junction and signal cabin. The line to the left ran to Clynderwen via Rosebush and Maenclochog. In recent years only the branch to the RNAD facility at Trecwen remained. *(John Gale)*

before the point of junction. The signal box, a typical GWR structure opened in 1906, was situated in the 'V' of the junction; it is not clear how many levers it had, one description referring to 43 and another to 78 – the latter figure may refer to the enlarged layout with the additional loops. Morris refers to the installation on 30 July 1972 of a new signal box ex west Drayton with 26 levers; it is not clear, however, when the original box was taken out of use. Jordanston Halt (284:08), opened on 1 October 1923, had a low-level platform on the up side with a small timber building at the Fishguard end. The halt finally closed on 6 April 1964.

Manorowen Signal Box (285:05) was opened on 5 August 1906 and controlled movements from the double to single line. It was another typical GWR box, initially with 9 levers, later increased to 15; and was eventually closed on 9 March 1958 when the line was singled between Letterston Junction and Fishguard. Until that time banking engines assisted up trains tackle the two-mile climb from Goodwick to the summit near Manorowen, much of it at 1 in 50. Following the singling of the line the banking engines had to run on to Letterston Junction. This entailed a good deal of light-engine running and so a 'Bank Engine Token' system was introduced. Under that arrangement, the driver of the train engine was handed a normal token at Goodwick while the banking engine driver was given the bank engine token. When the train no longer required the services of the banker, the latter

returned to Goodwick with the bank token; until this was replaced in the instrument there no other tokens could be withdrawn from the instruments at either end of the section.

The connection to Goodwick Brickworks siding (287:20) was on the down side facing down trains. The brick company operated a 2ft gauge line, their last locomotive being a diesel mechanical four-wheeled shunter purchased from Ruston & Hornsby in 1939. Traffic from the brickworks ceased in June 1969.

Fishguard & Goodwick Station (287:48), so called officially since 1904, was generally known simply by its original name of Goodwick. As opened, the station had a single platform on the up side with the station building on it. A 17-lever signal box was provided by the NP&FR for the opening on 1 July 1899, this being replaced by a new box with 37 levers on the down side on 29 July 1906, opposite to the station building. When the signal box at the Harbour Station was closed on 1 January 1965, all movements in the harbour area were controlled from the Goodwick box, the frame being enlarged to 53 levers. At the time of opening of the F&RR&H line, there was a run-round loop on the down side, this being later lengthened to become a goods loop. Then in 1907 a second platform was added on the down side, this being built round the signal box. On the up side at the Paddington end there was a two-road goods yard behind the platform for the handling of local goods traffic. These two sidings

Fishguard & Goodwick station looking towards the harbour with a pair of 0-4-2Ts Nos 1452 and 1431 working two auto-trains. That on the left has the road to run on to Fishguard Harbour. *(Great Western Trust)*

Fishguard & Goodwick station c1955. Apart from the goods facilities on the down (right) side, two sidings were located at the London end of the up platform; several vans can be seen in this view behind which is Goodwick Shed, a typical two-road Churchward design with the coaling plant on the right. *(Photographer unknown, Martin Lewis Collection)*

were lengthened in July 1906 and were worked from a ground frame released by a key on the section staff.

The locomotive yard, comprising of a two-road locomotive shed of typical Churchward design, 65ft turntable, watering and coaling facilities, was located on the down side. Access to the locomotive yard was gained by a crossover on the harbour side of the road overbridge which also provided entry to the goods yard which was again on the down side of the line at the Goodwick end of the harbour layout. This yard was known as Marsh sidings and consisted of seven roads capable of holding some 200 wagons.

Fishguard Harbour Station (288:18 from Paddington) had two island platforms, each 789ft in length; the faces being numbered 1 to 4 from the landward side, Nos 3 & 4 being used for passenger traffic. A booking office, waiting and refreshment rooms were located on this platform, and there was a separate office block located at the breakwater end of the same platform. An overall roof spanned the two platforms and this was later extended at the breakwater end and also over part of the quay. A subway linked the two platforms with the approach road, which originally came into the station area past the Fishguard Bay Hotel, in addition to which electrically-operated traversers, interlocked with the signalling, could be put in place between the platforms. There

were 12 cranes on the quayside, the largest of which was of 21-ton capacity. Fishguard Harbour handled a large volume of live cattle traffic from Ireland and had extensive cattle pens behind the platforms; there was a separate subway for cattle, which were removed from the ship at a lower level to passengers. The railway layout at Fishguard Harbour today is but a shadow of its former self with only a single platform in use – a reflection of the change in transport demands.

Fishguard Harbour signal box, situated right at the water's edge nearly opposite to the Fishguard Bay Hotel, was a timber structure containing 61 levers. Absolute block working was in operation on the main lines, with permissive block working on the down goods line, on which reversible working was allowed. An unusual signal was to be found on the edge of the quay near the signal box; this was a double-arm semaphore of standard GWR type but with black and white striped arms and used for signalling to ships. The signal box was only brought into use on the night of 29/30 August 1906.

There were no stop blocks at the ends of the platform roads at the breakwater end of the Harbour Station, the four platform lines merged into a single head shunt – unusual for a terminal station. However, this arrangement facilitated the release of locomotives from incoming trains and the attachment of banking

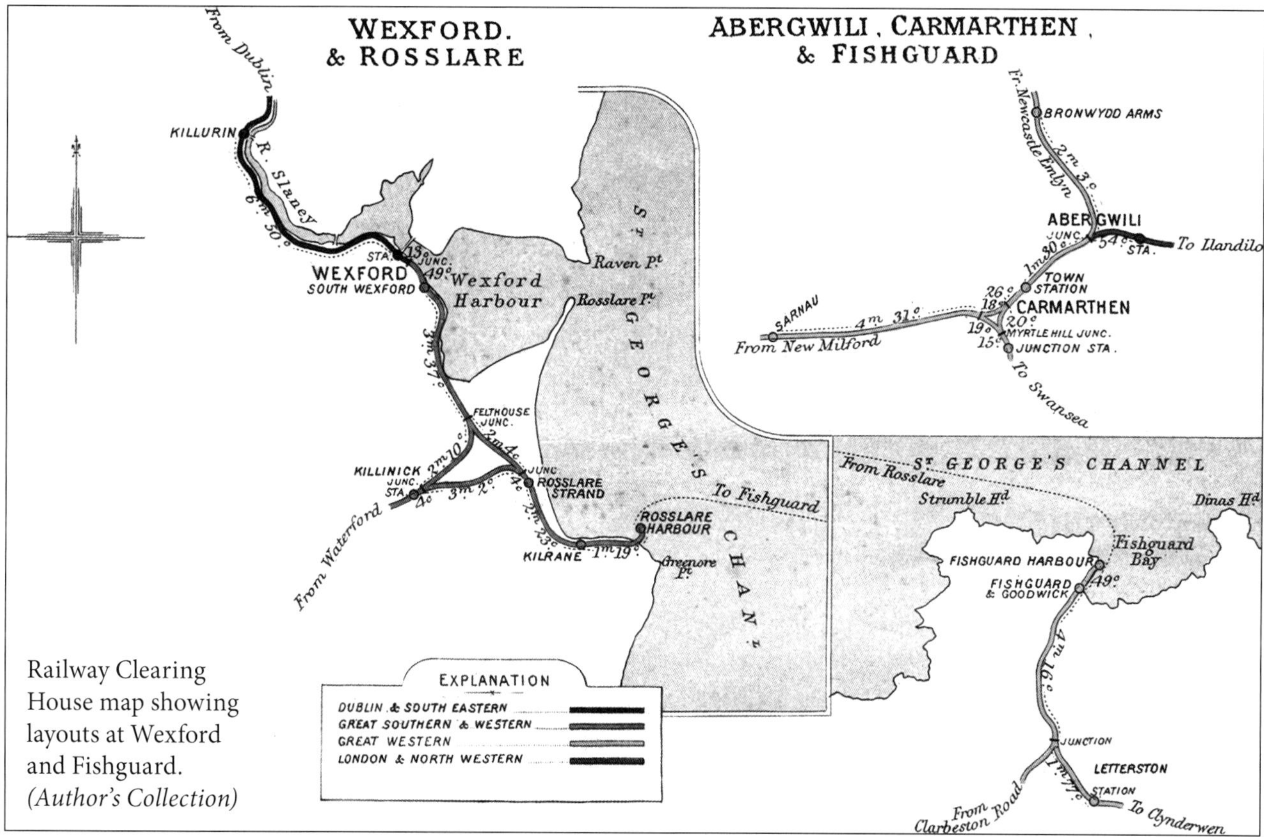

Railway Clearing
House map showing
layouts at Wexford
and Fishguard.
(Author's Collection)

engines to the rear of up trains. Initially there was a short spur on the North Breakwater, this later being extended and a second siding installed; the power station, located at the inner end of the breakwater in line with the Cow & Calf Rocks, was served by a short siding off the spur. The lighthouse on the end of the breakwater had a 4th Order light showing a red light every five seconds.

The route to Cork

Having proceeded by ship across St George's Channel the rail route resumes at Rosslare Harbour (114:20 from Mallow). Access to the mainland was achieved by means of an 11-span viaduct consisting of steel girders on concrete piers, originally with only one track across it. A pedestrian foot walk comprised of wooden planks was provided on the seaward side of the viaduct; the planks were not fastened to the viaduct, so preventing serious damage to the viaduct in storm conditions. On a number of occasions the planks were simply washed into the sea, later being recovered and replaced. On the landward side there was a cattle run which gave access to a tunnel on the pier that enabled the loading of cattle without disturbance to passengers. The viaduct remained more or less in its original condition until 1964.

To provide additional accommodation, the original pier was extended by a cant. The pier consisted of four berths for steamers; the respective length of each being as follows: No 1, 280ft; No 2, 230ft; No 3, 560ft; and No 4, 480ft. On the pier were two railway platforms, two sidings and two loading banks, the passenger line running along the back wall of the pier to the final cant, where it divided into the main platform road and two adjacent roads, respectively known as Middle and Wall Roads, which were mainly used as carriage sidings, although the Wall Road later became Platform No 2. The former goods line left the viaduct parallel to the passenger line and then curved left into a bay platform, from which trains bound for Dublin departed. A crossover connected the goods line to the passenger line. Trains starting from the pier often encountered adhesion problems on the salt encrusted rails. The platform at its outer end was covered by

Kilrane station looking towards Rosslare Harbour. The platform here was only 104ft in length. *(Photographer unknown, IRRS Collection)*

a glass roof supplied by Morton & Co of Liverpool. Both the end and back of the pier have a storm wall with a foot walk about half way up the back wall. A signal cabin was located on the back wall, closed on 12 January 1936, the lines on the pier then being worked from Ballygeary cabin. At the outer end of the pier is a lighthouse, with a fixed top showing red, green and white lights, depending on the direction in which it is sighted. It gives a flash of one second duration every four seconds.

On the landward side the main line from the pier curved sharply to the right, a 15mph restriction applying to all movements on the pier and through this curve. Continuing past the signal cabin, the running lines joined the lines leading to the two-road locomotive shed and 54ft 6in turntable, two-road carriage shed and sidings. A plan of the harbour facilities dated 1906 indicates that space was left for a possible extension of the locomotive shed to take four roads. The signal cabin, containing 15 levers, was in the 'V' of the junction beside the concrete bridge giving road access to the harbour. The original cabin at this location was closed on 10 September 1931, a new one being brought into use on 12 January 1936.[2] Originally there was a turntable, of unknown diameter, on the seaward side at the end of the curve from the viaduct. On the seaward side of the locomotive shed was an extensive cattle inspection yard, from which

point a subway gave access to the cattle run on the pier. On the landward side were the old gasworks and gasometer, which provided lighting for the pier and the yard; it was built for the opening of the line in 1906. Soon after the opening of the new line the public road from Kilrane to the pier, which ran parallel to the railway, was replaced by a new road, to which the railway contributed to the cost of construction. This road descends from the cliff overlooking the harbour and crossed the railway by a concrete bridge which, when constructed, was the longest span concrete structure in Ireland. Ballygeary (113:60) was a block post and, upon the closure of Kilrane on 12 October 1970, a passenger platform on the up side was brought into use.

Gradients from Rosslare Harbour to Rosslare Strand are generally easy. Kilrane Station (113:04) was originally known as Rosslare Harbour when it was the passenger terminus of the W&WR line; goods traffic was worked the remaining 1¼ miles to the pier as required. The name of the station was altered with the opening of the new route in 1906. The original track layout was unusual as, by means of a diamond crossing, a connection from the main line on the down side crossed the up side loop and terminated in two sidings on the landward (up) side. One of these sidings had a carriage shed for most of its curved length; this was removed in the spring of 1907. Kilrane had the distinction of having the second shortest platform in the country; the single platform on the up side being only 104ft in length. Some track alterations were carried out in 1917, and a small goods shed was

---

2 Signalling on the South Wexford line was worked on the electric tablet system rather than the more familiar staff system mostly used on the GS&WR lines. The Tyer's No 1 tablets were installed and maintained by the GS&WR, not by the Post Office authorities. Standard staff instruments were installed during the 1930s.

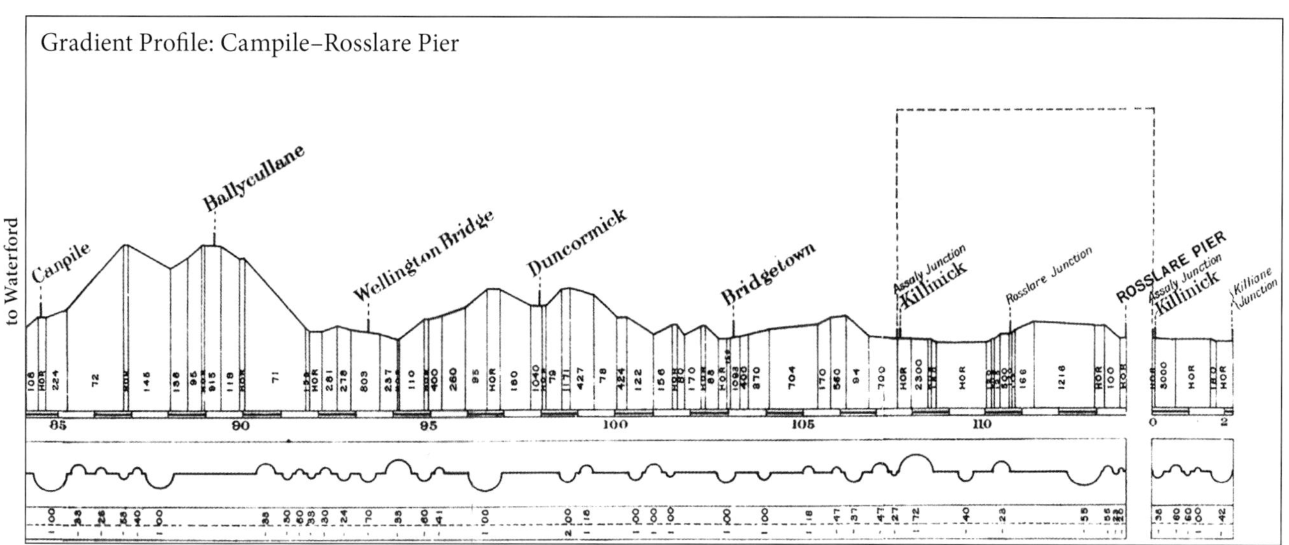

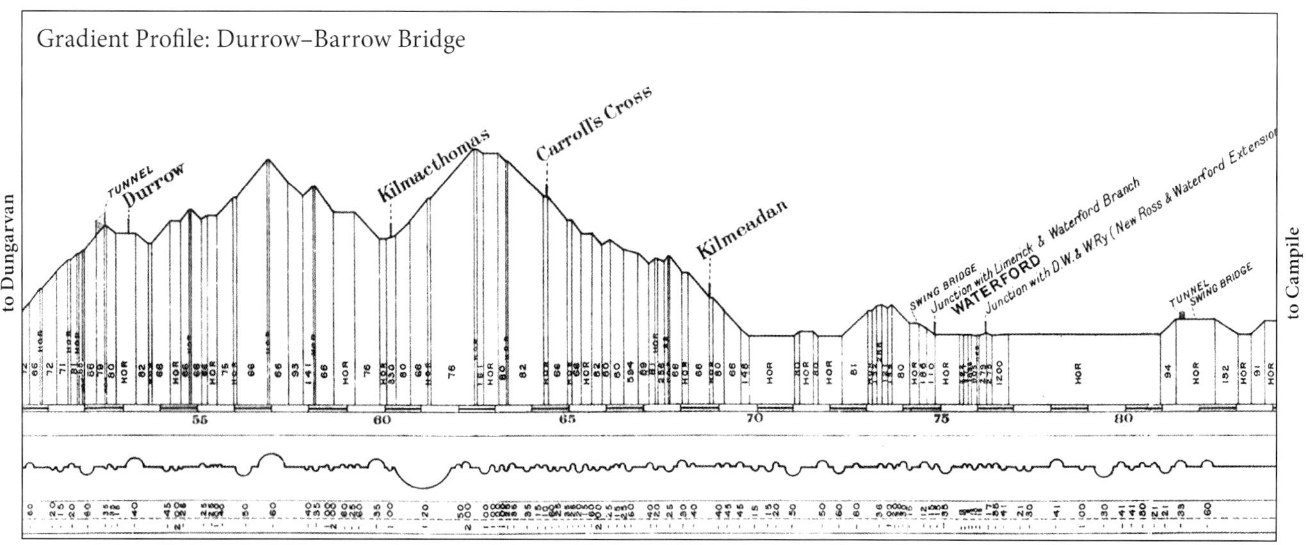

erected. Following these alterations, a signal cabin containing 18 levers, the superstructure for which came from Athy, was brought into use on 16 July 1918. The cabin was closed on 10 September 1931 and the loop removed; release of the siding points thereafter being obtained from a key on the Ballygeary–Rosslare Strand section staff. Kilrane became a halt under Rosslare Harbour as from 1 November 1950, and it was closed to all traffic on 12 October 1970 with the exception of seasonal sugar beet which continued to use the siding. The siding itself was disconnected in 1977 following the opening of the new beet loading facility at Wellington Bridge. The station site was razed shortly afterwards.

Rosslare Strand (110:60) is the point at which the F&RR&H route diverges from the former W&WR line to Wexford. Before the arrival of the F&RR&H, the station was simply known as Rosslare and comprised a single platform on the down (seaward) side, with a short siding facing to up trains. This platform was extended and a new up platform was provided. At the Harbour end, the up and down platform roads originally converged just short of the road overbridge, but in 1910 the connection point was moved beyond the bridge to permit the crossing of longer trains, and the signal cabin was moved slightly nearer to the Harbour. At the same time the up platform was extended at the northern end, a former siding at this site then becoming a bay platform road for the Waterford route.

4-4-0 No 314 at Rosslare Strand on 26 April 1955 while working the 10:05 train from Dublin, Westland Row, to Rosslare Harbour.
(RM Casserley)

The two routes diverged by means of a facing double junction just beyond the north end of the platforms, and there was a 40mph speed restriction for trains taking the Waterford route. On both routes the double tracks continued beyond the junction for sufficient distance to provide berthing to hold trains outside of the station if both platform roads were occupied, or to clear a platform road for direct access by an approaching train. Prior to May 1973 trains bound for Waterford could use either platform, but when the diamond crossing at the double junction became due for renewal a decision was taken, on financial grounds, not to replace it and, because access to the Waterford route was by means of a single facing connection off the up platform road, all trains to and from Waterford could thereafter only use the up platform. The down platform is now used by Wexford trains in both directions, except when a crossing is booked at Rosslare Strand, when trains to Wexford are routed via the up platform. The present signal cabin, containing 26 levers, is situated at the Wexford end of the down platform, the base of the original cabin at the Harbour end of the station still being used as part of a shed.

Killinick (107:54) was a block post and the junction station for the short-lived, virtually level, 2 mile 10 chain line which gave a direct connection from Waterford to Wexford via Felthouse Junction. The line from Felthouse Junction came in from the down side, the actual junction, originally known as Orristown Junction (during the construction phase) and later Assaly Junction, being at a point just before the Rosslare end of Killinick platform. The six stations between Rosslare Strand and the Barrow Bridge were all constructed to a standard design consisting of an island platform with station buildings located thereon. Pedestrian access to the platforms was gained via iron footbridges. The line to Felthouse Junction was closed on 28 May 1911, although it remained in situ as a siding worked from Killinick until it was lifted in 1918. At the time of its closure a direct connection to a loop on the up side, which served the goods store, was also dispensed with. The signal cabin at Killinick was maliciously damaged on 18 July 1922.

From Rosslare Strand the gradients were easy, providing train crews with a gently undulating road all the way to Bridgetown (103:72). In addition to the standard island platform arrangement at this station, there was a goods store, loading bank, horse & carriage dock, and siding on the up side. There was a manually operated public road level crossing at the Waterford end of the station and an 18-lever signal cabin at the Rosslare end; this cabin was yet another victim of the Civil War, being maliciously damaged on 21 September 1922, but it was rebuilt in 1924. There was a steady climb from the 101mp for just over two miles before a short descent at 1 in 79 brought the line to the three-arch Duncormick Viaduct at the Mill of Rags. Immediately beyond the viaduct the line entered Duncormick Station (98:02), which was another of the South Wexford line's standard island-platform layouts. There was a loop off the down side platform road and a loading bank on the up side. The signal cabin was at the Waterford end of the platform. From a summit about 1½ miles beyond Duncormick, the line was on a falling grade, swinging right before entering a 33-chain left hand curve to cross the Corock River on the approach to Wellington Bridge.

Wellington Bridge (93:27) was in recent years the most important station on the South Wexford line, after its conversion as a centre for sugar beet loading. The 20-lever signal cabin, maliciously damaged on 2 September 1922 and rebuilt in 1924, was at the Waterford end of the island platform. Sidings existed on both sides of the platform to cater for the sugar beet traffic.

Shortly after leaving Wellington Bridge the line curves right and commences the climb up Taylorstown bank, 2½ miles at 1 in 71 and 1 in 191 with sharp curves; a section that was the graveyard of many a heavy train on a bad night. The 9-arch Taylorstown Viaduct, is on one of the curves, and provides a view on the up side out towards Bannow Bay. At Ballycullane (89:25) the signal cabin was at the Rosslare end of the island platform and goods facilities were provided on the up side. The line is on a falling gradient of 1 in 72 on the way to Campile (84:48), the last of the more or less identical stations on the South Wexford line to be described, which had an additional loop on the down side and an 18-lever signal cabin at the Rosslare end of the island platform. This signal cabin, together with that at Abbey Junction, jointly released the controls for the opening of the Barrow Bridge. The goods sidings,

Left: A short goods train in Killinick station in the 1970s with laden beet wagons on right. Top right is the station master's house. *(Barry Carse)*

Right: Bridgetown station on 4 September 1977. The train was run in connection with the All-Ireland Hurling final, and consisted of B168+B171 with five bogies. The train has just arrived empty from Waterford. It was reported that the return working, again running via Waterford, was poorly patronised over the South Wexford line. *(Barry Carse)*

The famed Dunbrody Abbey on 12 October 1991 with Co-Co No 048 passing with 18 laden beet wagons. Note by this time Irish Rail were using the larger wagons, fabricated in Limerick Wagon Works by placing two of the Bulleid designed corrugated wagon bodies on top of one another. *(Barry Carse)*

loading bank and goods store were all situated on the up side, in addition to which a facing connection gave access to a siding serving the Shelburne Co-operative Society premises. On leaving Campile the line continues to fall at 1 in 72 before crossing the River Pill on a steel girder bridge and passing the remains of Dunbrody Abbey on the down side. There is a short rise at 1 in 192 to the Barrow Bridge just before which is the site of Kilmokea Halt (81:76), the remains of the temporary platform still being visible on the down side. The halt opened on 22 August 1966 to serve workers employed on the construction of the Great Island power station, but it has been out of use for many years.

The regulation speed limit across the 2,131ft Barrow Bridge was 40mph but this was further reduced in recent years. The bridge has been described in detail in Chapter Twelve, and electrical power for the operation of the swinging span, originally produced by a generator, with back-up battery supply, located on the dolphin below the central pivot, was switched to mains electricity supply in January 1961. Immediately on leaving the Barrow Bridge the line enters the 217 yard long Snow Hill tunnel and a falling grade at 1 in 94 brings it down to shore level beside the River Suir, which it runs alongside on the level for five miles into Waterford. A loop and two sidings were installed at Belview (79:58) for the opening of the Bell container terminal (known as Bellport) on 22 August 1993. This latter provided considerable traffic for the railway for

some years until Bell went into liquidation, however the sidings are still in use. A facing connection to a private siding at 77:04 was installed in 1927 on the down side to provide access to the Clover Meats factory; it was closed in 1976.

Abbey Junction (76:20) is the point at which the F&RR&H line joined the former D&SER line from New Ross and Macmine which converged from the down side. The original signal cabin, situated in the 'V' between the two lines, was destroyed on 9 March 1923 during the Civil War and was replaced later that year by a new cabin on the up side, a small distance nearer Waterford and adjacent to Pier Head level crossing. Apart from controlling the junction, this 26-lever cabin also, jointly with Campile, released the controls for the opening of the Barrow Bridge. The junction was simplified in February 1956, a new crossover near Pier Head level crossing being installed to allow the double line junction to be replaced with a single turnout for the New Ross line. The short stretch of jointly (D&SER and F&RR&H) owned double-track line ended just before the junction to the 34-chain New Wharf siding trailed in on the up side at 75:73 and passing under the main Waterford–New Ross road, the line enters Waterford (North) Station (75:56). The Wharf sidings were under the control of Waterford East Cabin (26 levers).

In the station were three through roads, Up, Down and Platform, the latter served by the second longest platform in Ireland, at 1,210ft. It was in effect two

Abbey Junction, Waterford. This photograph taken by the Author in autumn 2009, shows the lines immediately after crossing over Pier Head level crossing. The line to Rosslare swings to the right and becomes single, the line to the left is the ex-D&SER New Ross branch. Prior to the Civil War, Abbey Junction signal cabin was situated in the vee of the two lines. *(Ernie Shepherd)*

platforms, numbered 3 and 4, the latter at the western end. Access was provided to the two ends by means of a scissors crossing in the middle. At the Rosslare end were two bay platforms, 1 and 2, which were used by D&SER trains. Following the closure in 1963 of the New Ross branch to passenger trains these bays were used for the storage of diesel locomotives; in 1967 they were filled-in and used for car parking. At the Limerick end of the through platform was Waterford Central Cabin, unusual in that it is in effect a bridge spanning the platform and through lines. Currently on the up side there are two bay platforms, originally numbered 5 & 6. Originally there were two more, Nos 7 & 8, but these were converted into a bus parking area prior to the opening of the new Bus Eireann bus station on Waterford Quays in 2000.

Leaving Waterford Station the line passed under the main Waterford–Limerick (N24) road. Beyond the bridge on the down side there were two goods sheds (GS&WR & D&SER) and a cattle bank, then two locomotive sheds (W&CIR & WL&WR), opposite to which on the up side, adjacent to a wharf, were a coal depot and turntable. Further on, on the up side, two sidings served the fertiliser factory of Messrs Goulding.

Suir Bridge Junction (75.05), where the F&RR&H line diverged from the former W&LR and W&CIR mainline that proceeded on to Dunkitt Junction where it split into separate routes for Limerick and Kilkenny, was controlled by the adjacent Waterford West signal cabin. This cabin also controlled connections to the extensive goods yard. Leaving the junction the

Waterford North station showing central cabin with 2-6-0 No 461 on an enthusiasts' special. *(RM Casserley)*

F&RR&H line curved sharply left to enter onto the 1,205ft Suir Bridge, which has already been described in detail. Control of the bridge opening was from the signal cabin on the bridge; release of the operating levers being jointly controlled by Waterford West and Grace Dieu Junction signal cabins. The signal cabin at Grace Dieu Junction (73¾mp) controlled the connection between the line from the Suir Bridge and the entry into Waterford (South). It was maliciously destroyed on 5 November 1922, and the release of the bridge controls was subsequently transferred to Kilmeaden; the junction being closed as a block post on 22 September 1924.

Waterford South (75½mp), as it was re-named following the line's takeover by the F&RR&H to distinguish it from the former W&LR terminus on the north side of the River Suir, was the terminus of the WD&LR line and was situated near Bilberry Rock on the south side of the river. As built the station only had a single passenger platform, a second one not being provided until 1891. It had all of the facilities as befitted a terminal station of an independent line, including a goods store, coal and cattle banks, carriage and locomotive sheds. All repairs to rolling stock were undertaken at Waterford, so we also find a fitting shop and smithy, two wagon shops, carriage painting shop, carpenters' shops and sail-maker's stores. The station was closed for passenger traffic on 31 December 1907, all passenger trains thereafter running to Waterford North Station via the Suir Bridge. The signal cabin was on the down side at the west end of the station and was closed on 3 July 1911; all signals being dispensed with at that time. However, the line into the station yard was retained and served as a siding to the premises of Waterford Ironfounders Ltd until 1974. It was finally closed on 5 September 1976.

From Grace Dieu Junction the line followed the bank of the River Suir for four miles, winding back and forth on a narrow shelf of land below the heavily wooded banks of the Mount Congreve estate, and as it left the river bank near the 69½mp it started a long climb through Kilmeaden and Carroll's Cross to a summit at the 62½mp. Kilmeaden (69mp) was one of seven intermediate stations on the former WD&LR line and was a block post with the signal cabin positioned in the middle of the up platform. The station building was also located on the up platform. The running loop on the up side stretched out beyond the bridge over the main Waterford to Portlaw road at the east end of this two-platform station, which today serves as the headquarters of the Waterford & Suir Valley Railway. Leaving Kilmeaden the line crossed over the Dawn River, with the goods siding trailing in on the down side, the 1 in 66 grade presenting a tough task for up trains that had stopped at the station.

The final stretch into Carroll's Cross (64½mp) was also at 1 in 66 and on sharp curves, the station itself being located on a very short level stretch of line. This was not the original station opened in 1882, which had a single platform on the down side, but a new station that was built in 1909 when the line was diverted to ease curvature. The new station also had a single down side platform, but was provided with a loop on the up side; release of the Annett's lock for the points providing entry into the loop being by means of a key on the section staff. Having passed through the station the climb recommenced at 1 in 82, another

Right: The site of Waterford South station following its closure and subsequent occupation by Waterford Ironfounders. *(Photographer unknown, IRRS Collection)*

Left: Kilmeaden station looking east towards Grace Dieu Junction, date unknown. Today this station is the headquarters of the Waterford & Suir Valley narrow-gauge railway. *(Photographer unknown, IRRS Collection)*

Right: Looking towards Carroll's Cross with the station buildings on left. The goods store on left replaced an earlier one which had been removed in 1928. The one shown, erected in 1937, was originally a carriage shed at Portarlington. *(T Cott, IRRS Collection)*

hard task for up trains, the overbridge at the summit being referred to as the 'bridge of hope' by locomotive men. From the summit the line ran downhill at 1 in 72, 1 in 68, and 1 in 80 for just over two miles into Kilmacthomas (60¼mp), the last 1¾ miles on a long 120-chain radius right-hand curve; a noteworthy start for trains leaving that station in the opposite direction.

Kilmacthomas, nestling at the foot of the Comeragh mountains was an important town on the line. The station had two platforms with the main building on the down side. A siding on the down side trailed back to run for a short distance parallel to the River Mahon and served cattle pens in connection with the nearby Fair Green. The main goods facilities were also on the down side; the former goods store was removed in 1928, being replaced some nine years later by a carriage shed removed from Portarlington. The signal cabin was at the Mallow end of the up platform. The signalling was altered in January 1939 to permit bi-directional running on each road, and mechanical staff exchanging apparatus was installed in January 1944 to allow nonstop trains to run through at higher speeds. These staff exchangers were replaced in May 1953 by the Manson-Guthrie type. On leaving the station the railway crossed above the town on a viaduct comprising four stone arches, a steel bridge across the main street and a further three stone arches; and shortly after it curved across the River Mahon on another stone viaduct of eight arches. Between the two there was a connection to a siding serving Flahavan's mill.

There were 81 sets of public road level crossing gates between Waterford and Mallow, and 10 of these were to be found in the 14-mile section from Kilmacthomas to Dungarvan. From Kilmacthomas there was a steady climb to the 57mp, including a 1-mile stretch at 1 in 93 and 1 in 66 to the summit. The 3½ miles down hill into Durrow & Stradbally Station (53½mp) presented a challenge for down trains starting from that station as the last mile to the summit was at 1 in 66. The station had two platforms with a short siding on the up side at the Waterford end. A signal cabin, which had been maliciously damaged by fire on 21 November 1922, was situated at

the Waterford end of the up platform. The departure from Durrow & Stradbally was at the beginning of a rapid downhill stretch that commenced with a 1 in 79 through the narrow and wet, 418-yard long Ballyvoyle tunnel. The line emerged from the tunnel on high ground with fine distant views to the sea at Dungarvan Bay, probably the most scenic stretch on the line. Just ¼ mile beyond the tunnel was Ballyvoyle Viaduct, another of the impressive structures on the line. One of the centre arches of this 8-arch stone structure was blown up during the Civil War on 8 August 1922, but in the two weeks following the remainder of the arches collapsed into the valley and river below. In the following January, a ballast train was sent to its destruction at the collapsed viaduct, '101' class 0-6-0 No 189 receiving irreparable damage. The line was out of use until the replacement structure, a braced steel bridge supported on concrete piers which was completed in June 1924.

In 1970 a facing connection to the 1 mile 48 chain Ballincourty branch was installed close to the 49½mp to serve the Quigley magnesite works. This was necessary as, although the line had been closed for three years, lifting had not been completed. The Ballincourty branch remained in use until 28 July 1982. From this point the line generally followed a series of gentle undulations, through Dungarvan and Cappagh to the 37mp, where it commenced a descent on grades of 1 in 66 and 1 in 80 for the final mile into Cappoquin. On the approach to Dungarvan the line crossed four

public roads in quick succession; that at the Causeway, which was crossed at an angle, giving rise to many complaints from local residents of severe disruption to traffic. After the Causeway the line crossed the River Colligan and Shandon Road level crossing before arriving at Dungarvan (46½mp), the county town of Waterford. This was the most important intermediate station on the line and had two platforms connected by a footbridge. The main goods facilities were on the up side towards the Waterford end, although there was a coal bank on the down side at the opposite end. A connection to a livestock siding, secured by an Annett's Lock, was added in 1946. At the Waterford end on the up side there was a 44ft 9in diameter turntable that had been installed by the GS&WR in 1908. A new signal cabin, constructed immediately adjacent to its predecessor, was brought into use on 17 May 1953. A post war fashion to boost tourism saw a number of redundant passenger carriages converted to camping coaches; these were each equipped with eight beds, a living room, and kitchen. Two of these vehicles were placed in a siding at Dungarvan for the 1960 summer season, where they remained in use for several years.

Cappagh (40½mp) was a halt with a single platform on the down side and a short siding to a goods store, cattle pens and carriage dock accessed by a connection facing up trains. There had been a signal cabin at Cappagh until 25 May 1903, after which the points to the siding were released by a key on the

Right: Dungarvan station with single cab General Motors Bo-Bo No B131 on a passenger train. *(Jimmy Navin, Waterford County Museum)*

Opposite: Durrow & Stradbally station in July 1962. *(T Cott, IRRS Collection)*

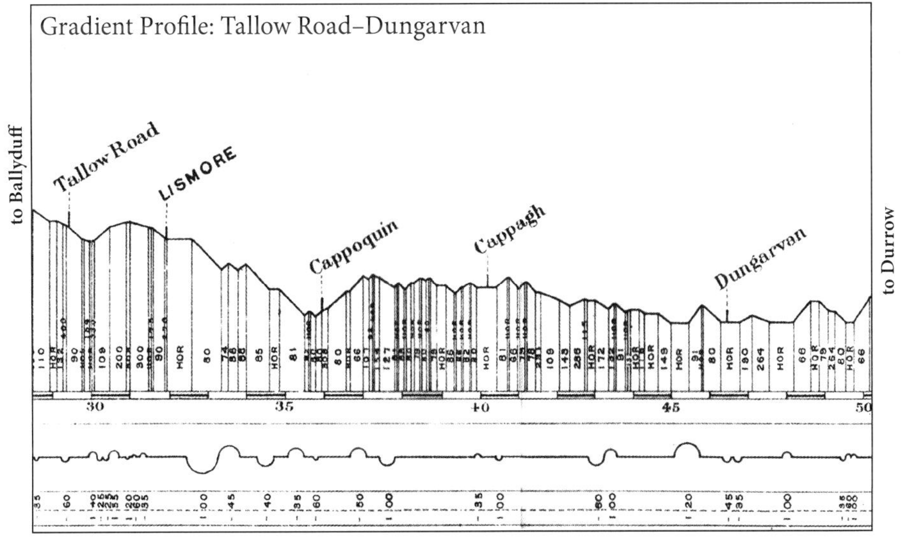

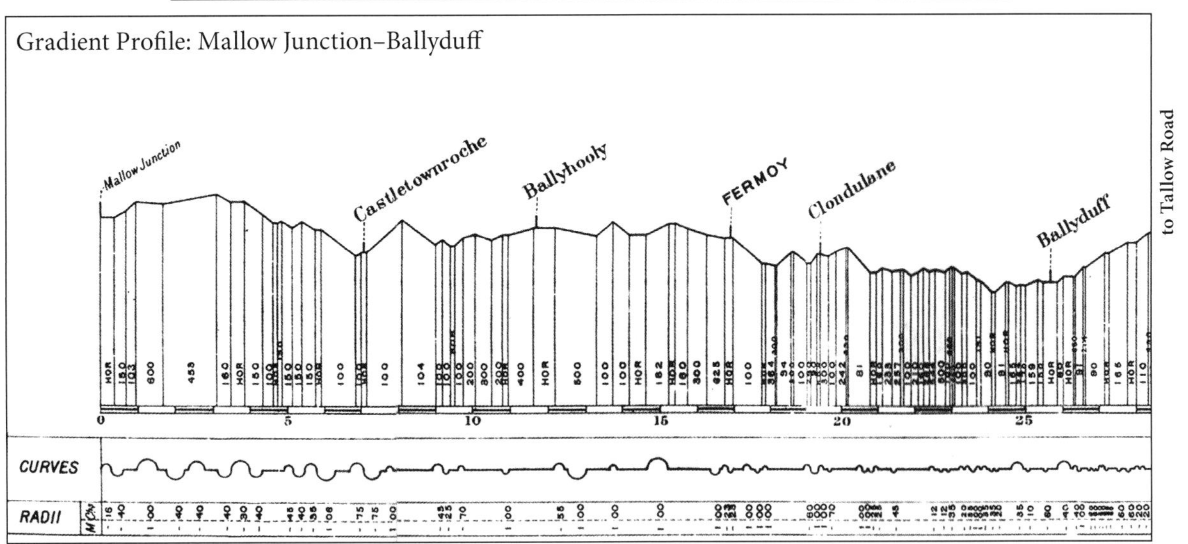

Cappagh station in August 1962 with its single platform and the goods shed in the middle distance. *(T Cott, Courtesy IRRS)*

Cappoquin station on 7 July 1934. *(HC Casserley)*

Cappoquin–Dungarvan section staff. Cappoquin (36mp) was situated in a hollow with a heavy grade out of the station in either direction. On the west side there was an arduous 3-mile climb at 1 in 80, and we have already described the downhill approach in the up direction, which presented a hard start for down trains. Approaching Cappoquin the line kept close to the River Blackwater as it ran south to enter the sea at Youghal Harbour. A long viaduct, comprising five stone arches followed by seven steel girder spans, carried the railway over the river shortly before entering the station. A facing connection at the Waterford end gave access from the up line to a goods siding on the up side which ran behind the signal cabin, whilst opposite on the down side there was a goods shed which was served by a siding that trailed into the down line. The passenger facilities included two platforms with the signal cabin at the Waterford end of the up platform and the main station building on the down platform. The station was noted for its annual floral display for which it won many awards. Close to the station was the site of the works of the South of Ireland Wagon Company, owned by Richard Keane, and which supplied rolling stock to a number of Irish railway companies. The firm went out of business in 1886 when sawing and

wagon building machines were offered for sale by the liquidator.

Just before Ballyea level crossing, on a falling gradient of 1 in 80 near the 33¼mp, a siding serving a ballast pit trailed in on the up side. The last ¾ mile into Lismore, the ancient ecclesiastical capital of the Decies, was on the level. The station (32¼mp), was originally the terminus of the F&LR, which explained the presence on the down side of a locomotive shed and 39ft 3in turntable. There were originally two signal cabins at Lismore, one on the up side at the Waterford end of the station just beyond the bridge carrying the Lismore–Ballinaspick road over the railway, the other at the Mallow end on the down side of the line; these were later replaced by one cabin on the down side at the Mallow end of the station. The single passenger platform was on the down side, goods facilities being located on the up side. The station building was an ornate structure, being somewhat similar in architectural design to Lismore Castle.

The Fermoy to Lismore section, although gently undulating in nature except for the last mile into Fermoy, which on a rising grade of 1 in 100, was plagued with many curves much sharper than found elsewhere on the route. This was due to the fact that this was the mountain country of the Knockmealdowns and the line followed the twists and turns of the Blackwater valley, a renowned fruit-growing district. Tallow Road (29½mp) had a single platform on the up side and a facing connection from a goods siding, also on the up side. The station at Ballyduff (25¾mp) served a locality in which the inhabitants could find that they lived in Co Waterford, went to school in Co Cork, and worshipped in Co Tipperary, for the three counties met at this place. The station possessed two platforms, with the loop serving the up platform on which the signal cabin was located at the Mallow end. At the same end of the station were the goods and coal stores, which were served by a siding on the down side. Clondulane Halt (19½mp), originally known as Clondulane (Glenwick), had a single platform on the down side immediately before a level crossing, beside which was a small gatekeeper's hut. A facing connection led to sidings behind the platform that gave access to a goods store and granary, the latter being provided in connection with a local corn mill.

Just before Fermoy Station the line passed the remains of Carrickabrick castle on the up side and crossed the River Blackwater on the Carrickabrick Viaduct (17). This impressive structure consisted of masonry piers and abutments supporting a main lattice girder with a span of almost 150ft over the river and six shorter fish-bellied girder spans, on top of which was the deck carrying the railway 100ft above the river. Rebuilt in 1910 it had a later claim to fame, being used in the film *The Blue Max*, starring George Peppard, James Mason and Ursula Andress, directed by John Guillermin, and released in 1966. The climax to the film was the flying of a German World War I aircraft beneath two spans of the viaduct. This was carried out by a UK stunt pilot, Derek Piggott, who had to fly under the main span 15 times and no less than 17 times under one of the narrow spans; this feat was carried out despite only about 4ft clearance on each side of the wingtips!

While passenger traffic at Fermoy (16¾) was always dealt with at the GS&WR station, the F&LR had separate goods facilities on east side of the bridge that carried the railway across the main Dublin–Cork road. These consisted of four sidings which were accessed from a facing connection on the down side, with goods and coal stores; beyond which were a separate locomotive shed and turntable. The latter was removed to Cashel in 1904 while the goods store was maliciously burnt in 1922. There was a single passenger platform with a through road on one side and a bay on the up side at the Mallow end, the latter being provided for the Mitchelstown branch trains. Part of the platform and the terminal end of the bay was covered by a short overall roof. There was also a long running loop on the down side, which was used for crossing goods trains. The goods facilities, including a store and cattle bank, were located on the down side as were a locomotive shed and 50ft turntable for the branch locomotive. There were originally two signal cabins, the West cabin on the up side opposite the branch turnout and East cabin at the Waterford end on the down side. Both were replaced in 1921 by a new cabin at the rear of the up platform. The F&LR line made connection with the GS&WR line by an end-on junction at the west end of the bridge over the main Dublin–Cork road. On leaving Fermoy, the 12-mile Mitchelstown branch diverged by a trailing junction on the down side of the line. This branch, opened on 23 March 1891, had intermediate stations at Glanworth and Ballindangan. It was closed to passenger services on 27 January 1947 with complete closure on following withdrawal of goods services from 1 December 1953.

Although not part of the F&RR&H system, the GS&WR line from Fermoy to Mallow was an integral part of the through route from Rosslare to Cork and so deserves some mention. The ruling gradient was 1 in 100 and the line twisted and turned crossing no less than eight public roads in the 16¾-mile section. There were two intermediate stations, Ballyhooly (11¼) and Castletownroche & Killavullen (7). Approaching Ballyhooly there were cattle pens and a goods store

Mallow station on 7 July 1934 with 4-4-0 No 311 taking water on the 13:50 to Cork. On left is J15 0-6-0 No 129. *(HC Casserley)*

on the up side. Originally there was only a single platform on the down side, on which the signal cabin and station buildings were located, and a loop on the up side opposite the platform. A second platform with a passenger shelter was added on the up side in 1913, which made it possible to cross passenger trains at this station. At the same time the road behind the station was diverted to allow of the installation of a carriage dock and horse loading bank behind the goods store. In conjunction with these additional facilities, a new signal cabin at the Waterford end of the new up platform was brought into use from 10 August 1913. Between Castletownroche and Ballyhooly the line crossed over a tributary of the River Blackwater by means of Kilcummer Viaduct (9½); this consisted of a multi-span steel girder supported on stone piers. Castletownroche & Killavullen had a short passenger platform on the down side with goods store, coal store and carriage dock on the same side; there was also a crossing loop on the up side. The original signal cabin adjoined the level crossing at the Fermoy end of the station; this cabin was maliciously destroyed by fire on 16 January 1923 and was replaced by a new one located on the platform between the station building and the Station Master's house. Both of these intermediate stations were ETS block posts with provision for long-section running between Mallow and Fermoy, the latter being the normal method of operation.

Mallow (144½ miles from Dublin on the Cork main line) was the junction point for the line from Waterford via Fermoy and also for trains to Killarney and Tralee. Originally opened in March 1849, it became a junction in May 1854 when the branch to Killarney was opened, followed in May 1860 by the Fermoy line. Approaching Mallow on a left hand curve the line from Waterford and Fermoy passed over the main Cork–Limerick road and then divided into a double tracked stretch leading to the 'Fermoy' bay platform on the down side and by a facing crossover to the down Cork main line. In addition to the bay there were three other platforms at Mallow Station; the down mainline and an island platform that served the up mainline and branch line services to Killarney and Tralee. There was a small locomotive shed on the down side at the Dublin end of Mallow Station, two signal cabins (North and South), and extensive siding accommodation on the up side.

Towards Dublin

Returning to Rosslare Strand, we have to make the short journey over the former W&WR line to Wexford; on this line mileages read northwards from Rosslare Strand (00:00). There were no intermediate stations between Rosslare Strand and Wexford South. Felthouse Junction (02:02), also referred to as Killianne Junction, was the junction for the direct line from Killinick with the controlling signal cabin on the up side at the junction. At Drinagh (03:18) a

Wexford Quays photographed from the leading carriage of a down passenger train. *(HC Casserley)*

siding trailing to up trains served the cement works of Messrs Cooper; the works were in operation between 1882 and about 1924.

Wexford South (05:25), one-time terminus of the W&WR, was initially known as White Walls, later as South Wexford and finally Wexford South, and was a block post until 1982. Facilities consisted of an island platform on which the station buildings were located. The signal cabin was at the Rosslare end of the platform. Goods facilities consisted of several sidings on the up side serving two oil depots, a goods store and carriage dock. At the Rosslare end there was also a short siding on the down side which served the premises of the Wexford Engineering Company and on the up side there was, for a time, a turntable that had been transferred from Waterford South.

Leaving Wexford South, the line crosses a small inlet by means of the Crescent Bridge and then runs along the quayside with the harbour on one side and the public road on the other; there is a permanent speed limit of 5mph on this stretch of line. The Bridge originally opened to allow vessels access to the Crescent, but this has been fixed for many years. Beyond the Crescent Bridge there was, until recent times, a second line on the seaward side which ran the length of the quays and served as a siding for the loading and unloading of vessels moored alongside. This was connected to the running line by crossovers at several points. At the north end of the Quays the line crosses on the level the approach to the road bridge over the River Slaney. Flashing lights and bells to warn road users are triggered by track circuit occupancy, which is also used to interface with the road traffic signals.

The line then enters former D&SER territory,

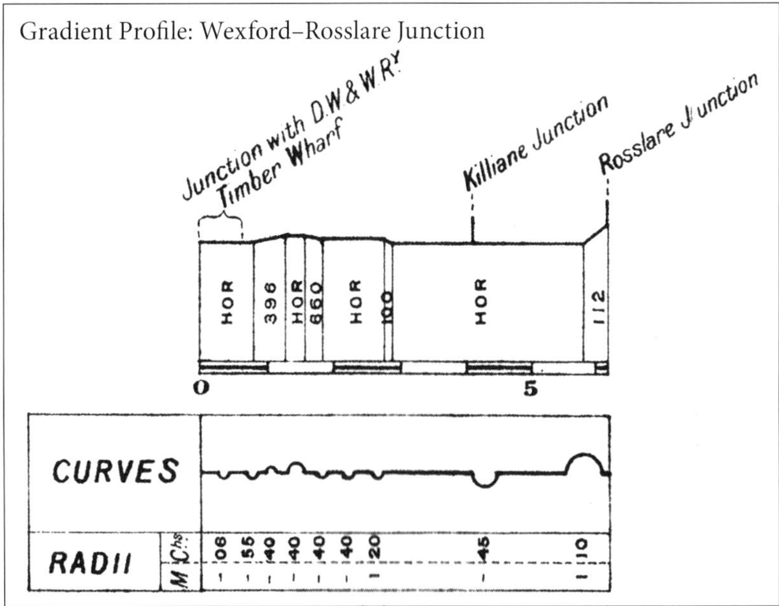

Wexford level crossing guarded only by track-circuited road traffic lights. This arrangement and the use of a mainline unguarded alongside a road is somewhat unique in these islands, the only other such to the author's knowledge being the line at Southampton Docks. No 071 is departing from Wexford for Rosslare Harbour on a down passenger train. *(Ernie Shepherd)*

passing the old goods store to enter Wexford North Station (06:00 & 92:60 from Dublin, Harcourt Street), the southern terminus of the D&SER. Here there is a 542ft long single platform on the up side. The goods facilities were on the down side as were a locomotive shed and turntable. Today there is only the running line through the station, with a single siding on the seaward side for the use of permanent way trains. Modernisation of the Rosslare line signalling in 2009 included the provision of a 132m loop just to the north of the station to facilitate the crossing of trains. For many years prior to the installation of this loop trains could not be crossed between Rosslare Strand and Enniscorthy.

CHAPTER NINETEEN

Locomotives & Rolling Stock

Taking first the WD&LR, each of the contractors are known to have used at least one locomotive on the construction works. John Ashwell, on behalf of Messrs Smith Finlayson & Company, purchased an 0-4-0 saddle tank new from the Hunslet Engine Company in March 1876, Works No 156. Named *Waterford*, all we know of this locomotive is that it had two outside cylinders 10in by 15in and 2ft 9in wheels. It was later converted to 4ft 8½in gauge and transferred to England in 1881. The late George Mahon also referred to the sale by Ashwell to the WD&LR in January 1879 of a small vertical-boilered locomotive, but nothing is known about this and there is no mention of it in the WD&LR board minutes. JW Stanford of Dublin purchased a Sharp Brothers 2-2-2 No 13 from the GS&WR in 1876 for use on his contract between Dungarvan and Lismore. It was one of 20 locomotives purchased new by the GS&WR from Sharps between 1846 and 1848, and had 15in by 20in cylinders and 5ft 6in driving wheels. Nothing is known of its fate after use on Stanford's contract but seeing that it was by then some 30 years old the chances are that it was scrapped.

Nearly two years prior to the opening of the line, the Directors gave some consideration in November 1876 to the provision of locomotives and rolling stock, the Engineers being ordered to report to the Board as to the quantity and description of stock likely to be required. The matter was again discussed at a board meeting on 14 December, the result of these deliberations being a request for the Chairman and Mr Currey to confer with George Ilberry of the GS&WR to see whether that Company might be disposed to working the new line. Nothing further transpired at that time and it was not until 9 August 1877 that seven tenders were considered for the provision of four locomotives. However, it is clear that Daniel McDowell, Locomotive Engineer of the W&CIR, had been consulted and requested to draw up a specification for locomotives and rolling stock. When the tenders were discussed at the meeting, four of them – from Messrs Sharp Stewart & Company, Beyer Peacock & Company, Kitson & Company and Dübs & Company – were excluded as they did not conform to McDowell's specification. The tender of the Avonside Engine Company of Bristol was accepted at £2,550 per locomotive; this figure was later reduced by £30 per locomotive, delivery to be made at Waterford in April 1878. It is of interest to note that when the Directors wished to have the new locomotives under construction inspected, it was not to McDowell that they turned, but to Henry Waugh, Locomotive Superintendent of the Waterford & Tramore Railway.

Early in May 1878 the Chairman and Mr Currey were requested to confer as to what steps were to be taken with Messrs Avonside who had failed to deliver any of the locomotives, and if deemed necessary, to authorise the serving of notice of cancellation of their contract. In fact Avonside were served with notice of cancellation on 23 May. At the same meeting that this announcement was made, the Chairman intimated that the DW&WR had consented to the loan of two locomotives to enable the WD&LR to open their new line. This is hardly surprising as William Wakefield had been appointed Locomotive Engineer of the WD&LR in the previous March. His father, John Wakefield, was at that time Locomotive Superintendent of the DW&WR. It would appear that Messrs Avonside approached the Board at the end of May endeavouring to have the contract reinstated, but the Directors decided to remain with their decision, particularly as there was reference to a possibility that the DW&WR might actually work the Dungarvan line. The locomotives in question were 0-4-2s numbered 20 and 22 on the DW&WR. They were worked in steam to Lismore on 31 July 1878, making

In early GS&WR days a passenger train for Waterford crosses the Shandon Bridge just to the east of Dungarvan. *(Waterford County Museum)*

a journey of 301 miles from Dublin, via Macmine Junction, Bagenalstown, Carlow, Kildare and Mallow. The GS&WR also agreed to loan one locomotive at £2 per day, this being accepted; no details are known of the locomotive concerned.

The Secretary reported to the Board on 22 August 1878 that Messrs Beyer Peacock had offered to supply four two-coupled engines at £2,050 each, to be delivered at Waterford in four months, or the same number of three-coupled engines at £2,100 each in three months. At the same board meeting Sharp Stewart offered four locomotives at £1,950 each, again to be delivered in three months. The Sharp Stewart tender was reported to be acceptable to the Chairman, but was to be subject to certain alterations as suggested by Wakefield. Meanwhile, following a further approach from Avonside in June 1878, the Board considered whether they might take two of the locomotives, provided Avonside would pay half of the expenses that the Company might incur due to late delivery. This proposition was put to Sir James Ramsden, who advised against such action. By the time the contract was cancelled Messrs Avonside had virtually completed the order. In an attempt to dispose of the locomotives, they were offered initially to the DW&WR and the W&LR, both declining to take them although the former company offered to store them for a limited period. In due course they were offered to the Midland Great Western Railway (MGWR) at £1,800

each plus carriage. This was declined, a subsequent offer of £1,600 by that company being accepted. They were delivered to Broadstone in January 1880 and were numbered 96–99. They were rebuilt in 1906–8 with larger boilers, No 99 as CIÉ 622 being withdrawn in 1945, the remaining three surviving until 1949. Some sources relate that they were refused by the WD&LR due to being overweight, but it seems unlikely that an engineer of McDowell's experience would have made such an elementary mistake in drawing up a specification.

Sir James Ramsden wrote to the Board at the end of July stating that he was aware of a locomotive on offer from Messrs Sharp Stewart & Company, the Secretary being requested to obtain full details. At the same time, the DW&WR intimated that they did not intend to loan their two locomotives long term, this obviously concentrating minds as to the acquisition by the Company of their own locomotives. Tenders were again sought in August, a contract being entered into with Messrs Sharp Stewart for the supply of four locomotives. The Locomotive Superintendent reported in January 1879 that No 1 was in service and that No 4 was running on trial; it was hoped that in a few days these two would be sufficient to operate the service, enabling the DW&WR locomotives to be returned by the end of the month. At a board meeting on 21 November 1878 reference was made to the DW&WR's account for the hire of the two locomotives from 28 July to 18 October amounting to £608 0s 6d. The Directors, in consultation with Wakefield, considered a sum of £395 17s 3d more appropriate; the minutes are silent as to what sum was actually paid. In the following February Sharp Stewart submitted their account for locomotives 2 and 3, amounting, with three months interest, to £4,380 0s 6d; they were informed that they would shortly be paid in cash, less the interest.

The four Sharp Stewart locomotives, WD&LR Nos 1–4 (Works Nos 2818–21), were of the 0-4-2 wheel arrangement and had 17in by 24in cylinders and 4ft 9½in wheels. Following their takeover by the GS&WR they were initially allocated GS&WR numbers 211–4, these being renumbered 244–7 in 1901. They had comparatively short working lives, being withdrawn respectively in 1909, 1906, 1914 and 1905. No 213 (246) was rebuilt in 1901 as an 0-4-2ST. The Engineer was ordered in November 1882 to communicate with Sharp Stewart regarding terms on which an additional locomotive of the same type as those in use would be supplied, both for prompt and deferred payment. However, when the builders replied in December it was to the effect that delivery would not be for 12 months and that they would not accept deferred payments. Otway then informed the Board that he believed that the GS&WR might be willing to dispose of a spare engine. So it was that the Company purchased ex GS&WR No 71. This was a 2-4-0ST, one of five originally purchased from Messrs Neilson & Company in 1859 by the Cork & Youghal Railway and taken over by the GS&WR in 1866. Originally numbered 1 and named *Lewis*, it carried maker's number 542. Principal dimensions were 15in by 24in cylinders, 5ft 9in driving wheels and 1,027sq ft heating surface. When sold to the WD&LR it was estimated to have run a total of 430,193 miles. The purchase price of £500 was defrayed out of funds provided by the Directors.

It was decided in November 1889 to obtain two further locomotives, if possible by deferred payments. In particular, Sharp Stewart refused to entertain this idea but offered to supply another locomotive similar to those already in service for £2,400, with delivery by the end of 1890. In February of the following year

Sharp Stewart offered one locomotive for £2,700 cash on delivery or £2,934 with payment spread over three years, this latter offer being accepted. At about the same time, Sharp Stewart agreed to supply a pair of cylinders for £90. Two further locomotives were in fact purchased from Sharp Stewart, No 6 delivered in 1891 and No 7 the following year (Works Nos 3665 & 3813). They were basically similar to the previous four, but with some minor changes. No 7 was slightly larger at the trailing end and had an improved cab with round instead of square spectacles; in addition the front sandboxes were combined with the splashers. Both carried 60 gallons less water than the earlier locomotives. They initially became 216/7 on the GS&WR and 248/9 in 1901. They had short working lives, No 248 being scrapped in 1913 and No 249 in 1910.

Otway reported in May 1894 that he had received an offer for the purchase of No 5, its disposal being left in the Engineer's hands. However, it remained with the WD&LR, probably seeing little if any service following the delivery of Nos 6 & 7. It was believed to have been condemned just before the line's takeover by the GS&WR, but nevertheless was allocated GS&WR No 215 in 1898. It was condemned by the GS&WR and was quickly scrapped, although outliving its sister engines from the C&YR by more than ten years.

At a board meeting of the F&RR&H on 26 October 1898 it was agreed that the GS&WR should take over the rolling stock of both the WD&LR and the W&WR, subject to any liabilities there might be on them, and that the GWR should take over the plant and stock at Fishguard on similar terms. At the same meeting it was noted that though all three of the Irish companies had been vested in the F&RR&H since 1 July 1898, the working of the WD&LR was still being carried on by that Company, so it was resolved to take over the working as from 1 November. The *Railway Times* for 5 November, in announcing the formal transfer, confirmed that all the existing locomotives and rolling stock had been removed to Inchicore and replaced by locomotives and carriages belonging to the GS&WR.

As recorded in Chapter Three the W&WR Company's line was worked by the DW&WR between June 1882 and May 1889; motive power was provided by that Company, frequently No 1, a Fairbairn 2-2-2 of 1854. Two new locomotives were purchased by the F&RR&H Company for the re-opening of the line in August 1894, both being supplied by the Hunslet Engine Company. First to be delivered was an 0-6-0ST (Works No 610), named *Erin*, which was reported by the *Wexford Independent* to have arrived in Wexford on Wednesday 16 June 1894. *Erin* was used in connection with the harbour works at Rosslare and worked the opening train on 6 August. The second locomotive, an 0-4-0ST (Works No 609) named *Cambria*, must have only recently arrived as it was reportedly inspected by the officials on arrival of the first train at Ballygeary. Both were to a standard Hunslet design. Apart from the differing wheel arrangements, there were some other differences. *Cambria* had outside cylinders with the saddle tank covering only the boiler barrel, while the lower cab sheets were extended forward to form small coal bunkers. *Erin* had inside cylinders, full length saddle tanks, and had a larger cab with rear bunker; she also had a brass safety valve bonnet over the firebox. It is interesting to record that both locomotives carried the letters 'R&WR' on their buffer beams. The local press generally referred to the line as the Rosslare & Wexford Railway; it appears that the F&RR&H Company did this for accounting reasons to keep the separate entities distinct. When the line was inspected on behalf of the BoT in July 1894, Hutchinson suggested that the Company should purchase a second six-wheeled tank locomotive as he considered that *Cambria* was unsuitable for passenger working and was not fitted with automatic brake equipment. This of course was never done.

Both locomotives were taken over by the GS&WR in 1898. *Erin* was allocated the number 300 but this was purely for accounting purposes and was never carried by the locomotive. *Erin* was withdrawn from service in 1930 but *Cambria* had a more colourful career, being purchased by the Dublin & Blessington Steam Tramway (D&BST) in 1918. Two years prior to this the D&BST had acquired an 0-4-0WT from the D&SER. This diminutive locomotive, D&SER No 70, had started life as the locomotive portion of one of two steam railmotors purchased by the D&SER in 1906 from Messrs Manning Wardle (Works Nos 1692/3). Fayle and Newham, in their history of the D&BST

published by Oakwood Press in 1963, incorrectly refer to the railmotors being supplied by Kerr Stuart & Company. The railmotors proved less than ideal on the D&SER, largely due to excessive vibration; this led to the locomotives being separated in 1907–8 from the carriage portions which were then successfully used as ordinary carriages. When No 70 was sold to the D&BST it had its side tanks replaced by well tanks and it became No 2 on the tramway. It was soon found to be too heavy for the Blessington Company's track (weight being quoted as 23t 14c), in addition to which the outside cylinders fouled lineside structures. So it was that *Cambria* found its way onto the D&BST, ex No 70 returning to the D&SER.

It seems quite likely that when the GS&WR began operating the W&WR on behalf of the F&RR&H in 1898 that the motive power consisted of the above two locomotives. However, at a DW&WR board meeting on 16 February 1899 the GS&WR sought permission to bring a locomotive from Ballywilliam to Wexford as a spare engine for the Rosslare line, this request being granted. This was almost certainly one of the 0-4-4T locomotives of Class 47. With the opening of the line from Rosslare Strand to Waterford in August 1906 the entire line between Wexford and Waterford via Rosslare was worked by the GS&WR, the local service between Wexford and Rosslare continuing to be worked by the 0-4-4Ts. In addition some other GS&WR 'imports' were employed, including an ex WL&WR 0-4-2, GS&WR No 278, which as related in Chapter 21, was derailed at Felthouse Junction while working a goods train.

With the opening of the through route to Rosslare in August 1906, the GS&WR provided '301' class 4-4-0 locomotives for the Rosslare Express. Designed and built at Inchicore by Robert Coey, the '301' class were an advance on Aspinall's 4-4-0s and were initially employed on Dublin–Cork services. They proved to be poor steamers, but following modifications they were transferred to the Rosslare line. However, with their 6ft 7in driving wheels and lack of tractive effort, they proved to be unsuited to the steep gradients of the Dungarvan line. Coey, reporting to the GS&WR Board on 28 October 1906 following the opening of the Rosslare line, requested the provision of six new locomotives, this request being granted. So it was

Woolwich 2-6-0 class No 380 approaches Waterford on a Cork train, believed to be in 1939. *(J O'Neill)*

that Coey designed a new class of 4-4-0 specifically for the Rosslare and Kerry lines. These were the '333' class which were introduced to service in 1907. These locomotives had the same coned boilers as fitted to Nos 305–308, with an identical wheelbase. The principal difference between the '333' class and their predecessors was a reduction in driving wheel diameter from 6ft 7in to 5ft 8½in, making them more suited to the Dungarvan line with its steep gradients. Members of the class allocated to Rosslare included Nos 333/4/7 and 340, while Cork had Nos 335/6/8/9. The '301' class continued to work the stopping passenger trains along with the '305' and '308' classes, also large wheeled; from 1936 onwards they were joined by the new '342' class.

When the 'Woolwich' 2-6-0 class was introduced from 1925 onwards they took over the boat train workings and remained on this duty until the end of steam on the route in 1956. Of these, Nos 374/7 and 380 went to Rosslare in 1930. Other members of the class known to have been on the Rosslare Express for extended periods were Nos 382/4/5/8/9, 390/4/7. It has been recorded by the late Bob Clements that the Rosslare men were not entirely happy with the new motive power. Particularly in later years, with poor maintenance, they were rough riding; they were also very dirty locomotives to work on with a good deal of dust from the ashpan blowing around the cab. One driver commented that "in summer the short cab would roast you, while in winter you'd freeze with all the draughts up through the floor." The wooden tip-up seats were regarded as a joke and seldom used by crews. Injectors were temperamental and liable to waste a good deal of water. The Irish locomotives were never equipped with smoke deflectors and the short chimneys resulted in a lot of smoke blowing back across the cab restricting visibility. Finally, on the move they had a peculiar motion which caused something akin to seasickness, even with experienced crews. All these faults aside, the Woolwich locomotives brought improvements in time keeping on the Rosslare Expresses.

With the arrival of the 'Woolwich' engines, the '333' class took over the stopping services. AEC railcars were tried on the Rosslare Express during the winter of 1954/55 but they were underpowered for the line and soon departed. Passenger trains on the line then became the preserve of 'A' (Metrovick) and 'B' (Sulzer) diesel locomotives in 1956. Goods traffic was worked by the ubiquitous '101' class 0-6-0s, assisted by members of the '249' and '257' classes. Towards the end members of the General Motors '121' and '141' classes worked virtually all the traffic, passenger and goods, on the line.

There is some confusion regarding the total number of locomotives employed by Sir Robert McAlpine on the construction of the Rosslare–Waterford line. Rowledge lists six locomotives but the F&RR&H board

AEC three-piece railcar set headed by 2633 traverses northwards along the Wexford Quays and approaches the road crossing beside Wexford Bridge before arriving in Wexford North station. *(Ernie Shepherd)*

minutes appear to suggest a total of ten locomotives in use at one point. Sir Benjamin Baker confirmed the use of three locomotives in March 1902, six in July 1902 and ten by 26 June 1903. Of those definitely known to have been used on this contract, details can be found in Appendix C2.

Welsh locomotives

Three locomotives are known to have worked on the NR&MR, at least one of which was later employed on the construction works at Goodwick. The first to arrive was a Hudswell Clarke & Rogers 0-4-0ST dating from 1875. Named *Prescelly*, it was the only one of the three with outside cylinders. It was sent to Swindon for repairs in 1898 and became GWR No 1379. Next was a Manning Wardle 0-4-0ST delivered in 1876 and named *Ringing Rock*. She is described as being to the maker's class 'Q', although recorded as being an "extensive alteration of the class" though many of the alterations were of a minor nature; one feature of note was the large non-standard cab. This locomotive remained in Pembrokeshire and was photographed at Goodwick during construction works; it was numbered 1380 by the GWR and like *Prescelly* also received repairs at Swindon in September 1898. However, compensating beams and a spark arrestor in the smokebox were fitted. Following these repairs *Ringing Rock* spent some time working the Goonbarrow branch of the Cornwall Minerals Railway. She returned to Swindon in 1902, at which point she was heavily rebuilt with

a standard GWR boiler, saddle tank and new wheels, but retaining the large cab; she also received a GWR style copper-capped chimney and safety valves.

Ringing Rock was sold by the GWR in 1912 to the Bute Works Supply Company in Cardiff, eventually ending up as No 8 on the Kent & East Sussex Railway, one of a number of lines under the ownership of Colonel Holman Fred Stephens; she arrived at Robertsbridge on 27 November 1912. At an unrecorded date in 1915 the locomotive was renamed *Hesperus*, the original plates going to another K&ESR locomotive. As *Hesperus*, she was finally withdrawn on 17 March 1939 and was scrapped two years later. The final locomotive, yet another 0-4-0ST, came from Fox, Walker & Company, later Peckett & Sons, of Bristol, in 1878. Named *Margaret*, after Sir Hugh Owen Owen's wife, it remained in the area and was stationed at Letterston by September 1898; it was numbered GWR 1378. *Margaret* has been preserved and is on display at Scolton Manor in Pembrokeshire, not far from her original home.

The exact number of locomotives employed by the contractor, JT Firbank, on the original construction works at Fishguard is unclear. A total of 14 locomotives are listed in John de Havilland's *Industrial Locomotives of Dyfed & Powys*, published in 1994 by the Industrial Railway Society, this being qualified by the comment that "it is probable that all of these locos were used here but there is little direct confirmation." A full list of these locomotives is included in Appendix C2.

Manning Wardle built 0-4-0ST *Ringing Rock*.

Ex Maenclochog Railway 0-6-0ST Margaret at Scolton Manor from a colour postcard. *(Scolton Manor)*

What we do know is that a total of 17 locomotives were advertised for sale at Fishguard in September 1907, some of which were reported to have remained unsold in March of the following year. As Firbank also carried out the construction works on the Clarbeston Road–Letterston section of line, it is quite possible that some of the locomotives may have been employed on that contract. The Manning Wardle 0-4-0ST *Caldew* is the only one definitely known to have been so employed.

The F&RR&H also owned a total of seven locomotives during the construction works at Fishguard, six of which were built by Messrs Manning Wardle of Leeds. In addition, at least one of the NP&FR locomotives, *Ringing Rock*, as mentioned before was photographed at Goodwick in 1899. As early as 8 July 1898 approval had been given for the purchase of a locomotive, this being ordered in the following October from Manning Wardle at a price of £810. It would appear that this locomotive, Works No 1380 and named *Mermaid*, had already been built as it was delivered on 2 November. Fred Harman lists *Pioneer* as having been delivered on 8 April 1897; if this is correct, then this particular locomotive had been ordered by the original F&RR&H Syndicate. It was stipulated that the locomotive was to be supplied in pieces weighing no more than 2 tons, excluding the boiler; this was due to the fact that the line to Goodwick had not been completed by this time and it had to be brought across country from Letterston.

Another new locomotive was offered by the makers in October 1901 at a cost of £825; this was *Wyncliffe*, Works No 1549. June 1903 saw a fourth locomotive ordered at a cost of £815. *Nipper*, Works No 1610 was also obviously already built as she was delivered on 21 July. All four locomotives delivered up to this time were built to the maker's standard 'E' class. They were 0-4-0ST type and had outside cylinders. Harman states that with No 1368, the 'E' class design was modified with new style frames, buffer beams, frame stays, footplating, coke boxes and boiler mountings. No 1380 incorporated the further use of cast steel components, while with *Nipper* a new pattern of 2ft 9in wheels was introduced. Two further Manning Wardle locomotives are listed, *Gallo* (Works No 1040), another 'E' class, and *Hook Norton* (No 1127), a slightly larger 0-6-0ST; both were acquired second-hand. *Hook Norton* had originally belonged to the Hook Norton Ironstone Partnership and dated from 1889; she was sold to the GWR in 1904 and became GWR No 1337. She was then sold to the F&RR&H in 1907, returned to the GWR in 1913 and eventually withdrawn in 1926. On 3 July 1909 the F&RR&H Board discussed the inconvenience being experienced at Fishguard due to a shortage of locomotives when they were laid up for repairs. They decided to purchase a second-hand locomotive from Messrs CH Walker & Company for the sum of £250; it was estimated that a further £150 would be required to bring *Gallo* up to standard. The final locomotive was *Elfin*, an 0-4-0ST purchased from Hudswell Clarke in 1898, Works No 460, a locomotive about which we know nothing.

Contractor's locomotive 0-4-0ST *Wyncliffe*. The maker's plate confirms she was built by Manning Wardle in Leeds in 1901 (Maker's No 1549). *(The National Archives, Kew)*

Another of the contractor's locomotives, *Elfin*, an 0-4-0ST, this one by Hudswell Clarke (Maker's No 466). Both locomotives sport a crude weather board and cab roofs. *(The National Archives, Kew)*

In connection with the breakwater contract of 1913, Messrs Topham Jones & Railton appear to have utilised four locomotives, two from Avonside and two from Manning Wardle. *Roath* was an 0-6-0ST, Avonside Works No 1412 of 1900; she was scrapped in 1924. Avonside 1509 of 1907, an 0-4-0ST named *Test*, was bought new in connection with the widening of Trafalgar Graving Dock at Southampton for the London & South Western Railway. Following use at Fishguard she went in December 1920 to Brancepeth Colliery. *Abertawe* was an 0-6-0ST by Manning Wardle (No 1672 of 1906) and was first used on the King's Dock works at Swansea before going to Fishguard; she was sold to Perry & Company Limited in 1926. The fourth engine was Manning Wardle 0-6-0ST *Dynevor* (Works No 1726 of 1908), also first used at Swansea; she is shown about 1920 as being the property of the executors of LP Nott.

It would not be possible, or practicable, to detail all the locomotive types which operated from Goodwick Shed over the years. What follows, therefore, is intended purely as an example of what might be found there at different periods. Originally known as Goodwick Shed (GWK), it later became Fishguard (FGD) and later still in the early 1950s it became 87J. The original allocation at Goodwick comprised about 15 locomotives, which included three 'Bulldog' 4-4-0s, 3710, 3714 and 3729; the first of these was transferred from Pembroke, while the other two came new from

Swindon. The shed also included an allocation of saddle tanks, of which Nos 652, 864, 888, 1935, 1938 and 1958 must be noted. An 'Aberdare' double-framed 2-6-0 No 2635 arrived in November 1906 to handle heavy freight traffic. Worth brief mention was 'Atbara' class No 3408 *Ophir*; she was used on the first Killarney excursion train, being renamed *Killarney* for the occasion, a name which she retained. The first steam railmotor (SRM) arrived at Goodwick on 2 September 1906, entering service the next day on a shuttle service of up to 24 trains a day between Goodwick and Fishguard Harbour, this practice continuing for some time. SRMs noted at Fishguard in the early days included Nos 37, 63 and 83. The SRMs tended not to remain long, except for No 83 which remained in service there until June 1917.

The arrival of the ocean liners at Fishguard brought about a necessity for larger, more powerful, locomotives. The first of these to arrive in June and July 1908 were 'Flower' class 4-4-0s, numbered 4113 *Hyacinth* and 4117 *Narcissus*, later renumbered respectively 4161 and 4165. Details of the locomotives which worked the initial ocean specials are given elsewhere and will not be repeated here. The first 4-6-0 to be allocated to Goodwick Shed was No 4008 *Royal Star*, which arrived in August 1911, although her stay was reported to be of short duration. Some of this class later went on to be rebuilt as Castle class. The same year saw three 'Saint' class 4-6-0s arrive,

Hall class 4-6-0 No 4981 *Abberley Hall* in course of being turned on the turntable at Fishguard & Goodwick. *(Photographer unknown)*

Nos 2937 *Clevedon Court*, 2938 *Corsham Court* and 2940 *Dorney Court*, all new ex Swindon. Members of this class remained at Fishguard until 1926. The 'Hall' class were first introduced to Fishguard in 1929 with the arrival of No 4914 *Cranmore Hall* in February, followed by No 4942 *Maindy Hall* in the following August. Apart from the larger passenger locomotives, there was also an allocation of 43XX 2-6-0s.

In early British Railways days, Goodwick usually had four 'Hall' class and at least one 'Grange'. Regular 'Halls' at that time included 5905 *Knowsley Hall*, 5908 *Moreton Hall* and 5928 *Haddon Hall*, along with 6823 *Oakley Grange*. The 1950s also saw 53XX 2-6-0s, 2251 0-6-0s and four 48XX (later 14XX) 0-4-2T type for auto trains and up to half a dozen pannier tank, including 5716 and 9602. The auto trains on the Fishguard to Clarbeston Road service were withdrawn in 1957, the service thereafter being worked with pannier tanks and conventional carriages. With dieselisation taking hold, redundant 'Hall' and 'Castle' class locomotives appeared at Goodwick in 1963. However, this was to be short-lived, as steam traction in Pembrokeshire officially came to an end on 9 September of that year.

Carriages & Wagons

With the line still almost two years away from opening, the question of providing rolling stock for use on the WD&LR was raised at a board meeting held on 9 November 1876; the result of the deliberations

was that the Engineers were instructed to report, furnishing "such details as they may consider necessary for the Board's information." Arising from these deliberations, Messrs Denny and Currey were requested to confer with Mr Ilberry of the GS&WR to ascertain upon what terms that Company might be disposed to make arrangements for working the line. However, by January 1877 it was clear that negotiations were also ongoing with the GWR regarding the possible working by that Company of the Dungarvan line. In fact there was a good deal of correspondence between the Chairman on the one hand and Sir Daniel Gooch and Sir Alexander Wood, respectively Chairman and Deputy Chairman of the GWR (the latter also a Director of the WD&LR), on the subject. The Directors, at their meeting on 8 March 1877, appeared to be in some doubt regarding an offer being made for the conversion of broad-gauge rolling stock for use on the WD&LR.

By the end of 1877, about 727 miles of the GWR broad-gauge lines had been converted to standard-gauge out of a total of 1,063 miles, thus making redundant a large number of carriages and wagons. The GWR proposition appeared to be that a certain quantity of this redundant stock was to be suitably converted at a cost of £31,375. Of this amount, the Duke of Devonshire was to pay directly to the GWR a sum of £16,000, the balance representing a GWR loan, the payment of which was to be taken out of the gross receipts of the WD&LR. James Grierson, the GWR General Manager, attended the board meeting at Waterford on 4 April to clarify matters and confirmed that if an order for rolling stock was sent to Swindon in July, then it could be delivered by January of the following year. Having reconsidered the matter, it was decided in June, following an intervention by the Duke of Devonshire, that paying a sum of £32,000 for second-hand rolling stock was not a good bargain. It is of interest to record that the W&LR, urgently in need of additional rolling stock, approached the GWR in 1877 seeking to have some of the redundant broad-gauge stock converted, the GWR advising them against it.

Finally, at a board meeting on 9 August 1877, various tenders were read for the supply of locomotives, carriages and wagons, the former being referred to earlier in this chapter. Six companies in all tendered for rolling stock as follows, the stock required to comprise of 3 firsts, 3 seconds, 9 thirds, 3 passenger brake vans, 3 horse boxes, 2 carriage trucks, 2 goods brake vans, 100 covered goods, 30 ballast wagons and 4 timber trucks, viz:

Ashbury	£22,790 0s 0d
Metropolitan	£21,590 15s 0d
Lancaster	£21,421 0s 0d
Oldbury	£23,878 0s 0d
Midland	£21,219 0s 0d
SJ Claye	£19,260 0s 0d

The South of Ireland Wagon Company, based in Cappoquin, tendered in an amount of £13,960 only for the covered goods, ballast wagons and timber trucks. Whilst the Directors did briefly consider mixing the order to procure carriages from Metropolitan and wagons from Midland, this would have cost £21,014 and it was decided to accept Messrs Claye's tender, even though it was increased by £500. The revised figure of £19,760 was broken down as follows:

3 Firsts @ £300 each	£900
3 Composites @ £275 each	£825
3 Seconds @ £210 each	£630
9 Thirds @ £195	£1,755
3 Passenger Brake Vans @ £180 each	£540

3 Horse Boxes @ £170 each	£510
2 Carriage Trucks @ £110 each	£220
4 Timber Trucks @ £75 each	£300
2 Goods Brake Vans @ £150 each	£300
30 Ballast Wagons @ £76 each	£2,280
100 Covered Goods Wagons	£11,500

It was agreed that one-third of all kinds of stock was to be delivered by 30 April 1878, a further one-third by 31 May and the balance on or before 30 June, with payment in full due by 1 September 1878. While Messrs Claye's tender was accepted and separate tenders for passenger and goods stock were received from Metropolitan and Midland, it was in fact the former who actually built the carriage stock and Midland the goods stock; it would appear that the former provided advice, possibly at the instigation of Sir James Ramsden as they were located at Barrow-in-Furness.

Reporting on the rolling stock order in December 1877, Daniel McDowell, the Locomotive Superintendent of the Waterford & Central Ireland Railway, expressed himself unhappy with Messrs Claye's suggestion to substitute Barrow steel for crucible steel as defined in the original specification, most likely prepared by McDowell, although not referred to in the minutes; as a result of this Messrs Claye were informed that such a substitution could not be allowed. It is of interest to note that when an inspection of the locomotives and rolling stock under construction was considered advisable in January 1878, it was Henry Waugh of the W&TR who accompanied the Directors.

All the passenger stock, with the exception of the composites, was delivered in 1878, the latter arriving in the following year. Originally the different classes of stock were numbered in a separate series, each beginning at No 1. While the order shows 3 seconds and 3 composites, the Company's half-yearly returns clearly show 2 seconds and 4 composites, all other categories as being per the orders. There is some doubt as to whether the passenger stock was all four-wheeled or whether some of it may have been six-wheeled. The only extant drawing, of a passenger brake van, clearly shows it to have had four wheels, but it is just possible that the firsts were six-wheeled. Alan Newham, in his history of the Waterford & Tramore Railway (W&TR), refers to one of the ex WD&LR firsts, No 4 (ex composite) as being identical to some other ex WD&LR stock purchased in 1900 apart from being six-wheeled. There is also some doubt as to the lengths of the different classes; firsts appear to have been 26ft 1in, seconds 28ft 5in, thirds, composites and brake vans 26ft, although we cannot be absolutely sure on this point. Metropolitan also provided the goods brake vans, horse boxes and carriage trucks. An additional goods brake van, No 6 in the van series and 24ft 8in in length, was supplied by Metropolitan late in 1893. A board minute dated 23 April 1879 refers to a draft agreement with the South of Ireland Wagon & Wheel Company for the hire and repair of rolling stock. It would appear that some additional stock may have been hired, but was actually paid for by Messrs Denny and Currey; we have no details of this stock nor do we know how long it was on hire.

With the abolition of second class on the WD&LR on 1 May 1894, the two seconds shown on the half-yearly returns were altered to thirds, becoming Nos 10 and 11. One of the composites became third No 12, another became first No 4, while Composite No 3 was altered from first and second to first and third class accommodation in 1894. All of the WD&LR rolling stock was quickly removed to Inchicore following the takeover of the line's working by the GS&WR in 1898. Following an inspection by Coey, it was initially decided in December 1898 to dispose of all of the carriages, and then in August of the following year the decision was taken to break them up. Subsequently, however, in December 1900 the W&TR offered to purchase four ex WD&LR carriages for £180 each, delivered at Waterford South Station or £200 at the W&TR Manor Street Station, the latter being accepted by the GS&WR. Following an inspection by the W&TR, it was decided to renovate two of the firsts and to fit all the acquisitions with roof lamps; acetylene lighting was later provided in July 1911, while they were all fitted with upholstery in February 1908.

Eight coaching vehicles were also sold to the Cork & Macroom Direct Railway in 1899 and 1900. These were first No 3, converted to a tri-composite in 1906,

to a third in 1930 and scrapped in 1938. The remainder were all thirds, one of which, No 12, was broken up in 1935, four more, Nos 11 and 13–15, being converted in 1941 to carry turf and No 16, which became a Tool Van with the Signal Department in 1943. In addition, one of the passenger brake vans, C&MDR No 27, became a Red Cross Van at Rosslare Harbour in 1941.

All of the goods stock dated from 1878, and all appear to have been retained by the GS&WR, although covered van No 38, to which GS&WR No 5038 was allocated but probably not carried, was scrapped in 1899. The four timber trucks, Nos 132–35, were allocated GS&WR Nos 5146–49, but were renumbered 8143–46 in 1899, and were scrapped between 1913 and 1916. In 1900 the WD&LR goods vehicles, with the above exceptions, were allocated numbers between 5010 and 5131, not all of these numbers being utilised (as eg 5010/1, 5112/3 and 5145); in addition, Herbert Richards states that three opens were actually renumbered 5241–43.

The W&WR owned a small amount of rolling stock, and is easily dealt with, although we do not have full details of all of the vehicles concerned. On the coaching side, there were only four passenger carriages, numbered 1 to 4, all six-wheeled and 33ft in length. No 1 was a first with 40 seats, surviving until 1960 as GS&WR/GSR/CIÉ No 341. Nos 2 and 3 were 72-seat thirds, probably becoming GS&WR Nos 604 and 606. No 604 was scrapped in 1920, while No 606 became a Sight Testing vehicle in 1917 and became part of the Cork Workmen's train in 1919. Finally, No 4 (GS&WR No 608) was a third brake, seating capacity unknown; it was withdrawn in 1946.

Henry Wynne, the W&WR Secretary, wrote to the DW&WR at the beginning of February 1886 seeking to hire ballast wagons to carry stone to Rosslare Pier, the DW&WR saying they had none to spare. It would appear that the hire would only have been temporary as it is clear that ballast wagons had already been ordered on behalf of Mr Mann as in March Messrs Brown Marshall & Company of Birmingham prepared drawings for 5ft 3in gauge ballast wagons to Order No 6273. The wagons in question were two plank four-wheeled vehicles 15ft 5in long over body. A note signed by J Mann on the drawing shows inside dimensions were to be 15ft × 7ft 6in × 1ft 4in. The note also states that the wagons were to carry "as a rule 7 tons but to be sufficiently strong to carry 9 tons in case of necessity". We have no information as to the number, if any, ordered, but it is just possible these are the open wagons Nos 1–6 on the F&RR&H list, although these are shown as timber wagons in the half-yearly return for June 1898. They have a body length of 15ft 6in (probably outside), no date of delivery being shown against them. They were later numbered 5244–49 in the GS&WR list and were further renumbered in the series 8244–84 as shown in Appendix D3. There were 12 covered goods wagons, all presumably delivered in 1894; we know nothing whatsoever about these vehicles. Finally, there were 6 cattle wagons, Nos 1–6, which were scrapped between 1909 and 1911, having become GS&WR Nos 7320–25.

In regard to the NR&MR, we have no details regarding the original rolling stock which, with the exception of the three locomotives, had been withdrawn quite early on, so eight new passenger vehicles were ordered in 1894 by the NP&FR Company, these being initially leased from the Birmingham Railway Carriage & Wagon Company (BRCW) and later purchased. They comprised two composites, each with two first and two third class compartments, NP&FR Nos 1 & 8, two five-compartment thirds, Nos 2 & 3, and three brake and luggage thirds, each with three passenger compartments, Nos 4–7. All carriages were 27ft 6in long, four-wheeled with a 15ft wheelbase. Nos 1–5 were delivered in 1894, the remaining three in the following year. Further details of these vehicles can be found in Appendix D2, including later GWR numbers. One further vehicle is shown on the GWR list, a 16ft wheelbase third which appears to have come from the Swansea Wagon Company at an unknown date. Perhaps it was one of the original Rosebush Company's vehicles. It is listed as 'Past use', with a note appended in red stating "This vehicle belongs to Messrs Holme & King, Contractors. It was sold by the NP&FR some time ago. See Mr A Nichol's letters of 12th & 14th September 1898."

The half-yearly return for December 1897 shows 3 locomotives, 8 carriages and a total of 15 goods vehicles, comprised of 6 open goods, 6 cattle wagons, 2 timber trucks and 1 goods brake van. This does not correspond either with the GWR records or a letter dated 29 September 1898 from JC Hughes, the Company Secretary, and addressed to the GWR. The latter refers to 16 goods vehicles while the GWR list shows 20, this latter appearing to be correct. BRCW supplied 6 open goods wagons (Nos 1–6), 4 twin timber trucks (Nos 7–10) and 6 medium cattle wagons (Nos 11–16), presumably in 1894, while the Midland Railway Carriage & Wagon Company supplied 3 large cattle trucks, Nos 17–19. All of these vehicles were reported to be in good condition when inspected in August and October 1898. In addition the Company had purchased an ex GWR goods brake van, that Company's No 23777, for £40 and described as being in "very bad condition" by August 1898. All of the foregoing goods stock was lease purchased from the manufacturers and eventually taken over and numbered by the GWR. Finally there was a travelling crane, ex Young for £165, along with two 'check trucks'. Both the passenger and goods stock was subsequently purchased and in due course passed into the hands of the GWR.

A F&RR&H Board Minute dated 27 October 1899 refers to a recommendation from James Inglis for the purchase from the GWR of 37 tipping wagons at a cost of £36 each, this purchase being approved. All but one were side-tipping wagons originally built at Swindon between March and June 1896 to Lot No 119. Prior to going to the harbour works at Fishguard, most of them had previously been on the NP&FR. The odd-one out was No 65, an end-tipping wagon built in April 1898 to Lot No 215. As noted in Appendix D4 this wagon was somewhat smaller than the remainder; it was replaced in November 1902 by another No 65, even smaller, with a capacity of only 1½ cu yd. Apart from the Fishguard wagons, a further batch, Nos 75–83 and 98–115, were sent to Goodwick in October 1901. Of these, Nos 100 to 114 appear in the GWR Wagon Register as "Sent to Mr Mann, Goodwick, NP&FR."

Another three ballast wagons, Nos 62–64, although apparently having no connection with the Fishguard works, are of some interest as the GWR purchased them in May 1896 from Messrs Buggins & Company. Some sources state that the Hunslet locomotive

The new rolling stock built for the Rosslare Express at Islandbridge Junction. In the background, above the signal cabin, is the Wellington Monument in Dublin's Phoenix Park. *(H Fayle, IRRS)*

Cambria supplied to the W&WR in 1894 was ordered by a Joseph Buggins. The firm of Joseph Buggins & Company, dealers in railway plant, including permanent way, locomotives and rolling stock, was based initially at Great Charles Street in Birmingham, and later had a depot at Cambridge Street. It is likely, therefore, that Buggins was known to Joseph Rowlands, and may indeed have been responsible for arranging the purchase of the locomotives for the W&WR.

Finally we need to take a brief look at the coaching stock provided by the GS&WR and the GWR for the working of the Rosslare Express trains and the Ocean specials. A set of 66ft long bogie coaches were built at Inchicore in 1906/7 for the Rosslare to Cork trains. Nos 861–63 of 1906 were first and third class composite brakes built on six-wheeled bogies and providing accommodation for 12 first and 40 third class passengers, they also included two lavatories in each carriage.

The late Bob Clements made reference to the fact that some of the third class compartments were marginally longer than others and always suspected that there might initially have been three classes in use on the Rosslare Expresses. A couple of GS&WR Traffic & Works Committee minutes shed some light on this. One dated 26 January 1906 refers to a letter received from the GWR stating that that Company was willing to restrict bookings on the Fishguard–Rosslare route to first and third classes if the GS&WR were prepared to do the same; this was approved. Then on 5 February it was reported that the Locomotive Engineer had

submitted plans to the Board of new carriages for the Rosslare branch showing alterations from first/second/third to first/third classes, again this alteration being approved. It is clear from this that the composites were originally intended to be tri-composite vehicles, the alteration being made in February 1906; as time was now of the essence, it would seem that the decision was taken to go ahead on the basis of the plans already drawn up rather than have fresh plans prepared.

The remainder of the vehicles entered service in 1907, Nos 869–874 being first/third composites, with 18 first and 56 third class seats. No 875 was another composite brake with the same accommodation, but on four-wheeled bogies. Finally, No 876 was a diner. Sketch plans for this vehicle were submitted to the GS&WR Board in December 1906. Once again, the vehicle was to be a composite, 66ft in length. Two interior arrangements were shown to the Directors, one with the kitchen at one end, the other with it in the centre. It was agreed that the kitchen should be placed at the opposite end of the carriage to the first class seating. It was also ordered that only the first class section was to be marked. All, with the exception of the dining car, were side corridor. The first class section originally had individual chairs, but on 26 September 1910 the GS&WR Board ordered that fixed seats be fitted owing to several instances of passengers falling over. Withdrawal dates and other dimensions are shown in Appendix D2.

For the Ocean Express traffic, the GWR built two 11-coach sets at Swindon. Each set consisted of

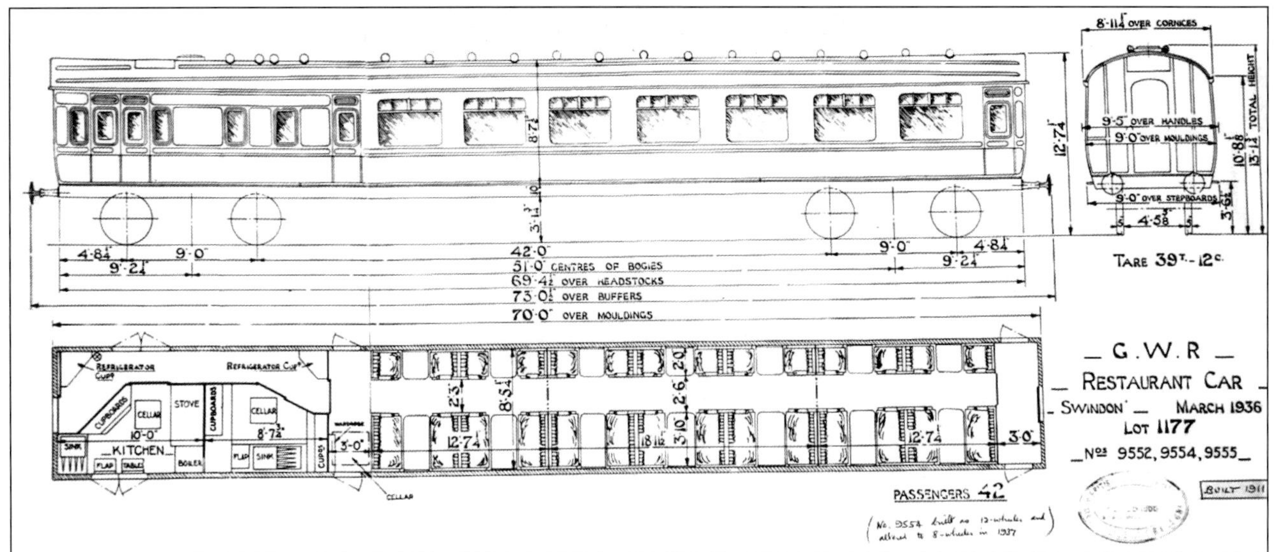

Diagram for the rebuilding in March 1936 of the three GWR Restaurant Cars Nos. 9552/4/5. These 70ft vehicles were originally built at Swindon in 1911 in connection with the Ocean Express trains, operating between Fishguard and Paddington. *(Graham Carpenter)*

eight firsts, a restaurant car, with a brake first at one end and a baggage van at the other end. Two 70ft centre-gangwayed baggage vans of 20 ton capacity, numbered 874 and 875, were built in 1908, the former being stationed at Old Oak Common and the latter at Fishguard. These were followed by two more in 1910, Nos 876–877, which had six-wheeled bogies; all had four sliding doors on each side. With the demise of the Cunard special trains, these vehicles became newspaper vans after World War I. Also in 1910, brake firsts 8178–80 and firsts 8181–96, appeared, followed by four Restaurant Cars, 9552–55, in the following

year. The restaurant cars had high-backed seats and were divided by partitions; the bodies had large windows in the sides like the GWR 'Dreadnoughts'. All were withdrawn in 1958. Michael Harris states that No 9554 had six-wheeled bogies. The first brakes survived until 1961 for use on the 'Members Only' Newbury Race specials, their longevity being attributed to the lack of brake firsts of GWR design until the construction by British Railways of standard vehicles in 1960. No 8179 had the distinction of being the only one of these carriages, and one of very few toplights, to be repainted in lined maroon livery.

CHAPTER TWENTY

Services

In connection with the opening of the WD&LR the Board approved a service of two trains each way daily, departing Waterford at 10.10 and 14.50, and from Lismore at 07.20 and 15.20. By March of the following year the service had been increased to three trains each way, from Waterford at 08.44, 14.50 and 18.40, while departures from Lismore were at 08.00, 15.10 and 18.00. There are no further references in either the Board or Traffic Minutes to provide details of train services, nor apparently have any of the Company's timetables survived. Before referring to the service provided by the GS&WR from 1898 onwards, we must take a brief look at the service on the short W&WR from the time of its opening in 1882.

As already detailed in Chapter Three, the DW&WR had agreed to operate a service of two trains each way daily, leaving Wexford at 09.30 and 16.00; the return service was timed so as to connect with the DW&WR mainline service for Harcourt Street, Dublin, which departed from Wexford at 12.25 and 17.30. On Sundays, trains left Wexford at 11.00 and 15.00. The *Wexford Independent* for 17 June 1882 provides us with a few additional details. Trains stopped intermediately at Rosslare (later Kilrane), journey time from Wexford to Ballygeary being 40 minutes in each direction. Return services from Ballygeary were at 10.30 and 16.30 on weekdays, and 14.00 and 18.00 on Sundays. It also stated that trains would be first and third class only. Henry Wynne, the W&WR Secretary, wrote to the DW&WR towards the end of June asking that a third train be run daily, this being agreed to at a rate of 18s per day. A revised timetable from 1 July 1882 saw trains leave Wexford at 07.30, 13.30 and 18.20, and Ballygeary at 09.00, 16.40 and 19.20. There were, however, still only two trains each way on Sundays, down at 11.00 and 14.00, and up at 13.00 and 19.10. July also saw the introduction of weekly return tickets at 5s 3d first and 3s 6d third.

The weekday service was reduced back to two trains each way as from 1 October 1882, this being the pattern of services in following years. Sunday services were also withdrawn for the winter months, but were reinstated on 15 April 1883 "to enable the inhabitants (of Gorey and Enniscorthy) to visit the beautiful strand of Rosslare and neighbourhood." It was agreed in October 1882 to issue weekly return tickets to Naval Reserves at a special rate of 3s third class. The *Wexford Independent* for 14 April 1883 reported that a well-appointed car would run between Ballygeary and Carne in connection with the trains on Mondays, Wednesdays and Saturdays. The same newspaper, while reporting favourably on the revised train service, stated that the want of a refreshment room at either Rosslare or Ballygeary, "where ladies and children could be supplied with tea, coffee or milk" was much felt.

A special train was run in September 1883 to bring children from the Wexford Workhouse to Rosslare and Ballygeary. The children left the train at Rosslare and it was reported that they were brought to visit the nice little church and graveyard in the "neat and clean village of Kilrane." They then went on to Ballygeary pier head, following which a Miss Duggan of Rosslare provided the children with tea.

The new station at White's Wall (South Wexford and later Wexford South), stated to be nearly opposite Miss Carr's, was opened on 1 October 1885, a station which the *Wexford Independent* claimed would be of great advantage to people frequenting the Faythe market. From the same date the winter service of two trains each way came into effect. It was to be 6 June before Sunday services resumed in 1886. One train was to leave the Dublin (DW&WR) station at 14.00, while a second train would depart White's Wall at 15.00, "going down to the pier." It would seem that all three weekday trains operated from the Dublin station, leaving at 07.30, 14.00 and 18.30. The first Sunday train of 1887, at the beginning of June, was reported to be a most successful one, with 14 carriages packed with passengers, and indeed a number left behind for want of seats. In May 1888 the W&WR introduced return tickets to Rosslare at single fares, only valid for use on the 07.30 down and 09.00 up trains; these tickets would have been of very limited use.

As recorded in Chapter Three the DW&WR withdrew services on the W&WR line in May 1889, resulting from the latter company's refusal or inability to pay the DW&WR arrears for working the line, which now remained dormant for the next five years. The *Wexford Independent* for 4 August 1894 reported under the heading of the F&RR&H that the line was to be re-opened on that day with a train leaving the Harbour Station at 11.40 and arriving at South Wexford (White's Wall) at 12.10. In the opposite direction a train was to leave Wexford at 13.50 and arrive at the Harbour Station at 14.30; the newspaper does not record whether this train was to run from North or South Wexford, but as the time allowed was 40 minutes it would appear to have gone from the North station. A full timetable, showing four trains each way appeared in the following Saturday's newspaper as follows:

Rosslare Harbour	dep	07.30	09.30	11.40	17.00
South Wexford	arr	08.00	10.00	12.10	17.30
Wexford	arr	08.10	10.10	12.20	17.40

Wexford	dep	08.20	10.40	13.50	18.50
South Wexford	arr	08.30	10.50	14.00	19.00
Rosslare Harbour	arr	09.00	11.20	14.30	19.30

The *Free Press* of Wexford dated 1 January 1896 shows a revised service operating from 1 November 1895; there were to be no Sunday trains until further notice. A full timetable appeared in the *Free Press* for 20 May 1896 as follows:

					Sunday	Sunday
Wexford	08.20	11.45	14.00	18.30	14.30	19.00
South Wexford	08.30	11.55	14.10	18.40	14.40	19.10
Rosslare	08.45	12.10	14.30	18.55	15.00	19.25
Rosslare Harbour	08.55	12.20	14.40	19.05	15.10	19.35

					Sunday	Sunday
Rosslare Harbour	06.55	09.30	12.30	17.30	13.30	18.00
Rosslare	07.05	09.40	12.40	17.40	13.40	18.10
South Wexford	07.20	09.55	12.55	17.55	13.55	18.30
Wexford	07.30	10.05	13.05	18.05	14.05	18.40

Fares (ex Wexford)

	1st Single	3rd Single	1st Single	1st Return
South Wexford	2d	1d	3d	1½d
Rosslare	1s 0d	6d	1s 4d	10d
Rosslare Harbour	1s 3d	9d	1s 11d	1s 2d

The last timetable published under the heading of the F&RR&H and the signature of FW Gelling was that for November 1898 showing two trains from Wexford, at 08.00 and 15.30, returning at 09.00 and 17.25. In addition, on Saturdays only, there was a train leaving Wexford at 11.00 and returning at 12.00. Journey time in both directions for all trains was now 35 minutes, and, as in previous years, there was no Sunday service during the winter months.

Operation by the GS&WR and its successors

Turning now to the operation of the two lines by the GS&WR, the working timetable for 1898 indicates three trains from Mallow to Waterford (all three classes) at 08.50, 13.45, 18.05 and 19.40, the latter only running from Lismore to Waterford on Saturdays. Journey times varied from 2h 25m to 3h 05m. In addition to the weekday service, on Sundays there was a 14.40 from Cork to Lismore. Similar services operated in the opposite direction, with one goods train each way on weekdays, this train taking 6¾ hours for the journey. The Rosslare–Wexford service for May 1899, referred to as the Rosslare and Wexford branch, shows four trains in each direction on weekdays, at 08.00, 10.45, 14.15 and 16.30 from Wexford, 09.00, 12.00, 15.30 and 17.30 from Harbour Station. There was one train each way on Sundays, from Wexford at 14.30 and Harbour Station at 18.00; journey time on weekdays was 35 minutes and 40 minutes on Sundays. A goods train appears for the first time in the November 1899 timetable, an engine and van leaving Wexford on Wednesdays and Thursdays at 10.45 with an arrival at the pier at 11.15; a goods train returned from the pier at 12.00.

Table No. 51.   **UP—ROSSLARE PIER, WEXFORD, WATERFORD, LISMORE AND FERMOY TO MALLOW AND CORK.**

Miles	Stations	1 PAS.	2 Express PAS.	3 PAS.	4 PAS.	5 PAS.	8 PAS.	9 PAS.	11 Express PAS. (Oct. only)	14 PAS.	15 PAS.	16 Goods	18 Through Goods	Sundays 17 PAS.	Sundays 18 PAS.	Sundays 19 PAS.	Sundays 20 PAS.
—	ROSSL'RE H'BOUR	—	5 30	—	8 10	—	—	—	—	—	—	—	—	5 30	—	—	—
1	KILRANE	—	—	—	—	—	—	—	—	—	—	—	—	—	—	—	—
3½	ROSSLARE STRAND	—	—	8 16	8 17	—	—	—	—	—	—	—	—	—	—	—	—
—	WEXF'D	—	—	—	—	—	—	—	6 15	—	—	—	—	—	—	—	—
—	WEXFORD (STR.)	—	—	—	—	—	10 30	4 20	4 30	—	—	—	—	—	—	—	—
—	FELLHOUSE JUNCTION	—	—	—	—	—	—	—	4 25	—	6 55	8 30	—	—	—	—	—
6½	KILLINICK	—	—	[illegible]	[illegible]	—	10 40	4 40	4 41	—	7 37	6 40	—	—	—	—	—
11	BRIDGETOWN	—	—	[illegible]	[illegible]	—	11 2	4 50	4 51	—	7 16	7 14	—	—	—	—	—
16½	DUNCORMICK	—	—	[illegible]	[illegible]	—	11 23	5 1	5 3	—	7 25	7 27	—	—	—	—	—
21	WELLINGTON BRIDGE	—	—	[illegible]	[illegible]	—	11 41	5 11	5 12	—	7 55	7 45	—	—	—	—	—
23	BALLYCULLANE	—	—	[illegible]	[illegible]	—	11 55	5 22	5 23	—	—	8 1	—	—	—	—	—
24½	CAMPILE	—	—	[illegible]	[illegible]	—	12 5	5 32	5 34	—	8 13	8 21	—	—	—	—	—
34½	W'TORD (NORTH)	—	—	6 35	9 32	—	12 22	5 50	6 25	—	7 19	8 41	7 30	10 30	—	—	—
39	W'TORD (SOUTH)	—	—	—	9 40	—	—	2 45	—	—	7 19	—	—	—	8 30	—	—
45½	KILMEADAN	—	—	—	9 44	9 55	2 57	3 44	—	7 22	7 23	—	7 50	7 55	8 43	8 43	—
48½	CARROLL'S CROSS	—	—	—	10 5	10 6	3 9	3 10	—	7 33	7 33	—	—	9 5	9 5	—	—
52½	KILMACTHOMAS	—	—	—	10 16	10 17	3 20	3 21	—	7 43	7 44	—	8 19	8 20	9 9	9 6	—
60½	DURROW	—	—	—	10 32	10 33	3 36	3 37	—	7 57	7 58	—	8 50	9 0	9 21	9 22	—
67½	DUNGARVAN	—	—	7 25	10 43	10 55	3 51	3 53	7 25	8 10	8 13	9 20	1 33	2 9	9 35	9 39	—
72½	CAPPAGH	—	—	—	11 3	11 9	4 5	4 6	—	8 23	8 23	—	2 47	2 23	9 53	9 55	—
78	CAPPOQUIN	—	—	—	11 15	11 19	4 15	4 16	—	8 33	8 33	—	2 46	3 0	10 3	10 3	—
82	LISMORE	—	—	7 51	8 30	11 26	4 23	4 25	7 51	8 40	8 43	9 30	3 10	3 30	10 10	10 15	—
84½	TALLOW RD.	—	—	—	8 36	11 35	4 33	4 35	—	8 46	8 47	—	3 30	3 35	10 21	10 22	—
88½	BALLYDUFF	—	—	—	8 43	11 46	4 50	4 51	—	8 56	9 0	9 50	3 47	4 2	10 30	10 31	—
92½	CLONDULANE	—	—	—	8 53	9 0	12 0	4 55	4 56	—	9 13	9 13	10 25	4 15	4 37	10 43	10 44
97½	FERMOY	—	7 15	8 19	8 21	9 5	9 13	12 20	5 0	8 19	8 21	9 23	10 55	11 25	10 50	10 55	—
102½	BALLYHOOLY	—	7 24	7 25	—	9 19	9 24	12 30	5 10	8 41	9 41	—	11 37	11 50	11 4	11 5	—
107	O'TOWNSHEND	—	7 34	7 30	—	9 54	9 58	12 42	5 20	8 53	9 56	—	—	11 15	11 16	—	—
114	MALLOW	—	7 50	8 48	8 51	9 52	—	12 55	—	3 55	5 46	10 16	—	12 45	5 45	5 55	11 32	11 40
—	CORK	—	—	9 28	10 35	—	12 0	—	4 52	—	6 65	11 30	—	7 5	—	12 30	—

A page from the GS&WR Working Timetable for October 1906 shows the initial service provided in the up direction with two boat trains leaving Rosslare at 05.30 and 17.30. It should be noted that on Sundays only the morning train operated, and that only as far as Waterford. *(Herbert Richards)*

The following service is shown in the working timetable for the summer of 1905. A goods train left Cork at 00.30 and Mallow at 02.50, stopping at all stations to Dungarvan, which was reached at 07.15. This train left Dungarvan at 07.45 as a mixed train, arriving at Waterford South at 09.20. In the opposite direction this train ran throughout as a goods service, leaving Waterford at 19.20 and arriving in Cork at 05.30 the following morning. There was also a down goods which left Fermoy at 12.20 and arrived in Waterford at 17.55. Passenger trains operated from Cork at 07.20, 13.00, 15.30 and 18.50 (the latter to Lismore only). There was one through passenger train on Sundays, leaving Cork at 14.45; in addition, there was a 14.30 from Fermoy to Dungarvan and a 19.10 Lismore to Waterford, the latter being a return working of the 15.00 Waterford to Lismore. Through services from Waterford to Cork on weekdays left the former at 07.30, 10.00, 14.45 and 18.40, the latter mixed as far as Dungarvan.

The introduction of the new steamer service and the opening of the South Wexford line at the end of August 1906 brought about a recasting of the timetable and the introduction of the Rosslare Express. The down morning train left Cork at 08.30 with first and third class accommodation only, but with a breakfast car included in the train formation. This train only stopped at Mallow, Fermoy, Lismore, Dungarvan and Waterford, arriving in Rosslare Harbour at 12.20; the corresponding up working was scheduled to leave Rosslare Harbour at 05.30 but this was of course subject to the actual arrival time of the steamer from Fishguard. In the evenings an express left Cork at 19.40, with a dining car and, with the same intermediate stops, arrived in Rosslare Harbour at 23.30; in the opposite direction the up train left at 17.30, arriving in Cork at 21.20. In addition to these stops, this train stopped briefly at Ballyhooly to cross the down express. Some other passenger trains ceased to run, while others, such as the 16.12 from Mallow to Waterford South, now only ran as far as Fermoy. Some through passenger trains now ran to Wexford South via Killinick and Felthouse

Junctions, including the 09.30 and 12.45 from Cork. There were also some additional short workings, such as the 07.30 mixed from Waterford to Wexford and the 20.05 Waterford to Rosslare Harbour.

The steamer service between Fishguard and Rosslare was temporarily suspended as per GWR Circular dated 15 July 1922, being eventually reinstated as from Monday 17 September 1923. This explains why the GS&WR initially refused offers from the D&SER to run the Cork–Rosslare train service via Macmine Junction and New Ross. The following table shows the service provided by the GSR in July 1928:

Cork dep	23.45	Waterford arr	09.15	Goods	
Waterford	07.20	Wexford	09.00	Passenger	
Waterford	07.35	Rosslare Harbour	13.00	Goods	
Cork	09.30	Waterford	13.12	Passenger	
Waterford	14.00	Wexford	16.04	Mixed	
Dungarvan	14.45	Waterford	17.00	Goods	
Cork	13.00	Waterford	17.55	Passenger	
Waterford	18.30	Rosslare Harbour	20.20	Mixed	
Cork	16.00	Rosslare Harbour	21.30	Passenger	
Cork	19.00	Rosslare Harbour	23.10	EP*	* Empty Passenger
Rosslare Harbour	05.25	Cork	09.15	Passenger	Mixed RH to Waterford
Waterford	09.45	Dungarvan	13.05	Goods	
Lismore	08.20	Cork	10.24	Passenger	
Rosslare Harbour	07.40	Cork	15.00	Passenger	
Wexford	11.20	Waterford	13.22	Mixed	
Waterford	13.30	Cork	17.18	Passenger	
Rosslare Harbour	14.40	Waterford	16.15	Passenger	
Waterford	17.20	Cork	22.15	Passenger	Mixed Fermoy to Cork
Rosslare Harbour	15.00	Waterford	18.30	Goods	
Wexford	17.10	Waterford	19.20	Mixed	
Waterford	20.15	Cork	06.55	Goods	
Rosslare Harbour	05.45	Cork	11.30	Passenger	Sundays Only

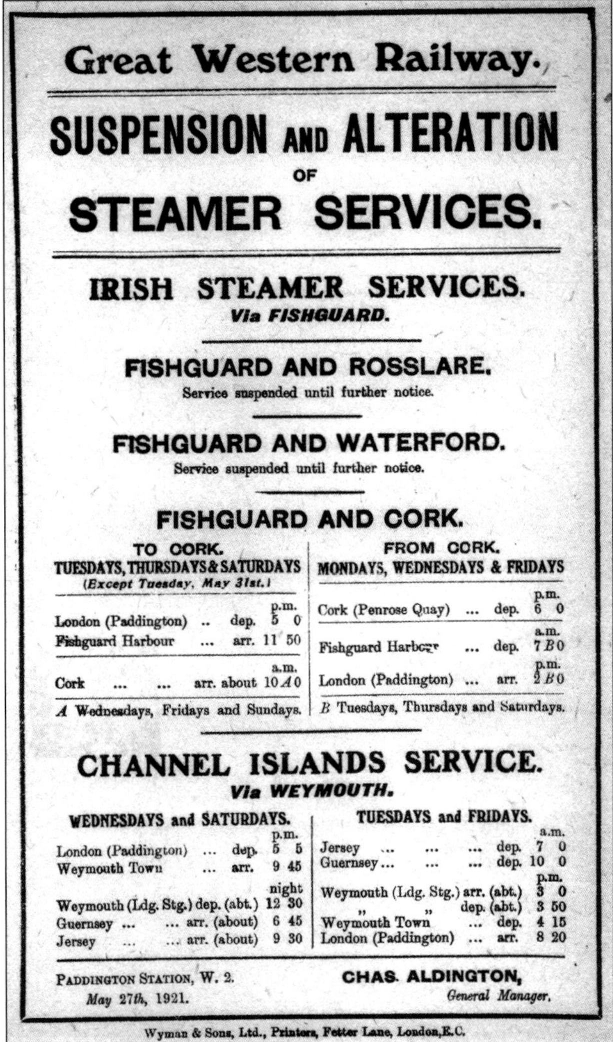

GWR poster announcing the suspension in May 1921 of the cross-channel steamer service between Fishguard and Rosslare & Waterford. *(Ernie Shepherd)*

Wartime shortages of fuel and other essentials saw reductions in the service provided throughout the country. The June 1942 timetable shows only one through passenger train from Cork to Waterford, leaving the former at 14.00 with an arrival 4h 35m later; there was also a through goods from Cork. One goods and one passenger ran from Waterford to Rosslare Harbour, respectively at 08.20 and 17.10; in addition there was a goods train path 'as required' from Dungarvan to Waterford and back. On the Wexford and Rosslare branch, one train ran from Wexford to Rosslare Harbour at 06.50, with two further trains at 14.00 and 18.00 which ran only as far as Rosslare Strand; these and their return workings at 08.20 (from Rosslare Harbour), 15.15 and 19.10 were all mixed. With the withdrawal of the steamer service during the war years the through train service from Cork to Rosslare was also withdrawn and it was not until the 1960s that the timetable once again reverted to showing Rosslare Harbour as the final destination.

The winter 1946 timetable had two separate tables, Cork–Waterford and Waterford–Wexford & Rosslare Harbour. There were two passenger trains from Cork to Waterford, departing at 08.00 and 14.00; progress was leisurely, in particular as regards the latter train which stopped in Mallow for 32 minutes and in Lismore for 17 minutes. There were two goods trains, which left Mallow at 04.20 (Mondays to Fridays only) and 16.10 with arrivals in Waterford some 12 hours later, respectively at 16.50 and 04.00. There was only one passenger train from Waterford to Rosslare Harbour, at 17.30 with a journey time of 146 minutes for the 38½ mile journey; there was also a passenger train leaving Waterford at 09.40 for Wexford. There were similar workings in the reverse direction on both lines. The 1946 timetable provided evidence of the hardships encountered during the war years and, indeed, several succeeding years. Time was allowed to goods trains at certain stations for fire cleaning purposes, viz 40 minutes each at Lismore and Dungarvan, and also at Duncormick in respect of the South Wexford line. It has to be said that scheduled running times were frequently exceeded due to breakdowns on the road.

The Rosslare Express had been reinstated by the time of the 1951 summer timetable but with only one train each way daily, from Cork at 18.00 and from Rosslare at 06.15; journey time was 4 hours even in the up direction with an additional 5 minutes in the opposite direction. For the winter of 1952, this train ran only on Saturdays with its running time having been extended by 15 minutes in each direction, to allow for additional stops.

The summer service for 1965 showed three passenger trains from Cork to Rosslare, at 07.25 (arr 11.30), 13.30 (19.45) and the Rosslare Express at 18.20 (22.15); in addition there was a service from

Rosslare Mainland station on 2 July 1988 with No 007 running round its train prior to departure for Dublin. *(Barry Carse)*

ROSSLARE HARBOUR, WATERFORD, LISMORE AND FERMOY TO MALLOW AND CORK

Trains 9–16 are WEEK-DAYS; trains 17–18 are SUNS.

Distance from Rosslare Hbr.	UP TRAINS	Sectional Running			9 PAS.		10 Goods		11 Rosslare Express T.S		12 PAS. T.S.		13 Goods		14 PAS. Path as Required		15 PAS.		16 Goods T.S.		17 Rosslare Express		18 PAS. Path if Required	
Miles		D	S	D	arr.	dep.	arr.	dep.	arr.	dep.	arr.	dep.	arr.	dep.	arr.	dep.	arr.	dep.	arr.	dep.	arr.	dep.	arr.	dep.
					a.m.	a.m.	a.m.	a.m.	a.m.	a.m.	a.m.	a.m.	p.m.	p.m.	p.m.	p.m.	p.m.	p.m.	p.m.	p.m.	a.m.	a.m.	p.m.	a.m.
—	**ROSSLARE H.** W ●	0	0	0	...	7 10	...	...	...	**11 00**	...	**11 10**	...	**2 40**	...	**6 05**	...	**6 25**	From		...	**1100**	...	**1115**
1¼	KILRANE ..	3	4	5	7 15	7 16	...	...	...	11 04	11 15	11 16	...	2 47	...	6 09	...	6 29	Wexford		...	1104	...	1119
3½	ROSSLARE STD. D	3	4	7	7 22	7 34	...	...	...	11 07	11 21	11 24	2 56	3 07	...	6 12	...	6 32	8 14	8 24	...	1107	...	1122
6½	KILLINICK .. D	4	4	7	7 40	7 41	...	...	11 12	11 17	11 30	11 31	3 18	3 33	...	6 16	...	6 36	...	8 33	...	1111	...	1126
11	BRIDGETOWN D	7	6	11	7 50	7 51	...	...	...	11 25	11 40	11 41	3 48	4 03	...	6 23	...	6 43	...	8 44	...	1118	...	1133
16¼	DUNCORMICK D W	8	8	14	8 01	8 02	...	...	...	11 33	11 51	11 52	4 21	4 35	...	6 31	...	6 51	...	8 58	...	1126	...	1141
21	WELLINGTON BRIDGE D	6	6	10	8 10	8 11	...	...	...	11 39	12 00	12 01	4 49	5 05	6 38	6 43	C.R.	6 58	...	9 08	C.R.	1133	...	1147
25	BALLYCULLANE D	7	7	12	8 20	8 21	...	...	...	11 46	12 10	12 11	5 21	5 33	...	6 51	...	7 06	9 22	9 46	...	1141	...	1154
29¾	CAMPILE .. D	6	8	11	8 29	8 31	...	...	...	11 52	12 19	12 21	5 48	6 25	...	6 57	...	7 12	...	9 59	...	1147	...	1200
38	ABBEY JUNCTION ..	...	...	...	...	...	...	...	...	...	...	...	...	...	...	...	...	...	...	...	...	...	...	...
38½	**WATERFORD** ●	10	11	18	8 45	9 20	...	9 40	12 03	12 08	12 33	12 50	6 50	...	7 08	7 40	7 23	7 30	1019	...	1158	1202	1211	1220
40½	GRACE DIEU ..	...	...	...	...	...	...	...	...	...	...	...	...	...	...	...	...	...	...	...	...	...	To	
45¼	KILMEADEN	11	12	18	9 33	9 34	10 02	10 15	...	12 20	To		...	...	To		...	7 42	...	...	...	1214	Limerick	
50	CARROLL'S CROSS ..	7	9	14	9 43	9 44	10 33	10 43	...	12 27	Limerick		...	...	Limerick		...	7 49	...	...	...	1221	...	...
54	KILMACTHOMAS D	6	7	11	9 52	9 57	10 58	11 25	12 34	12 35	...	...	...	...	...	...	7 56	7 57	...	...	1228	1229	...	...
60½	DURROW .. D	10	10	18	10 09	10 10	11 49	11 57	...	12 46	...	...	...	...	...	...	8 09	8 10	...	...	...	1240	...	...
67½	DUNGARVAN .. D W ●	9	9	15	10 21	10 24	12 16	1 18	12 56	12 59	...	...	...	...	...	...	8 21	8 25	...	...	1250	1252	...	...
74	CAPPAGH HALT ..	7	8	12	10 33	10 34	1 34	1 47	...	1 07	...	...	...	...	...	...	...	8 33	...	...	...	1 00	...	...
78¼	CAPPOQUIN .. D	5	6	11	10 41	10 44	2 02	2 35	1 13	1 15	...	...	...	...	...	...	8 39	8 40	...	...	1 06	1 07	...	...
82¼	**LISMORE** +	6	7	10	10 52	10 54	2 49	3 35	1 23	1 24	...	...	...	...	...	...	8 48	8 50	...	...	1 15	1 16	...	...
85	TALLOW ROAD ..	4	4	6	11 00	11 01	3 45	3 54	...	1 29	...	...	...	...	...	...	...	8 55	...	...	...	1 21	...	...
88¾	BALLYDUFF	5	5	9	11 08	11 10	4 07	4 20	...	1 34	...	...	...	...	...	...	9 01	9 02	...	...	...	1 26	...	...
95	CLONDULANE ..	7	8	14	11 19	11 20	C.R.	4 47	...	1 41	...	...	...	...	...	...	...	9 10	...	...	...	1 33	...	...
97¾	**FERMOY** .. + W ●	3	4	6	11 25	11 29	4 57	5 47	1 45	1 47	...	...	...	...	...	...	9 14	9 16	...	...	1 37	1 39	...	...
103	BALLYHOOLY HALT ..	5	5	12	11 36	11 37	...	6 01	...	1 53	...	...	...	...	...	...	...	9 22	...	...	...	1 45	...	...
107½	CASTLETOWNROCHE +	6	6	12	11 45	11 46	C.R.		...	1 59	...	...	...	...	...	...	...	9 28	...	...	...	1 51	...	...
114½	**MALLOW** .. W ●	11	11	20	12 02	12 15	6 45	...	2 11	2 20	...	...	...	...	...	...	9 40	9 44	...	...	2 03	2 08	...	...
—	**CORK** .. W ●	...	...	...	12 45	...	...	...	2 50	...	...	...	...	...	...	...	1015	...	...	...	2 40	...	...	...

C.R.—Calls if required.
T.S.—Operates Tuesdays to Saturdays only.

Summer 1965 timetable. (*Ernie Shepherd*)

Limerick which arrived in Rosslare at 22.00. There were corresponding trains in the opposite direction, the Rosslare Express leaving Rosslare Harbour at 11.00, followed by a train for Limerick at 11.10. In the down direction a goods train left Mallow for Waterford at 07.00, arriving at 19.10; there was also a goods train on Tuesdays and Saturdays from Waterford at 14.55 and running to Wexford.

Following the closure of the WD&L section in March 1967 the boat trains ran via Limerick Junction and the ex WL&W line through Waterford. As an example, the 1971 CIÉ working timetable lists two passenger trains each way, at 07.00 and 18.30 ex Cork, arriving respectively at 11.05 and 22.35; the evening train ran daily only to 2 October after which it ran on Tuesdays and Saturdays only. There was also a passenger train from Limerick at 12.15 to Waterford, with a long wait until 16.30 to continue the journey to Ballygeary only. At that time goods services such as they were ran to Wexford via Rosslare Strand. The current timetable shows only one train each way between Rosslare Europort and Waterford, at 07.00 with an arrival in Waterford at 08.20; to travel on to either Limerick Junction or Dublin involves a lengthy wait at Waterford. Likewise in the opposite direction, the train leaves Waterford at 17.20, before the Dublin train has arrived. These trains are worked by a two-car 2700 class railcar set.

With the opening of the new route, boat trains left Paddington at 08.45 and 20.45, arriving in Fishguard Harbour respectively at 14.15 and 02.15 with the steamers due to leave ten minutes later. In the opposite direction, trains were scheduled to leave Fishguard Harbour at 16.15 and 03.25, respectively 10 and

15 minutes after the steamer's arrival. The 08.45 down train included a luncheon car while the night train had buffet and sleeping cars. The overnight up train had a sleeping car as well as a breakfast car, the 16.15 departure a dining car. It should be pointed out that Irish time still applied at this time, being 25 minutes behind Greenwich, ie when it was midday in England and Wales, it was 11.35 in Ireland.

On the GWR, breakfast and luncheon cost 2s 6d, a four-course dinner 3s and five-course 3s 6d; tea or coffee on their own were charged at 3d, and with a variety of jams etc and salad, between 6d and 1s. In Ireland the cost of dinner was based on class, first was 3s 6d and third 3s. In addition to the foregoing, luncheon and tea baskets were available at a number of stations en route, on notice to the Train Guard. Finally, as regards the sleeping cars, a charge of 7s 6d was made for the full journey between Paddington and Fishguard and vice versa, or 5s between either Newport or Cardiff and Fishguard. Rugs and pillows could be hired at a cost of 6d for each such article.

Local services on the NP&F branch and also on the mainline to Clynderwen started from and terminated at Goodwick rather than the Harbour Station. Steam Rail Motor (SRM) services commenced running between Fishguard Harbour and Goodwick Station on 2 September 1906; numerous trips, allowed two minutes in each direction, operated for a number of years. The SRMs began operating over the mainline to Clynderwen as from 1 July 1907; they were subsequently replaced by auto trains (14XX and carriage), which were in turn replaced in 1957 by conventional coaching stock hauled by a pannier tank. The GWR working timetable for October 1906 gives us some details of train services and operation on the NP&F branch. Trains departed Goodwick at 07.55 (passenger to Clynderwen, arrive 08.45), 09.00 mixed to Clynderwen, 12.15 passenger to Clynderwen, 13.30 cattle from Maenclochog to Clynderwen and 15.45 goods from Letterston to Clynderwen. In the opposite direction, trains left Clynderwen at 10.45 mixed, 12.13 passenger and 11.05 goods, the latter to Letterston only and arriving at 12.31.

Two additional trains ran, 06.00 from Clynderwen to Letterston on fair days at the latter, which was the third Monday in each month, and 06.00 Clynderwen to Maenclochog on fair days at the latter place. This train commenced its journey at 04.30 at Carmarthen Junction and was to consist of a six-wheeled carriage and a heavy goods brake van. A cattle special was due to leave Maenclochog on fair days at 13.30 for Carmarthen Junction. Long distance cattle off this train were to be forwarded by the 15.15 Carmarthen Junction to Pontypool Road train. The timetable also indicated that two passenger trains were not authorised to cross at Rosebush, although a passenger and a goods might do so; in the latter instance, the goods train was placed in the loop to allow the passenger train to run through on the mainline. On both Letterston and Maenclochog fair days the 15.15 was rescheduled to leave Carmarthen Junction at 17.15, unless fair traffic was sufficient to warrant the running of a special train beyond the Junction. Additional notes clarify some of the working details. Ballast trains were limited to six 20 ton ballast wagons or nine of 10 tons, in each case to have a heavy goods brake van attached. Excursion traffic to Killarney commenced as early as 1907, with the first such ticket, numbered 0000, being purchased by the vicar of Fishguard, coincidentally the Revd William Rowlands, but not believed to be any relation of Joseph Rowlands of the F&RR&H.

A timetable for July 1920 shows the boat train leaving Paddington at 20.00 and arriving in Fishguard at 01.40. In the opposite direction a train left Fishguard at 04.55, 50 minutes after the scheduled arrival time of the steamer from Rosslare; this was in marked contrast to the connecting times when the line first opened. Passengers were, however, now allowed to remain on board the steamer at Fishguard until 08.00. Passengers wishing to upgrade from third or steerage to saloon on the steamer could do so on payment of an excess fare of 9s 7½d single or 13s 1½d return; these unusual figures were reduced in 1924 respectively to 6s and 11s 3d. Whilst sleeping berths were initially reserved for first class passengers, they could be booked by third class passengers for 2s 6d. Two-berth state cabins were charged at 15s on top of the first class fare. Timetables also noted that refreshment rooms were available for the use of steamer passengers at Rosslare Harbour Station.

The three *Saints* resumed operations on 1 January 1920 with rail services being restored to something like pre-war levels. Services were also restored on the NP&F branch in 1920, with the re-opening of the section between Maenclochog and Rosebush on 12 July, extended to Puncheston on 14 November 1921. It is believed that goods services recommenced between the latter station and Letterston on 23 October 1922, followed on 9 July of the following year by a passenger service, the latter shown as "Rail Motor – One Class Only"; it is not clear whether this was an SRM or an auto-train.

Bradshaw for July 1922 shows the following boat services operating to and from Fishguard Harbour:

Depart	Arrive	Name of service	Remarks
LP 08.45	FH 14.50	South Wales Express	Breakfast & Dining Cars to Landore
LP 17.00	FH 23.30		Tea & Dining Cars to Cardiff
LP 20.00	FH 01.40	Irish Mail	Dining Car to Fishguard Harbour
FH 03.25	LP 10.15	Irish Mail	Sleeping & Breakfast Cars from Landore
FH 04.55	LP 10.57		Breakfast Car Cardiff to Paddington
FH 08.00	LP 14.30		Luncheon Car Cardiff to Paddington

LP = London, Paddington; FH = Fishguard Harbour

World War II saw the boat trains reduced to one each way, viz 19.55 from Paddington and 06.05 from Fishguard Harbour. Sleeping cars were withdrawn, never to return. As referred to in Chapter 18 a new line was opened in 1938 from Letterston Junction northwards to Trecwn in connection with the establishment there of a base for the RNAD. Workmen's trains began operating from Goodwick to Trecwn in May 1950, consisting of two or three old carriages in charge of a pannier tank; the carriages remained at Trecwn during the day while the locomotive was utilised for other services.

A new innovation was introduced as from 18 June 1965, namely the Motorail train. Rather than departing from Paddington this train, which consisted of car flats and coaching stock, ran from Kensington Olympia. There was a standard charge of £18 single, irrespective of the size of the car or the number of passengers travelling with it; each family had a separate compartment on the train, which also included a buffet car in its formation. On arrival at its destination the train was shunted into the loading dock at Goodwick Station, only the drivers disembarking there so as to bring their vehicles down to the harbour. In the meantime the coaches were moved to the Harbour Station. In its first (short) season the new service proved to be very popular with the motoring public, with 2,900 cars and some 10,000 passengers carried. For some years in the mid-1970s GUVs were substituted for car flats, vehicles then being unloaded at the old horse loading bank at the Harbour Station. For the summer of 1980 the train ran only on Saturdays and Sundays, running for the last time on 19 September of that year. In later days the service was generally operated by Class 47s although it is reported that a HST appeared at least once, on 27 May 1978, as the result of a locomotive failure.

The re-privatisation of British Rail in the 1990s is of little relevance to our story, except to record that the service to and from Fishguard is currently operated by Arriva Trains Wales (ATW). There are two arrivals at Fishguard on weekdays, at 01.27 and 13.15. The former train is operated by First Great Western (GW) between Cardiff and Swansea, arriving at the latter at 23.20, the onward service leaving 25 minutes later. The later train runs direct from Cardiff at 10.54; there is an eight minute connection at Cardiff from a GW train which leaves Paddington at 08.45. Return workings depart Fishguard at 01.50 and 13.27. The 01.50 involves a wait of 137 minutes at Llanelli, arriving in Cardiff at 06.43, while the later train runs direct. Bad as these services are, Sunday services offer little if any incentive to travel. A train leaves Cardiff at 09.50, providing a 12 minute connection at Pembrey Burry Port. The through passenger has then to change at Carmarthen to a bus which arrives in Fishguard at 14.00, the up working being a bus to Carmarthen and then by rail to Cardiff, arriving at 05.35. All services to and from Fishguard are generally operated by ATW class 150 Sprinter diesel multiple units.

Ocean Liner Specials

To conclude the story of the services some mention must be made of the Ocean Special trains which operated between 1909 and the outbreak of war in 1914. In this context we are lucky in that three Operating Notices between July and December 1909 have survived, which together provide us with a detailed and interesting insight into the running of these trains, which were of such importance to the GWR, albeit for such a short period of time. Notice No 85 dated July 1909 under the signature of Joseph Morris, the Superintendent of the Line, runs to six pages. It states that the Ocean Specials were to start either from the Ocean Quay or the Harbour Station, an extra 10 minutes being allowed if starting from the former. While scheduled times were shown in the Notice, it was clear that departure times were entirely dependant on the arrival times of the liners, details of which were to be telegraphed to principal stations so as to enable a clear road to be kept for these trains. Special trains were to run whenever sufficient passengers disembarked from liners; these trains called at Cardiff so as to afford connections to such destinations as Birmingham, Bristol, Plymouth, the Midlands, the North and West of England. It was also stipulated that all such special trains were to operate via Badminton.

In the event of insufficient passengers offering, they were to be sent on by either the ordinary Irish boat trains or by special trains to Cardiff or Bristol to connect with ordinary trains. Daytime special trains to Paddington were to consist of an Ocean mail van, corridor brake composite, restaurant car and another corridor brake composite. If run at night, the train was also to include a sleeping car. Specials to Cardiff or Bristol were made up of the same carriages, one or both composites and the sleeping car working through to Paddington at the rear of ordinary trains. In such circumstances details were to be telegraphed forward to ensure the provision of adequate motive power. It was also stipulated that only the best rolling stock was to be used for the Ocean Specials, the composite to be 57ft and lettered "For Ocean Traffic – return to Fishguard." The trains also carried special roof label boards.

A one-page Notice, No 195 dated 26 October 1909,

shows Ocean Special intermediate timings, these being shown only from the Harbour Station. Finally, we have a more detailed Notice issued regarding arrangements to be made in connection with the expected arrival of the SS *Mauretania* on Monday 6 December 1909. Three empty trains were listed to work to Fishguard on the previous day with the necessary staff, including lady attendants. These were a 12.40 mail special from Paddington and two empty passenger trains at 14.10 and 16.38, arriving respectively at 18.45, 19.55 and 22.25. The following table shows the formation of the three empty trains:

Mail Train	First Passenger Train	Second Passenger Train
Ocean Mail Van 70ft	Corridor Brake Compo No 7531	Van Third No 3527
Ocean Mail Van 70ft	First No 8314	Corridor Third $
Ocean Mail Van 70ft	First No 8315	Third No 3611
Ocean Mail Van 70ft	First No 8319	First No 9051
Corridor Brake Van	Two Restaurant Cars	First No 8257
Lavatory Van	First No 8320	Two Restaurant Cars
Newspaper Van *	First No 8321	First No 8256
Newspaper Van *	First No 8322	First No 8255
	Two 70ft Vans	First No 9046
	First No 9047	Two Vans (one 8-wh & one 70ft)
	First No 9048	First No 9049 $

* One of the Newspaper Vans to be attached at Cardiff and the other at Landore.
$ First No 9049 and the additional Corridor Third are being sent to Fishguard for use if required.

Three tenders were to be provided, namely the SS *Pembroke* for mails, either the SS *Great Western* or the SS *Great Southern* for baggage and the SS *Sir Francis Drake* for passengers. The mail tender was to berth at the Ocean Quay, the two other vessels at the Station Quay. The mail special was then to run from the Ocean Quay via the cattle pen sidings. London and Continental mails were to be loaded in the first six vans with the last vehicle being reserved for Cardiff, Birmingham, Bristol and Plymouth. The first passenger special was not to convey passengers or baggage for destinations short of London, these being accommodated on the second special. Arrangements were to be made for Wolf's Castle Signal Box to be opened for the passing of the three trains. The final instruction stressed the importance of keeping a clear road ahead of each special.

CHAPTER TWENTY ONE

Accidents

The Company and its predecessors were remarkably free from serious accidents. The usual accidents occurred during construction, hardly surprising when one considers the lack of any sense of health and safety issues at the time. Two such accidents occurred in 1876 during the construction of the W&WR. On 29 January of that year Peter Aspel, a labourer employed on the works was engaged in filling wagons with spoil. While endeavouring to jump into the first of some wagons, he fell between them and the second one ran over his legs, fatally injuring him. It was remarked that he had previously been cautioned against leaping off the stage into wagons. In the following December, three workmen were killed and a fourth was described as being in a "most precarious state." In this instance, a locomotive was engaged in pushing some wagons along the track near Hill of Sea when an axle broke derailing the wagons. The men, who had been in the wagon next the locomotive, were tipped out and run over. Shortly after the re-opening of the W&WR, a special train of three livestock wagons and a van was run from Gorey for Wexford. When arriving in Wexford the train collided with a Rosslare train standing at the platform, damaging some wagons on the latter train, damage being estimated at £50. It was lucky that the passengers for Rosslare were in the carriage next the locomotive and thus escaped injury.

An accident occurred on 16 July 1888 at Kilmacthomas involving the 15.20 train. The accident was in due course reported on by the BoT. A fatal accident occurred at Lismore Station on 6 November 1890 when a man named James O'Donnell was run over and killed by the locomotive of the 15.20 train. He had apparently crossed the line to the goods store to collect a parcel for his employer. When re-crossing the line he did not hear the approaching locomotive due to the weather being exceptionally wet and windy. The Coroner's Jury exonerated the Company's servants including the driver, but recommended O'Donnell's widow to the consideration of the Company. The matter was referred to the Chairman and Deputy Chairman who in due course recommended a grant of £10; it was ordered that the money be placed in the hands of Mr Onions, the Lismore Station Master, with an instruction that he should consult, if considered necessary, one of "the Roman Catholic clergy as to the most beneficial application of the money on Mrs O'Donnell's behalf." A Mr Feely was paid a sum of £2 2s 0d for professional attendance at the inquest.

The Board were informed at their meeting on 19 February 1891 that Peter Power was found "in a dying state" on the line on 8 February, having apparently fallen from the top of the cutting at Ballyvoyle tunnel, no blame being attached to the Company. Ganger Blanche was killed in an accident at Waterford Station on 26 October 1891, the Board agreeing to a temporary payment of 12s per week to his widow. However, in December it was ordered that she be informed that no further assistance would be given until she consented to place her children in an industrial school. The Engineer was in fact instructed to make the necessary arrangements to carry this out and to assist the widow, who was reported to be ill at that time, with a gift of £5. There was a sequel to this in the following April, when the Clerk of Waterford Union wrote to the Company stating that Mrs Blanche had applied to the Board of Guardians for outdoor relief, and suggesting that she be paid a monthly allowance by the Company. The Directors, however, responded saying that Mrs Blanche and her children had already been liberally assisted by the Company and they were unable to act on the Guardians' suggestion.

The final accident on the WD&LR as an independent company refers to a Matthew Ivory who was run over and killed by the 14.30 train on 10 August 1897 at an unspecified location. In view of the destitute condition of his widow and five children it was agreed to grant a year's wages, quite a generous settlement at that time.

An unusual accident occurred on Saturday 4 January 1896 on the Quays at Wexford. A man named Connors, in the employment of Messrs Doran of Kilmuckridge, was in charge of a horse and cart with a load of timber. A train passing along the Quay startled the horse, Connors sustaining serious injuries when trying to control it, injuries from which he subsequently died. An inquest was held two days later and the jury considered the Rosslare Railway to be negligent in not having the usual danger flag in front of the locomotive and they recommended that the locomotive whistle and the danger flag be dispensed with. It subsequently came to light that the red flag was rarely if ever used, the flagman frequently being seen travelling along the Quays on the locomotive. Nine and a half years later, on 15 June 1905, a similar accident occurred at Wexford. William Hutchinson, a farmer, was driving a pony and cart out of the Wexford Dockyard premises when he was struck by the midday train. The trap was shattered and one of the horse's forelegs was so badly injured that the animal had to be put down. Luckily, Mr Hutchinson escaped with a fractured leg and a head wound. Down the years there have been a number of incidents involving collisions between vehicles and trains, almost all resulting from drivers breaking through the lights at the bridge crossing. On other occasions cars have been damaged as the result of parking too close to the line.

What *The Irish Times* described as a "Shocking Affair" occurred at Waterford on 25 January 1906. In the course of sinking the cylinders under air pressure for the Suir Bridge, an explosion occurred, killing two workmen, MacDonald (29) and Ryan (36), who were working 80ft below low-water mark. It was reported that one of the submerged cylinder rings, measuring 10ft in diameter and 5ft in height, exploded "with the noise of a bursting shell, precipitating the air locks and the rest of the superstructure into the water, which immediately inundated the exterior of the cylinder, drowning the wretched men below." Two other workmen, Kelly and Healy, who were about to go down to relieve their colleagues, escaped without injury. The foreman of works, Edward Tibbett, and

Ganger Patrick Kennedy were injured by flying debris and were removed to the City Infirmary for treatment. An inquest was held two days later by Dr Walsh, Coroner for South Kilkenny. John Edward Everett, the Resident Engineer on the bridge works, explained in technical terms the manner in which the cylinder was being worked. He stated that the air pressure at the time of the explosion was well within normal limits. Having considered all the evidence, the jury returned a verdict of accidental drowning.

The F&RR&H board minutes also refer to a number of accidents occurring in the early days. A Mr J Llewellyn who was employed on the works at Fishguard Harbour lost an eye as the result of a stone flying up and hitting him in July 1899. It was reported that he was awarded a sum of £150 in compensation, a generous sum when considered with other payments made. Two fatal accidents, in July and October 1902, saw payments of £167 and £100 paid out, while in November 1903 the Company agreed to pay £40 to the father of John Owen who had suffered fatal injuries at Fishguard in the previous June.

It was reported that the fireman of the 17.30 Rosslare–Waterford train was injured on 7 November 1906 in the course of exchanging the tablet at Bridgetown, his right thumb coming into contact with the delivery arm. At the time the train was estimated to have been running at about 30–35mph. Subsequent to the incident the GS&WR fitted rubber bulbs on the tablet delivery arms. However, the BoT Inspector did not consider that this would entirely prevent a repeat of the incident and recommended that speed should in future be limited to 10mph when exchanging tablets. The Company's response was that it was the only such accident of its kind to occur in the course of more than 10,000 tablet exchanges.

A little over two years later, on the morning of 13 February 1909, Fireman John Sullivan injured his right hand on the 05.10 Rosslare–Cork train in the course of taking the tablet loop from Signalman James Grehan at Duncormick. On the morning in question there was a strong wind blowing accompanied by heavy rain and it was difficult to see the loop. The speed of the train was variously estimated as being between 20 and 35mph. A later BoT note states that between 1906 and 1913 a total of five such incidents occurred throughout the GS&WR system.

A potentially serious incident occurred on an unrecorded date in 1913 involving the tablet instrument in Campile signal cabin. The Signalman had just taken a tablet for the Abbey Junction to Campile section from the crew of a through train. When he went to the instrument to give "line clear" to Abbey Junction, and, while still holding the tablet in his hand, he pressed against the bottom slide which to his surprise went home. He then gave a "line clear" and requested a tablet which was released as normal, so that he had two tablets for the same section. The Company's view was that the last tablet restored to the instrument had some grease on it which caused it to stick on the tilter, thus keeping the back lock disengaged from the slide and leaving the bottom slide free to go in. The GS&WR pointed out to Messrs Tyer, manufacturers of the instrument in question, the serious nature of the apparent design fault. However, in their defence, Messrs Tyer referred to a visit to Wexford in November 1909 by one of their Engineers when reference had been made to the dirty state of both the tablets and the instruments; at that time it was pointed out that instruments should be regularly cleaned and indeed some parts of them taken to pieces and properly cleaned. It was also the first such incident involving a Tyer instrument among some 5,000 sold to railways world-wide.

In July 1909 it was reported that Mr Inglis had sent two seriously injured workmen to Haverfordwest Infirmary, reported at the time to be the closest hospital to the works. The Infirmary submitted a claim for £44 2s 0d for medical attendance. It would appear that the Company may have had ideas of not paying this as the Solicitor advised the board that the Company was liable. However, the Infirmary authorities were persuaded to waive the claim, the Company agreeing to pay arrears of their subscription of £5 5s 0d, which had been allowed to lapse in 1905.

Subsequent to this event, some attempt at improving facilities for treating injuries was made. In July 1910 Inglis reported that it would be very desirable to make arrangements for more efficiently dealing with accident cases, having regard to the fact that the nearest hospital was at Haverfordwest. He reported that one of the Company's properties, Beach House, was dilapidated and in need of extensive repairs; Inglis suggested that a portion of the premises be fitted up as an accident ward at an additional cost of £30, this being approved. In February 1912 the Secretary reported receipt of an application from the Pembrokeshire & Haverfordwest Infirmary for a continuation of the Company's yearly donation of £5 5s 0d to the funds of the Institution. They were, however, informed that as the Company had recently expended "a considerable sum" in fitting out Beach House as an accident ward for the purpose of treating serious cases on the spot, that the Directors found themselves unable to continue the donation.

A serious accident occurred at Kilrane Station on the night of 18 September 1907 when the 21.00 up passenger train from Kilrane to Wexford was run into by a light engine proceeding from Wexford to Ballygeary. The crews of both locomotives suffered injuries, a locomotive foreman travelling on the light engine subsequently succumbing to his injuries. The locomotives involved were both 0-4-4Ts of GS&WR design, Nos 75 and 84. From the evidence it is clear that both the passenger train, which ran empty from Ballygeary, and the light engine were offered to and accepted by the Kilrane Signalman within minutes of each other. There was nothing untoward in this as Kilrane was able to cross both movements. A fault was, however, discovered in that the interlocking was inadequate.

The Company's regulations stated that the 'line clear' signal should not be given at a crossing station unless the facing points were set for the line on which the approaching train was to run. The Signalman had clearly not carried this out as regards the points at the north end of the station. In his defence, he stated that if he had set these points for the goods loop he would have been unable to admit the passenger train to the station; this Colonel von Donop confirmed to be the case as the up signal could not be lowered unless the loop points at the north end were set for the passenger line. What the Signalman should have done was to have set the points at the north end for the loop before accepting the light engine, and then holding the passenger train outside the station until the former had come to a halt at the signals. Following the arrival of the passenger train at the platform, all the down signals were maintained at danger so as to bring the light engine to a stand before admitting it to the goods loop; the facing points at the north end were, however, still set for the passenger line.

The weather at the time was foggy although there was some difference of opinion as to how bad it was. The driver of the light engine said he had failed to see the Kilrane distant signal and in fact thought that it may not have been lighted at the time; this was later disproved. He was only about 15 yards from the home signal when he spotted it at danger, but seems to have thought it might have been the distant signal, only realising his mistake when he reached the points. He estimated his speed approaching the station rather accurately at 23mph, immediately applied his brakes when he realised where he was but collided with the passenger train without having seen it and still travelling at 18mph. The driver of the passenger train also failed to see the approaching light engine. Although the Guard of the passenger train reported the fog to be dense he was still able to see the up starter about 60 yards away from where he was standing on the platform, while the Signalman claimed he could see the back light of his down home signal 172 yards away and the Station Master was able to see the same signal over 200 yards from his vantage point.

Colonel von Donop came to the conclusion that they were dealing with a 'rolling fog' and considered that the Station Master should have called out flagmen; evidence showed that neither flagmen nor fog signals were ever used at Kilrane Station. It was clear that the driver of the light engine was travelling too fast in the prevailing weather conditions, but he was not the only one to come in for criticism. Another contributing factor was the fact that there was no lamp in the disc signal allowing access to the goods loop; indeed this signal was seldom used, trains being called in by means of a hand signal from the cabin. The Signalman said he never used the signal as it was out of order, although he admitted that he had never reported the fact. This was, however, disproved by the Signal Inspector, who found it was satisfactory. The Signalman also asserted that there was no lamp

in the signal as there was a shortage of lamps at the station, a fact confirmed by the Station Master. All in all, Colonel von Donop was singularly unimpressed with the working arrangements at Kilrane. As we shall shortly see this was not peculiar to Kilrane.

Another accident occurred in South Wexford on the night of Wednesday 19 January 1910 with the derailment of the 20.05 goods from Wexford at Felthouse Junction. Regrettably Fireman Thomas Power of Clonmel was killed in the accident, while Driver John Doyle was seriously injured. The train consisted of No 278, an ex WL&WR 0-4-2 tender locomotive running tender first, 13 wagons, two 30ft six-wheeled carriages and a bogie brake van. The driver had just exchanged tablets at Felthouse Junction signal cabin and was approaching the points where the double line converged into single when the tender appeared to mount the rail, causing both it and the locomotive to fall on their side across the line, also derailing six wagons. Fireman Power was killed due to the tender frame falling on top of him while Driver Doyle was off work for some considerable time. The cause of the accident appeared to be a tight coupling between locomotive and tender on the sharp curve. Wexford Quays were the scene of a non-fatal accident when on 28 December 1946 a 7½ year old boy attempted to take a ride on a train going down the Quays, fell off and had a leg severed above the knee. A claim was lodged against CIÉ resulting in an ex gratia payment of £1,250 being made.

A collision occurred at about 19.10 on 13 December 1907 when the 19.00 passenger train from Waterford South to Mallow came into collision between Waterford and Kilmeaden, at a point about 2½ miles from the former, with two wagons which were standing on the line. The passenger train, consisting of '101' class 0-6-0 No 115, two thirds, a composite, a van and five wagons, was at the time travelling at between 40 and 50mph. The driver sighted the obstacle only a short distance away and had only just applied the brake when the collision occurred. One of the wagons was completely destroyed. Of the 17 passengers on the train only one complained of minor injuries.

The accident was investigated on behalf of the BoT by Colonel von Donop. It transpired that the two wagons had become separated from a goods train running from Waterford South to Waterford North. It was normal practice at the time to run a shipping train from the South station across the river where they were marshalled with another train running to Rosslare. It was quite usual for the wagons to be propelled from Waterford South to Grace Dieu Junction, where the locomotive then ran round its train and hauled the wagons across to the North station, a procedure at variance with Company regulations; Rule 179 which stated that engines were never to push trains upon running lines except under certain conditions, none of which applied on the occasion in question. The locomotive in question was a 4-4-0, which had no vacuum pipe at the front end, so, although the wagons were all fitted, they were not braked from the locomotive, nor was there a brake van, another practice at variance with Company Rules. Furthermore, red lamps were attached at both ends of the train. The driver brought his train to a stand just beyond the points leading to the Suir Viaduct at Grace Dieu Junction. At this point it would appear that the outer two wagons had not been coupled to the remainder of the wagons and, as the train was now standing on a falling gradient, they ran off down the line towards Kilmeaden. The final litany of mistakes occurred when the Signalman at Grace Dieu failed to notice that there was now no tail lamp on the train, nor did he notice how many vehicles were on the train as it came past him. Colonel von Donop considered that the shunter who marshalled the train and the Grace Dieu Signalman were primarily to blame. Had they been more vigilant the accident could have been prevented, despite other irregularities in working.

What potentially could have been a serious accident occurred on the night of Tuesday 24 July 1945 involving the afternoon train from Cork to Waterford. The train had left Mallow at about 16.05 and when approaching Waterford about four hours later the locomotive derailed just before reaching the Suir Bridge. The locomotive, '101' class No 188, climbed to the top of the bridge's sloping girder, where it remained pointing towards the sky. The tender jack-knifed and the driver, James Cleary, aged 60, was buried in coal up to his chest, where he remained for

In early 1945 as 0-6-0 No 188 was approaching the Suir Bridge from the west she became derailed. The driver had to be cut out of the wreckage, the fireman escaping by squeezing through the spectacle plate. *(J O'Neill)*

almost three hours. It was found necessary to cut away part of the cab roof to release him. Fireman Henry Flynn was also trapped but managed to crawl through the square spectacle plate in the front of the cab. The Guard and 32 passengers escaped unhurt.

An unusual collision occurred near Fishguard and Goodwick Station on the evening of 11 July 1951, luckily without injuries to any of the passengers, although both engine crews were badly shaken. The up passenger train from Fishguard Harbour Station to Clarbeston Road, operated by an auto-train consisting of one coach hauled by an 0-6-0T, had just left Fishguard & Goodwick Station when it came into collision with a down freight train. The force of the collision pushed the passenger train back for 110 yards. The accident was in due course investigated by Brigadier CA Langley on behalf of the BoT.

To set the scene, the single line section from Manorowen to Fishguard & Goodwick Station was on a falling gradient of 1 in 50 for about 1½ miles, being curved for most of its length, and was at the time subject to a speed restriction of 40mph. Shortly before the point of collision the line was in a deep cutting on a 38 chain left-hand curve, followed by a short straight section, and then a 35 chain right-hand curve, at the south end of which the collision occurred, some 260 yards from the entrance to the brickworks siding. The section from Manorowen was worked by ETS, the staff instruments not being interlocked with either of the starting signals.

The freight train, consisting of 4-6-0 No 6823 *Oakley Grange*, 6 empty vacuum-fitted vans next the locomotive, 15 loose coupled wagons and a brake van, was running some 40 minutes late. The Signalman at Fishguard & Goodwick accepted the train when offered by Manorowen as he was confident that he would have it clear of the single line section prior to the departure time of the passenger train. The latter arrived at the up platform at Fishguard & Goodwick Station a few minutes late, to find a large crowd gathered to see off a wedding couple on their honeymoon. The train stood at the platform for about five or six minutes and then departed to the accompaniment of a number of detonators and frequent engine whistles. It transpired that this was a local custom to see off newly married couples. When the Signalman realised that the passenger train had left without the staff he endeavoured, without success, to capture the driver's attention. The Guard of the auto train admitted that he did not see the aspect of the staring signal and rang the bell, as was normal on auto trains, when he was ready. The driver confirmed that he started as soon as he got the bell signal from the Guard, claiming not to have been distracted by the wedding party. It was lucky that the driver realised his mistake before the collision occurred as he had time to bring the train to a halt.

The driver of the freight train confirmed that all his signals were off at Manorowen and estimated his speed as he entered the left-hand curve at about 25 to 30mph with the train well under control. Just as they were leaving the cutting the fireman shouted that there was a train on the line ahead, the driver applying the brakes, but the distance was too short to avoid a collision which occurred at about 15mph.

Primary responsibility for the collision rested with the driver of the auto train, who left Fishguard & Goodwick Station without the train staff and against the starting signal, although it was in full view some 150 yards ahead of him. It was not the Guard's responsibility to check the position of the signal before ringing the bell, which only indicated to the driver that the station work had been completed. If he had checked the signal as the train departed, the outcome might have been different. Neither the crew of the freight train nor the Signalman were to blame for the collision. Brigadier Langley recommended the provision of trap points or a sand drag, which would have prevented the accident. He also commented on the practice of blowing whistles and exploding detonators at a wedding party send-off. Whilst accepting that it was a long standing custom, and not wanting to be a killjoy, he commented that detonators were supposed to be used to stop or warn trains in emergency and not to speed them on their way. He confirmed that instructions had been issued by the GWR "to prohibit the light-hearted abuse of these valuable safeguards."

We now move back to Co Wexford and the station at Rosslare Strand for our next accident. Reference has already been made to certain track alterations made there in March and May 1973, which were to have a bearing on a collision which occurred there on the evening of 13 August 1974. A brief recap will be made here to better explain the circumstances of the accident. Prior to May 1973 the connection between the Dublin and Waterford lines was a double junction and allowed Waterford line trains to use both platforms. When the crossing required renewal it was decided, on grounds of cost, not to replace the double turnout. Following the alteration, the facility for bringing Waterford line trains into the Wexford (down) platform was, therefore, no longer available.

On the evening in question the boat from Fishguard arrived late at Rosslare, as a result of which the departure of the 18.30 up train from Rosslare to Limerick was delayed by 70 minutes. The 16.00 down Limerick to Waterford was also running about

Aftermath of the collision at Rosslare Strand on the evening of 13 August 1974. Locomotive B192 on the left was on the 18:30 Rosslare Harbour to Limerick while B176 on the right was working the 16:00 from Limerick. Neither driver was injured although a Snatcherman on the down train was. *(Irish Rail)*

10 minutes late. Normally the two trains would have crossed at Wellington Bridge but it was decided on this occasion to cross them at Rosslare Strand. The 16.00 down arrived at the Waterford platform at Rosslare Strand at 19.44. As he handed up the staff for the section, the driver was informed by the Signalman that the two trains would be crossed in the Strand. It was anticipated that the down train would be reversed back onto the Wexford line, while the up train would be brought into the down platform, and then reversed back and brought in to the Waterford platform. As, however, the rear of the down train was fouling the turnout at the Dublin end of the station, it would be necessary for him to pull forward to clear the points and to then reverse. After a short interval the down starting signal on the Waterford platform (No 19 on drawing) was lowered; although the driver did not have the staff for the next section he took the lowering of the signal as authority to pull forward sufficiently to clear the points in rear of his train, which he proceeded to do without his Guard's signal. After sitting there for one or two minutes the driver observed the 18.30 up train approaching and realising that the latter had overrun the home signal he put on his brakes and jumped off the locomotive.

The 18.30 eventually left Ballygeary at 19.41, the driver being informed that he would be going in on the wrong road (Wexford platform) at the Strand. For some unexplained reason the driver of this train ran past the up home signal at danger and collided at about 15mph with the down train, the relevant points at the Rosslare end of the station also having been left facing the up (Waterford) line platform. Thirteen passengers and two employees were injured in the collision, three passengers requiring removal by ambulance to Wexford General Hospital. The locomotives and rolling stock of both trains sustained damage consistent with the type of stock in use at the time.

Mr JV Feehan, the Railways Inspecting Officer, established that neither driver had crossed another passenger train at Rosslare Strand since the track layout had been altered, nor indeed had the driver of the up train been instructed as to how trains should be crossed there. Worse still, it transpired that the relief Signalman, who normally worked as a porter, had not crossed trains since the station layout had been altered, nor had he received instructions and he only discovered some ten minutes before the arrival of the down train that a crossing was in fact to be made there.

Mr Feehan established that the immediate causes of the accident were the failure of the Signalman to set the points correctly when accepting the 18.30 and the failure of the driver of that train to observe in timely manner the position of the up home signal. He also criticised the lowering of the down home signal to allow a shunting movement (a practice quite common at Rosslare Strand) and indeed the passing of that signal by the driver of the down train. Some criticism was also made of the practice of withdrawing staffs well in advance of the arrival of trains at the station. This was explained by the fact that the Signalman, as the only employee on duty, was also expected to perform station duties, including the sale of tickets, booking luggage and attending to passengers.

Over the years there have been at least three incidents involving ships and the Barrow Bridge. The first of these occurred less than a year after the bridge was opened for rail traffic, on 24 July 1907 when the Norwegian barque *Venus* of Helsingborg, in tow of the tug *Heron* with a cargo of deals, collided with the bridge. The bridge received no damage although the barque lost her foremast. On the morning of 16 January 1975 the 1,350 GRT MV *Pool Fisher* inbound in ballast to New Ross struck the opening span of the Barrow Bridge, causing slight damage to the bridge. Considerable damage was caused to the vessel, the captain and first mate sustaining injuries. The operation of the bridge was conducted under bye-laws made subject to the approval of the New Ross Harbour Commissioners (NRHC).[1] The original bye-laws were promulgated in August 1906 with subsequent amendments in 1960 and 1965; these alterations resulted from pressure from the NRHC arising from delays to vessels using the port and provided for extended opening hours due to increases in shipping movements to and from the port. Prior to 1960 the bridge was only opened in daylight hours, the 1965 bye-laws allowing for 24-hour opening; as a result Barrow Bridge signal cabin is manned 24 hours a day all year round. This change necessitated the provision of flood lighting on the bridge and subsequently the installation of VHF radio equipment. In daylight a circular round ball

The Barrow Bridge was struck on the evening of 7 April 1986 by the 6,000 ton MV Balsa24 as she came through the opening span, causing severe damage necessitating a six months closure of the bridge. This view, as the repair work approaches completion, is looking through the bridge towards the Wexford shore. The total cost of repairs exceeded £½million. (*E Greene, Irish Rail*)

was raised over the opening span to indicate that it was open and secured, a green light being exhibited at night. The actual operation of the bridge is covered by an instruction in the Appendix to the Working Timetable.

At the time of the collision, the cabin was in charge of a relief Signalman from Campile Station. The Signalman confirmed that he was in communication with the New Ross pilot on board the *Pool Fisher* at 16.15 on the day of the accident, informing him that the bridge would be opened following the passing of the 16.25 Waterford–Rosslare Harbour passenger train, passenger trains having precedence over river traffic. The key for opening the bridge was released by Campile and Abbey Junction at 16.41, following

---

1 Section 17 of the F&RR&H Act of 1898 made provision for such bye-laws.

which the Signalman commenced to open the bridge. For some reason, although the Signalman turned off power as normal, the electric motor continued to run and the opening span continued on past the open position, thus fouling the shipping lane by about 9ft according to the Signalman; however, the extent of the damage to the ship indicated that the span had travelled somewhat further. Evidence also indicated that since the collision occurred at 16.48 the *Pool Fisher* must have commenced its approach to the bridge before the latter was opened and secured as required by the bye-laws.[2] The Signalman immediately radioed the pilot but by then the vessel was unable to reduce speed or alter its course.

The inquiry found that the bye-laws had been allowed to fall into partial disuse. In particular, it was clear that the black ball had not been used for some considerable time. It was also found that pilots were in the habit of beginning their approach even before the swing span had begun to open, a fact never brought to the attention of the NRHC. The inquiry found that the captain of the ship was primarily at fault in having allowed his ship to approach the bridge before he had received confirmation that the bridge was fully open; he was also at fault in beginning his approach from too close a point to allow him to take avoiding action in the event of the opening span failing to operate properly, as for example in the case of a power failure or incapacitation of the Signalman. However, it was also clear that the opening mechanism had malfunctioned due to a missing bolt, and that parts of the operating instructions had been allowed to fall into disuse.

Another collision occurred on the evening of 7 April 1986 when the 6,000 ton MV *Balsa24*, again proceeding up-river collided with the central dolphin, and with one of the supports of the opening span and that adjacent to it. On this occasion severe damage was caused to the bridge, it not being possible to close the opening span. It was to be 14 July before the bridge was re-opened to rail traffic; in the interim it was decided to drive tubular piles around the cylinders down to rock level and transfer the bridge load onto the piles. This work, initially estimated to cost £½million eventually worked out at £560,000, and was carried out by Irishenco Limited.

---

2 The ship must have been at the most 3 minutes away from the bridge when the opening span commenced to move.

CHAPTER TWENTY TWO

Steamers & Liners at Fishguard

Following the passing of the F&RR&H Act of 1895, the Company decided to charter a vessel to provide a service between Rosslare Harbour and the ports of Liverpool and Bristol. The iron-hulled steamer, SS *Voltaic*, had been built in 1867 by Messrs MacNab & Company of Greenock in Scotland for the Belfast Steamship Company, Yard No 17; she was launched on 9 October 1867. As built she had a two-cylinder simple engine, but was re-engined in Belfast in 1882 with a compound engine. She was sold in July 1896 to Messrs David & Charles MacIver of Liverpool[1], who intended to use her on a service between Liverpool and Dublin. She was, however, initially chartered to the F&RR&H, later purchased, and opened a new service on 26 August 1896 from Rosslare to Bristol. The *Voltaic* had a gross registered tonnage (GRT) of 612 tons, was 209ft long and had accommodation for 30 saloon passengers and an unspecified number of steerage passengers, livestock and goods.

Initially she was scheduled to leave Rosslare at 19.00 for Bristol on Tuesdays and at the same time on Saturdays for Liverpool. An advertisement in the local press announced that a special livestock train would leave North Wexford (the DW&WR station) for Rosslare at 13.00 on sailing days. On these schedules the *Voltaic* was operating in competition with the 697 ton SS *Menapia* running between Wexford and Bristol and the SS *Edenvale* between Wexford and Liverpool.

A later advertisement from November 1898 provides a few additional details. The *Voltaic* was now scheduled to depart on Saturday evenings for Liverpool, returning from the Clarence Dock (south–west side) on Mondays, while she was to leave Rosslare for Bristol on Tuesdays, returning on Thursdays. Departure times varied during the month to take account of tides at the English ports[2]. Average passage time on both routes was shown as 13 hours. Cabin fares on both routes were 10s single and 17s 6d return, while steerage passengers paid 5s and 7s 6d respectively; return tickets were valid for two months, but could be extended on payment of the difference between the return fare and the sum of two single fares. Servants in the cabin paid full fare, children between the ages of 3 and 12 being charged half fare. Apart from the advertisement being headed F&RR&H, it also included the name of Messrs C MacIver & Company as agents in Liverpool.

The *Voltaic* appears to have had a chequered career on the new route. The first mention of her was in October 1896. On the evening of Thursday 1 October, three pilots set out in their boat from the Fort for the purpose of piloting the *Voltaic* out of Rosslare Harbour at the start of her voyage to Liverpool. On their return the strong northerly gale which prevailed made it impossible to cross the Bar at Wexford and they spent Thursday night and Friday morning being tossed about in rough seas. At about 11.30 the pilot boat ran aground about 100 yards from the beach. They were eventually rescued by a member of Rosslare Coastguards who volunteered to swim out to the men to bring out a line so that the rocket apparatus could be used to save them.

With the opening of Rosslare Harbour, the pilots at Wexford saw the prospect of their livelihood disappearing or at least being diminished, so it was agreed that a pilot service would be provided for vessels using the new harbour, with pilot dues being collected. Captain Robert Keown, the Master of the *Voltaic*, refused to pay these dues, no doubt encouraged by his employers. Relations between the railway company and the Wexford Harbour Commissioners (WHC) had not been good for some years. By November 1896

---

1 David MacIver was a director of the 'new' F&RR&H from its incorporation until his death on 1 September 1907.

2 Tidal variation at Rosslare Harbour is only 6 feet.

there was reported to be an amount of £37 due and, as the Company refused to pay this sum, the Harbour Commissioners sent some men to Rosslare to seize the *Voltaic*. The arrears were then paid, under protest. However, Captain Keown persisted in his refusal to pay further dues, leading to two summonses against him being heard at Wexford Petty Sessions in January 1897 for recovery of an amount of £8. Keown's solicitor unsuccessfully argued that the whole situation was farcical, despite which a decree was handed down. Captain Keown resigned in November 1898. At a board meeting on 13 December, a memorial was read from residents and traders in Wexford recommending the appointment of Mr Codd, "the late Chief Officer of the *Voltaic*" as successor to Keown. However, as Codd had been dismissed on 21 October for being intoxicated on duty, the Company declined to consider the recommendation.

Obviously incensed by the WHC getting the better of him, it is perhaps not entirely surprising to discover that Joseph Rowlands gave notice of intention to apply for an Order to prevent the WHC from collecting port dues at Rosslare Harbour. Needless to say there was strong opposition from the Harbour Commissioners and the pilots themselves. Despite the opposition, the Pilotage Order Confirmation Act, 1897 Rosslare Pilotage, passed into law on 6 August 1897. This amended the Wexford Harbour Commissioners Act of 1874, and exempted masters of vessels using Rosslare from any obligation to pay pilotage rates imposed by that Act. In return, the F&RR&H were obliged to pay a sum of £1,000 to the WHC, to be divided between the pilots of Wexford and the Harbour Commissioners. A further sum of £1,000 was to be paid over to the WHC within a month of the passing of the Order, by which the F&RR&H "may obtain the right to make or acquire or partly to acquire a through railway route from Rosslare or Wexford to or near the city of Cork."

The *Voltaic* was included in the Schedule attached to the Memorandum of Agreement dated 15 February 1898 amongst the assets of the F&RR&H Syndicate being handed over to Alexander Henderson, on behalf of the GWR. In this context, a board minute dated 26 October 1898 reported that the GWR were liable as from 12 February of that year for the working of the

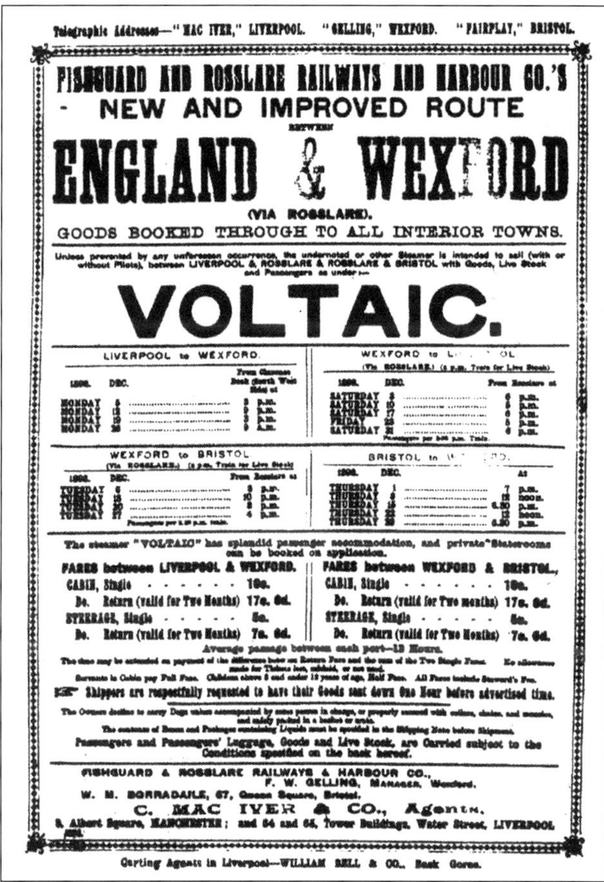

Poster advertising the short-lived cross-channel service operated by the F&RR&H with the steamer *Voltaic*. *(Author's Collection)*

Voltaic, but that the wages and repairs were payable by and receipts payable to the F&RR&H. At the same board meeting reference was made to a collision which had occurred on 15 April between the *Voltaic* and the SS *Devonia*. The owners of the 2,271 ton *Devonia*, the Anchor Line, had declined to pay the costs incurred in repairs to the *Voltaic* and the hire of another vessel during the time she was laid up. Mr Nelson, the Company's Solicitor, was instructed to take whatever steps were necessary for enforcement of the claim. Eventually, after the case had been submitted to arbitration, the Company's claim against the *Devonia* was settled for £109 1s 8d with £37 7s 0d costs.

Following her return to service, the *Voltaic* was reported to have run aground at Avonmouth on 9 September on her way from Bristol to Rosslare. She managed to get off the sandbank under her own power but she had to go for an inspection. Hardly back again in service, a second collision occurred on the night of 11 November 1898 when, outbound from Liverpool, she struck the SS *Cognac* near Holyhead, the latter vessel sinking. Owned by the Charente Steamship Company, the 503 ton *Cognac* was carrying a cargo of cognac and other cargo from France to Liverpool. The collision resulted in a very large claim being made against the F&RR&H, the cargo alone being estimated at £16,000. However, it was reported that the Company's liability under the Merchant Shipping Act of 1894 was limited to about £4,500, of which their underwriters would pay two-thirds. The case eventually went to the High Court where the F&RR&H sought to limit their liability. The outcome was that the claim was in due course assessed at a figure of £4,534 0s 0d; this figure was based on a rate of £8 per ton for each ton of the registered tonnage of the *Voltaic*. While the ship was undergoing repairs, she was replaced by the GWR steamer *Pembroke*.

The *Voltaic* was involved in one further collision; on the night of 1 December 1900 she collided with the SS *St Olaf* off the Skerries. The *St Olaf*, of 568 GRT and owned by Thomas Heiton & Co coal merchants of Dublin, sank with the loss of two crew members, while the badly damaged *Voltaic* limped back to Liverpool. It was lucky that the City of Dublin Steampacket Company's SS *Kerry* was nearby at the time, a boat was lowered and the *St Olaf*'s engineer was rescued. The remainder of her crew, with the exception of the two who were drowned, managed to scramble on board the *Voltaic*. The *Kerry* took all the survivors on board and brought them to Liverpool. Finally in April 1900 the *Voltaic* was sold to FH Powell & Co of Liverpool and the steamer service from Rosslare was suspended, not to resume for more than six years. In 1901 she was sold to V Tolstopjat of Kerch[3] in Russia, who renamed her the *Prince Oldenboursky*. The end came for the vessel when she was wrecked in the Black Sea in October 1903.

With work progressing well on all fronts, the Board at their meeting on 5 November 1903 discussed the question of the steamers that would be required when the new route was ready for traffic. Mr Inglis, the GWR Engineer, said that he hoped shortly to be in a position to report in some detail on the subject; it was agreed that the steamers should compare favourably with any of the existing cross-channel boats. It was not until 7 June 1904 that Inglis reported back to the Board, when he recommended that three vessels be provided for working a day and night service. He pointed out that they should be capable of steaming at 22 knots and make the passage between Fishguard and Rosslare in three hours under adverse conditions. The details of the design had not been fully determined, but it was proposed that they be about 350ft long with 40ft beam and a draft of 14ft; they should have engines upon the Parsons turbine principle and provide sleeping accommodation for about 220 first and 100 second class passengers. It was hoped to obtain a passenger certificate for the conveyance of about 1,000 passengers. There would be limited cargo space. Inglis estimated the cost at £100,000 per vessel.

Mr Inglis confirmed in November 1904 that with the assistance of Charles T Ramsay, a naval architect, plans had been prepared for the new steamers and, the plans having been generally approved of and subject to the approval of the GS&WR, it was suggested that a number of shipbuilding firms in Britain should be requested to submit tenders. Eleven firms tendered in January 1905 as follows:

Company	Location	1 Steamer	2 Steamers	3 Steamers
Denny Bros	Dumbarton	£120,500	£240,000	£358,500
Swan Hunter	Newcastle	£114,000	£226,000	-
Harland & Wolff	Belfast	£114,000	£226,000	£336,000
Earle's Shipbuilding	Hull	£119,000	£237,700	£356,100
London & Glasgow	Glasgow	£115,200	£229,800	£344,600
A & J Inglis	Glasgow	£128,000	-	-
John Brown & Co (1)	Clydebank	£ 99,000	£198,200	£297,300
John Brown & Co (2)	Clydebank	£111,126	£220,252	£327,378
John Brown & Co (3)	Clydebank	£109,126	£218,252	£327,378
Vickers Sons & Maxim	Barrow	£125,270	£249,340	£373,410
Fairfield Shipbuilding	Glasgow	£119,750	£238,000	£354,000
Sir WG Armstrong	Newcastle	£115,000	£228,000	£342,000
Cammell Laird	Birkenhead	£114,000	£226,000	£336,000

---

3 A city on the Kerch Peninsula in eastern Crimea, and now a part of the Ukraine.

(1) To guarantee 22 knots; (2) To guarantee 22½ knots; (3) To guarantee 23 knots.

First Class Dining Room on one of the 1906 Saints. Note the chains to anchor the chairs in position in rough weather. *(Great Western Trust)*

Before deciding the matter it was agreed that the tenders be referred to Mr Ramsay for his report. Finally, in May 1905 the tender of Messrs John Brown & Company was accepted for two steamers at £220,252 and Messrs Cammell Laird & Company for one steamer at a reduced figure of £111,000. A speed of 22½ knots was guaranteed in both cases, with penalties down to 22 knots. The Board approved of a recommendation from Mr Inglis that Mr Ramsay, who had in effect prepared the design for the new steamers and was to supervise their construction, should be paid on a commission basis at the rate of ¼% on the total cost of the three steamers with reasonable out-of-pocket expenses.

Some details from the Agreement dated 4 August 1905 between the F&RR&H and John Brown & Company are of some interest. As mentioned above, the speed of the new vessels was to be not less than 22½ knots, with penalties imposed for not meeting this figure. The penalty was to be £1,000 if only 22¼ knots could be achieved and £2,000 if only 22 knots. If less than the latter figure, the Company would not be bound to accept such vessel, the makers to refund any moneys paid or advanced with interest thereon at 5% per annum from date of payment. The vessels were to undergo sea trials to the satisfaction of the Company and to be delivered at Fishguard on or before 15 June 1906.

The specification attached to the Agreement gives us some further details of the vessels. They were to be constructed of Siemens Martin mild steel, to Class A1 Irish Channel service standard. They were to be of awning deck type, with lower, main and boat deck amidships with top gallant forecastle, and with straight stem from water line up and an elliptical stern. They were to have double bottoms in way of engine room so as to form a tank for carrying water ballast or fresh water for boilers. Draught with 215 tons on board, including bunker coal, all tanks full and 50 tons of cargo in the holds was to be 13ft 6in. It was stipulated that the rudder was to have an exceptionally large surface so as to convenience the quick handling of the vessel. They were to have nine watertight bulkheads and seven watertight doors; water tank was to carry a total of about 60 tons and coal bunkers 140 tons.

The dining saloon was to be on the main deck forward of the funnel, with a vestibule extending right across the vessel. Decoration was to be worked in India figured satin-wood panels with teak framing, and with two large mirrors over each sideboard at the forward end of the saloon. All furniture, including sofas, tables and revolving chairs (about 70 in number) were to be in American walnut.

The propelling machinery was to consist of three independent Parsons compound steam turbines and two condensers, the former designed with a working pressure of 185psi. The propellers were to be of manganese bronze about 7ft in diameter, all surfaces perfectly smooth and correctly balanced. Steam was to be provided by eight single-ended multi-tubular boilers, each with a grate area of 20sq ft and 2,300sq ft heating surface. Finally the funnel height was to be 50ft from the boat deck level, to have double funnels, oval in shape, the inner one 10ft by 6ft and the outer one 12ft by 8ft, both to be of ¼in plates near the bottom.

In August 1905 Mr Inglis recommended that the new steamers should be named *St George*, *St David* and *St Patrick*, this being approved both by the F&RR&H Board and that of the GS&WR. The *St George* was the first of the three to be launched, at Birkenhead on 13 January 1906, the ceremony being performed by David MacIver's wife. It was followed into the water by the *St David* twelve days later at Clydebank, with the *St Patrick* also being launched at Clydebank on 24 February. Mr Inglis reported that he had found it necessary to appoint three engineers to constantly supervise the vessels' construction. These men were being paid 70s per week plus 17s 6d per week for expenses, and it was suggested that they be appointed Chief Engineers of the three steamers when they commenced running on the service, this arrangement being approved. In order to carry out light and urgent repairs, there was a necessity for workshop accommodation to be provided at Fishguard at an estimated cost of £2,870 for the purpose, excluding machinery. The fitting out of the vessels included the provision of such items as cutlery, crockery and rugs, expenditure of about £1,600 being approved at the board meeting held on 1 November 1906. It is said that this expenditure, in particular the rugs, was first suggested by Mr Inglis following a rough crossing made by him and some of his colleagues shortly after the opening of the new route.

The *St George* encountered rough seas on a crossing from Fishguard on 20 February, resulting in her anchor being lost at sea; this was replaced by Cammell Laird at a cost of £231 5s 0d. At the same board meeting on 9 May 1907 at which the damage to the *St George* was reported, Mr Inglis pointed out the difficulties experienced in maintaining the day and night sailings with only three steamers available. There was insufficient time available for necessary repairs and overhauls, making it necessary on several occasions to substitute a reciprocating engined steamer with prejudicial results for timekeeping, and, ultimately, the reputation of the route. Apart from the shortage of steamers, the schedules demanded excessive hours being worked by the crews, in most cases 12 to 16 hours per day. Mr Inglis reported that he had instructed Mr Ramsay in conjunction with Mr Davidson, the GWR Steamboat Superintendent, and Mr Warden, a first class pilot in the port of Liverpool, to fully investigate and report. Their report was now to hand and it basically recommended the acquisition of a fourth turbine steamer. This would be similar to the existing steamers but with more space allocated for cargo. Messrs John Brown and Cammell Laird were requested to submit tenders for such a steamer.

It was in fact to Messrs John Brown that the contract was awarded at £111,000 and by the following October construction was reported to be well in hand. Following her successful sea trials the *St Andrew* was delivered at Fishguard on 1 May 1908. A board minute dated 3 July 1909 refers to damage to the extent of £2,000 sustained to the *St Andrew* "in July last", presumably 1908; it would appear that she struck submerged rocks to the north of the entrance to Rosslare Harbour, this resulting in a submarine survey of the harbour and its approaches being called for. Despite this damage, it was not, however, until October 1910 that Mr Gordon reported on the subject of dredging. It was hoped to

The *St Andrew* photographed during her speed trials is an impressive sight. *(Photographer unknown)*

Again, not of good quality, this view shows the *St Andrew* in use as a hospital ship during the First World War. *(Photographer unknown)*

dredge sufficient to obtain a minimum depth of 18ft at extreme low water over all the area within the harbour limits over which the GWR boats may manoeuvre; the material to be dealt with consisted of heavy boulders embedded in stiff clay. It would not be possible to safely carry out dredging during the winter months. Another complication was that the contractor employed had been unable to obtain a suitable dredger and it had been necessary to arrange to hire one from Wexford Harbour Commissioners at a cost of £120 per month.

A severe gale at Fishguard on 21 October 1912 caused the *St Patrick* to swing from her moorings on to the dredger *Porteur*, causing the latter to break adrift, finally striking and impaling herself on the rocks near Saddle Point. The dredger was eventually floated off and beached on Goodwick Sands, but repairs were estimated at £2,300; she was later sold for scrap to TW Ward of Sheffield, realising a sum of £450. The *St David* struck some hidden obstruction at Rosslare in October 1913, resulting in extensive damage to the keel plating on the starboard side for a distance of 30ft; this followed from further damage to the *St Andrew's* propellers and once again brought to the attention of the Board the necessity for a thorough survey of the area to ascertain definitely if an uncharted rock or other obstruction existed.

In the interim, and despite the apparent necessity for a fourth vessel only five years previously, the *St George* was sold to the Canadian Pacific Railway (CPR) in 1913 for the sum of £73,000; she made her last crossing from Fishguard on 1 March 1913. She was then handed over to her new owners on 3 June in the Mersey and was towed across the Atlantic as

her bunkers were unable to carry sufficient coal for the voyage. The vessel was used on the Bay of Fundy services, probably between Digby and St John, New Brunswick. Her stay in Canada was short as she was returned to Britain in 1915 and was pressed into service as a hospital ship. At the end of the war, the *St George* was sold to the Great Eastern Railway Company, operating the Harwich to Hook of Holland service; she was withdrawn in 1929 and broken up at Blyth in Northumberland.

Following the outbreak of World War I in August 1914, the three 'Saints' were commandeered to be used as hospital ships. For this role they were equipped with lifts and other items at the marine workshops at Fishguard to enable them to be used for loading and unloading casualties. They were replaced by the GWR vessels *Great Southern* or *Great Western* and the *Duke of Connacht*, the latter a London & North Western Railway steamer, and the former two from the GWR Fishguard-Waterford service; the *Great Southern* spent part of the war at Weymouth. In addition some vessels were chartered, including the Great Central Railway's *Dewsbury*, which prior to the war had been operating on the Grimsby to Hamburg service.

It was reported in October 1919 that the *St David* and the *St Patrick* had gone from Fishguard to Messrs John Brown's shipyard on the Clyde on 30 June and 16 July respectively for reconditioning prior to their return to service. The *St Andrew* was to follow as soon as accommodation at the shipyard came available. In conjunction with the reconditioning, the opportunity was taken to carry out some structural alterations and improve the hatchway facilities so as to increase cargo capacity by about 200 tons on each vessel. The estimated cost of the reconditioning and alterations was estimated at £48,000 per vessel. The Ministry of Shipping arranged for the work to be carried out under their supervision and to bear the cost of reconditioning but not the other alterations.

The Board were informed in December 1919 that the work on the *St David* had been completed and she had returned to her normal duties on 30 October. It was confirmed that the alterations which had been carried out were quite satisfactory and her cargo capacity had been increased to 430 tons as compared with her previous capacity of 150 tons; this had the effect of increasing her draught by 4½in, which had been approved by the BoT. The *St Patrick* returned to the route on 30 December, while the *St Andrew* was expected to be back in service by April 1920.

The *St David* was fitted with new geared turbines in late 1925, and as the results had proved satisfactory, it was proposed to deal with the *St Patrick* in a similar manner. It was hoped that this would obviate the necessity to withdraw the boats for boiler cleaning as it would then be possible to deal with two boilers at a time while running, and a stand-by vessel would not then be necessary. With a view to reducing overhead charges and maintenance costs in connection with the running of the service, the Board gave consideration in July 1928 to selling off the *St Andrew*, which was by then being maintained as a stand-by vessel and the SS *Reindeer*, which had been used in a similar capacity by the GWR on the Channel Islands service. The two vessels should then be replaced by one new ship similar in size to the GWR 1,885 ton SS *St Helier* built three years earlier, but suitable for running on either of the services as required. This proposal was approved and authority given for the sale of the *St Andrew* and its replacement by a new vessel as suggested.

Fate intervened, however, as the *St Patrick* was seriously damaged by fire shortly after arriving at Fishguard from Rosslare on the evening of 7 April 1929. Such was the ferocity of the blaze that it took the Fishguard fire brigade and crew members several hours to bring it under control. The fire was believed to have been electrical in origin. By that time an order had already been placed with Messrs Alexander Stephen & Sons Limited[4] of Linthouse, Glasgow for a new vessel. In the light of the damage to the *St Patrick*, it was decided to retain the *St Andrew*, transferring the *St Patrick's* comparatively new turbines to her. The *St Patrick* was sold for £8,160 to Thomas Ward Limited of Sheffield, and the amount paid to the GWR. It was decided to name the new vessel *St Patrick*. A credit note for £112,665 10s 5d was duly received from the GWR, being the amount shown in the Fishguard Company's Capital Account in respect of the vessel disposed of.

The second *St Patrick*, generally referred to as *St Patrick II*, was launched on 15 January 1930 by Mrs J Milne, wife of the GWR Chairman. This ship was smaller and slower than her predecessor, with a gross tonnage of 1,922 and a speed of 18 knots. She was intended for service on both the Fishguard–Rosslare route and the GWR Weymouth–Channel Islands service. While operating on the latter service, she struck rocks off the Corbiere lighthouse during a fog, but luckily was floated off with only minor damage. The Board heard in July 1930 that plans and specifications were being prepared as a preliminary to seeking tenders for the construction of two new oil-burning vessels to replace the aging *St Andrew* and *St David* by the time they were due for load-line survey in the spring of 1932. Resulting from this an order was placed with Messrs Cammell Laird & Company Limited in January 1931 for two new twin screw cross-channel passenger steamers at a cost of £342,000. It was agreed that the new vessels should carry the names of their predecessors, to give effect to which the older vessels were to be renamed *Fishguard* and *Rosslare* respectively; this was done in October 1931. John Maddock relates that when they came to be named, the actual letters of the names on the original ships were removed and put on the new ones. The new vessels were launched in January 1932 and were expected to undergo sea trials in February and March.

We have a few details of the new ships. Yard Nos were 981 and 982. Length overall was to be 335ft, this being altered in pencil on the specification to 327ft

---

4 The business had been started in 1750 by Alexander Stephen. It was at the Stephen shipyard that the comedian, Billy Connolly, served his apprenticeship as a welder.

9in, breadth 46ft 6in, depth moulded to main deck 18ft 9in. The vessels were to have straight stem and cruiser stern.[5] Fuel tanks, including settling tanks, were to have a total capacity of 180 tons. The trial trip, run at the builder's expense, was to consist of six runs on a certified measured mile, when the vessel was to average a speed of 21 knots. Fuel on the trial trips was to be Anglo-Persian oil fuel, and the fuel, fresh water and ballast tanks were all to be full. The ships were to have two steel pole masts, with a crow's nest fitted on the foremast. There were to be three lifeboats each side, situated amidships, to hold 50 persons each and an additional boat on each side of the afterdeck to hold 25 passengers. Cargo space was to be sufficient to allow about 450 tons of cargo to be carried so that the vessel when loaded should have a mean draft not exceeding 14ft 6in.

The machinery was to consist of two sets of Parsons steam turbines, each comprising a high pressure and a low pressure turbine, driving the propeller shafts through separate pinions and single-reduction mechanical gearing. Steam was to be supplied by four water-tube Babcock & Wilcox boilers with a total tube heating surface of 18,120sq ft, arranged to burn fuel oil on the closed stokehold system of forced draught. Propellers were to be three-bladed and of solid bronze. There were to be three electric generators and the vessels were to be equipped with the latest Marconi Siemens, or other approved, wireless telegraph system. The whistle was to be secured to the forward funnel and to be of a deep organ tone with two notes. The *Irish Times* reported that the new trend was for two-berth cabins and they understood the new ships would have a number of these available; the old vessels had only four-berth cabins.

The *St Andrew II* entered service on the Fishguard route on 27 February 1932, the *St David II* on 22 March. The final cost of the two vessels, less the value of spare parts taken into stock, was £339,478; as the estimated replacement cost of the two former vessels was £300,000, the Company ended up with a betterment value of £39,478, a debit note for this

This view of the *St David* tied up at Fishguard Harbour shows to good effect the beautiful lines of these vessels. (*Great Western Trust*)

amount being received from the GWR. The *Fishguard* and the *Rosslare* were sold in November 1933 to Mr John Cashmore of Newport for £4,425 each.

Following the outbreak of World War II the three vessels were requisitioned, the *St Andrew* on 11 September 1939 as a Hospital Ship, the *St David* on 23 September for similar purposes and the *St Patrick* on 20 September as a Military Transport. This latter only lasted until 11 October. As a result of these requisitions it became impossible to operate more than a tri-weekly service, this being introduced as from 16 November. As recorded elsewhere an Order was in due course issued relaxing the Company's obligations for the duration of the war. In addition, a licence was issued in respect of the *St Patrick* under the Control of Trade by Sea (No 2) Order of 1939. While the *St Patrick* was undergoing repairs at Fishguard between 15 January and 16 February 1940, the service was operated by the SS *Porthrepta*, chartered from Care Lines Limited of

---

5 A cruiser stern ran in a curve upwards from a ship's after waterline; one advantage over the previous arrangement was that at normal loads the vessel's rudder was completely submerged.

Cardiff, passengers being diverted to the Waterford route. She may also have operated for a short time following the *St Patrick's* sinking.

To offset the danger from magnetic mines, the three 'Saints' were equipped in July 1940 with demagnetising apparatus; most of the cost was paid by the Government, the Company having to contribute £100 per vessel. In addition, echo-sounding machines were purchased from the Marconi Sounding Device Company for the *St Andrew* and the *St David* at a cost of £225 each.

The *St Patrick* suffered two enemy attacks in August 1940; on the seventeenth of the month while on a westbound voyage, she was machine-gunned about 20 miles from the Irish coast. Two people on board were injured and it is to be regretted that Moses Brennan, a crewman from Wexford, died of his injuries in Wexford County Hospital. Only three days later she was bombed by three German bombers; by that time the vessel had been equipped with machine guns for self protection, and these were immediately used. None of the bombs actually hit the *St Patrick* although she was shaken by the attacks. After zig-zagging at full speed, the ship managed to escape and arrived safely in Rosslare. She again was in difficulties in November 1940 when a mine exploded about 70 yards away. The 92 passengers and 45 crew arrived unhurt but shaken at Rosslare.

Worse was to come as she was dive-bombed about 12 miles off Strumble Head[6] as she neared the port of Fishguard on the morning of Friday 13 June 1941. The first bomb struck the ship between the bridge and the funnel, penetrating the fuel tanks and setting them on fire. The vessel was broken in two by the explosion and sunk within five minutes of the attack commencing and, sadly on this occasion of the 45 crew and 44 passengers on board, 17 of her crew, a gunner and 12 passengers were lost. Included among these were Captain James Faraday[7] and his son Jack, a 20 year old Merchant Navy officer cadet who had decided to travel with his father for experience; Captain Faraday's nephew, Joe Wallace of Duncannon,

was one of the lucky survivors. Included among those missing crew members was John Brennan, whose father Moses had been killed in the earlier attack on the ship on 17 August 1940. The survivors were picked up by a warship and a merchant ship and brought to Milford Haven. Arising from this tragedy, Stewardess Elizabeth May Owen was awarded the George Medal in the following September for her bravery in saving female passengers trapped on the lower deck. A claim was made by the GWR in the following month under the War Damage provision of the Railway Control Agreement.

Meanwhile, the *St Patrick's* two sister ships saw action at Dunkirk in May 1940, both making several voyages to bring home wounded soldiers. They were both later involved in the Anzio landings on 24 January 1944. Despite being clearly marked as a Hospital Ship, the *St David* was bombed and sunk, with the loss of Captain Evan Owen and 56 others. The *St Andrew* picked up 60 survivors, she also suffering damage. Later, she was towed back to Newport for extensive repairs after hitting a mine.

With the loss of the *St Patrick*, the service between Fishguard and Rosslare had to be suspended for the duration of hostilities. Following her repairs, the *St Andrew* returned to the route on 22 May 1947. A daily service, except Sundays, was put on during the summer months, with sailings on three days a week during the winter period. Two new ships, bearing the names of their predecessors, were ordered from Cammell Laird in 1947 at a cost of £570,000. The *St David III* was launched on 6 February 1948 and made her first visit to Rosslare on 22 July. Officials of CIÉ and public figures from Wexford were brought on a cruise along the south coast as far as Cork. She commenced her routine sailings from Fishguard four days later, with a complement of 1,300 passengers. She was followed by the *St Patrick III* launched on 4 February 1948 and put into service on 20 May 1948. It is of interest to note that the masthead pennant from the *St Patrick II*, washed ashore at Fishguard some time after the sinking of the vessel, was transferred to the new ship of the same name. These new ships had a gross registered tonnage of 3,500. A board minute of 1 February 1950 approved the use of the

---

6 At co-ordinates 52° 04'N & 5°25'W.

7 Captain Faraday, originally from Arthurstown, but living at Goodwick, was at that time also Commodore of the GWR fleet.

St David as a relief ship on the Harwich to Hook of Holland service in January and February of that year, with either one of the new ships relieving between 22 February and 1 April on the Holyhead to Dun Laoghaire (shown as Kingstown in the minutes) route. It was also mentioned that the *St David* had been allocated to operate an excursion from Fishguard to Belfast on 11 March. Later, it was decided to send the *St Patrick* to operate as a relief vessel for the summer season between Weymouth and the Channel Islands, remaining on that route until 1964.

In November 1950 the Fishguard Board approved the design of a house flag depicting the crosses of St George and St Patrick, on which a representation of the Company's seal was imposed. The design had already been agreed with CIÉ, and, subject to the Admiralty seeing no objection, a suitable number of flags were to be obtained. A detailed investigation of the working of the Rosslare to Fishguard service was carried out at the beginning of 1959, leading to the conclusion that there was no necessity to retain three vessels, and that the withdrawal of the third ship would produce economies of approximately £50,000 per annum. It was also felt that the passenger traffic via Waterford should be diverted to Rosslare, a decision likely to cause opposition from Waterford. Following correspondence with Dr Andrews, Chairman of CIÉ, the approval of the latter Company was given for the withdrawal of the *St Patrick*. The F&RR&H directors approved of the ship's transfer to the BTC as from

17 December 1959, resulting in a credit to Capital Account of £365,704.

The question needed to be addressed of providing a new stern-loading car-carrier passenger and cargo ship for the Rosslare service to replace the *St Andrew* and the *St David*, which would be retained for a period not exceeding twelve months after the delivery of the new ship. This new vessel would have seating capacity of approximately 900 passengers under cover, and accommodation for either 160 cars or 120 cars and 20 large containers or commercial road vehicles. Likewise, a new stern-loading cargo and livestock ship would be required for the Waterford service. In order that this new ship could be used to augment the Rosslare service and carry unaccompanied motor cars, it would be necessary to provide side-loading facilities similar to those on the *St David*. All of this would require the provision of stern-loading facilities at both Fishguard and Rosslare as outlined in Messrs Coode's report of 13 October 1964.

Mr Lemass said that works would be put in hand to enable side-loading and unloading of cars on and off the *St David* in time for the 1965 summer traffic; these works were completed in time for the 1965 summer season. The total cost of all of these changes would be about £3.63 million, including £1,880,000 for the new Rosslare ferry and £625,000 for the new Waterford ship. Harbour facilities at Fishguard were estimated to cost £750,000, at Rosslare £380,000 and at Waterford £144,000. Deducted from these figures would be scrap

The F&RR&H house flag as flown at the masthead of the Company's vessels. *(Ernie Shepherd)*

The *St David* with FR on the funnel, denoting ownership by the F&RR&H. These letters were carried between 1964 and 1967. Otherwise the vessels' livery was identical to other British Railways' ships. *(Brian Boyce)*

or sale value of the three ships. At the same meeting, Dr Andrews expressed a wish that the vessels on the route should have a distinctive livery to distinguish them from the BR vessels. The Fishguard Board did not agree to this and ordered that they be painted in the new BRB livery but approving of the letters 'F' and 'R' being painted on the funnels of the two remaining vessels when they were next withdrawn for annual overhaul. The two ships carried these letters on the funnels for about three years.

As well as putting in doors at the side of the *St David*, her second class accommodation was improved at a cost of £11,000. The total cost of converting the vessel and providing drive-on/drive-off facilities at Fishguard amounted to £77,847. It was announced in February 1967 that the *St Andrew* was being withdrawn from service, and in fact she was sold in October to Joseph de Smedt of Antwerp for £35,017 for breaking up. It was also announced that she was to be replaced by the *Duke of Rothesay*, which had been operating the Heysham to Belfast route, and which was to be converted to side-loading and would be chartered from British Railways. This charter was initially for five years from 12 May 1967. The *Duke of Rothesay* proved to be popular with the travelling public and the two ships operated the route until the spring of 1969. Early in that year it was announced that the *Caledonian Princess* (affectionately known by her crew as the 'Cale P') would be transferred on

charter for five years from 1 January 1971 from the Stranraer to Larne route to work alongside the *Duke of Rothesay*; the *Caledonian Princess* also required the fitting of side-loading doors for use on the new route. It was about this time that the *St David* was withdrawn from the Rosslare service. She was sold in 1971 to Greek owners, but not before she had served on the Dun Laoghaire to Heysham route, following the destruction of the Menai Bridge by fire.

British Railways set up a new shipping division as from 1 January 1968 known as the Shipping & International Services Division; this had little if any effect on the F&RR&H. However, British Railways began using a new brand name in 1971, Sealink, this being applied to the ships in the following year. It was not until January 1979 that a new BR subsidiary, Sealink UK Limited, was officially established, the F&RR&H becoming a subsidiary of Sealink UK. The charter for the *Duke of Rothesay* was renewed for another five years from 11 May 1972; alterations at Fishguard in 1972 included a new link-span enabling lorries, coaches and caravans to use the route for the first time.

From this time on, a number of different ships appeared on the route and it is not feasible to deal with all of these in this work. The story of these ships has been adequately told in the official centenary book, *Fishguard–Rosslare 1906–2006*, and the reader is referred to that publication for further details. In

1975 the Harwich ferry *Avalon* was converted into a stern-loading car ferry and was intended for use as a replacement for the *Caledonian Princess*, which made her last crossing on the route on 19 June 1975. After withdrawal from service she became a floating night club in Glasgow. The *Avalon* was, however, sent to Holyhead and a number of different ships operated the Rosslare service until the arrival of the *Stena Normandica*.

In October 1978 British Rail announced that a new ferry had been ordered from Harland & Wolff in Belfast, to be named the *St David IV*. A month prior to this the large ferry *Stena Nordica* was chartered, and arrived in Rosslare to carry out berthing trials; at 24,206 GRT, this was by far the largest ferry which had used the port up to that time. Pending the delivery of the new ferry, Sealink chartered the *Stena Nordica*'s sister ship, the *Stena Normandica*, beginning service on the route on 2 April 1979. This vessel had an enormous impact, traffic soon jumped by 10%. However, tragedy struck in June when the ship suffered a serious engine failure[8], and the *Avalon* was quickly brought back to Fishguard. *Stena Normandica* was missing until 23 September, when the *Avalon* returned to Holyhead. Side-loading doors were cut in her upper vehicle deck during her annual overhaul early in 1980, thus allowing her to use the facilities at Fishguard. The *St David IV* was eventually delivered in September 1980, by which time it had been decided to send her to Holyhead.

It was announced in the House of Commons in July 1984 that Sealink UK Limited was to be sold for £66 million to Sea Containers Limited, a Company based in Bermuda, the Company becoming known as Sealink British Ferries. The new Company decided to purchase the *Stena Normandica*, which was renamed *St Brendan*. Then in early 1990 it was announced that the Swedish shipping Company, Stena Line, had put in a bid for Sea Containers Ltd. Despite attempts to thwart this, an offer of £226 million was eventually accepted for the Company in March 1990. This acquisition made Stena the world's largest ferry company. The takeover coincided with the acquisition

The *Stena Europe* approaches her berth at Fishguard on arrival from Rosslare in May 2008. *(Ernie Shepherd)*

on charter of the Swedish ferry *Visby* of 15,001 GRT. Renamed *Felicity*, later the *Stena Felicity*, she made her appearance at Fishguard on 2 March 1990 and entered service three days later.

The *Stena Felicity* remained in service until 1997, when she left the route and was replaced by the 31,189 tonne *Koningin Beatrix* with a passenger capacity of 2,100. The *Koningin Beatrix* first arrived in Rosslare on 22 June 1997, and following berthing trials took up service three days later on the evening sailing from Rosslare. It was announced at the end of 2001 that the *Koningin Beatrix* was to be transferred to Stena's Poland to Sweden service as from March 2002, and would be replaced by the vessel already operating that route. So it was that the *Stena Europe* of 24,828 tonnes began service on the Fishguard to Rosslare route on 12 March 2002. Originally built for Sessan Line and used on their Gothenburg to Frederikshavn service and named *Kronprinsessan Victoria*, Sessan Line was taken over by Stena, and she was renamed *Stena Saga* in 1989, becoming the *Stena Europe* in 1998. She remains on the Rosslare route today.

Fishguard saw an even bigger change in June 1994 with the introduction of the twin-hulled catamaran *Stena Sea Lynx*, which with a service speed of 38 knots, could cover the 54 nautical miles between the two ports in 99 minutes. This vessel operated during the summer months until 1998, apart from 1996 when the *Condor 10* was chartered from Condor Ferries. The *Stena Lynx III* came on to the route in 1998 but in

---

8 One of five such failures to beset what was otherwise an excellent ship on the route.

The *Stena Lynx III* near Strumble Head, west of Fishguard Harbour. The catamaran service was marketed under the Stena Express brand. This service was withdrawn in autumn 2010 and the vessel sold to a South Korean operator. *(Stena Line)*

2004 she suffered a major crankshaft failure, causing the fast-ferry service to be suspended for almost two months. She weighs 4,113 tonnes, is 264ft 6in long and has a capacity of 620 passengers and 145 vehicles. She was later marketed as the Stena Express and worked the Rosslare–Fishguard service for her last season on the route between July and September 2011. She was then sent to Dun Laoghaire but it was soon announced that she had been sold to Dae A Gosok Ferries of Busan in South Korea. Renamed the *Sunflower 2*, she departed Dun Laoghaire on 21 October on her delivery voyage to Korea, estimated to last up to 25 days. Disaster struck, however, when she suffered a major engine failure in the Bay of Biscay and spent some time undergoing repairs in La Coruna. She was photographed in December 2011 in the Philippines and was reportedly laid up in Busan in 2012.

Liner traffic at Fishguard

In September 1859 JO Lever[9], founder of the Galway Line, bought up the fleet of the former General Screw Steam Shipping Company and started a new line of Royal Mail steamships to undertake a monthly service between Milford Haven, Lisbon, St Vincent, Pernambuco, Bahia and Rio de Janeiro under the title of the Real Companhia de Navegacao a Vapor Anglo-Luso-Brasileira (Anglo-Luso-Brazilian Royal Mail Steam Navigation Company). The directors of the new company included CRM Talbot, chairman of the SWR, and Captain Robert Ford of Messrs Ford & Jackson. The vessel *The Milford Haven* of 1,850GRT[10], sailed from Milford on 1 October 1859, followed by two other vessels in November and December. However, the port of Milford Haven was found to be inconvenient and it was announced in May 1860 that Liverpool would in future be the port of departure; in the event this was also short-lived, the company being sold in 1861. The GWR had from the earliest days expressed an interest in attracting transatlantic traffic. Brunel's famous *Great Eastern*, launched in 1858, arrived at Neyland in August 1860 with a view to commencing such a service. She eventually sailed for New York in May 1861, returning to Neyland in February 1862 where she was laid up. However, this was to be the end of the GWR's aspirations in this venture.

Some hopes were raised in 1889 when the 8,415 GRT Anchor Line steamship *City of Rome* arrived off Milford to offload a circus en route from New York. Once again, however, it proved to be a one-off call. Following negotiations between the GWR and the Canadian Steamship Company in 1898 it was announced that the latter would operate a service between Paspebiac[11] and Milford. The GWR agreed to co-operate by putting on connecting boat trains to and from London. In due course the liner *Gaspesia* arrived at Milford on 7 December 1898 to inaugurate the first westbound service on the following day. She returned to Milford on 9 January 1899, but became trapped in thick ice off the Canadian coast on the return voyage, following which the service was abandoned. By that time the writing was on the wall for the port of Milford so far as the GWR was concerned. Not only was it not to see any further transatlantic traffic but, because of the F&RR&H, within seven years it was also to lose its

---

9 John Orrell Lever, born in Lancashire, established with Fr Peter Daly, a Galway priest, member of Galway Harbour Commissioners and also a director of the MGWR, the Galway Bay Steam Navigation Company to provide a service to the Aran Islands. Later, in June 1858, the two set up the Atlantic Steam Navigation Company, also known as the Galway Line.

10 Originally built by CJ Mare of Blackwall in 1852 for the General Screw Steam Shipping Co as the *Queen of the South*. Renamed *The Milford Haven* in 1859, she was wrecked near Sandy Hook in November 1885.
11 Paspebiac (current population 3,654) is a small port in the Gaspe Peninsula region of Eastern Quebec. Its only apparent claim to fame is that it was established in 1767 as the first permanent cod fishing port in the Gaspe.

cross-channel service to Waterford, thereafter having to rely solely on the fishing industry for its future survival.

Within months of the opening of Fishguard harbour for the cross-channel service, negotiations were commenced with various companies with a view to attracting liners to the port. The parties approached included Cunard, Elder Dempster and Booth Lines. Only the latter company initially agreed to their liners calling at Fishguard. Booth Line had been founded in 1866 to operate services from Liverpool via Oporto and Lisbon to Brazil and the Amazon. History was made on 2 April 1908 when the Booth Line liner *Lanfranc* entered the harbour and disembarked passengers from South America. A special four-coach train, including a dining car, was laid on by the GWR but only 21 passengers travelled on it to London. Three weeks later, the *Antony* disembarked passengers and mails. On this occasion the special train ran the 262 miles to Paddington in 4h 55m at an average speed of 53mph. Further details indicate that the tender was alongside the *Antony* only seven minutes after the liner had anchored in the bay, taking 22 minutes to load and bring passengers to the quayside. The special train left Fishguard just 50 minutes after the liner's arrival. At least six of Booth Line's vessels called at Fishguard over the next four years, the last such sailing calling in February 1914. For details of the various vessels involved, see Appendix F1.

It was soon realised that the facilities at Fishguard, good as they might be for the cross-channel shipping, were unsuitable for liner traffic. Reporting in December 1908, Inglis stated that the Quay at the Dolphins was then nearing completion, but to render it suitable for ocean liners he recommended that it be covered in and accommodation provided for both passengers and customs officials at an estimated cost of £2,180. Having considered the matter, the Board approved of this expenditure. Twelve months later it was decided to extend the main station roof by 190ft to provide better shelter in inclement weather. The main drawback to the use by ocean liners of Fishguard harbour was the inadequate depth of water available inside the breakwater; this meant that large vessels could not actually enter the harbour

itself, necessitating transfer of passengers, mails and baggage to tenders which caused inconvenience to disembarking passengers, particularly in bad weather. The *Railway Times* for 29 January 1910 reported that the GWR had decided to hire a powerful dredger from the Mersey Docks & Harbours Board; this was then engaged in deepening the water to 40ft alongside the Ocean Quay, which should enable the large Cunard vessels to come right up to the quay. This was clearly a short-term measure as it was announced in May 1910 that negotiations had been opened with Mr CH Campbell of Dashwood House, New Broad Street, London, for the dredging of an area which would involve the removal of one million tons of material; Campbell quoted a figure of 8¼d per ton, subject to a minimum payment of 8½d for the first 500,000 tons. These figures were approved and authority given for the work to proceed, the overall estimate being £40,000. Formal approval had to be obtained from the BoT, this being granted in October, allowing dredging down to 38ft below LWOST[12]. In April 1911 it was decided to extend the area of dredging and it was expected that by the autumn the harbour would be sufficiently dredged to admit the Cunard ships inside the breakwater.

While the dredging works were proceeding at Fishguard, plans were submitted to the Board meeting on 14 October 1910 for the building of a quay 900ft long on the inner side of the northern breakwater to more effectively deal with ocean liner traffic. It was agreed that this should be constructed in ferro-concrete, Inglis being authorised to enter into negotiations with Messrs LG Mouchel & Partners[13] for their assistance; the estimated cost of this work amounted to £100,000. Mouchel & Partners agreed to act as superintending constructors on the basis of a payment of 5% of the total cost of the ferro-concrete work, this being accepted by the Board.

---

12 LWOST = Low water over spring tides.
13 The company was started by Louis Gustave Mouchel, born Cherbourg in 1852. The concept of reinforced concrete had been pioneered by another Frenchman, Francois Hennebique, and was first used in Britain in 1897 for Weaver's flour mill in Swansea. Mouchel gained the British agency for Hennebique and founded the LG Mouchel company. Among Mouchel's structures were a sea wall for the L&SWR at Southampton and the Royal Liver Building of 1909, Britain's tallest building until the 1960s. The company's offices were at 38 Victoria Street, London.

Prior to the commencement of dredging operations, matters had progressed as Cunard had finally agreed to stop at Fishguard on their eastbound service from New York. The announcement followed a similar notification in the *New York Times* of 20 June 1909 that the White Star liner *Cedric* was to call at Holyhead to land the English and Continental mails and passengers. Officials of White Star had travelled to meet the *Cedric* at Queenstown, and it was confidently hoped that this would lead to the permanent opening of Holyhead for the disembarkation of the American mails. This was undoubtedly a coup for the LNWR and made it even more imperative that the GWR provide sufficient facilities at Fishguard so as to attract traffic. So it was finally that the Cunard liner *Mauretania*, under the command of a Welshman, Captain John Pritchard, anchored just outside the breakwater at Fishguard at 13.20 on Tuesday 31 August 1909, having created a new record for an eastbound crossing by the shorter, summer route from New York. The crossing occupied 4 days 14 hours and 27 minutes, at an average speed of 25.41 knots for the 2,807 nautical miles.[14]

Prior, however, to the arrival of the first transatlantic liner, a six-page circular was issued to GWR staff in July 1909 under the signature of Joseph Morris, Superintendent of the Line. In it reference was made to the new Ocean Quay being brought into use, accommodation there including Customs Room, booking and telegraph offices. Trains carrying passengers berthing at the new quay were to be started from there. As the hours of special trains could not be fixed in advance, it was arranged that telegraphic advice should be forwarded to the principal stations right through to Paddington as soon as convenient, a clear road being kept ahead of the trains. An instruction was given that whenever sufficient passengers had cleared Customs, a special was to be immediately despatched, such trains to call at Cardiff so as to provide onward connections to Birmingham, the Midlands and North, Bristol and the west of England. Should the number of passengers landing be insufficient to warrant the running of a special train throughout, arrangements were to be made to send passengers forward either

The following notice is reproduced:

PRIVATE AND NOT FOR PUBLICATION. Notice No. 241.

GREAT WESTERN RAILWAY.

SUPPLEMENTARY NOTICE

OF

Arrangements to be made in connection with the arrival of the S.S. "Mauretania" at Fishguard Harbour on Monday, December 6th, 1909.

Empty Trains Paddington to Fishguard.

1. On **SUNDAY, DECEMBER 5th**, the Empty Trains will run from Paddington to Fishguard as shewn below:—

STATIONS.	Mail Special.		First Passenger.		Second Passenger.	
	Arr. p.m.	Dep. p.m.	Arr. p.m.	Dep. p.m.	Arr. p.m.	Dep. p.m.
PADDINGTON	A	12 40	— B F	2 10	— C	4 38
Ealing	—	—	—	2 20	—	4 48
Slough		1 4		2 35		5 3
Reading		1 26		2 53		5 21
Didcot		1 48		3 12		5 40
Swindon	2 15	2 16	3 38	3 39	6 8	6 10
Badminton		2 41		4 3		6 34
Severn Tunnel Junction		3 10		4 33		7 4
Newport		3 27		4 48		7 19
Cardiff	3 44	3 54	5 5	5 10	7 36	7 40
Bridgend		4 20		5 36		8 6
Landore	4 54	5 0	6 10	6 11	8 40	8 41
Carmarthen Junction		5 45		6 56	G	9 26
Clarbeston Junction		6 16		7 27		9 57
Fishguard & Goodwick	—	—	—	7 53	—	10 23
FISHGUARD HARBOUR	6 45	—	7 55	—	10 25	—

Empty Trains to carry "A" Head lights, and be signalled as Express Passenger Trains. Express Passenger Trains must not be shunted for the Empty Trains.
A To leave Old Oak Common at 12.0 noon.
B To leave Old Oak Common at 1.0 p.m. C To leave Old Oak Common at 3.30 p.m.
F The 12.40 p.m. Milk Empties from Paddington to be kept clear.
G Precede 11.45 a.m. Paddington to Neyland from Carmarthen Junction.

Formation of Empty Trains.

2. Formation of Empty Trains:—

MAIL TRAIN.	FIRST PASSENGER TRAIN.	SECOND PASSENGER TRAIN.
Ocean Mail Van 70 feet.	Engine	Engine
Do. Do.	Corridor Brake Compo. 1 and 3 (No. 7531)	Van Third (No. 3527)
Do. Do.	First (No. 8314)	Corridor Third
Do. Do.	First (No. 8315)	Third (No. 3611)
Brake Van Corridor	First (No. 8319)	First (No. 9051)
Lavatory Van	Restaurant Car	First (No. 8257)
Newspaper Van D	Restaurant Car	Restaurant Car
Do. D	First (No. 8320)	Restaurant Car
	First (No. 8321)	First (No. 8256)
D One of the Newspaper Vans will be attached to this train at Cardiff and the other at Landore.	First (No. 8322)	First (No. 8255)
	Van (70 feet)	First (No. 9046)
	Van (70 feet)	Van (8-wheel)
	First (No. 9047)	Van (70 feet)
	First (No. 9048)	First (No. 9049)
	Note.— Corridor Firsts Nos. 9047 and 9048 are being sent to Fishguard for use if required.	First No. 9049 and the additional Corridor Third are being sent to Fishguard for use if required.

Three page circular issued from Paddington on 3 December 1909 outlining arrangements for the two Mauretania specials on Monday 6 December 1909. *(Author's Collection)*

on the ordinary Irish boat trains or by special train to Cardiff or Bristol, there to connect with the ordinary train service.

Running time for Ocean Specials not exceeding five eight-wheeled vehicles and stopping only at Cardiff was shown as five hours to London, with an additional ten minutes allowed if starting from the Ocean Quay. Within months a fresh circular was issued on 26 October 1909 showing a running time of 4 hours and 50 minutes, with an additional five minutes allowed if an extra stop was made at Southall. Through specials to Paddington were to consist of an Ocean mail van, corridor brake composite, restaurant car and brake composite (in both cases first and third class); if a night train was required, a sleeping car was also to be included in the formation in rear of the restaurant

---

14 In fact, *Mauretania* recorded the fastest crossings in both directions, retaining the coveted Blue Riband for 20 years until July 1929.

The *Mauretania* outside Fishguard Harbour sometime between 1909 and 1914. *(Martin Lewis Postcard Collection)*

car. Only the best stock was to be used for the specials, the composites to be 57ft vehicles, lettered 'For Ocean Traffic – return to Fishguard', although when necessary 70ft stock might be used; roof label boards were to be used, and returned after use to Fishguard. As noted in Chapter 19 dedicated stock was later built for these trains.

Such was the prestige associated with the arrival of the first liner that three Cunard directors, including Ernest Cunard himself, Lord Barrymore, chairman of the GWR, accompanied by a number of officials, travelled to Queenstown on the westbound *Lusitania* to meet the inbound liner and journey back to Fishguard. The *Irish Times* reported that at Fishguard a great demonstration had been organised to which "the neighbourhood for some miles around enthusiastically contributed". The railway station, the harbour, quays and the narrow streets around were all decorated with bunting. There was a march of the Pembrokeshire Territorials, a procession of tradesmen, school children, municipal dignitaries and a group of eight red-cloaked and tall-hatted Welsh ladies,[15] giving an historical perspective to the event; the ladies presented each passenger with a bunch of heather. Staff and reporters descended on the port on the previous Sunday, many of the latter being quartered on board the *St Andrew*, some of the staff in the Fishguard Bay

Hotel, every available bed in Goodwick having been taken in advance.

As this was a momentous event in the history of Fishguard, some details of the operation involved might be of interest to the reader. The tender *Smeaton*, specially transferred from Plymouth for the occasion, was alongside the liner within minutes of dropping anchor, removing 881 bags of mail and 5 hampers of parcel post in the space of 14 minutes. The *Smeaton* then headed for the Ocean Quay where the mails were off-loaded in pallets by crane and quickly transferred to the mail train. The latter, consisting of two mail vans and a brake van, headed by 'Atbara' class 4-4-0 No 3381 *Maine*, departed at 14.07 via the cattle siding behind the passenger platforms; at Cardiff, *Maine* was replaced by 'Star' class 4-6-0 No 4023 *King George* for the run to Paddington, reached at 18.35, having dropped off one of the mail vans at Cardiff.

Meanwhile, the passenger tender *Sir Francis Drake* pulled alongside *Mauretania* and off-loaded 238 passengers, who were disembarked at the Irish Quay, where their baggage, taken off the liner by the *Great Western*, was checked by a squad of no less than 25 customs officers.[16] Such was the speed of the entire operation that the *Mauretania* weighed anchor at

---

15 In 1797 a group of similarly dressed local women led by the famous Jemima Nicholas captured 12 French soldiers in what was to be the last foreign invasion of Britain.

16 It appears that the 478T tender *Sir Walter Raleigh*, built by Cammell-Laird of Birkenhead in April 1908, following her sea trials at Liverpool on 19 May, also spent a year at Fishguard before being transferred to Plymouth, although there is no mention of her exact role there. She was 151ft 6in long, 38ft 6in beam, twin-screwed, with accommodation for 590 passengers in smooth water.

The first Mauretania special to leave Fishguard in 1909. The train is in charge of 4-4-0s Nos 3402 *Halifax* and 4108 *Gardenia*, respectively of the City and Flower classes. Two locomotives were required to tackle the 1 in 50 gradient up to Manorowen. A second train on the left is to be hauled by two Flower class locomotives, Nos 4111 *Anemone* and 4164 *Mignonette*. (Martin Lewis Postcard Collection)

14.00, barely ¾ hour after her arrival. Two special trains were laid on for the embarking passengers. The first of these, standing at No 2 platform, consisted of a mail van, 3 firsts, 2 restaurant cars, 3 more firsts and a bogie brake van, totalling 273t 18c tare and about 325t gross. The vehicles were side-corridor and vestibuled, and all carried destination boards labelled 'Cunard Ocean Express: Fishguard–London'. The two vans had been detached from the carriages and placed alongside No 3 platform so as to expedite the loading of baggage. This done, the leading van was taken by the two locomotives, Nos 3402 *Halifax* and 4108 *Gardenia* and placed at the head of the train; the second van was placed at the rear of the train by the Fishguard Harbour shunter. The first special left Fishguard Harbour at 14.51½, arriving at Cardiff at 17.03; there 'Star' 4-6-0 No 4021 *King Edward* was substituted in the creditable time of 3m 55s. The 145 mile run from Cardiff to Paddington was made by Driver Butcher in 141m 39s at an average speed of 61.9mph. Apart from the transatlantic passengers, this train also carried the GWR chairman and officials.

The second train, consisting of a 70ft van, 3 firsts, 2 restaurant cars, 2 firsts, a ten-compartment third and a third brake, all vestibuled and centre-corridor, departed at 15.05 behind Nos 4111 *Anemone* and 4116 *Mignonette*, arrived in Paddington at 19.56, No 4002 *King William* being substituted at Cardiff.

A special train had been provided at Paddington to bring Continental passengers to Dover via Southall, Kensington and the South Eastern & Chatham Railway. Special boards had been prepared reading 'Cunard Ocean Express: Fishguard–Dover', but as only a small number of passengers were travelling through to Paris, these boards were not used. In the event, passengers were brought by omnibus to Charing Cross in time to catch the 21.00 boat train. The passengers and mails reached Paris at 05.45 on the Tuesday morning, ensuring that the mails were delivered some 12 hours earlier than by the normal route, Queenstown to Dublin and Holyhead. A sign of the times was the delivery of some of the mails in London on Monday night, only five days after leaving New York. Subsequently the *Mauretania* was to bring some distinguished visitors to Fishguard, including Princes Albert and Radziwell and Mr Carlisle, Managing Director of Harland & Wolff, in December 1910. She arrived at Fishguard on 20 June 1911, two days before the Coronation of George, Duke of York, as King George V, with in excess of 2,000 passengers, many of whom travelled solely for that event. *The Times* (of London) reported that many of them expected to return to America on the *Mauretania's* return voyage on the following Saturday. In total, 750 passengers disembarked at Fishguard along with 1,510 bags of mail; three special passenger trains ran to London, one each to Cardiff and Dover.

The *Lusitania* first called at Fishguard on 4 October 1909 with little publicity. Whilst the people of Fishguard and district were pleased to see the Cunard liners calling at their port, not everyone was happy. The *Irish Times* reported in its issue for 24 November 1909 that a specially convened meeting of Queenstown Urban District Council (UDC) had been held to consider what steps should be taken in reference to rumours that Cunard were to abandon the eastbound call there during the first three months of 1910, an action much to be deplored. This would affect not only Queenstown, but would also be to the detriment of the GS&WR and its shareholders (although it seemed that the GS&WR were of the view that the Queenstown traffic was "altogether over-rated", a statement which hardly endeared them to the people of Cork!) The UDC unanimously resolved to hold a conference with Cork Harbour Board, the Chamber of Commerce, and the Corporation and County Council, to take immediate steps to urge Cunard to rethink their decision.

Worse news came in March 1910 with a report in the *New York Times* to the effect that Cunard had decided to eliminate Queenstown altogether as a port of call for the eastbound mail ships. However, it was understood that a service would be provided by the slower liners *Caronia* and *Carmania,* which would call there in both directions between 1 April and 1 November; during the winter months these ships were employed on the Company's Mediterranean service. Appendix F1 shows a list of both Booth and Cunard Line vessels which called at Fishguard during the period 11 April to 18 July 1910. The question of the Queenstown stopover continued to rumble on for some time to come. Representations to the Postmaster General, supported in Parliament by representatives of both of the Irish parties, failed to gain any concessions. Part of the argument put forward was that the American mails for Ireland were brought direct to Fishguard and then returned on the cross-channel service, causing considerable delays. In addition the liners had, on at least three occasions, failed to call at Fishguard owing to adverse weather conditions, whereas they could have safely put in at Queenstown.

The night of 22 December 1910 saw the arrival at Fishguard of the *Mauretania* carrying a large number of passengers home from America for the Christmas season. *The Times* (of London) described the atmosphere at Fishguard as being more like the return of soldiers from a hard campaign rather than "voyagers completing a pleasure trip surrounded by every luxury that science can furnish and money can buy". Cunard had made a special effort to turn round the *Mauretania* in record time in New York so as to have her back home for Christmas. Once again, a special corps of Customs Officers was drafted in for the occasion. Both the *Great Western* and the *Pembroke* acted as tenders for the transfer of mails and baggage. Not only did the exclusion of the Queenstown stop benefit passengers disembarking at Fishguard, but also those continuing their journeys from Liverpool to Sweden and Germany, the Great Central Railway laying on special trains to connect with their ships from Grimsby and Hull. It was the *Lusitania* which did the honours for Christmas 1911 with a record 720 passengers disembarking as well as a large volume of mail. On this occasion, she arrived off Fishguard an hour earlier than expected, catching the tenders still tied up at the quays. The *Mauretania* was responsible for both the 1912 and 1913 Christmas sailings. In the case of the former, she carried a record 6,361 bags of mail and specie[17] to the value of £216,000, while passengers included Mr & Mrs AG Vanderbilt.

Blue Funnel Line ships called at Fishguard between November 1910 and March 1912 to pick up passengers en route from Liverpool to South Africa and Australia. Vessels included the *Aeneas* which called on 19 November 1910, the *Ascanius* on 31 December and the *Anchises*. A further development in the port was announced by the *Railway Times* on 20 May 1911, when it reported that the Cunard liner *Franconia* had recently arrived at Fishguard, marking the adoption of the port for the Boston service. The *Franconia's* sister ship the *Ivernia*, also called at Fishguard, although we have no specific details. Later, in June it was learned that of twenty-nine transatlantic steamships from New York conveying the American mails for Britain during the month of May, seventeen were handled at the GWR docks at Plymouth, seven at Fishguard and five at Queenstown.

---

17 Specie refers to coin money as opposed to bullion or paper money.

Improvements were made in October 1909 in the running of the connecting Ocean Mail trains, with timings of 4h 45m and 4h 50m respectively for mail and passenger trains between Fishguard and London. Due to the uncertainty in arrival times of the liners, no specific times were shown in the Working Timetables of the period. On the arrival of a liner, Fishguard Signal Box sent a box-to-box message up the line, the actual train departure time then being wired through each section right through to Paddington. Signalmen were directed to ensure that these trains were given absolute priority. To further improve the rail connection, new rolling stock was introduced in 1910-11, details of which are given in Chapter 19 and more powerful locomotives were allocated to Fishguard & Goodwick shed. The first such was No 4008 *Royal Star* in August 1911, followed later in the year by 'Saint' class Nos 2937 *Clevedon Court*, 2938 *Corsham Court* and 2940 *Dorney Court*, all newly constructed at Swindon.

The Cunard liners continued to call at Fishguard until the outbreak of war in August 1914. A notable event was that the *Aquitania* of 45,647 GRT departed Liverpool on her maiden voyage to New York on 30 May 1914, calling at Fishguard on 16 June on her return voyage; 437 first and 169 second class passengers were disembarked along with 1,246 mail bags and gold bullion, necessitating the running of no less than five special trains on that day. The last liner to call at Fishguard was the *Lusitania*, on 14 September. Some eight months later, on 7 May 1915, she was torpedoed by the German submarine U-20 about eight miles off the Old Head of Kinsale, tragically with the loss of 1,198 lives.

Shortly after the Cunard liners ceased to call at Fishguard, approaches were made in January 1915 to the GWR by the Anglo-Persian Oil Company, who were seeking a suitable site for the construction of a refinery close to an existing port. It was proposed that the refinery should be built at Manorowen, crude oil being brought in at Fishguard and pumped through a pipeline to the refinery for processing. Negotiations continued for some three months but the plan was dropped as tankers would have required the use of a portion of the northern breakwater and would have interfered with the cross-channel steamers. Coaling of tankers would have taken place at the Parrog (eastern) breakwater, necessitating the completion of the rail connection, work on which had been suspended, and never to be completed. In addition, the GWR were confident that Cunard would return to the port once the war was at an end. In the event the refinery was built at Llandarcy, close to Swansea. So came to an end the aspirations for Fishguard as an ocean liner port. From this point on it returned to its status as a cross-channel port, albeit a successful one in recent times.

Hotels

The property today known as the Fishguard Bay Hotel overlooking Fishguard Harbour began life as Wyncliffe (sometimes referred to as Windcliffe or Wyndcliffe) House. There has been a house on the site of the hotel since the eighteenth century, at which time, it was called Wyndcliffe; the house and the quay at Goodwick were at that time held under lease by the Rogers family, who hailed from Minehead in Somerset. The house was apparently sold in 1805 to David Harries of Dinas Island.[1] The house was described by Fenton in his *Historical Tour through Pembrokeshire*, published in 1811, as "niched like an eagle's nest above the pier." In the 1891 census, the head of household is shown as an Alfred Morrison, who was living there with his wife, two daughters and a son; there were, in addition, three visitors and no less than eighteen servants. The house was purchased in 1896 by the F&RR&H Company under powers granted by Section 62 of the FBR&P Company's Act of 1893; Section 62 authorised the Company to take, by agreement, any land not exceeding 20 acres on which they might erect or build an hotel, or acquire any houses or buildings and carry on the business of hotel keepers. Other properties were purchased at the same time, including the Rose and Crown public house, Ivy Cottage and Rock House and adjoining cottage, the latter three adjoining Wyncliffe House. Rock House was described in October 1899 as being an integral part of the hotel, while the small cottage to the rear was considered necessary for the hotel's purposes. To effect the purchase of these properties, a subsidiary company, the Pembrokeshire Estates Company, was set up, the directors of the F&RR&H also being the directors of the Estates Company.

It is not clear exactly when Wyncliffe was converted to a hotel but it was certainly in use as such when the Memorandum of Agreement with Alexander Henderson was signed in February 1898. Complaints were made in February 1900 regarding the very bad condition of the roadway from Goodwick station to the hotel, an order being given to widen and improve a portion of it at a cost of £20. This matter was still causing some concern in June of the following year, Mr Inglis recommending that additional land be acquired on the east side of the road. Powers were taken under Section 23 of the Company's Act of 1903 for the purchase of additional land adjoining the north-western side of the railway and between the bridge carrying the public road over the railway at Goodwick station and the Wyncliffe Hotel, and between Ivy Cottage and the public road.

In March 1902 it was reported that Ivy Cottage was also in a bad state of repair and it was agreed to expend £65 in putting it in order, following which it was to be rented to Mr Brown, the foreman for the contractor carrying out the harbour works; Brown agreed to pay a rent of £20 per annum for a period of three years. At the same board meeting the Engineer was authorised to negotiate for the purchase of four cottages near to the hotel, along with additional land on which the Company would erect housing for the accommodation of staff.

The decision was taken in August 1906 to change the name of the property to the Fishguard Bay Hotel as better befitting its location overlooking the harbour. With the opening of the new steamer service business became brisk at the hotel. The gardens were landscaped by a well-known Cornish gardener; apart from the gardens, the grounds also featured a tennis court, croquet lawns and ¾ mile of woodland walks. In addition, licences could be purchased allowing fishing in the Western Cleddau River alongside the railway line.

---

1 Not actually an island but a promontory to the east of Fishguard Bay. It would seem that the Davies family also owned a property known as Pen-Rhiw overlooking Goodwick; portion of this estate was sold to the F&RR&H in connection with the construction of the Harbour Village.

Hotel Wyncliffe in its original form.
(*The National Archives, Kew*)

Inglis reported in October 1908 on the inadequate accommodation existing at the hotel; this was most likely prompted by the Company's aspirations to attract cruise liners or transatlantic traffic to the port. Inglis recommended extending the hotel by the provision of a wing so as to provide a total of 50 bedrooms and other alterations at an estimated cost of £8,000. The scheme was approved in principle, Inglis being instructed to prepare and submit detailed plans, these being placed before the board on 18 December 1908, by which time the estimated cost had risen to £11,684. Various tenders were received over the next eighteen months, including £1,955 6s 6d for internal plastering, £1,186 for joinery work and £1,050 for painting and papering. By the time the work was finally completed in October 1911 the total cost had risen to £23,215. This was explained by Inglis as resulting from the work being carried out in a more expensive manner than originally contemplated in the light of experience gained during the construction works and also the necessity to put the old building into a proper state of repair. The opportunity was taken to provide electricity in the hotel. The new section was in fact the four-storey section to the left of the original two-storey building.

As mentioned in Chapter 22 the transatlantic liner trade was short-lived, coming to an end with the outbreak of the First World War. In addition, since only the eastbound liners called at Fishguard it is likely that few disembarking passengers stayed over, but rather took the Ocean Express trains for London. The hotel was, however, used to some extent as a stopover for passengers using the Irish ferries. Some problems were encountered in December 1914 in relation to the water supply to the hotel and the harbour village provided by the Pembrokeshire Water Company. As a result it was found necessary to supplement the supply from the Company's own mains at a cost of £169. During the war years the hotel was used as a rest home for officers; we know that the RNAS officers were housed there by April 1917 as we are told that following his accident on Sunday 22 April, Lieut Richard E Bush was taken to his quarters in the hotel. It was similarly used as a rest home during the Second World War.

An advertisement for the hotel in 1930 shows the accommodation as consisting of forty bedrooms (not fifty as planned in 1908) and two suites of apartments. The dining hall was capable of seating 75 people; there were also a smoking room, two lounges and a billiard room. The tariff at that time was as follows:

Single rooms from 5s, dressing room 1s 6d, bath (either hot or cold) 1s, fires (morning or evening) 1s, fires (all day) 2s, breakfast 2s, luncheons from 2s and dinners from 3s 6d. Visitors' servants were charged at the rate of 2s 6d for bed and 5s 6d for board. All of the foregoing charges were "inclusive of electricity".

The 1935 issue of the GWR Company's "Holiday Haunts" confirms that the hotel also boasted an electric lift, central heating and a service telephone in every room, while there were 12 lock-up garages. Winter terms (1 October to 31 May, excluding Christmas,

Poster advertising the Fishguard Bay Hotel. Although stressing the fact that it adjoined the port, few cross-channel travellers appear to have availed of the opportunity to stop over, most likely due to somewhat unsocial sailing times. The Holiday Haunts Centenary number for 1935 expands on the facilities which included central heating, an electric lift and twelve lock-up garages. Winter terms in 1935 were quoted as 4½ guineas per week (1 Guinea = £1 1s 0d), which included all meals, accommodation, baths and early morning tea. The hotel porter was available to carry luggage to and from the harbour free of charge. *(Great Western Trust)*

Easter and Whitsuntide) amounted to 4½ guineas (£4 14s 6d), which included all meals, accommodation, baths and early morning tea.

In January 1938 the decision was taken to improve the accommodation at the hotel by constructing nine additional bathrooms, installing a cocktail bar and modernising the hot water system at an estimated cost of £3,495. Of this amount it was anticipated that approximately £2,995 would be chargeable to the F&RR&H capital account. Despite these improvements the hotel was not very successful at attracting guests and it was reported at the F&RR&H board meeting on 8 November 1950 that the Railway Executive had, in view of the hotel's unfavourable trading results, taken the decision to close down the hotel. The closure took effect from 3 September 1951. The property then lay idle until it was leased in April 1959 by a Mrs Burscough, apart that is from a brief

lease to the makers of the film *Moby Dick* in 1956.[2] Mrs Burscough provided accommodation for workmen during the construction of the Esso oil refinery at Milford Haven. Following this, plans were made to re-open the hotel but tragically Mrs Burscough passed away before this was accomplished.

The hotel was then put on the market, being purchased by a consortium of local businessmen. When the hotel was sold in 1967, included in the purchase was the access road to the harbour and the station. However, British Railways were only allowed the use of the road until the end of 1971, by which time an alternative route had to be provided. Major alterations at the port in connection with the provision of an end-loading vehicle ferry ramp included a new road at an estimated cost of £50,000. Following extensive renovations the Fishguard Bay Hotel re-opened in December 1967. The hotel had a second short period of fame in 1971 with the making of the Dylan Thomas film *Under Milk Wood*. The stars in this film included Richard Burton, Elizabeth Taylor, Peter O'Toole and Glynis Johns. In 1979 the hotel was designated as a building of historic and architectural interest.

The hotel is currently a listed building (Grade II), described as part three and part four storied, situated on a levelled shelf on the steep, rocky slope above the west side of Fishguard Harbour. It is rendered, with a slate roof and sash windows. The south block is four-storey, with barge-boarded gables over the top windows and balconies with pent glass roofs and iron railings, supported on decorative iron piers, outside

---

2 Directed by John Huston, the film's stars included Gregory Peck and Orson Welles.

Fishguard Bay Hotel in May 2008. There is quite an extensive two-storey connection to the right of the main building. What used to be the main A40 access road to the port now stops here. *(Ernie Shepherd)*

the first-floor windows. The southeast facing block is three storey, with a taller tower, topped by a flagpole, over the entrance. At its north end a modern block has been added and rooms have been extended outwards from the original front in recent years. An interesting feature at the rear of the hotel, on the west side which faces the rock-cut slope behind, is the remains of a bridge between the hotel and the gardens; this ran from the second floor across to the path at the top of the rock face.

There were extensive gardens in GWR days, lying on the steep slope to the north, west and southwest of the hotel. The garden was bounded by a high stone wall, which occupied the slope up to the lane to Harbour Village. Although the original Wyndcliffe House had ornamental gardens, they were developed in association with the hotel, between 1900 and 1910, reputedly by a Cornish gardening firm, possibly Treseders, who were known to have operated in Wales.[3] It would seem that the terraced area at the south end of the garden was associated with former small houses in that area, which were removed when the hotel was built/enlarged; this possibly refers to Rock Cottage mentioned above.

Section 76 of the F&RR&H Act of 1898 gave the Company powers to erect an hotel at Rosslare either on lands owned by the Company or acquired by them.

It was not, however, until November 1903 that the question of providing an hotel appears to have been discussed. The matter was then referred to the General Managers of the GWR and GS&WR to consider the question, authority being granted to negotiate for the acquisition of the necessary lands if considered expedient. Brief mention was made of the matter at the board meeting of 7 June 1904 but it was at a further board meeting held on 1 March 1906 that the Secretary again raised the question and suggested that the powers be allowed to lapse. The directors, however, were of the view that it was desirable that a hotel be provided in connection with the harbour and the general managers were once again requested to report. It is not clear why the general managers found it necessary to defer a decision, but finally on 9 May 1907 the Board took the decision out of their hands and agreed to put the matter to rest.

An announcement was made on 18 September 1967 by the CIÉ hotels subsidiary, Ostlanna Iompair Éireann, that four hotels were to be built, to be known as 'Great Southern Inns'. Intended to cater mainly for the motoring tourist, one of these was to be built at Rosslare Harbour. Accommodation was to consist of 100 bedrooms and was to cost in the region of £350,000.

Whilst the hotel was built in Rosslare Village, as the property of Ostlanna Iompair Éireann, the subsidiary of CIÉ, it thus had no further part in our story.

---

3 *A passion for plants – the Treseders of Truro* by Suzanne Treseder refers to extensive contracts with the GWR in Cornwall, South Devon and Wales.

Appendices

F&RR&H Chairmen and Secretaries

Date	Chairman	Secretary	Date	Chairman	Secretary
1894	J Rowlands	A Nichols	1929	Viscount Churchill	FC Hockridge
1895	J Rowlands	A Nichols	1930	Viscount Churchill	FC Hockridge
1896	J Rowlands	A Nichols	1931	Viscount Churchill	FC Hockridge
1897	J Rowlands	JC Hughes	1932	Viscount Churchill	FC Hockridge
1898	Earl Cawdor	GJ Whitelaw	1933	Viscount Churchill[3]	FC Hockridge
1899	Earl Cawdor	GJ Whitelaw	1934	RS Horne	FC Hockridge
1900	Earl Cawdor	GJ Whitelaw	1935	RS Horne	JW Griffin
1901	Earl Cawdor	GJ Whitelaw	1936	RS Horne	JW Griffin
1902	Earl Cawdor	GJ Whitelaw	1937	RS Horne	JW Griffin
1903	Earl Cawdor	GJ Whitelaw	1938	RS Horne	JW Griffin
1904	Earl Cawdor[1]	GJ Whitelaw	1939	RS Horne	JW Griffin
1905	Alfred Baldwin	GJ Whitelaw	1940	Horne of Slamannan	WN Connah
1906	Alfred Baldwin	GJ Whitelaw	1941	Sir Charles J Hambro, MC	WN Connah
1907	Alfred Baldwin[2]	GJ Whitelaw	1942	Sir Charles J Hambro, MC	WN Connah
1908	Viscount Churchill	GJ Whitelaw	1943	Sir Charles J Hambro, MC	WN Connah
1909	Viscount Churchill	GJ Whitelaw	1944	Viscount Portal	WN Connah
1910	Viscount Churchill	GJ Whitelaw	1945	Viscount Portal	WN Connah
1911	Viscount Churchill	GJ Whitelaw	1946	Viscount Portal	WN Connah
1912	Viscount Churchill	GJ Whitelaw	1947	KWC Grand	WN Connah
1913	Viscount Churchill	GJ Whitelaw	1948	KWC Grand	AH Curtis Welch
1914	Viscount Churchill	GJ Whitelaw	1949	KWC Grand	AH Curtis Welch
1915	Viscount Churchill	FJ Richins	1950	KWC Grand	AH Curtis Welch
1916	Viscount Churchill	FJ Richins	1951	KWC Grand	AH Curtis Welch
1917	Viscount Churchill	FJ Richins	1952	KWC Grand	AH Curtis Welch
1918	Viscount Churchill	FJ Richins	1953	KWC Grand	AH Curtis Welch
1919	Viscount Churchill	FRE Davis	1954	KWC Grand	AH Curtis Welch
1920	Viscount Churchill	FRE Davis	1955	KWC Grand	AH Curtis Welch
1921	Viscount Churchill	FRE Davis	1956	KWC Grand	AH Curtis Welch
1922	Viscount Churchill	FRE Davis	1957	KWC Grand	AH Curtis Welch
1923	Viscount Churchill	FRE Davis	1958	KWC Grand	AH Curtis Welch
1924	Viscount Churchill	FRE Davis	1959	KWC Grand	AH Curtis Welch
1925	Viscount Churchill	FRE Davis	1960	KWC Grand	AH Curtis Welch
1926	Viscount Churchill	FC Hockridge	1961		AH Curtis Welch
1927	Viscount Churchill	FC Hockridge	1962	SE Raymond	AH Curtis Welch
1928	Viscount Churchill	FC Hockridge	1963	SE Raymond	AH Curtis Welch
			1964	GF Fiennes	AH Curtis Welch

1   Cawdor resigned prior to 11 May 1905.
2   Baldwin died suddenly on 13 February 1908.

3   Churchill died 3 January 1934.

Date	Chairman	Secretary	Date	Chairman	Secretary
1965	GF Fiennes	AH Curtis Welch	1993		
1966	LW Ibbotson	AH Curtis Welch	1994		
1967	LW Ibbotson[4]	AH Curtis Welch	1995		
1968	JL Harrington	GE Snelling	1996	M Storey	CJ Polkinghorne
1969	JL Harrington	GE Snelling	1997		CJ Polkinghorne
1970	JL Harrington	PJ Trinder	1998		CJ Polkinghorne
1971		PJ Trinder	1999		CJ Polkinghorne
1972	J Posner	PJ Trinder	2000	Mary Finola Gallagher	CJ Polkinghorne
1973	J Posner	PJ Trinder	2001		CJ Polkinghorne[5]
1974	DD Kirby	PJ Trinder	2002		LD Stracey[6]
1975	DD Kirby	PJ Trinder	2003		LD Stracey
1976	DD Kirby	PJ Trinder	2004		LD Stracey
1977	DD Kirby	PJ Trinder	2005		LD Stracey
1978		PJ Trinder	2006	G Williams	LD Stracey
1979		PJ Trinder	2007	G Williams	LD Stracey
1980		PJ Trinder	2008	G Williams	LD Stracey
1981	LC Merryweather OBE	PJ Trinder	2009		LD Stracey
1982	LC Merryweather OBE	PJ Trinder	2010	LD Stracey	LD Stracey
1983	LC Merryweather OBE	PJ Trinder	2011	LD Stracey	LD Stracey
1984	LC Merryweather OBE	PJ Trinder	2012	LD Stracey	LD Stracey
1985	LC Merryweather OBE	FJ Leese	2013	LD Stracey	LD Stracey
1986	CD Lenox-Conyngham	FJ Leese	2014	LD Stracey	LD Stracey
1987	CD Lenox-Conyngham	FJ Leese	2015	LD Stracey	LD Stracey
1988	CD Lenox-Conyngham				
1989	CD Lenox-Conyngham				
1990	CD Lenox-Conyngham	TG Dick			
1991					
1992					

The 2015 Board consists of Les Stracey (Chairman & Secretary), AR Fearn (Deputy-Chairman), John P Lynch, Aidan Cronin, Ian Davies and Michael McGrath. There is one vacancy waiting to be filled.

5   Polkinghorne retired as Director 15 April 2002.
6   Stracey appointed Director 2 November 1999.

4   Ibbotson resigned 2 August 1968.

APPENDIX B

Stations between Fermoy & Rosslare Harbour & Wexford[1]

Distance from Mallow	Station	Opened	Closed	Platform Lengths		Turntable Diameter
				Down	Up	
16.60[2]	Fermoy	1860	1967		775' 0"	50' 0"
19.40	Clondulane	1872	1967	301' 0"		
25.60	Ballyduff	1872	1967	320' 0"	320' 0"	
29.40	Tallow Road	1872	1967	300' 0"		
32.20	Lismore	1872	1967	404' 0"		39' 3"
32.40	Lismore (WD&LR)	1878	1893			
36.00	Cappoquin	1878	1967	198' 0"	198' 0"	
40.40	Cappagh	1878	1967	200' 0"		
46.40	Dungarvan	1878	1967	439' 0"	451' 0"	44' 9"
53.20	Durrow & Stradbally	1878	1967	250' 0"	250' 0"	
60.20	Kilmacthomas	1878	1982	207' 0"	207' 0"	
64.38	Carroll's Cross	1882	1967	211' 0"		
68.78	Kilmeaden	1878	1967	268' 0"	233' 0"	
75.40	Waterford South	1878	1908			
75.56	Waterford North	1864	Open			44' 9"
76.02	Abbey Junction	1904	2010			
81.76	Kilmokea Halt	1966	1970			
84.48	Campile	1906	2010	400' 0"	405' 0"	
89.25	Ballycullane	1906	1976	200'0"	200' 0"	
93.27	Wellington Bridge	1906	2010	250' 0"	250' 0"	
98.02	Duncormick	1906	1976	250' 0"	250' 0"	
103.72	Bridgetown	1906	2010	250' 0"	250' 0"	
107.54	Killinick	1906	1976	250' 0"	250' 0"	
110.66	Rosslare Strand	1906	Open	406' 0"	402'0"	
113.04	Kilrane		1970	104' 0"		
113.60	Ballygeary					
114.20	Rosslare Harbour			846' 0"		54' 6"
	Rosslare Europort		Open			
2 [3]	Felthouse Jct.					
3½ [3]	Drinagh					
5½ [3]	Wexford South		1977	302' 0"	303' 0"	

---

1 For those interested in further information, lists of level crossings are to be found in the GS&WR Appendix to the Working Timetable dated November 1912 and the GSR Appendix dated 1 March 1935. The former also includes a list of signal cabins, while the latter includes details of turntables and locomotive watering facilities at stations.

2 Distances between Fermoy and Waterford were shown in the WTT in miles and fractions rather than in miles and chains, hence distances shown may not be entirely accurate.

3 Measured northwards from Rosslare Strand.

APPENDIX C1

F&RR&H (R&WR section) and WD&LR Locomotive Stock

Company	No	GS&WR No	Name	Wheels	Date	Builder	Works No	Scrapped	Remarks
F&RR&H		300*	*Erin*	0-6-0T	1894	Hunslet	610	1930	
F&RR&H			*Cambria*	0-4-0T	1894	Hunslet	609	1928	To D&BST 1918 as No 5 †
WD&LR	1	211		0-4-2	1878	Sharp Stewart	2818	1909	R/N 244 in 1901
WD&LR	2	212		0-4-2	1878	Sharp Stewart	2819	1906	R/N 245 in 1901
WD&LR	3	213		0-4-2	1878	Sharp Stewart	2820	1914	R/B as 0-4-2ST & R/N 246 in 1901
WD&LR	4	214		0-4-2	1878	Sharp Stewart	2821	1905	R/N 247 in 1901
WD&LR	5	215*		2-4-0T	1859	Neilson	542	1898	Ex C&YR 69 & GS&WR 71 in 1883
WD&LR	6	216		0-4-2	1891	Sharp Stewart	3665	1913	R/N 248 in 1901
WD&LR	7	217		0-4-2	1892	Sharp Stewart	3813	1910	R/N 249 in 1901

* These numbers were allocated but never carried.

† Dublin & Blessington Steam Tramway.

APPENDIX C2

Contractors' Locomotives Employed on Various Contracts in Ireland and Wales

Name	Built	Maker	Wks No	Class	Wheels	Remarks
Ringing Rock	1876	MW	630	Q	0-6-0ST	Later to Kent & East Sussex Railway
Pioneer	1897	MW	1368	E	0-4-0ST	
Mermaid	1898	MW	1380	E	0-4-0ST	
Wyncliffe	1901	MW	1549	E	0-4-0ST	
Nipper	1903	MW	1610	E	0-4-0ST	
Elfin	1898	HC	460		0-4-0ST	To GWR 1913? and then to Noah Hingley & Sons
Gallo	1888	MW	1040	F	0-4-0ST	
Hook Norton	1889	MW	1127		0-6-0ST	To GWR 1904, to F&RR&H 1907, to GWR 1913

Locomotives possibly employed by JT Firbank on Fishguard Harbour contract

Name	Built	Maker	Wks No		Wheels	Remarks
Bristol	1873	FW	171		0-6-0ST	Sold for Scrap c1907
Weaste	1888	HC	302		0-4-0ST	
Portsmouth	1865	HE	4		0-6-0ST	On Chingford Reservoir contract by 1908
Hunslet	1866	HE	7		0-6-0ST	Sold for Scrap c1907
Brockenhurst	1885	RWH	2023		0-6-0ST	Sold for Scrap c1907
Cliftonville	1876	HE	165		0-6-0ST	Dyffryn Steel & Tinplate, Morriston by November 1912
Wellington	1872	HE	72		0-6-0ST	Sold for Scrap c1907

Amesbury	1890	MW	1190	L	0-6-0ST	
Henry Appleby	1870	HE	45		0-6-0ST	On Chingford Reservoir contract by 1908
Bradford	1870	MW	291	M	0-6-0ST	To Graigola Merthyr Co by 1919
Fox	1862	FW	14		0-6-0ST	Sold for scrap c1907
Walsall	1877	HE	188		0-6-0ST	
Newport	1877	HE	170		0-6-0ST	To Charles Williams, Morriston c1907
Caldew	1867	MW	225	E	0-4-0ST	Also on Clarbeston Road–Letterston contract
Ely	1885	MW	927	M	0-6-0ST	Ex Kirk & Parry No 9

Locomotives employed by Topham, Jones & Railton at Fishguard 1913+

Roath	1900	AE	1412		0-6-0ST	Scrapped 1924
Test	1907	AE	1509		0-4-0ST	To Brancepeth Colliery December 1920
Abertawe	1906	MW	1672	M	0-6-0ST	To Perry & Co (Bow) Ltd 1926
Dynevor	1908	MW	1726	M	0-6-0ST	To Exors of LP Nott c1920

Robert McAlpine is known to have used seven locomotives in Ireland, viz HC759, HC794, HE404, HE457, ex DW&WR No 6A, and possibly HE536. The F&RR&H Board Minutes suggest that as many as ten locomotives were in use on the South Wexford contract. Messrs Brand are also believed to have had two locomotives on the Rosslare Harbour contract, but we have no details. HE457 *Limerick* was initially used by Pearson and went to McAlpine between March 1903 and May 1905.

Waterford	1876	HE	156		0-4-0ST	Used by Smith & Finlayson on WD&LR contract
	1846/7	Sharp	459		2-2-2	Ex GS&WR in 1876 to JW Stanford on WD&LR

APPENDIX D1

WD&LR Passenger and Goods Rolling Stock

Passenger Rolling Stock List

Number	GS&WR No	Class	Length	Wheels	Date	Builder	Compts	Seats	Scrapped	Remarks
1		First	26'1"	6	1878	Metro	3	?24	N/K	
2		First	26'1"	6	1878	Metro	3	?24	N/K	
3		First	26'1"	6	1878	Metro	3	?24	N/K	
4		First	26'1"	6	1879					Ex Composite
1		Second *	28'5"	6	1878	Metro	5	50	N/K	
2		Second *	28'5"	6	1878	Metro	5	50	N/K	
3		Second *	28'5"	6	1878	Metro	5	50	N/K	
1		Third	26'0"	?4	1878	Metro	?5	?50	N/K	
2		Third	26'0"	?4	1878	Metro	?5	?50	N/K	
3		Third	26'0"	?4	1878	Metro	?5	?50	N/K	
4		Third	26'0"	?4	1878	Metro	?5	?50	N/K	
5		Third	26'0"	?4	1878	Metro	?5	?50	N/K	
6		Third	26'0"	?4	1878	Metro	?5	?50	N/K	
7		Third	26'0"	?4	1878	Metro	?5	?50	N/K	

Number	GS&WR No	Class	Length	Wheels	Date	Builder	Compts	Seats	Scrapped	Remarks
8		Third	26'0"	?4	1878	Metro	?5	?50	N/K	
9		Third	26'0"	?4	1878	Metro	?5	?50	N/K	
10		Third		?4	1878	Metro			N/K	?Ex Second in 1894
11		Third		?4	1878	Metro			N/K	?Ex Second in 1894
12		Third							N/K	?Ex Composite in 1894
1		Composite †			c1879				N/K	
2		Composite †			c1879				N/K	
3		Composite †			c1879				N/K	
4		Composite †			c1879				N/K	
1		Brake			1878	Metro			N/K	
2		Brake			1878	Metro			N/K	
3		Brake			1878	Metro			N/K	
4		Goods Brake			1878	Metro			N/K	
5		Goods Brake			1878	Metro			N/K	
6		Brake	24'8"	4	1893	Metro			c1962	To C&MDR as No 6 in 1900 ††
1	293	Horse Box		4	1878	Metro			1911	
2	294	Horse Box		4	1878	Metro			1911	
3	295	Horse Box		4	1878	Metro			1911	
1	232	Truck	15'0"	4	1878	Metro			1914	
2		Truck	15'0"	4	1878	Metro			N/K	

* Two seconds altered to Third in 1894.
† One Compo altered to First and another to Third in 1894.
†† C&MDR = Cork & Macroom Direct Railway

Wagon Stock List

No.	GS&WR No.	Class	Date	Builder	Scrapped	Remarks
1 to 11	5101-5111	Covered Goods	1878			May never actually have carried GS&WR Numbers
12 to 100	5012-5100	Covered Goods	1878			May never actually have carried GS&WR Numbers
101-104	5141-5144	Open	1878			Did not carry GS&WR numbers
105-106	5132-5133	Open	1878			Most never carried GS&WR numbers
107-110	5137-5140	Open	1878			Most never carried GS&WR numbers
111-113	5134-5136	Open	1878			Most never carried GS&WR numbers
114-131	5114-5131	Open	1878			Most never carried GS&WR numbers
132	5146	Timber?		Midland?	1914	Renumbered 8143 in 1899
133	5147	Timber?		Midland?		Renumbered 8144 in 1899
134	5148	Timber?		Midland?	1913	Renumbered 8145 in 1899
135	5149	Timber?		Midland?	1916	Renumbered 8146 in 1899

Three of the Opens were renumbered 5241 to 5243 by the GS&WR but it is not known which wagons.

APPENDIX D2

GS&WR, GWR and NP&FR Passenger Rolling Stock

GS&WR Passenger Stock for Rosslare–Cork Express service

Nos	Built	Wdn	Length	Width	Weight	Seats-1st	Seats-3rd	Type	Lavs	Bogies	Corridor
861	1906	1964	66'0"	9'0"	38½T	12	40	1/3Brake	2Lav	6wh	SC
862	1906	1959	66'0"	9'0"	38½T	12	40	1/3Brake	2Lav	6wh	SC
863	1906	1964	66'0"	9'0"	38½T	12	40	1/3Brake	2Lav	6wh	SC
869	1907	1961	66'0"	9'0"	36T	18	56	1/3Compo		4wh	SC
870	1907	1961	66'0"	9'0"	36T	18	56	1/3Compo		4wh	SC
871	1907	1965	66'0"	9'0"	36T	18	56	1/3Compo		4wh	SC
872	1907	1960	66'0"	9'0"	36T	18	56	1/3Compo		4wh	SC
873	1907	1963	66'0"	9'0"	36T	18	56	1/3Compo		4wh	SC
874	1907	1957	66'0"	9'0"	36T	18	56	1/3Compo		4wh	SC
875	1907	1966	66'0"	9'0"	36T	12	40	1/3Brake	2Lav	4wh	SC
876	1907	1957	66'0"	9'0"	35¾T	16	30	Diner		4wh	CC

GWR Passenger Stock for Ocean Express traffic from Fishguard

Nos	Built	Length	Width	Type	Bogies
874-875	1908	70'0"	9'0"	Baggage	
876-877	1910	70'0"	9'0"	Baggage	6wh
8178-8180	1910	70'0"	9'0"	Brake Firsts	
8181-8196	1910	70'0"	9'0"	Firsts	
9552-9555	1911	70'0"	9'0"	Restaurant	

NP&FR Passenger Stock

No	Built	Withdrawn	Length	Width	GWR No	Compts	Wheels	Builder
1	1894-5	Feb 1932	27'6"	8'0"	7893	2F2T[1]	4wh	BRCW
2	1894-5	Withdrawn between Dec 1927 & Oct 1931	27'6"	8'0"	3983	5T	4wh	BRCW
3	1894-5		27'6"	8'0"	3984	5T	4wh	BRCW
4	1894-5		27'6"	8'0"	3985	5T	4wh	BRCW
5	1894-5		27'6"	8'0"	3986	3T/L&G	4wh	BRCW
6	1894-5		27'6"	8'0"	3987	3T/L&G	4wh	BRCW
7	1894-5	Mar 1910	27'6"	8'0"	3988	3T/L&G	4wh	BRCW
8	1894-5	Oct 1929	27'6"	8'0"	7894	2F2T[1]	4wh	BRCW

1 Later altered to 2S & 2T and then probably 4T (GWR Nos as Thirds unknown). Body height given as 7'0". Dimensions may be internal for all vehicles.

APPENDIX D3

F&RR&H (R&WR section) Wagon Stock

Number	GS&WR No	R/N	Class	Length	Date	Builder	Scrapped	Remarks
1	5244	8273	Open	15'6"?	1894?	Br Marshall?	1913	Nos. 1 to 6 probably ex Mann wagons of 1886.
2	5245	8247	Open	15'6"?	1894?	Br Marshall?	1914	Date of renumbering unknown for these wagons.
3	5246	8304	Open	15'6"?	1894?	Br Marshall?	1913	
4	5247	8244	Open	15'6"?	1894?	Br Marshall?		
5	5248	8364	Open	15'6"?	1894?	Br Marshall?		
6	5249	8384	Open	15'6"?	1894?	Br Marshall?		
1			Covered		1894?		Not Known	
2			Covered		1894?		Not Known	
3			Covered		1894?		Not Known	
4			Covered		1894?		Not Known	
5			Covered		1894?		Not Known	
6			Covered		1894?		Not Known	
7			Covered		1894?		Not Known	
8			Covered		1894?		Not Known	
9			Covered		1894?		Not Known	
10			Covered		1894?		Not Known	
11			Covered		1894?		Not Known	
12			Covered		1894?		Not Known	
1	7320		Cattle		1894?		1911	
2	7321		Cattle		1894?		1910	
3	7322		Cattle		1894?		1910	
4	7323		Cattle		1894?		1911	
5	7324		Cattle		1894?		1910	
6	7325		Cattle		1894?		1909	

APPENDIX D4

NP&FR Wagon Stock as handed over to GWR in 1898

Number	GWR No	Class	Length	Wheel Dia	Wheel Base	Weight	Load	Builder	Cost
1	30177	Open	14'6"	3'0"	9'0"	5t15c0q	8t	Birmingham	£68
2	30178	Open	14'6"	3'0"	9'0"	5t13c3q	8t	Birmingham	£68
3	30179	Open	14'6"	3'0"	9'0"	5t15c1q	8t	Birmingham	£68
4	30180	Open	14'6"	3'0"	9'0"	5t15c1q	8t	Birmingham	£68
5	30181	Open	14'6"	3'0"	9'0"	5t15c1q	8t	Birmingham	£68
6	30182	Open	14'6"	3'0"	9'0"	5t15c2q	8t	Birmingham	£68
7	48987	Twin Timber	13'7"	3'0"	8'0"	5t6c1q	n/k	Birmingham	£69
8	48988	Twin Timber	13'7"	3'0"	8'0"	5t7c1q	n/k	Birmingham	£69
9	48989	Twin Timber	13'7"	3'0"	8'0"	5t5c0q	n/k	Birmingham	£69
10	48990	Twin Timber	13'7"	3'0"	8'0"	5t5c3q	n/k	Birmingham	£69
11	68992	Cattle (Med)	16'0"	3'0"	9'0"	6t0c2q	n/k	Birmingham	£77-10-0
12	68993	Cattle (Med)	16'0"	3'0"	9'0"	6t1c1q	n/k	Birmingham	£77-10-0
13	68994	Cattle (Med)	16'0"	3'0"	9'0"	6t0c1q	n/k	Birmingham	£77-10-0
14	68995	Cattle (Med)	16'0"	3'0"	9'0"	6t0c3q	n/k	Birmingham	£77-10-0
15	68996	Cattle (Med)	16'0"	3'0"	9'0"	6t0c0q	n/k	Birmingham	£77-10-0
16	68997	Cattle (Med)	16'0"	3'0"	9'0"	6t0c2q	n/k	Birmingham	£77-10-0
17	68998	Cattle (Lge)	18'0"	3'0"	10'6"	6t17c1q	10t	Midland	£98
18	68999	Cattle (Lge)	18'0"	3'0"	10'6"	6t17c2q	10t	Midland	£98
19	69000	Cattle (Lge)	18'0"	3'0"	10'6"	6t17c0q	10t	Midland	£98
	56984	Gds BV	15'4"	3'0"	9'0"	Not marked			£15 *
		Tvlg Crane			8'7"			Not plated	£120 †
		Check Trucks		3'6"	6'7"				£5 each ††

* Van in bad condition, ex GWR in April 1896.

† In good order.

†† Two trucks to run with crane.

GWR Engineering Tip Wagons to NP&FR and sold on to F&RR&H in 1899.

Number	Type	Built	To NP&FR	To F&RR&H	Length	Wheel Base	Tare Weight	Load	Lot No
1	Side Tip	25 Apr 1896	Mar 1899	25 Oct 1899	10'9"	3'5"	4t9c2q		119
4	Side Tip	25 Apr 1896	Dec 1898	25 Oct 1899	10'9"	3'5"	4t9c2q		119
5	Side Tip	25 Apr 1896	Mar 1899	25 Oct 1899	10'9"	3'5"	4t9c2q		119
6	Side Tip	25 Apr 1896		25 Oct 1899	10'9"	3'5"	4t9c2q		119
7	Side Tip	25 Apr 1896		25 Oct 1899	10'9"	3'5"	4t9c2q		119
10	Side Tip	25 Apr 1896	Mar 1899	25 Oct 1899	10'9"	3'5"	4t9c2q		119
11	Side Tip	25 Apr 1896	Mar 1899	25 Oct 1899	10'9"	3'5"	4t9c2q		119
12	Side Tip	25 Apr 1896	Mar 1899	25 Oct 1899	10'9"	3'5"	4t9c2q		119
13	Side Tip	25 Apr 1896	Dec 1898	25 Oct 1899	10'9"	3'5"	4t9c2q		119
14	Side Tip	25 Apr 1896		25 Oct 1899	10'9"	3'5"	4t9c2q		119
15	Side Tip	25 Apr 1896	Mar 1899	25 Oct 1899	10'9"	3'5"	4t9c2q		119
17	Side Tip	25 Apr 1896	Mar 1899	25 Oct 1899	10'9"	3'5"	4t9c2q		119
18	Side Tip	25 Apr 1896	Dec 1898	25 Oct 1899	10'9"	3'5"	4t9c2q		119

No	Type	Built	To NP&FR	To F&RR&H	Length	Wheel Base	Tare Weight	Load	Lot No
21	Side Tip	25 Apr 1896		25 Oct 1899	10'9"	3'5"	4t9c2q		119
22	Side Tip	25 Apr 1896	Dec 1898	25 Oct 1899	10'9"	3'5"	4t9c2q		119
23	Side Tip	25 Apr 1896	Dec 1898	25 Oct 1899	10'9"	3'5"	4t9c2q		119
24	Side Tip	25 Apr 1896	Dec 1898	25 Oct 1899	10'9"	3'5"	4t9c2q		119
28	Side Tip	25 Apr 1896	Dec 1898	25 Oct 1899	10'9"	3'5"	4t9c2q		119
30	Side Tip	25 Apr 1896	Dec 1898	25 Oct 1899	10'9"	3'5"	4t9c2q		119
32	Side Tip	25 Apr 1896		25 Oct 1899	10'9"	3'5"	4t9c2q		119 [1]
34	Side Tip	25 Apr 1896	Dec 1898	25 Oct 1899	10'9"	3'5"	4t9c2q		119
35	Side Tip	25 Apr 1896	Mar 1899	25 Oct 1899	10'9"	3'5"	4t9c2q		119
38	Side Tip	25 Apr 1896	Mar 1899	25 Oct 1899	10'9"	3'5"	4t9c2q		119
42	Side Tip	25 Apr 1896	Dec 1898	25 Oct 1899	10'9"	3'5"	4t9c2q		119
43	Side Tip	25 Apr 1896	Mar 1899	25 Oct 1899	10'9"	3'5"	4t9c2q		119
44	Side Tip	25 Apr 1896	Mar 1899	25 Oct 1899	10'9"	3'5"	4t9c2q		119
46	Side Tip	25 Apr 1896	Mar 1899	25 Oct 1899	10'9"	3'5"	4t9c2q		119
48	Side Tip	25 Apr 1896	Mar 1899	25 Oct 1899	10'9"	3'5"	4t9c2q		119
50	Side Tip	25 Apr 1896	Mar 1899	25 Oct 1899	10'9"	3'5"	4t9c2q		119
51	Side Tip	25 Apr 1896	Mar 1899	25 Oct 1899	10'9"	3'5"	4t9c2q		119
54	Side Tip	25 Apr 1896	Mar 1899	25 Oct 1899	10'9"	3'5"	4t9c2q		119
57	Side Tip	25 Apr 1896	Mar 1899	25 Oct 1899	10'9"	3'5"	4t9c2q		119
58	Side Tip	25 Apr 1896	Mar 1899	25 Oct 1899	10'9"	3'5"	4t9c2q		119
59	Side Tip	25 Apr 1896	Mar 1899	25 Oct 1899	10'9"	3'5"	4t9c2q		119
61	Side Tip	25 Apr 1896	Dec 1898	25 Oct 1899	10'9"	3'5"	4t9c2q		119
65	End Tip	23 Apr 1898		25 Oct 1899	7'4"	3'6"	2t18c2q	4cu yds	g215 [2]

The following additional tip wagons were sent to Mr Mann at Goodwick in 1901:

No	Type	Built	Length	Wheel Base	Load
75 to 80	Side Tip	21 Oct 1901	6'4½"		
81 to 83	Side Tip	21 Oct 1901	5'0"		
98 & 99	End Tip	21 Oct 1901	5'2"	1'11"?	
100 to 114	Side Tip	Oct 1901	10'0"	4'5½"	4½cu yds
115	End Tip	21 Oct 1901	5'2"	1'11"?	

---

1   May not have been with NP&FR.

2   Sold direct to F&RR&H.

APPENDIX E

An incomplete list of staff at various stations on the WD&LR and W&WR

Stations	Surname	First Name	Position	Appointed	Notes
Lismore	Onions	Joseph	Station Master	Mar 1893	Originally appointed 1 March 1861 Pensioned 1 October 1899
	Maher	William	Signalman	27 Apr 1857	Wages 21s per week
	Miller	William D	Station Master	29 Oct 1903	To Waterford
	Ryan	William F	Station Master	5 Oct 1878	To Ballyduff 19 May 1899

All staff allowed 2s additional per week for lodgings. Porter allowed 3s per week extra for acting as Guard. Opened for passengers on 1 October 1872 and for goods on 25 November 1872.

Stations	Surname	First Name	Position	Appointed	Notes
Fermoy	Berry	George	Station Master		Originally appointed 26 April 1858
	O'Callaghan	Edward	Head Porter	19 Dec 1879	Appointed Station Master on 14 October 1890
Tallow Road	Hederman	William	Station Master	28 Nov 1849	
	O'Keeffe	John	Station Master		To Queenstown 18 December 1899
	Duffy	Christopher	Station Master	19 Dec 1899	To Kingsbridge 4 June 1900
	Sheedy	James	Station Master	1 July 1900	
Clondulane	Sullivan	Michael	Station Master	12 Jan 1874	
	Power	Thomas	Station Master	1 Apr 1880	7 June 1904
Ballyduff	Jones	James	Station Master	4 Jan 1866	To Bruree 8 July 1892
	O'Keeffe	Thomas	Station Master		Resigned 18 April 1899
	Regan	Denis	Station Master	19 May 1899	
Kilmeaden	Burgess	John	Station Master	Sep 1889	
	Mulcahy	George	Station Master	1 May 1892	To Kilmeaden 25 April 1904
Carroll's Cross	Quinn	Elizabeth	Station Master	5 Sep 1894	Retired 30 September 1900
	Power	Michael	Station Master	1 Oct 1900	
Kilmacthomas	Hill	James	Station Master	1878	Resigned 1 February 1899
	Hill	Edward	Station Master	1 Feb 1899	
	Walsh	Maurice	Signalman	3 Dec 1892	
Durrow	Greene	RJ	Station Master	20 May 1890	
	Flynn	John	Station Master	1 June 1899	
Dungarvan	Cunningham	Patrick	Station Master	1 July 1878	Died 25 May 1902
	Dixon	William	Station Master	15 June 1902	To Cahir 19 February 1903

Porter is allowed 2s for relieving Signalman. Two extra porters sanctioned 1 January 1901 consequent on improved train service.

Stations	Surname	First Name	Position	Appointed	Notes
Cappagh	Reynolds	John	Station Master	20 June 1878	Resigned 30 September 1899
	Ottley	William	Station Master	18 Nov 1899	

Stations	Surname	First Name	Position	Appointed	Notes
Cappoquin	Keily	John	Station Master	21 Aug 1878	
	Kelleher	U	Signalman	1 Aug 1878	
Wexford (Dist. Supt. Office)	Gelling	Frederick W	District Supt		To DS, Dublin 1 Jan 1901 & Tuam 1 Jan 1902. No trace after.
	Redmond	TS	Clerk	28 July 1895	Resigned 31 July 1902
	Edwards	PR	District Agent	5 Sep 1896	To Cork 10 April 1900
	Doyle	Lewis C	District Agent	1 Aug 1902	To Naas 27 May 1904
	Moore	William	District Agent	27 May 1904	
South Wexford	Spratt	William	Station Master		To Ballindine 5 January 1903.
	Cousins	Andrew	Clerk	29 Aug 1904	
	Callaghan	Daniel	Guard	6 Aug 1894	To Rosslare Harbour as Station Master 1 October 1901.
	Spratt	Joseph	Assistant Guard	23 Jan 1902	5 December 1902
	Healy	Michael	Gateman		

Extra man allowed during summer months. Station Master removed to Ballindine owing to station being worked by Agent.

Stations	Surname	First Name	Position	Appointed	Notes
Rosslare [presumably later Kilrane]	Spratt	Thomas	Station Master		
	McKenna	John	Lightkeeper		Died 1 February 1903
	Williams	James	Lightkeeper	26 Feb 1903	

Lightkeeper allowed 2s additional for Sunday duty.

Stations	Surname	First Name	Position	Appointed	Notes
Rosslare Harbour	Canning	William John	Station Master	4 Sep 1894	Absconded 15 September 1901
	Callaghan	Daniel	Station Master	1 Oct 1901	
Waterford South [closed 1 Feb 1908]	O'Keeffe	John	Station Master		
	Gaule	Lawrence	Signalman	15 June 1895	Wages initially 18s per week
	Grant	Thomas	Signalman	29 Aug 1906	18s
	Caulfield	Joseph	Signalman	15 Apr 1907	18s
	Kenny	Michael	Signalman	30 Sep 1907	18s. All four signalmen transferred to Waterford North.
Wexford South [also see above]	Hayes	Patrick J	Station Master	15 Oct 1906	
	Langton	William	Ticket Collector	3 May 1909	
	Hanrahan	Edward	Guard	15 Aug 1906	Wages 15s 6d
	Cleary	James	Guard		15s 6d
	Hackett	Patrick	Head Porter	8 Oct 1906	Wages 20s
	Meade	Patrick	Signalman	24 Apr 1907	Wages 15s 6d
	Kenny	Michael	Signalman	1 July 1906	Signalman at Felthouse
	Hanan	James	Signalman	1 July 1906	
	Daly	Jeremiah	Signalman	11 Oct 1906	
	Landy	Stephen	Foreman	25 July 1906	Wages 27s 6d
	Madden	Thomas	Signalman	27 Sep 1907	
	McCarthy	Daniel	Signalman	9 Dec 1907	
	Phillips	Henry	Signalman	17 Feb 1908	
	Treacy	James	Signalman	30 Dec 1908	
Ballycullane	Connolly	John	Station Master	25 Jun 1906	Station opened for Goods traffic 25 June 1906 and Passenger 1 August
	McEvoy	Denis	Signalman	25 July 1906	
	Meade	Patrick	Porter	12 Oct 1906	

Stations	Surname	First Name	Position	Appointed	Notes
Bridgetown	Glavin	Patrick	Station Master	25 June 1906	Wages 20s per week
	Moylan	Stephen	Signalman	24 July 1906	Wages 18s
	Connor	Patrick	Porter	8 Oct 1906	Wages 15s 6d
	Porter is allowed 2s per week for relieving Signalman, same applying at Ballycullane.				
Campile	Callanan	John	Station Master	25 June 1906	
	Walsh	Robert	Signalman	24 July 1906	
	Brien	William	Signalman	24 July 1906	
	Stone	Michael	Signalman	24 July 1906	
	Tynan	Patrick	Signalman	29 Aug 1906	
	Walsh	Michael	Porter	15 Oct 1906	
Duncormick	Dwyer	John	Station Master	25 Jun 1906	
	Grehan	James	Signalman	25 July 1906	
	McGuinness	Patrick	Porter	1 Nov 1906	
Killinick	Mannion	Thomas	Station Master	25 Jun 1906	
	McCarthy	Daniel	Signalman	15 Oct 1906	
	Dempsey	Michael	Porter	28 July 1906	
	Somers	Michael	Porter	8 Oct 1906	Appointed Signalman on 24 June 1908
Wellington Bridge	Walsh	JH	Station Master	25 June 1906	? To Rosslare Pier as Assistant to Harbour Master [see below]
	Wallace	Edward	Signalman	29 Aug 1906	
	Tynan	Patrick	Porter	2 July 1906	
	O'Neill	Richard	Porter	22 Nov 1906	
Rosslare Pier	Adderley	Thomas	Foreman		Discharged 30 November 1901
	Leary	William	Timekeeper		Discharged 30 November 1901
	Roche	Paul	Timekeeper	30 Nov 1901	Discharged 15 March 1902
	Harris	John	Porter		
	White	James	Porter		
	Ennis	James	Porter		
	White	Patrick	Lightkeeper		
	McKenna	John	Lightkeeper		Lightkeeper at Hill of Sea
	Moore	William	Harbour Master	31 Aug 1906	
	Radford	William J	Harbour Master	1 Mar 1907	
	Walsh	JH	Asst Hrb Master	31 May 1907	
	Mitchell	Thomas	Asst Hrb Master	11 May 1910	
	Moroney	Michael	Inspector	29 Aug 1906	
	Mooney	Michael	Inspector	4 June 1907	
	Clery	James	Guard	15 Feb 1909	
	Linegar	Thomas	Passenger Guard	30 Aug 1906	
	Ottley	James	Signalman	1 Nov 1906	
	Dempsey	Michael	Signalman	4 Jan 1907	Signalman at Ballygeary
	White	Patrick	Lightkeeper	20 Aug 1906	Wages 15s per week
	O'Toole	Richard	Policeman	3 Oct 1906	Allowed 2s 6d for working evening trains
	Dooley	Christopher	Carriage Cleaner	9 Oct 1906	Ex Locomotive Department. Wages 20s per week
	Mooney	Peter	Head Checker	22 Nov 1906	

APPENDIX F1

Ocean Liners known to have called at Fishguard during the period 1908–14

Name of Vessel	Built	GRT	Remarks	Scrapped
Anchor Line				
City of Rome	1891	8,415T	Originally owned by Inman Lines; t/t. Anchor Lines 1882.	1902
Booth Line				
Ambrose	1903	4,588T	AMC 1914; purchased by Admiralty 1915 and renamed HMS *Ambrose*.	n/k
Anselm	1905	5,442T	Sold to Argentina 1922 and renamed *Commodoro Rivadavia*.	n/k
Antony	1907	6,446T	Torpedoed & sunk off Coninbeg lightship 1917 with loss of 55 lives.	1917
Augustine	1880	3,849T	Ex *Grantully Castle*; purchased from Castle Mail Pkt Co 1896 and renamed *Augustine*.	1912
Hilary	1908	6,329T	Torpedoed and sunk off Shetland Islands in 1917 while an AMC.	1917
Lanfranc	1906	6,287T	Torpedoed and sunk off Havre 1917 while in use as Hospital Ship; loss of 34 lives.	1917
Cunard Line				
Aquitania	1914	45,647T	AMC 1914; TS 1915; HS 1916: TS 1918-9; Rtnd 1919; TS 1939-48:	1950
Campania	1893	12,950T	AC 1914; Broke moorings Firth of Forth 1918 and sunk after collision with HMS *Revenge*.	1918
Carmania	1905	19,524T	AMC 1914; Rtnd. 1916.	1932
Caronia	1905	19,687T	AMC 1914; TS 1916; Rtnd 1919; Sold 1932 to Japan and renamed *Taiseiyo Maru*.	n/k
Lusitania	1907	31,550T	Torpedoed May 1915 off Old Head of Kinsale with loss of 1,198 lives.	1915
Mauretania	1907	31,938T	TS 1914-9.	1935

AMC = Armed Merchant Cruiser
HS = Hospital Ship
Rtnd = Returned (to owners)
TS = Troop Ship

APPENDIX F2

List of Vessels known to have worked at Fishguard under F&RR&H

Name	Built	Acquired	Disposed of	Builder	Length	Breadth	Depth	GRT	Notes
Atalanta (or *Atlanta*)	1907	Oct 1910	1924	Gourlay Bros.	170.3'	32.2'	15.3'	577	Originally for London & South Western Rly.
Great Southern	1902	1902	1934	Laird Bros	275.8'	36.3'	15.2'	1339	
Great Western II	1902	1902	Sep 1933	Laird Bros	275.8'	36.3'	15.2'	1339	
Great Western III	1934	1934		Cammell Laird	282.9'	40.4'	16.1'	1659	

Name	Built	Acquired	Disposed of	Builder	Length	Breadth	Depth	GRT	Notes
Melmore[1]	1892	1905	1912	D J Dunlop Port Glasgow	156.2'	25.8'	11.3'	412	Built for Earl of Leitrim
Mercury	1903	1903	1933	Robert Napier, Glasgow					
No 1	1906	1906	n/k		95.0'	25.0'	5.0'		Flush-deck Lighter
No 182	1906	1906	n/k		18.4'	5.9'			Motor Launch
Palmerston	1864	1883	n/k	Simpson, London	96.5'	18.5'	9.4'	109	Purchased from Dover Harbour Board 1883
Pembroke	1880	1880	1925	Laird Bros	235.5'	27.6'	13.1'	927	
Pen Cw	1912	24 Oct 1912	Jun 1927	JT Eltringham	105.1'	21.1'	9.1'	168	Paddle Tug
Pen Cw II	1922	1922	1938		40.0'	11.0'			Motor Launch
Porteur No 5	1884	1898	n/k	Holland - actual bldr n/k					
Roebuck	1897	1897	1915	Naval Constn. Barrow	280.0'	34.5'	16.8'	1281	Registered to F&RR&H Company
Sir Francis Drake II	1908	1908	1954	Cammell Laird	148.9'	38.8'	14.1'	478	Twin screw Tender Unusually tall funnel
Sir John R Wright	1909	1921	Mar 1938					95	Tug
Sir Walter Raleigh II	1908	1908	1947	Cammell Laird	148.9'	38.8'	14.1'	478	
Smeaton	1883	1883	1929	W Allsup & Son Preston	125.2'	35.1'	11.1'	369	Tender. At Fishguard 1909-10
St Andrew I	1908	1908	Sep 1933	John Brown	351.1'	41.1'	16.5'	2495	Renamed *Fishguard* in 1930
St Andrew II	1932	1932	1966	Cammell Laird	327.2'	46.7'	17.7'	2702	
St David I	1906	25 Jan 1906	Sep 1933	John Brown	350.8'	41.1'	16.5'	2529	Renamed *Rosslare* in 1932
St David II	1932	1932	Jan 1944	Cammell Laird	327.2'	46.7'	17.7'	2702	Sunk at Anzio
St David III	1947	Jul 1947	1969	Cammell Laird	300.0'	48.0'	18.5'	3352	
St George	1906	1906	May 1913	Cammell Laird	352.0'	41.1'	16.2'	2456	To Canadian Pacific Rly
St Patrick I	1906	24 Feb 1906	Sep 1929	John Brown	350.8'	41.1'	16.5'	2531	Sold for scrap after fire at Fishguard
St Patrick II	1930	1930	Jun 1941	A Stephen & Sons, Linthouse	281.3'	41.1'	16.3'	1922	Bombed & sunk near Fishguard 13 June 1941
St Patrick III	1947	May 1947	1949	Cammell Laird	300.0'	48.0'	18.5'	3352	Transferred to English Channel 1949
Voltaic	1867	1896	1900	McNab & Co. Greenock	209.4'	26.7'	14.3'	580	See text
Magnetic[2]	1863			Tod & McGregor	210.1'	27.1'	14.1'	571	
Waterford II	1912	1912	Sep 1924	Swan Hunter & Wigham	275.2'	38.7'	16.5'	1204	
Stena Lynx III	1996	1998	2011	Incat, Tasmania, Australia	264'5"	85' 4"	10'2"		Sold to South Korea & renamed *Sunflower 2*
Stena Europe	1981	2002	Current	Gotaverken, Gothenburg	489'02"	87'1"	20'1"	24828	1400 passengers

1 Only on Fishguard–Rosslare service August 1906 to April 1907. Generally employed Weymouth–Channel Islands and Plymouth–Nantes.
2 Although not a sister ship to the *Voltaic*, *Magnetic* was also owned by the Belfast SS Co and had almost identical dimensions.

APPENDIX G

Some Personalities

As the two most important individuals involved in the formation of the F&RR&H, it is important that we take a look at the background to Joseph Rowlands and James Cartland. Joseph Rowlands was born about 1841 in Whittington, about three miles east of Oswestry in Shropshire. His father, John, is described in the 1841 census as being an agricultural labourer, aged in his forties, while his mother, Jane, is shown as being 43 years of age. Joseph had five older siblings, in addition to which there was at least one younger brother, Edward, born about 1850. Both Jacob, aged 9 in 1841, and Joseph were to enter the legal profession in later life.

Joseph married Comfort Williams in 1864, one of four children of Richard and Esther Williams of Bloxwich in Staffordshire, where Richard was employed as a Blast Furnace Manager. Comfort had taken her name from her paternal grandmother, who lived in Whitchurch. Joseph Rowlands obviously did well in his chosen career, as in 1880 he had a mansion built for himself and his family at Bromsgrove. Lickey Grange was contemporaneously described as a large, brick, gabled house, "mildly Gothic in design", with two-storey canted bays; the estate comprised the mansion, a lodge and about 100 acres of land. By the time of their move to Lickey Grange, Joseph and Comfort had six children, at least one of whom was destined to enter the family legal business, located at 41 Temple Row, Birmingham, also the offices during the Syndicate period of the F&RR&H. Comfort passed away in 1911, by which time Joseph had already sold Lickey Grange some three years earlier to Sir Herbert Austin, founder of the Austin Motor Company at Longbridge, near Birmingham.[1] By 1911 Joseph Rowlands was living in more modest surroundings at Hill Crest on Richmond Hill Road in King's Norton

along with his son, Osbert. By co-incidence this was the area in which his partner in the F&RR&H, James Cartland, had also lived. It seems likely that the financial burden imposed by his involvement in the Fishguard Company may have contributed to the sale of the Lickey estate and the acquisition of the more modest accommodation. Joseph Rowlands passed away on 28th June 1926, by which time he was living in Malvern.

James Frank Howard Cartland, born about 1852, was one of at least seven children of John and Ann Cartland of Birmingham, where the family had set up a brass foundry business some 30 years earlier at Constitution Hill. The family originally came from Lanarkshire where they are chronicled back to at least 1200; a small village several miles northwest of the county town of Lanark has taken the family name. James married Flora Falkner, another Scot, reputed to be a direct descendant of Robert the Bruce, in 1875 in the fashionable London district of Kensington. James was a notable figure in Birmingham public life and was twice offered a Baronetcy and a Knighthood for his services to the city, all of which he turned down. The family lived in a large house in what was then open countryside in King's Norton. James Cartland became overstretched in financing the F&RR&H and, when the banks called in their loans, he tragically took his own life in 1903.

The couple had only one son, James Bertram Falkner Cartland, who later married Mary (Polly) Hamilton Scobell[2]; a daughter, Mary Barbara Cartland, was born on 9th July 1901, who was later to become famous as a prolific writer of romantic novels. Her father, Major James Cartland, served as an officer in the 3rd Worcester Regiment and was reported as missing in action, presumed killed, in France on 27th May 1918, shortly before the end of the war.

---

1 Herbert Austin, after spending some time in Melbourne, Australia, became manager of the newly formed Wolseley Tool & Motor Car Company in 1901. He left Wolseley in 1905 to form his own Company. Sir Herbert remained at Lickey Grange for 31 years.

2 The Scobells were an even older family than the Cartlands, one of them being High Sheriff of Devon in 1032.

Among other early directors of the Syndicate were Richard Henry Combe, George Watkins Yardley, a barrister of Knightsbridge, J. Farquharson Remnant, MP, of Farnham in Surrey, Frederick Lee, another barrister of London and Robert William Broomfield. We know nothing regarding the latter gentleman, other than as a director of the NP&FR and of the F&RR&H Syndicate. However, as he had two addresses in Lincoln's Inn, it is reasonable to assume that he was also a member of the legal profession. Richard Henry Combe was a member of a London brewing firm which had been in the family since the late 18th century. Harvey Christian Combe[3] had acquired Messrs Gyfford & Company, a small brewery at Upper Thames Street in the Long Acres district of London in June 1787, along with a London sugar refiner, George Shum. In the years following various other London breweries were acquired. In due course Harvey Combe Junior succeeded his father, the firm becoming Combe & Company in 1839. Harvey Junior died in 1858, leaving his share in the business to two of his nephews, Richard Henry and Charles Combe, and by the end of the 1880s it had become the fourth largest brewery in London. Richard Henry Combe was born in April 1829 and died on 8th April 1900. The firm merged in July 1898 with two other breweries to form Messrs Watney, Combe, Reid & Company, Messrs Combe & Company going into voluntary liquidation in January of the following year. However, the Combe family were to maintain an interest until the 1960s in what eventually became Messrs Watney Mann Limited, the UK's largest brewing concern.

Alexander Henderson was the intermediary between the GWR and the F&RR&H when it became clear at the beginning of 1898 that the latter company was not in a position to go forward on its own. Henderson was born on 28th September 1850, the second child of George and Eliza Henderson of Langholm, Dumfriesshire. At the age of 17, he entered the City firm of Messrs Deloitte, who were Accountants to the GWR. He moved to the stock-broking firm of Eyton, Greenwood & Eyton, and became a member of the Stock Exchange at the young age of 22. He

married Jane Ellen Davis in 1874 and they had seven children. Alexander, along with his younger brothers, was involved in the development of the Buenos Aires Great Southern Railway, for which the Government had guaranteed a 7% dividend. In 1888 Alexander Henderson became a director of the Manchester Ship Canal Company and subsequently was involved in efforts to bail out Barings Bank. Through this latter connection he became a director of the Manchester Sheffield & Lincolnshire Railway, forming a syndicate to underwrite that Company's London extension. He has been credited with obtaining the services of Sam Fay, and possibly John G Robinson and Dixon Davies, respectively as Locomotive Superintendent and Solicitor, for that Company. Henderson was a Liberal-Unionist MP for West Staffordshire from 1906 to 1913, and then for St George's Hanover Square from 1913 to 1916; he was raised to the peerage as Lord Faringdon in the latter year, having already been knighted in 1902. He was deputy-chairman of the London & North Eastern Railway at the time of his death on 17th March 1934.

One of the leading characters in the story of railways in the south of County Waterford was the Duke of Devonshire. The Cavendish family descended from Sir John Cavendish, who reportedly took his name from the Suffolk village of Cavendish, where he held an estate in the fourteenth century. The 6th Duke never married, being popularly known as the "Batchelor Duke". He first visited Lismore in 1812 and made great efforts to develop his estates there and at Chatsworth, sparing no expense. Following a stroke in 1854, the 6th Duke died on 18th January 1858, and was succeeded by his cousin, William Cavendish, 2nd Earl of Burlington, and son of William Cavendish and the Hon. Louisa O'Callaghan, eldest daughter of Cornelius O'Callaghan, 1st Baron Lismore. The 6th Duke married in 1829 Lady Blanche Georgiana Howard, the fourth daughter of the 6th Earl of Carlisle. They in turn had four children. His wife died in 1840, and William devoted his energies to the management of the Burlington estates in Lancashire and Sussex.

After succeeding as 7th Duke of Devonshire in 1858, he took an active interest in his Irish estates, under the control of Francis Edmond Curry. In England,

---

3 Harvey Christian Combe was later an Alderman of the City of London, Lord Mayor in 1799 and later still an MP.

the Duke was responsible for the development of the Furness Railway, steel works and shipbuilding and dock facilities at Barrow in Lancashire. By 1874 he was reported to be one of the richest men in England, with a personal fortune of over £300,000. As is related in the relevant chapters, the 7th Duke was responsible for the building of the F&LR and was heavily involved financially in the WD&LR. An Obituary in *The Irish Times* for 23rd December 1891 referred to the Duke as being with no exaggeration the best landlord in Ireland. Lismore Castle is still owned by the Dukes of Devonshire but is lived in for only a short period each year. The 7th Duke was succeeded by his second son, who became the 8th Duke, having used the title Marquess of Hartington until 1891.

When dealing with the Duke of Devonshire's involvement with the F&LR and the WD&LR, some mention must be made of the Currey family. Benjamin Currey (1786-1848) was a lawyer and worked for some years on the Duke's legal affairs before being appointed auditor in 1827. He was also prominent in Parliament and on the day of his death it was announced that Queen Victoria had appointed him to the important office of Clerk Assistant of the Parliament. Benjamin Currey was closely involved in the formation of the Furness Railway as the line ran through the lands of the Duke of Devonshire; in fact, Currey was the line's first Chairman until his sudden death on 13th March 1848. Benjamin was succeeded in 1848 as auditor of the Devonshire Estates by his eldest son William, who remained in the role until 1886. In turn William's son, Francis Alfred Currey (incorrectly referred to in some references as Frederick Alfred), born in London in 1851, succeeded his father and continued as auditor until 1916. His name appears on a number of occasions in the WD&LR minute books. Benjamin's third son, Henry, became an architect and was responsible for the design of St Thomas's Hospital in London.

Benjamin Currey's younger brother, William Samuel Curry (note different spelling of the surname), was the resident agent at Lismore. His eldest son, Francis Edmund acted as assistant to his father from 1837, becoming head agent of the Lismore estate in 1839, retaining this role until 1885, apart from the year 1882. He went to Cambridge University where he studied law, later serving as a local magistrate and poor law guardian in Co. Waterford. Francis Edmund was a shareholder and director of a number of railway companies and was a pioneer in photography in Ireland. He was a director of the WD&LR from the time of its formation in 1872, becoming Deputy Chairman of the Company in 1887 and Chairman in 1891 on the death of Abraham Denny; he remained as Chairman until his death on 6th June 1896 at the age of 82. In making reference to his passing, the Board stated that he was since "its (the Company) formation was so actively identified with its interests, and which, to the close of his valuable life, he did so much to sustain and promote."

James Ramsden was born in Liverpool in 1822 and served his apprenticeship with the Liverpool firm of Bury, Curtis & Kennedy, later working under Edward Bury at the Wolverton Works of the London & Birmingham Railway. Ramsden was appointed Locomotive Superintendent of the Furness railway as from 1st January 1846. With the death of the Chairman, Benjamin Currey, in 1848, Ramsden was appointed to the post of general manager, a position he held until becoming managing director in 1866; he remained in the latter position until 1895. Ramsden was responsible for the establishment of the Barrow Shipbuilding Company in 1871, much of the capital for the new enterprise reported to have come from Furness Railway shareholders, including the Duke of Devonshire. The first vessel launched at the new yard, on 12th May 1873, was Ramsden's personal yacht, *Aries*. This was followed by an order for four passenger/cargo vessels for the Indian trade. James Ramsden was knighted by Queen Victoria in 1872 in recognition of his services to the town of Barrow-in-Furness. He became the town's first Mayor, serving five consecutive terms. Sir James Ramsden died in Barrow-in-Furness on 19th October 1896; a year after his death the shipyard was sold to Messrs Vickers and was to become synonymous with building ships for the Royal Navy.

APPENDIX H

Lifeboats at Fishguard and Rosslare

As far as is known, no history of the lifeboat station at Fishguard has been written, but we do know that a lifeboat was first established in 1822, presumably based in the old harbour on the opposite side of the bay to the present ferry terminal. This boat was built locally for a sum of £95 and was involved in a number of rescues prior to being replaced about 1846. The Royal National Lifeboat Institution (RNLI)[1] established their first station at Fishguard in 1855 at the request of local inhabitants, a new boat, the *Sir Edward Perrott*, being provided from RNLI funds in 1862 at a cost of £153. During its 23 year sojourn at Fishguard a total of 117 lives were saved in 32 launches. Numbered among these were 46 sailors rescued on the night of 16th November 1882; on that date the lifeboat launched no less than five times to the rescue of 15 different vessels.

A second *Sir Edward Perrott* was on station for four years, being replaced in 1889 by the *Elizabeth Mary* which remained until 1907, when the station at Fishguard Harbour was closed. A second lifeboat station had been opened in 1869 on the Goodwick side of Fishguard Bay and up until 1994 has saved a total of 521 lives in 439 launches.

Complaints were made to Mr Inglis in October 1899 by Capt. Nepean, the Chief Inspector of Lifeboats that the harbour works were prejudicially affecting the working of the lifeboat, Inglis recommending the carrying out of temporary works at an estimated cost of £150. Section 14 of the F&RR&H Act of 1899 obliged the Company to construct, at their own cost, a new lifeboat house and slipway in lieu of the existing one, which required to be removed to allow railway works to proceed. Correspondence with Capt. Nepean led to a recommendation from the engineer in November 1904 that a sum of £200 should be contributed towards the cost of a temporary lifeboat house. Inglis reported

again in February 1910 that further harbour works on the Quay Wall extension would necessitate the removal of the lifeboat house at an estimated cost of £767, a new house being opened in the following year.

How cost escalated with the provision of lifeboats is illustrated by a comparison with the figures quoted above and the provision of an Arun class boat in 1981, which cost approximately £300,000. An inshore 'D' class lifeboat first arrived at Fishguard on 21st April 1995, being replaced on 24th July of the following year by D505 *Arthur Bygraves*. Currently the inshore service is provided by D652 *Team Effort*, which arrived on station on 10th April 2006. The current off-shore lifeboat is a Trent class ON-1198 (14-03) *Blue Peter VII*, provided in 1994 with funds donated by viewers of the BBC children's programme.

A lifeboat operated between 1838 and 1925 at Rosslare Point or Fort at the southern entrance to Wexford Harbour, with some short gaps in service. Following an inspection in February 1896 by the deputy chief inspector of the RNLI, he recommended the establishment of a station at, and the transfer of

Fishguard Harbour's RNLI Trent Class lifeboat ON-1198 (14-03) *Blue Peter VII* awaits its next call-out in May 2008. First introduced in 1994, the Trent class are 14.26m in length (46ft 9in) and have a top speed of 25knots. Thirty of them are currently in service, at a cost of £1.1 million each. *(Ernie Shepherd)*

---

1 Founded in March 1824 and known until 1854 as the Royal National Institution for the Preservation of Life from Shipwreck

A Watson class lifeboat (ON 932) *Howard Marryat*, of the RNLI based at Fishguard from 1956–1981. *(RNLI)*

Severn Class lifeboat ON1276 (17-43) *Donald and Barbara Broadhead*, based at Rosslare Harbour from 9 July 2004. Powered by twin 1,050hp Caterpillar diesels, she was capable of 25 knots. *(RNLI)*

the lifeboat, to Rosslare Harbour. The lifeboat *Tom and Jenny* duly arrived on 22nd May 1896, with a temporary shed being provided for the storage of equipment. An agreement was necessary with the F&RR&H before permanent buildings could be provided in the area of the harbour. A decision was taken in May 1913 that the station at Rosslare Harbour was unnecessary, but before this could be put into effect World War I intervened. The lifeboat was eventually withdrawn in 1921 and the station formally closed in September 1921.

As mentioned above, the Wexford area lifeboat had been located at Rosslare Point. Nature now intervened to see a resumption of services at Rosslare Harbour, when a succession of storms and high seas led to the effective erosion and removal of land at the Fort. The first new boat at Rosslare Harbour was a 45ft 6in Watson class cabin motor boat which arrived on 27th April 1927. Six cottages were purchased on the cliff overlooking the harbour for the accommodation of employees, these eventually being sold in the 1960s and 1970s.

Among lifeboats to serve at Rosslare was the

Watson class *Douglas Hyde*, which was on station from 1952 to 1969. She was involved in the rescue of crew from the 20,125T tanker *World Concord* on 26th November 1954. She also took part in the search and rescue operation for the Aer Lingus Viscount aircraft which disappeared in March 1968 near Tuskar Rock while en route from Cork to London. The Arun class boat *St Brendan*, ON-1092 (52-26) arrived at Rosslare Harbour on 1st June 1984. Powered by twin 485hp Caterpillar diesels, this vessel had a top speed of 18 knots. Her career came to an abrupt end on 9th September 2001 when the Stena Line ferry *Koningin Beatrix*, in course of reversing on to her berth collided with the *St Brendan*, which was damaged beyond repair. The lifeboat currently on station is Severn class *Donald and Barbara Broadhead*, ON-1276 (17-43). Provided at a cost of £2 million, this 17.28m long boat is powered by twin 1,050 Caterpillar diesel engines, giving her a top speed of 25 knots. Since November 2002, Wexford harbour has had its own inshore 'D' class rib, the present one being the *Philip Robert Booth*, named after the late Philip Booth, known to the writer, and over the years a tireless volunteer for the RNLI.

Bibliography

Newspapers and Periodicals consulted include:

Belfast Telegraph, Bradshaw's Shareholders' Railway Guide, Engineering, Freeman's Journal, Great Western Railway Magazine, Herepath's Railway Journal, Industrial Railway Record, Irish Independent, Irish Railfans' News, Irish Railway Gazette, Irish Railway News, Irish Times, Journal of the Irish Railway Record Society, Railway Gazette, Railway Magazine, Railway News, Railway Times, Saunders Newsletter, The Locomotive, The People (Wexford)*, The Times of London, Waterford News, Western Mail* (Cardiff)*, Wexford Independent.*

Other printed sources referred to:

Board & Traffic Minutes of the DW&WR/D&SER, F&RR&H, GS&WR, GSR, GWR, WD&LR, WHC and WL&WR, Various Acts of Parliament, Parliamentary Plans and Books of Reference, Public and Working Timetables, Minutes of Parliamentary Proceedings, Board of Trade Inspection and Accident Reports.

Across Deep Waters – Bridges of Ireland: Barry, Michael; Frankfort Press, Dublin, 1985

Civil Engineering Heritage Ireland: Cox, RC & Gould, MH; Thomas Telford Publications, London, 1998

Cork Bandon & South Coast Railway: Shepherd, Ernie: Midland Publishing Ltd, Leicester, 2005

Dublin & South Eastern Railway: Beesley, G & Shepherd, E; Midland Publishing Ltd, Leicester, 1998

Fishguard's Great War Seaplanes: Hale, Martin; Paterchurch Publications, Pembroke Dock, 2007

Fishguard–Rosslare 1906–2006: Cowsill, Miles (Ed); Ferry Publications, Ramsey, 2006

GWR Service Timetable Appendices 1945: Bradford Barton, Truro

History of the Great Western Railway, Vols 1&2: MacDermot, ET & Clinker, CR; Ian Allan, London, 1964

Industrial Locomotives of Dyfed & Powys: de Havilland, John; Industrial Railway Society, London, 1994

Irish Industrial and Contractors' Locomotives: Cole, D; Union Publications, London, 1962

Irish Passenger Steamship Services, Vol 2: McNeill, DB; David & Charles, Newton Abbot, 1971

Irish Steam Locomotive Register: Rowledge, JWPR; Irish Traction Group, Stockport, 1993

Isambard Kingdom Brunel, Knight Errant: Vaughan, Adrian; John Murray (Publishers) Ltd, London, 1991

Johnson's Atlas & Gazeteer of the Railways of Ireland: Johnson, S; Midland Publishing, Leicester, 1997

Let Go Fore and Aft, A History of the F&RR&H: Merrigan, J & Cleare, B; Nautical Signals, 1996

Locomotives of the Great Southern Railways of Ireland: Rowledge, JWPR; Unpublished Mss.

Locomotives of the GSR: Clements, J & McMahon, M; Colourpoint Books, Newtownards, 2008

Maenclochog Railway Miscellany: Gale, John, Privately Published, 2004

Making the Connection: Share, Bernard (Ed); Iarnród Éireann, Dublin, 2006

Memoranda of the Late Col John Owen: Owen, John; (Reprint) General Books, 2009

Newport Pem and Fishguard: Lewis, Martin; Tempus Publishing, Stroud, 1996

Newport Pem and Fishguard Revisited: Lewis, Martin; Tempus Publishing, Stroud, 2003

Neyland, A Great Western Outpost: Parker, Richard, KRB Publications, Bishops Waltham, 2002

Official Handbook of Railway Stations, Various Editions: Railway Clearing House, London

Packet to Ireland: Elis-Williams, M; Gwynedd Archives Service, Caernarfon, 1984

Rails to Rosslare: Hitches, Mike; Amberley Publishing Ltd, Stroud, 2010

Railway and Other Steamers: Duckworth, C & Langmuir, G: Shipping Histories Ltd, Glasgow, 1948

Rosslare Europort Centenary: Doyle, Carmel (Ed); South East Business Magazine, Waterford, 2006

Rosslare Harbour: Coy, L, Cleare, B, Boyce, J & Boyce, B; Nonsuch Publishing, Dublin, 2008

Rosslare Harbour Sea & Ships: Maddock, John; Harbour Publications, Portmarnock, 1996

Second Report of the Commissioners appointed to consider and recommend a General System of Railways for Ireland; Her Majesty's Stationery Office, London, 1838

The Cambrian Railways, Vols 1&2: Christiansen, R & Miller RW; David & Charles, Newton Abbot, 1971

The Campile Bombing August 26th 1940: The Horeswood Historical Society, 2010

The Chester & Holyhead Railway, Vol 1: Baughan, Peter; David & Charles, Newton Abbot, 1972

The Furness Railway: Rush, RW; The Oakwood Press, Tarrant Hinton, 1973

The Great Southern & Western Railway: Murray, KA & McNeill, DB; IRRS, Dublin, 1976

The Lifeboats of Rosslare Harbour and Wexford: Leach, Nicholas; Nonsuch Publishing, Dublin, 2007

The Locomotives built by Manning Wardle & Co Vol 3: Harman, Fred; Century Locoprints, Bridlington

The Maenclochog Railway: Gale, John; Privately Published, 1992

The Manchester & Milford Railway, Second Revised Edition: Holden, JS; The Oakwood Press, Usk, 2007

The North Pembrokeshire and Fishguard Railway: Morris, JP; The Oakwood Press, Lingfield, 1969

The Pembroke and Tenby Railway: Price, MRC; The Oakwood Press, Headington, 1986

The Railways of Pembrokeshire: Morris, John: HG Walters Ltd, Tenby, 1981

The Railways of Pembrokeshire: Parker, Richard; Noodle Books, Southampton, 2008

The Railway Year Book: The Railway Publishing Company Ltd, London, Various Editions

The Ships of Rosslare Harbour: Cleare, B, Coy, L, Boyce, J & Boyce, B; Nonsuch Publishing, Dublin, 2008

The Slate Railways of Wales: Richards, Alun John; Gwasg Carreg Gwalch, Llanrwst, 2001

track diagrams Volume 1 Mallow–Rosslare: Richards, H; Transport Research Associates, Dublin

Waterford Limerick & Western Railway: Shepherd, Ernie; Ian Allan, Hersham, 2006

Index